To my fabulous wife, Melissa

About the Author

Steven Bragg, CPA, CMA, CIA, CDP, CSP, CPM, CPIM, has been the chief financial officer or controller of four companies, as well as a consulting manager at Ernst & Young. He received a master's degree in finance from Bentley College and an MBA from Babson College. He has also written *Just-in-Time Accounting, Advanced Accounting Systems, Outsourcing, Accounting Best Practices,* and *Managing Explosive Corporate Growth,* and has co-authored *Controllership* and *The Controller's Function.* Mr. Bragg resides in Englewood, Colorado.

Contents

PART FOUR   Other Analysis Topics

APPENDICES

Preface

This book is designed to assist a company controller, or any other member of the accounting and finance staffs, in the analysis of all corporate activities. These activities include the ones covered by most traditional financial analysis books—the evaluation of capital investments, financing options, cash flows, and the cost of capital. However, these topics are not nearly sufficient for an active controller who is concerned with not only the performance of every department, but also potential acquisition candidates, the capacity levels of company equipment and facilities, and the relative levels of risk associated with new or existing investments. This book covers all of these additional topics and more. Within these pages, the reader will find a thorough analysis of all the following topics:

- *Evaluating capital investments, financing options, and cash flows.* The first portion of the book attends to these traditional financial analysis topics.

- *Evaluating acquisition targets.* The analysis of acquisition candidates is a major activity for those organizations that grow by this means. The book itemizes the specific analysis activities to complete.

- *Increasing shareholder value.* The book describes a number of areas in which shareholder value can be improved.

- *Determining the breakeven point.* The book covers the mechanics of the breakeven calculation, as well as how to use it to recommend changes to operations.

- *Forecasting future business conditions.* The book notes a number of factors useful for predicting business cycles.

- *Evaluating operations, processes, and managers.* The book discusses the specific measurements and corrective actions that can be used for all major company departments, process cycles, and manager performance evaluations.

- *Evaluating capacity utilization.* The book describes how to measure capacity utilization and what corrective action to recommend in cases in which there are bottlenecks or excess available capacity.

- *Using Microsoft Excel to conduct financial analysis.* The book describes the specific Excel formulas that can be used to conduct reviews of the financial statements, as well as capital expenditures, investments, and project risk analyses.

- *Using sample analysis reports.* The book presents a wide array of standard financial analysis reports that can be adapted for use by the reader, such as weekly management reports, payroll reports, and utilization reports.

- *Determining the cost of capital.* The book describes the reasons for using the cost of capital, how to calculate it, and under what conditions to modify or use it.

- *Analyzing risk.* The book discusses the concept of risk, how it should be integrated into a financial analysis, various tools for calculating risk, and how to integrate it into an analytic report for use by management.

With the particular attention given to operational analysis in this book, as well as the wide-ranging coverage of all other financial analysis topics, the corporate controller will find that this is a handy reference that can be used time and again for a variety of analytic purposes.

A special note of thanks to my editor, Sheck Cho, who has assisted in the completion of so many manuscripts.

Steven M. Bragg
Englewood, Colorado
March 2000

PART ONE

OVERVIEW

1

Introduction

A controller is responsible for a wide array of functions, such as processing accounts payable and receivable transactions, properly noting the transfer of assets, and closing the books in a timely manner. Properly completing these functions is critical to a corporation, which relies on the accurate handling of transactions and accurate financial statements. These activities clearly form the basis for anyone's successful career as a controller. However, the outstanding controller must acquire skills in the area of financial analysis in order to be truly successful.

By obtaining a broad knowledge of financial analysis skills and applying them to a multitude of situations, a controller can acquire deep insights into why a company is performing as it does, and can transmit this information to other members of the management team, along with recommendations for improvements that will enhance the corporation's overall financial performance. By knowing how to use financial analysis tools, a controller can rise above the admittedly mundane chores of processing accounting transactions and make a significant contribution to the management team. By doing so, the controller's understanding of the inner workings of the entire corporation improves and raises his or her visibility within the organization, which can eventually lead to a promotion or additional chances to gain experience in dealing with other departments. Thus, the benefits of using financial analysis are considerable, not only for the company as a whole, but for the controller in particular.

This book is designed to assist the controller in obtaining a wide and in-depth view of the most important financial analysis topics. Toward this end, the book is divided into four parts.

Part One covers the overall layout and content of the book, as well as the role of financial analysis and making management and investment decisions. This includes notations regarding the several types of financial analysis, as well as the various kinds of questions that one can answer through its use. Part One concludes with a discussion of the need for judgment by a controller in interpreting analysis results.

Part Two covers the primary financial analysis topics. Chapter 3 discusses the evaluation of capital investments, which involves assembling cash flow information into a standard cash flow format for which a net present value calculation can be used to determine the discounted cash flow that is likely to be obtained. Chapter 4 describes the various financing options that a controller may be called on to review. For example, is it better to lease an item, and if so, should it be an operating or capital lease? Alternatively, should it be rented or purchased? What are the risks of using each financing option, and can the current mix of company financial instruments already in use have an impact on which option to take? All of these questions are answered in Chapter 4. Chapter 5 covers the essentials of why cash inflows and outflows are the key forces driving financial analysis and notes the wide variety of situations in which cash flow analysis can be used, as well as how to construct and interpret cash flow analysis models.

Chapter 6 is full of checklists and advice regarding how to conduct an analysis of any prospective merger or acquisition candidates, with an emphasis on making a thorough review of all key areas so that there is minimal risk of bypassing the review of a key problem area that could lead to poor combined financial results. Chapter 7 notes several ways to increase shareholder value and discusses the reasons why enhanced cash flow is the predominant method for doing so, as well as how to use leverage to increase shareholder value, while being knowledgeable of the dangers of pursuing this strategy too far.

Chapter 8 covers the deceptively simple topic of breakeven analysis, which is the determination of the sales level at which a company makes no money. The discussion covers how to calculate the breakeven point, why it is important, the kinds of analysis for which it should be used, and how to use subsets of the breakeven analysis to determine breakeven levels of specific divisions or product lines.

Finally, Chapter 9 covers the forecasting of business cycles. Although this is an issue normally left to bank economists or chief financial officers (CFOs), the controller is sometimes called on to forecast expectations for the industry in which a company operates. This chapter gives practical pointers on where to obtain relevant information, how to analyze it, and how to make projections based on the underlying data. These chapters comprise the purely *financial* analysis part of the book. Though Part Two alone is adequate for the bulk of all analysis work that a controller is likely to handle, there are still many *operational* analysis issues that a controller should be able to review and render an opinion about. That is the focus of Part Three.

Part Three covers operational analysis, which is the detailed review of information about company operations, department by department. Chapter 10 covers the methods for choosing an appropriate set of performance review measures for each member of the management team, how to measure and report this information, and the types of behavioral changes that can result when these measures are used. Though the specific performance measures used are typically made by the CFO or the human resources director, these people may (and should) ask the controller's opinion regarding the best measures. If so, this chapter gives the controller a good basis on which to make recommendations.

Chapter 11 reviews how to analyze process cycles. These are the clusters of transactions about which a company's operations are grouped, such as the purchasing cycle and the revenue cycle. If there are problems with the process cycles, then there will be an unending round of investigations and procedural repairs needed to fix them; because the controller is usually called on to conduct the repair work, it makes a great deal of sense to analyze them in advance to spot problems before they fester.

Chapter 12 covers a *major* topic—the analysis of all primary departments, such as sales, production, engineering, and (yes) accounting. Specific measurements are noted for determining the efficiency and effectiveness with which each department is managed, alongside suggestions regarding why measurement results are poor and what recommendations to make for improving the situation.

Chapter 13 concludes the operational analysis section with a review of capacity utilization, how to measure it, why it is important, sample report formats to use, and recommendations to make based on the measured results. All these chapters are designed to give a controller an excellent knowledge of how all company operations are performing, and what to recommend to the management team if problems arise.

Part Four covers a number of other analysis topics. Chapter 14 covers the primary formulas that a controller can use in the Microsoft Excel program to analyze financial statements, projected cash flows, investments, and risk. Chapter 15 includes many report formats that the reader can use for the reporting of such varied analyses as employee overtime, capacity utilization, and key weekly measures for the management team.

Chapter 16 discusses how to meld the cost of debt and equity to arrive at the cost of capital, and also notes how it should be used and where to use it. Finally, in Chapter 17, there is a discussion of risk—what it is, how it can impact a financial or operational analysis, what kinds of measurement tools are available for calculating its extent, and how to report a risk analysis to management in an understandable fashion.

There are also two appendices in the book. In Appendix A, there is a list of the most common symptoms of financial problems that a controller will encounter, alongside a list of recommended analyses and solutions for each symptom that will point one in the direction of how to obtain a fix to the problem. Appendix B contains a list of the most commonly used ratios, which are useful for analyzing both overall financial results and the specific operational results of individual departments.

This book is designed to give a controller, or anyone in the accounting and finance fields, a thorough knowledge of how to analyze an organization, from individual projects upward to complete departments, and on to entire divisions and companies. For those who are searching for specific analysis tools, it is best read piecemeal, through a search of either the table of contents or the index. However, for those who wish to gain a full understanding of all possible forms of analysis, a complete review of the book is highly recommended.

2

The Role of Financial Analysis

Historically, the primary purpose of the accounting department has been to process transactions: billings to customers, payments to suppliers, and the like. These are mundane but crucial activities that are unseen by the majority of company employees, but still necessary to an organization's smooth operations. However, the role of the accounting staff has gradually changed as companies encounter greater competition from organizations throughout the world. Now, a company's management needs advice as well as a smooth transaction flow. Accordingly, the controller is being called on not only to fulfill the traditional transaction processing role, but also to continually review company operations, evaluate investments, report problems and related recommendations to management, and fulfill requests by the management team for special investigations. All of these new tasks can be considered financial analysis, for they require the application of financial review methods to a company's operational and investment activities.

There are several types of financial analysis. One is the continuing review and reporting of a standard set of measures that give management a good view of the state of company operations. To conduct this type of analysis, a controller should review all key company operations, consult the literature for examples of adequate measures that will become telltale indicators of operational problems, develop a timetable and procedure for generating these measurements on a regular basis, and then devise a suitable format for issuing the results to management. For these operational reviews, there are several points to consider:

- *Target measurements.* There is no need to create and continually recalculate a vast array of measures that will track every conceivable corporate activity. Instead, it is best to carefully review operations, with a particular view of where problems are most likely to arise, and create a set of measurements that will track those specific problems.

- *Revise measurements.* No measurement will be applicable forever. This is because a company's operations will change over time, which calls for the occasional review of the current set of measurements, with an inclination to replace those that no longer yield valuable information with new ones that focus on new problems that are of more importance in the current operating environment.

- *Educate management about the measures used.* Though most financial analysis measurements appear to be very straightforward and easily understood, this is from the perspective of the accounting staff, which has been trained in the use of financial measurements. The members of the management group to whom these measurements are sent may have no idea of the significance of the information presented. Accordingly, the controller should work hard not only to educate managers about the contents of financial analysis formulas, but also to keep reeducating them to ensure that explanations do not fade in their memories.

- *Add commentary to measurements.* Even a well-trained management team may not intuitively understand the underlying problems that cause certain measurement results to arise. To forcibly bring their attention to the key measurements, a controller should add a short commentary to any published set of measurements. This is an excellent way to convert a numerical report into a written one, which many people find much easier to understand.

In short, the financial analysis that relates to the continuing evaluation of current operations involves a great deal of judgment regarding the applicability of certain measures, as well as a great deal of work in communicating the results to management for further action.

A second type of financial analysis that a controller will sometimes be called on to perform is the analysis of investments. Though this work should fall within the range of responsibility of the treasurer's staff in the finance department, many smaller organizations have no finance staff at all, which means that the work falls on the accounting staff instead. Three subcategories of analysis fall under the review of investments:

1. *The analysis of securities.* When a company either has or is contemplating investing its excess funds in various investment vehicles, such as bonds or stocks, the controller can evaluate the rate of return on each one and render an opinion regarding it. The tools for making this analysis were developed long ago and are simple to calculate. However, the controller may also be called on to evaluate the relative risk of each investment, which is not so subject to quantitative analysis. Instead, the controller must have an excellent knowledge of the liquidity of an investment, as

well as its risk of default. This requires additional security analysis skills, heavily seasoned with judgment.

2. *The analysis of financing options.* The controller is frequently called on to review the cost of various financing options when a company is considering acquiring assets. To do so, the controller must not only be able to provide an accurate and well-documented answer that clearly reveals the least expensive alternative, but also have a sufficient knowledge of available options to suggest other financing variations that have not yet been tried.

3. *The analysis of capital expenditures.* When a company wishes to make a capital expenditure, the ultimate test of whether the right decision was made is if the acquisition eventually creates a cash flow that exceeds the cost of financing it. The controller is called on to analyze predicted cash flows in advance, determine the cost of capital, calculate the net present value of cash flows, and pass judgment on the reasonableness of the acquisition, while factoring in the risk of cash flows being inaccurate. These tasks require not just a knowledge of cash flow analysis and discounting methods, but also how to rationally judge the accuracy of predicted cash flows and estimate the risk associated with them.

In the final type of financial analysis, the controller receives a special request from management to perform a financial analysis. Such a request can cover any topic at all. Some examples of one-time management requests that require financial analysis are:

- What would happen to sales if credit levels were tightened?

- What would happen to the accounts receivable balance if credit levels were loosened?

- What would happen to the raw material turnover rate if purchases were made in weekly increments instead of monthly?

- What will be the inventory investment if the company adds one distribution warehouse?

- What will be the savings if the company passes through freight costs to customers?

- What will happen to the total gross margin if the price of one product is cut by 10 percent?

- What will happen to the corporate medical expense if the company requires employees to pay an extra $10 per month on their medical insurance?

These questions represent a wide range of queries, all of them valid, and all of them likely to be encountered on a regular basis. A controller's reputation within a company will be partially based on his or her ability to quickly and accurately respond to these requests. Alternatively, late or inaccurate responses can create a great deal of damage, not only for the controller, but for the reputation of the entire accounting department. To enhance the controller's credibility and give management accurate responses to their questions, a controller should follow these steps:

- *Clarify the question.* There is nothing worse than trying to remember the question asked by a requestor; making an assumption about what is being asked, rather than confirming with the requestor; and then finding later on that the resulting financial analysis answered the wrong question. To save a great deal of wasted effort, one must always write down the request at once, read it back, and clarify any points before beginning the analysis.

- *Verify assumptions.* There are some assumptions built into any financial analysis. For example, what is the cost of capital to be used for a discounted cash flow analysis? What is the assumed rate of customer retention if prices are dropped by 10 percent? Rather than guess at an assumption that will be an integral part of a financial analysis, it is much better to confirm the information before proceeding. Otherwise, the person who requested the information may receive an incorrect answer.

- *What answer is the requestor looking for?* This does not mean that the controller is angling for the correct answer for which to provide a backup set of financial analysis. However, it is important to reduce the investigation to as small an area as possible in order to save analysis time. For example, if a manager asks for a complete printout of all unpaid accounts payable, further questioning may reveal that the person wants to see only what is unpaid for one specific supplier, which reduces the accounting staff's work in compiling the requested information.

- *Investigate from the top down.* A common error for many people involved in financial analysis is to conduct a top-to-bottom analysis in great detail. Instead, it is best to start at the most summary level and proceed downward through successive layers of detail until sufficient information has been accumulated to provide an answer. Do not ever proceed further, because the question has already been answered, and lower levels of detail usually require the largest amounts of research work. For one exception to this rule, see the following item.

- *Answer follow-up questions in advance.* Once the results have been compiled, it is worthwhile for the controller to inspect it from the perspective of the recipient and anticipate any additional questions that may be raised. Obtain the answers to the additional questions and include them in the analysis. Not only does this approach keep the recipient from having to return to the controller for more follow-up questions, but it also shortens the time that management must take to arrive at a decision based on the analysis. Also, the controller will quickly earn a reputation for being a discerning analyst who reads deeply into the results of his or her work. This situation occurs, for example, when an accounts receivable turnover calculation results in a significantly worsened turnover ratio over the previous month. The obvious follow-up question is to find out which customers are not paying as quickly, and why. The controller can determine the answers to these questions before being asked, and add them to the turnover analysis prior to presenting it to management.

- *Confirm all data.* Before conducting the actual analysis, confirm that the sources of data are for the correct time period, cover the correct entity, and contain all needed information. If not, dig further to obtain the correct data. By not taking this step, one can conduct a comprehensive set of analyses with the wrong information, and then have to go back and start over again.

- *Verify all formulas.* Even with the correct underlying data, one can still issue the wrong results if the formulas used are the wrong ones. This is a particular problem when the analysis is an addition to work done in previous periods, when a slightly different formula may have been used. Consequently, when adding to a trend line of analysis results, be sure to re-create the results from the last period to verify that the formula currently in use resulted in the previously calculated amount. This method ensures calculation consistency from period to period.

- *Suspect unusual results.* If the end result of a financial analysis is a highly unusual result that does not intuitively make sense, then it probably doesn't. The controller should assume that either a data gathering or computational error has been made and review the work papers. It may be useful to have someone else review the work, because they can review the information from a fresh point of view and are more likely to spot mistakes. Only after an intensive internal review should one assume that the results are correct and present the results to management. The reason for this lengthy review process is that management will react to an unusual result with a full-blown investigation of its own, so the accounting staff should review its documentation before management does so, too.

- *Add supporting commentary.* If the financial analysis is full of ratios, percentages, and statistical measures, it is a good bet that the recipient will have no idea regarding the conclusion that is buried somewhere among all the numbers. To be more clear, add supporting commentary that translates the math into an easily readable conclusion.

- *Find the appropriate form of presentation.* Even with the analysis and commentary in hand, it is important to consider how this information should be passed along to the requestor. Is a brief voice mail or e-mail sufficient to relay the results, or is a formal presentation or written report necessary? This is where a good knowledge of the requestor's preferred form of communication comes in handy. This is not a trivial step, since preparing a full presentation instead of an e-mail can consume a large part of the accounting staff's time, whereas being too informal can injure the reputation of the department.

- *Determine if a calculation system is needed.* Once the requested information has been provided, ask the recipient if the information should be recalculated and presented on a regular basis. In most cases it will not, because the bulk of requests are to answer situational questions that do not require continuing analysis. It is important to ask this question, because some controllers will mistakenly assume that the same information will be requested in the future and will then consume an inordinate amount of the accounting staff's time in regenerating information that no one needs.

Throughout this overview of the role of financial analysis, the focus has been on three main points. The first is that proper financial analysis requires a solid grounding in financial analysis tools. This book is designed to provide the backbone of that knowledge. However, two more tools are needed. One is the ability to convert the results of a financial analysis into a format that can be easily communicated to and understood by the targeted recipient. For this, a controller must have a fine-tuned ability to convert accounting and financial terminology into everyday terms. Finally, and of greatest importance, is the use of judgment in several areas. A controller must be able to correctly discern what question is being asked by management so that the resulting financial analysis work is focused on the collection of the correct data and its interpretation with the correct formulas. Further, a controller must exercise judgment in interpreting the results and deciding if additional work is needed to ensure that the root causes of any problems have been found. Judgment is needed to ensure that the most critical results are quickly and forcefully communicated to management. Only by showing a mastery of all three items will a controller become an expert in the use of financial analysis. The knowledge for the first item is contained in this book. The other two must be learned through diligence, repetitive analysis, and by watching how analysis is conducted by others who have mastered the trade. In short, knowledge must be supplemented by experience.

PART TWO
FINANCIAL ANALYSIS

3

Evaluating Capital Investments

One of the most common financial analysis tasks with which a controller is confronted is evaluating capital investments. In some industries, the amount of money poured into capital improvements is a very substantial proportion of sales, and so is worthy of a great deal of analysis to ensure that a company is investing its cash wisely in internal improvements. This section reviews the concept of the hurdle rate, as well as the three most common approaches for evaluating capital investments. It concludes with reviews of the capital investment proposal form and the postcompletion project analysis, which brings to a close the complete cycle of evaluating a capital project over the entire course of its acquisition, installation, and operation.

HURDLE RATE

When controllers are given capital investment proposal forms to review, they need some basis on which to conduct the evaluation. What makes a good capital investment? Is it the project with the largest net cash flow, the one that uses the least capital, or some other standard of measure?

The standard criterion for investment is the hurdle rate—the discounting rate at which all of a company's investments must exhibit a positive cash flow. It is called a hurdle rate because the summary of all cash flows must exceed, or hurdle, this rate, or else the underlying investments will not be approved. The use of a discount rate is extremely important, for it reduces the value of cash inflows and outflows scheduled for some time in the future, so that they are comparable to the value of cash flows in the present. Without the use of a discount rate, we would judge the value of a cash flow 10 years in the future to be the same as one that occurs right now. However, the difference between the two is that the funds received now can also earn interest for the next 10 years, whereas there is no such opportunity to invest the funds that will arrive in 10 years. Consequently, a discount rate is the great equalizer that allows us to make one-to-one comparisons between cash flows in different periods.

The hurdle rate is derived from the cost of capital, which is covered in depth in Chapter 16. This is the average cost of funds that a company uses, and is based on the average cost of its debt, equity, and various other funding sources that are combinations of these two basic forms of funds. For example, if a company has determined its cost of capital to be 16 percent, then the discounted cash flows from all of its new capital investments, using that discount rate, must yield a positive return. If they do not, then the cash flow resulting from its capital investments will not be sufficient for the company to pay for the funds it invested. Thus, the primary basis on which a controller reviews potential capital investments is the hurdle rate.

A company may choose to use several hurdle rates, depending on the nature of the investment. For example, if the company must install equipment to make its production emissions compliant with federal air quality standards, then there is no hurdle rate at all—the company must complete the work or be fined by the government. At the opposite extreme, a company may assign a high hurdle rate to all projects that are considered unusually risky. For example, if capital projects are for the extension of a current production line, there is very little perceived risk, and a hurdle rate that matches the cost of capital is deemed sufficient. If the capital expenditure is for a production line that creates equipment in a new market in which the company is the first entrant, however, and no one knows what kind of sales will result, the hurdle rate may be set a number of percentage points higher than the cost of capital. Thus, different hurdle rates can apply to different situations.

Although the hurdle rate is the fundamental measuring stick against which all capital investments are evaluated, there is one exception to the rule: the payback period.

PAYBACK PERIOD

The primary criterion for evaluating a capital investment is its ability to return a profit that exceeds a hurdle rate. However, this method misses one important element—it does not fully explain investment risk in a manner that is fully understandable to managers. Investment risk can be defined as the chance that the initial investment will not be earned back, or that the rate of return target will not be met. Discounting can be used to identify or weed out such projects, simply by increasing the hurdle rate. For example, if a project is perceived to be risky, an increase in the hurdle rate will reduce its net present value, which makes the investment less likely to be approved by management. Management may not be comfortable dealing with discounted cash flow methods when looking at a risky investment, however; they just want to know how long it will take until they get their invested funds back. Though this is a decidedly unscientific way to review cash flows, the author has yet to

Exhibit 3.1   Stream of Cash Flows for a Payback Calculation

Year	Cash Flow
1	$1,000,000
2	1,250,000
3	1,500,000
4	2,000,000
5	3,000,000

find a management team that did not insist on seeing a payback calculation alongside other, more sophisticated analysis methods.

There are two ways to calculate the payback period. The first method is the easiest to use but can yield a skewed result. That calculation is to divide the capital investment by the average annual cash flow from operations. For example, Exhibit 3.1 shows a stream of cash flows over five years that is heavily weighted toward the time periods that are farthest in the future. The sum of those cash flows is $8,750,000, which is an average of $1,750,000 per year. We will also assume that the initial capital investment was $6 million. Based on this information, the payback period is $6 million divided by $1,750,000, which is 3.4 years. However, if we review the stream of cash flows in Exhibit 3.1, it is evident that the cash inflow did not cover the investment at the 3.4-year mark. In fact, the actual cash inflow did not exceed $6 million until shortly after the end of the fourth year. What happened? The stream of cash flows in the example was so skewed toward future periods that the annual *average* cash flow was not representative of the annual *actual* cash flow. Thus, the averaging method can be used only if the stream of future cash flows is relatively even from year to year.

The most accurate way to calculate the payback period is to do so manually. This means that we deduct the total expected cash inflow from the invested balance, year by year, until we arrive at the correct period. For example, the stream of cash flows from Exhibit 3.1 have been re-created in 3.2, but now with an extra column that shows the net capital investment remaining at the end of each year. This format can be used to reach the end of year four; we know that the cash flows will pay back the investment sometime during

Exhibit 3.2   Stream of Cash Flows for a Manual Payback Calculation

Year	Cash Flow	Net Investment Remaining
0	0	$6,000,000
1	$1,000,000	5,000,000
2	1,250,000	3,750,000
3	1,500,000	2,250,000
4	2,000,000	250,000
5	3,000,000	—

year five, but we do not have a month-by-month cash flow that tells us precisely when. Instead, we can assume an average stream of cash flows during that period, which works out to $250,000 per month ($3 million cash inflow for the year, divided by 12 months). Because there was only $250,000 of net investment remaining at the end of the fourth year, and this is the same monthly amount of cash flow in the fifth year, we can assume that the payback period is 4.1 years.

As already stated, the payback period is not a highly scientific method, because it completely ignores the time value of money. Nonetheless, it tells management how much time will pass before it recovers its invested funds, which can be useful information, especially in environments such as high technology, in which investments must attain a nearly immediate payback before they become obsolete. Accordingly, it is customary to include the payback calculation in a capital investment analysis, though it must be strongly supplemented by discounted cash flow analyses, which are described in the next two sections.

NET PRESENT VALUE

The typical capital investment is composed of a string of cash flows, both in and out, that will continue until the investment is eventually liquidated at some point in the future. These cash flows include the initial payment for equipment, continuing maintenance costs, salvage value of the equipment when it is eventually sold, tax payments, receipts from product sold, and so on. The trouble is that the cash flows are coming in and going out over a period of many years, so how do we make them comparable for an analysis that is done in the present? As noted earlier, in the section on hurdle rates, a discount rate can be used to reduce the value of a future cash flow into what it would be worth right now. By applying the discount rate to each anticipated cash flow, we can reduce and then add them together, which yields a single combined figure that represents the current value of the entire capital investment. This is known as its net present value.

For an example of how net present value works, listed in Exhibit 3.3 are the cash flows, both in and out, for a capital investment that is expected to last for five years. The year is listed in the first column, the amount of the cash flow in the second column, and the discount rate in the third column. The final column multiplies the cash flow from the second column by the discount rate in the third column to yield the present value of each cash flow. The grand total cash flow is listed in the lower right corner.

Notice that the discount factor in Exhibit 3.3 becomes progressively smaller in later years, because cash flows farther in the future are worth less than those that will be received sooner. The discount factor is published in present value tables, which are listed in many accounting and finance textbooks. They are also a standard feature in mid-range handheld calculators. Another variation is to use the following formula to manually compute a present value:

Exhibit 3.3   Simplified Net Present Value Example

Year	Cash Flow	Discount Factor*	Present Value
0	−$100,000	1.000	−$100,000
1	+25,000	.9259	+23,148
2	+25,000	.8573	+21,433
3	+25,000	.7938	+19,845
4	+30,000	.7350	+22,050
5	+30,000	.6806	+20,418
		Net Present Value	+$6,894

* Discount factor is 8%.

$$\text{Present value of a future cash flow} = \frac{(\text{Future cash flow})}{(1 + \text{Discount rate})^{\text{(squared by the number of periods of discounting)}}}$$

Using the above formula, if we expect to receive $75,000 in one year, and the discount rate is 15 percent, then the calculation is:

$$\text{Present value} = \frac{\$75,000}{(1 + .15)^1}$$

$$\text{Present value} = \$65,217.39$$

The example shown in Exhibit 3.3 was of the simplest possible kind. In reality, there are several additional factors to take into consideration. First, there may be multiple cash inflows and outflows in each period, rather than the single lump sum that was shown in the example. If a controller wants to know precisely the cause of each cash flow, then it is best to add a line to the net present value calculation that clearly identifies the nature of each item and discounts it separately from the other line items. (An alternate way to create a net present value table that leaves room for multiple cash flow line items while keeping the format down to a minimum size is shown in Chapter 5.) Another issue is which items to include in the analysis and which to exclude. The basic rule of thumb is that it must be included if it impacts cash flow and excluded if it does not. The most common cash flow line items to include in a net present value analysis are:

- *Cash inflows from sales.* If a capital investment results in added sales, then all gross margins attributable to that investment must be included in the analysis.

- *Cash inflows and outflows for equipment purchases and sales.* There should be a cash outflow when a product is purchased, as well as a cash inflow when the equipment is no longer needed and is sold off.

- *Cash inflows and outflows for working capital.* When a capital investment occurs, it normally involves the use of some additional inventory. If there are added sales, then there will probably be additional accounts receivable. In either case, these are additional investments that must be included in the analysis as cash outflows. Also, if the investment is ever terminated, then the inventory will presumably be sold off and the accounts receivable collected, so there should be line items in the analysis, located at the end of the project time line, showing the cash inflows from the liquidation of working capital.

- *Cash outflows for maintenance.* If there is production equipment involved, then there will be periodic maintenance needed to ensure that it runs properly. If there is a maintenance contract with a supplier that provides the servicing, then this too should be included in the analysis.

- *Cash outflows for taxes.* If there is a profit from new sales that are attributable to the capital investment, then the incremental income tax that can be traced to those incremental sales must be included in the analysis. Also, if there is a significant quantity of production equipment involved, the annual personal property taxes that can be traced to that equipment should also be included.

- *Cash inflows for the tax effect of depreciation.* Depreciation is an allowable tax deduction. Accordingly, the depreciation created by the purchase of capital equipment should be offset against the cash outflow caused by income taxes. Though depreciation is really just an accrual, it does have a net cash flow impact caused by a reduction in taxes, and so should be included in the net present value calculation.

The net present value approach is the best way to see if a proposed capital investment has a sufficient rate of return to justify the use of any required funds. Also, because it reveals the amount of cash created in excess of the corporate hurdle rate, it allows management to rank projects by the amount of cash they can potentially spin off, which is a good way to determine which projects to fund if there is not enough cash available to pay for an entire set of proposed investments.

The next section looks at an alternative discounting method that focuses on the rate of return of a capital investment's cash flows, rather than the amount of cash left over after being discounted at a standard hurdle rate, as was the case with the net present value methodology.

INTERNAL RATE OF RETURN

The end result of a net present value calculation is the amount of money that is earned or lost after all related cash flows are discounted at a preset hurdle rate. This is a good evaluation method, but what if management wants to know the overall return on investment of the same stream of cash flows? Also, what if the net present value was negative, but only by a small amount, so that management wants to know how far off a project's rate of return varies from the hurdle rate? Or, what if management wants to rank projects by their over-all rates of return, rather than by their net present values? All of these ques-tions can be answered by using the internal rate of return (IRR) method.

The IRR method is very similar to the net present value method, because the same cash flow layout is used, itemizing the net inflows and outflows by year. The difference is that, using the IRR method, a high–low approach is used to find the discount rate at which the cash flows equal zero. At that point, the discount rate equals the rate of return on investment for the entire stream of cash flows associated with the capital investment. To illustrate how the method works, we will begin with the standard net present value format that was listed in the last section. This time, there is a new set of annual cash flows, as shown in Exhibit 3.4. The difference between this calculation and the one used for net present value is that we are going to guess at the correct rate of return and enter this amount in the "Internal Rate of Return" column. We enter the discount rates for each year, using a low-end assumption of a 7 per-cent rate of return.

The end result of the calculation is a positive net present value of $13,740. Because we are shooting for the IRR percentage at which the net present value is zero, the IRR must be increased. If the net present value had been negative, the IRR percentage would have been reduced instead. We will make a higher guess at an IRR of 9 percent and run the calculation again, as shown in Exhibit 3.5.

The result of the calculation in Exhibit 3.5 is very close to a net present value of 9 percent. If we want to try a few more high–low calculations, we can zero in on the IRR more precisely. In the example, the actual IRR is 8.9 per-cent.

This approach seems like a very slow one, and it is. A different approach, if the reader has access to an electronic spreadsheet, such as Microsoft Excel, is to enter the stream of cash flows into it and enter a formula that the com-

Exhibit 3.4 Internal Rate of Return Calculation—Low Estimate

Year	Cash Flow	Internal Rate of Return = 7%	Present Value
0	−$250,000	1.000	−$250,000
1	+55,000	.9345	+51,398
2	+60,000	.8734	+52,404
3	+65,000	.8163	+53,060
4	+70,000	.7629	+53,403
5	+75,000	.7130	+53,475
		Net Present Value	+$13,740

Exhibit 3.5 Internal Rate of Return Calculation—High Estimate

Year	Cash Flow	Internal Rate of Return = 9%	Present Value
0	−$250,000	1.000	−$250,000
1	+55,000	.9174	+50,457
2	+60,000	.8417	+50,502
3	+65,000	.7722	+50,193
4	+70,000	.7084	+49,588
5	+75,000	.6499	+48,743
		Net Present Value	−$517

puter uses to instantly calculate the IRR. For example, the screen printout shown in Exhibit 3.6 contains the same stream of cash flows shown earlier in Exhibits 3.4 and 3.5. In this case, we have used the Excel formula for the internal rate of return to give us the IRR automatically. For the sake of clarity, we have duplicated the formula in a text format immediately below the main formula.

The internal rate of return is best used in conjunction with the net present value calculation, because it can be misleading when used by itself. One

Exhibit 3.6 Internal Rate of Return Calculation in Microsoft Excel

	A	B	C	D	E	F	G	H	I	J
1										
2										
3		Internal Rate of Return Calculation:								
4										
5				Year	Cash Flow					
6				0	($250,000)					
7				1	55,000					
8				2	60,000					
9				3	65,000					
10				4	70,000					
11				5	75,000					
12										
13		Internal Rate of Return (IRR):			8.9%					
14										
15		Text of IRR Formula:			=IRR(E6:E11)					
16										
17										
18										
19										
20										
21										
22										
23										
24										

problem is that it favors those capital investments with very high rates of return, even if the total dollar return is rather small. An example of this is when a potential investment of $10,000 has a return of $3,000, which equates to a 30 percent rate of return, and is ranked higher than a $100,000 investment with a return of $25,000 (which has a 25 percent rate of return). In this case, the smaller project certainly has a greater rate of return, but the larger project will return more cash in total than the smaller one. If there were only enough capital available for one of the two projects, perhaps $100,000, and the smaller project was selected because of its higher rate of return, then the total return would be less than optimal, because many of the funds are not being invested at all. In this situation, only $3,000 is being earned, even though $100,000 can be invested, which yields only a 3 percent return on the total pool of funds. Thus, if there are too many capital investments chasing too few funds, selecting investments based on nothing but their IRR may lead to suboptimal decisions.

Another issue is that the IRR calculation assumes that all cash flows thrown off by a project over the course of its life can be reinvested at the same rate of return. This is not always a valid assumption, because the earnings from a special investment that yields a uniquely high rate of return may not be investable at anywhere close to the same rate of return.

Despite its shortcomings, the IRR method is a scientifically valid way to determine the rate of return on a capital investment's full stream of cash flows. However, because it does not recognize the total amount of cash spun off by an investment, it is best used in conjunction with the net present value calculation in order to yield the most complete analysis of a capital investment.

CAPITAL INVESTMENT PROPOSAL FORM

When a controller is called on to conduct an analysis of a potential capital investment, the largest task is collecting all necessary data about it. This can involve meeting with a number of employees who are working on the capital investment to determine the timing and cost of all up-front and continuing expenditures, as well as the timing and amount of all future cash inflows, not to mention the eventual salvage value of any equipment to be purchased. Once the controller assembles this information, it may become apparent that there are a few items still missing, which will require another iteration of data gathering. In the end, the controller may find that the data collection task has grossly exceeded the time needed to analyze the resulting information. If there are many capital proposals to review, the data collection phase of the analysis can easily turn into a full-time job.

A good way to entirely avoid the data collection phase of the investment proposal process is to make the department managers do it. The controller can create a standard form, such as the one shown in Exhibit 3.7, that itemizes the exact information needed. This form can be created in a template format, perhaps in an electronic spreadsheet, and distributed by e-mail to all managers. They then fill out the necessary fields (all user-entered fields in the

Exhibit 3.7   Sample Capital Investment Proposal Form

Name of Project Sponsor: *H. Henderson*   **Submission Date:** *09/09/01*

Investment Description: *Additional press for newsprint.*

Cash Flows:

Year	Equipment	Working Capital	Maintenance	Tax Effect of Annual Depreciation	Salvage Value	Revenue	Taxes	Total
0	-5,000,000	-400,000		800,000				-5,400,000
1			-100,000	320,000		1,650,000	-700,000	1,170,000
2			-100,000	320,000		1,650,000	-700,000	1,170,000
3			-100,000	320,000		1,650,000	-700,000	1,170,000
4			-100,000	320,000		1,650,000	-700,000	1,170,000
5		400,000	-100,000	320,000	1,000,000	1,650,000	-700,000	2,570,000
Totals	-5,000,000	0	-500,000	2,400,000	1,000,000	8,250,000		1,850,000

Tax Rate:	**40%**
Hurdle Rate:	**10%**
Payback Period:	4.28
Net Present Value:	(86,809)
Internal Rate of Return:	9.4%

Type of Project (check one):

Legal requirement _____

New product-related _____

Old product extension _____   Yes

Repair/replacement _____

Safety issue _____

Approvals:

Amount	Approver	Signature
<$5,000	Supervisor	_____
$5–19,999	General Mgr	_____
$20–49,999	President	_____
$50,000+	Board	_____

example are in italics), and e-mail it back to the controller for review. This eliminates the data collection chore, while also putting the data into the exact format needed to yield basic calculations for the controller, such as the payback period, net present value, and internal rate of return, thereby keeping not only the data collection work, but much of the related analysis, to a minimum.

The form shown in Exhibit 3.7 is divided into several key pieces. The first is the identification section, in which the name of the project sponsor, the date on which the proposal was submitted, and the description of the project are inserted. For a company that deals with a multitude of capital projects, it may also be useful to include a specific identifying code for each one. The next section is the most important one; it lists all cash inflows and outflows, in summary form, for each year. The sample form has room for just five years of cash flows, but this can be increased for companies with longer-term investments. Cash outflows are listed as negative numbers and inflows as positive ones. The annual depreciation figure goes into the box in the "Tax Effect of Annual Depreciation" column. The column of tax deductions listed directly below the depreciation box are automatic calculations that determine the tax deduction, based on the tax rate noted in the far right column. All of the cash flows for each year are then summarized in the far right column. A series of calculations are listed directly below this "Total" column, which itemize the payback period, net present value, and internal rate of return, mostly based on the hurdle rate noted just above them. In the example, the rate of return on the itemized cash flows is 9.4 percent, which is just below the corporate hurdle rate of 10 percent. Because the discount rate is higher than the actual rate of return, the net present value is negative. Also, this can be considered a risky project, since the number of years needed to pay back the initial investment is quite lengthy. The next section of the form is for the type of project. The purpose of this section is to identify those investments that *must* be completed, irrespective of the rate of return; these are usually due to legal or safety issues. Also, if a project is for a new product, management may consider it to be especially risky, and it will therefore require a higher hurdle rate. This section identifies those projects. The last section is for approvals by managers. It lists the level of manager who can sign off on various investment dollar amounts and ensures that the correct number of managers have reviewed each investment. This format is comprehensive enough to give a controller sufficient information to conduct a rapid analysis of most projects.

Though the capital investment proposal form is a good way to have project sponsors assemble information for the controller, it does not guarantee that the finished product will be free of errors—far from it. Department managers may not have a clear understanding of what information goes into each field of the form, so they may enter incorrect information, which the controller will then use to arrive at an incorrect analysis. To keep this from happening, there are several steps to take. One is to create a short procedure to accompany all forms when they are given to managers, which clearly describe what information goes into each field in the form. Another option is to meet with all new managers to go over the form, so that they have a clear understanding of how to fill it out. Yet another option, if the form is distributed in Excel, is to include instructions in a "Comments" field that can be attached to each cell in the spreadsheet; by positioning the cursor on the field, the comment appears on the screen, describing how to fill in each field. Finally, and of greatest importance, the controller should meet with the sponsor of any large project to carefully review all aspects of the proposal form. For a large project, it is critical to verify all information, because even a small mistake can yield the wrong analysis results, possibly leading to significant and unexpected financial losses.

A final issue regarding the use of capital investment proposal forms is that a bureaucratically minded person can create a behemoth of a form. This happens when the accounting department wants to see all possible underlying details to justify every cash flow in the analysis. Though the accounting staff thinks it is just being careful, the managers who must fill out the novella-sized forms will certainly think otherwise. For them, creating a proposal form will become a major chore that is to be delayed or avoided at all costs. To keep this situation from arising, the controller must remember that most capital requests are very small, usually hovering near the low-end capitalization limit, and so do not require a vast analysis. Only a few very large capital investments are worthy of in-depth review, and so should be treated as the exception, not the rule. Based on this logic, the investment proposal form should be a small one, which the controller can investigate in greater detail if the size or uncertainty of the investment appears to warrant it.

The capital investment proposal form is a relatively easy one to create, and, with an accompanying procedure, is one of the best ways to improve the flow of information to the controller for the analysis of capital investments.

POSTCOMPLETION PROJECT ANALYSIS

The greatest failing in most capital review systems is not in the initial analysis phase, but in the postcompletion phase, because there isn't one. A controller usually puts a great deal of effort into compiling a capital investment proposal form, educating managers about how to use it, and then setting up control points around the system to ensure that all capital requests make use of the approval system. However, if there is no methodology for verifying that managers enter accurate information into the approval forms, which is done by comparing actual results to them, then managers will eventually figure out that they can alter the numbers in the approval forms in order to beat the corporate hurdle rates, even if this information is incorrect. However, if managers know that their original estimates will be carefully reviewed and critiqued for some time into the future, then they will be much more careful in completing their initial capital requests. Thus, analysis at the back end of a capital project will lead to greater accuracy at the front end.

Analysis of actual expenditures can begin before a capital investment is fully paid for or installed. A controller can subtotal the payments made by the end of each month and compare them to the total projected by the project manager. A total that significantly exceeds the approved expenditure would then be grounds for an immediate review by top management. This approach works best for the largest capital expenditures, where reviewing payment data in detail is worth the extra effort by the accounting staff if it can prevent large overpayments. It is also worthwhile when capital expenditures cover long periods of time, so that a series of monthly reviews can be made. However, it is not a worthwhile approach if the expenditure in question is for a single item that is made with one payment, although this type of purchase can still be reviewed by comparing the company's purchase order total to the amount noted on the capital investment proposal form.

Once a project is completed, there may be cash inflows that result from it. If so, a quarterly comparison of actual to projected cash inflows is the most frequent comparison to be made, with an annual review being sufficient in many cases. Such a review keeps management apprised of the performance of all capital projects and lets the project sponsors know that their estimates will be the subject of considerable scrutiny for as far into the future as they had originally projected. For those companies that survive based on the efficiency of capital usage, it may even be reasonable to tie manager pay reviews to the accuracy of their capital investment request forms.

An example of a postcompletion project analysis is shown in Exhibit 3.8. In this example, the top of the report compares actual to budgeted cash out-

Exhibit 3.8 Comparison of Actual to Projected Capital Investment Cash Flows

Description	Actual	Projected Actual	Budget	Actual Present Value*	Budget Present Value*
Cash Outflows					
Capital Items	$1,250,000	—	$1,100,000	$1,250,000	$1,100,000
Working Capital	750,000	—	500,000	750,000	500,000
Total Outflows	$2,000,000	—	$1,600,000	$2,000,000	$1,600,000
Cash Inflows					
Year 1	250,000		$250,000	$229,350	$229,350
Year 2	375,000		400,000	315,638	336,680
Year 3	450,000		500,000	347,490	386,100
Year 4		450,000	500,000	318,780	354,200
Year 5		450,000	500,000	292,455	324,950
Total Inflows	$1,075,000	$900,000	$2,150,000	$1,503,713	$1,631,280
Net Present Value	—	—	—	–$496,287	+$31,280

* Uses discount rate of 9%.

flows, while the middle compares all actual cash outflows to the budget. Note that the cash outflows section is complete, since these were all incurred at the beginning of the project, whereas the inflows section is not yet complete, because the project has only completed the third year of a five-year plan. To cover the remaining two years of activity, there is a column for estimated cash inflows, which projects them for the remaining years of the investment, using the last year in which actual data are available. This projected information can be used to determine the net present value. We compare the actual and projected net present values at the bottom of the report, so that management can see if there are any problems worthy of correction. In this case, the initial costs of the project, both in terms of capital items and working capital, were so far over budget that the actual net present value is solidly in the red. In this case, because working capital is the single largest cash drain in excess of the budget, management should take a hard look at reducing it while also seeing if cash inflow can be increased to match the budgeted annual amounts for the last two years of the investment.

SUMMARY

In this chapter, some of the most fundamental analyses that a controller will see were discussed: the use of the payback period, net present value, and internal rate of return measures to determine whether a company should invest in a capital project. Just as important to this analysis—though unfortunately overlooked by all too many companies—is the postimplementation review of partially or fully completed capital investments, because this information tells a company which investments have succeeded and which have failed. Only by mastering all the techniques noted in this chapter can a controller become an efficient analyzer of capital investment issues.

4

Evaluating Financing Options

In a larger corporation, the choice of how to fund the purchase of assets falls on the chief financial officer (CFO). However, there is generally no CFO in a smaller organization, so this task falls on the controller. Also, the funding for smaller purchases, even in a larger company, will frequently be left up to the controller to decide. To assist the controller in making the correct determination of which types of financing options to select under different circumstances, this chapter includes discussions of the types of funding options available, as well as all related cost, risk, and control issues. This chapter is intended to give a controller a sufficient amount of information to properly select the correct financing option that matches a company's specific circumstances.

TYPES OF FUNDING OPTIONS

There are two types of funding options: (1) debt and (2) equity. Later sections of this chapter will discuss a number of variations and crossover instruments, but essentially, every type of funding choice is based on one of these two options. In the case of *debt*, the funding is contingent on some obligation to pay interest in exchange for the use of the invested funds, which are also to be returned at the end of a stipulated period. The most pure version of debt is the long-term loan, which is usually collateralized against some group of company assets, carries a stated interest rate that may move with an underlying interest rate or pricing indicator, and which must be paid back either in installments or in total on a specified date. Variations on this concept are the lease, in which the creditor may own the underlying asset, and preferred stock, in which there is no obligation to pay back the funds on a specific date, but there is an interest payment obligation.

In the case of *equity*, the funding is not contingent on any specified interest payment, but the holder of the underlying common stock expects either a periodic dividend payment, an appreciation in the share price on the open market, or a combination of the two. Equity has no underlying collateral, so the holder is at much greater risk of losing the invested funds, which is why the expected return is much higher for equity than for debt. Preferred stock is also a variation on equity, because it is not collateralized and there is no obligation to pay it back on a specific date. Another variation on the equity concept is stock rights, which can be issued to current shareholders, giving them the right to purchase more shares of stock. Also, warrants can be attached to various debt instruments to make them more attractive; warrants give the holder the right to buy common stock at a specific price. These are all forms of funding that fall under the general concept of equity.

It is also possible to convert debt into equity. This is called a convertible security and is sometimes used when selling bonds, so that buyers can later switch their bonds over to debt if a specific stock price point is reached at which the conversion is an attractive one. This is not a third form of funding option, however—just a hybrid form that shifts from debt to equity at the buyer's option. Preferred stock can also be considered something of a hybrid, because it contains characteristics of both debt (with a fixed interest payment) and equity (with no specified payback date for the underlying investment).

The following sections discuss the cost, risk, and control issues associated with the major financing options.

COSTS OF FUNDING OPTIONS

There are significant differences between the costs of the two main kinds of funding. In the case of debt, there is an interest payment that must be paid to the lender on specified dates. If payments do not reach the lender on those dates, then penalty payments will also be charged. The interest rate charged will vary greatly, depending on the willingness of the borrowing organization to put up its assets as collateral. If it is not willing to do so or has no significant assets to use as collateral, then the risk of the lending institution is correspondingly greater, because it will have no specified assets at its disposal for liquidation purposes if the borrower is unable to pay for the borrowed funds. For this type of debt, the interest rate can be quite a few percentage points higher than the prime rate charged by local lending institutions. Also, if the borrower has a spotty earnings or debt payment record, lenders will charge the highest possible interest rates for use of their funds.

This may sound as though debt is an expensive option, but it can be extraordinarily inexpensive for those companies with a large base of available assets for use as collateral. Also, if the borrowing company is a very large one with an excellent financial credit rating, it can borrow well below the prime rate, perhaps only a fraction of a percent above the London Interbank Offer Rate (LIBOR), which is the minimum borrowing rate available. For these institutions, it makes a great deal of sense to use debt as a major financing source as much as possible.

In the case of equity, there is the surface appearance of free money, because the company receiving the equity is under no specific obligation to pay it back or to issue dividends. However, this is not the case for two reasons. First, the investments of shareholders are not secured by any form of collateral—if the company falls into financial difficulty and is liquidated, shareholders are likely to lose all their funds. Because of this increased level of risk, they want an inordinately high level of return, which they can receive either through dividend payments, stock appreciation, or a combination of the two. Second, interest payments on debt are tax deductible, whereas dividend payments are not, thereby making payments to shareholders more expensive than payments to creditors. Thus, the more expensive option is equity.

When deciding between the use of debt or equity, the management team may have a tendency to lean toward the acquisition of more debt, because it is less expensive than equity. However, there are serious risk issues associated with having an excessively leveraged company, which are discussed in the next section.

RISKS ASSOCIATED WITH FUNDING OPTIONS

All forms of financing involve some degree of risk. A controller must be cognizant of all the forms of risk to ensure that management is made aware of the potential shortcomings of each one. There are five types of risk that accompany the use of various kinds of debt or equity. One or more will be present for virtually every kind of financing option.

1. *Risk of not paying interest on debt.* If a company acquires more debt than it can support through the cash from its continuing operations, then there is a high risk that it will be unable to service even the periodic interest payments on the debt, which will result in either renegotiation of the debt with lenders or a default that can result in the liquidation of the company as a whole or the assets that were used as collateral for the debt.

2. *Risk of not paying principal on debt.* This is a lesser risk than the preceding situation, because many companies simply roll their debt over into new debt instruments as soon as the old ones become due and payable. However, for those companies whose financial fortunes have significantly declined since the last time they acquired debt, there may be no lenders available who are willing to take the risk of issuing new debt to cover the now-due principal on the old debt. If so, a company can face dissolution or liquidation of any assets used as collateral.

3. *Risk of experiencing a loan acceleration.* Lenders sometimes have the option to force the acceleration of payments on debt owed to them. This is usually brought about by a change in the lender's perception of the ability of a company to do business, such as a string of poor earnings reports. In such a situation, a company is obligated to pay off the debt

by whatever means, such as a refinancing or liquidation of any assets used as collateral. If it cannot meet the lender's demand, it may be necessary to take the company into bankruptcy.

4. *Risk of tighter loan covenants.* If a lender finds that a company is unable to meet its minimum loan covenants, such as a minimum current ratio or inventory turnover rate, then it can impose much more restrictive covenants that can actively interfere in the running of the business. Essentially, the lender can alter the company's objective to be that of paying off the loan, possibly by requiring lender approval of major business decisions involving the use of cash for purchases of any kind outside of the normal course of business activities.

5. *Risk of shareholder revolt.* Common stockholders own a company, and if they are dissatisfied with the existing level of return on their investment, then they can band together and replace the board of directors, which in turn can replace the management team. Thus, the consequences of not generating an adequate return for shareholders is severe.

At least one of the above five types of risk will apply to any form of financing. For example, the risk when using a lease is that nonpayment will result in the loss of the asset, while poor overall profitability can result in a new board of directors that may replace the management team. Thus, a controller must convey to management the risks of using each type of financing; this should be a continuing message to management as circumstances change, for the risks will rise if a company finds itself either unable to service its debt or provide an adequate return to investors.

CONTROL PROBLEMS ASSOCIATED WITH FINANCING OPTIONS

There is a major problem with issuing common stock or any variation that gives any entity the future right to purchase additional shares of stock, because this can alter the balance of power in the ownership structure of the corporation. This is a particular problem when a company is owned by a small group that wants to retain ownership. In this instance, the owners will continually opt for raising funds through any source *but* more equity. When this happens, the only options left for raising funds are through the spin-off of cash from continuing operations, or by adding on more debt, which will eventually raise the debt/equity ratio to such a high point that creditors will be willing to lend more funds only if the interest rate is extremely high (because the lenders are risking their capital while the owners earn all the profits). The end result is a highly leveraged organization that is at considerable risk of failure if its cash flow drops to the point where it cannot cover its continuing debt payments.

This problem is at its worst when the ownership group is absolutely unwilling to bring in new investors and has no funds of its own with which to increase the amount of equity. Under this scenario, the owners do not even have recourse to the use of stock rights (see the Stock Rights section later in this chapter), which would allow for all current owners to buy the same proportion of new shares that they currently own. A lesser situation occurs when the current owners *can* contribute more funds, in which case the absence of other owners is not a problem, and new equity is brought in as needed. Thus, the control problem as it relates to the acquisition of new funding is a combination of close control of an organization as well as the ability of the current owners to put more equity into a company as needed.

LEASING

In a leasing situation, the company pays a lessor for the use of equipment that is owned by the lessor. Under the terms of this arrangement, the company pays a set (usually monthly) fee, while the lessor records the asset on its books and takes the associated depreciation expense, while also undertaking to pay all property taxes and maintenance fees. The lessor typically takes back the asset at the end of the lease term, unless the company wishes to pay a fee at the end of the agreement period to buy the residual value of the asset and then record it on the company's books as an asset.

A leasing arrangement tends to be rather expensive for the lessee, because it is paying for the interest cost, profit, taxes, maintenance, and decline in value of the asset. However, it would have had to pay for all these costs except the lessor's profit and the interest cost if it had bought the asset, so this can be an appealing option, especially for the use of those assets that tend to degrade quickly in value or usability, and which would therefore need to be replaced at the end of the leasing period anyway. Examples of commonly leased items are autos, airplanes, copiers, and computers. However, the cost of a lease tends to be higher than necessary, since the number of variables included in the lease calculation (e.g., down payment, interest rate, asset residual value, and trade-in value) makes it very difficult for the lessor to determine the true cost of what it is obtaining. Consequently, when using leasing as the financing option of choice, a controller must be extremely careful to review the individual costs that roll up into the total lease cost, to ensure that the overall expenditure is reasonable.

Another use of the leasing concept is the sale and leaseback. This option is typically used by cash-poor companies with real estate holdings; they sell their real estate holdings to a leasing company for a cash payment, and then lease the property back from the lessor for a guaranteed minimum period. This approach releases a large amount of cash for immediate uses in exchange for a long-term series of lease payments.

LOANS

A company can obtain a loan either by borrowing funds from a lending institution or by issuing its own bonds to investors and paying interest to all of them on preset payment dates. In the case of debt owed to a lender, the lending institution may require collateral in the form of company assets, personal guarantees by company officers (usually the case only for the smallest companies), and restrictive covenants that require a company to operate in a specified manner that is designed to raise sufficient cash to ensure that the debt will be paid on time. These covenants may be so restrictive that the lender must approve of any significant asset sales or purchases. There may also be an annual audit by the lender, which is paid for by the borrower. In the case of a bond offering, however, there is not normally any required collateral, guarantee, audit, or covenant, though the company must pay for the cost of registering, issuing, and tracking the bonds.

The cost of a loan is based on the interest rate. This interest rate will vary considerably based on the perceived ability of the company to pay back the debt. If it has received a sterling credit rating from any of the various credit rating agencies, or if there are plenty of assets to use as collateral, then a company can expect to pay the lowest possible rate; however, a company that has a track record of failing to make payments or requiring renegotiated loan deals will pay a much higher rate in order to cover the default risk of the lender. If a company chooses to issue its own bonds, then it will state an interest rate that it is willing to pay on the bonds; purchasers of the bonds will pay either more or less than the face value of the bond in order to arrive at the interest rate they are actually willing to pay. For example, if a company offers a bond for sale at a face value of $1,000 and a stated interest rate of 6 percent (or $60 per year), a bond purchaser who wants to receive an interest rate of 8 percent will pay only $750 for the bonds, which will yield 8 percent ($60/$750 = 8%).

Debt is generally the least expensive form of financing, because the interest expense is tax deductible. This differs from dividend payments on equity, in which dividends are *not* tax deductible. Accordingly, the typical company that needs to increase its available funding will first increase its debt load to a considerable degree before obtaining other types of financing. The main limit on the amount of debt one can use is the issue of risk. As noted earlier, a company with too much debt will be put in the uncomfortable position of not being able to pay the interest cost if cash flow drops, possibly due to a downturn in the business or some unusual usage of cash. Thus, debt is inexpensive but can land a company in considerable trouble if it uses it to an excessive degree.

A final issue in regard to debt is that, as lenders perceive a company's risk to increase as it piles on a large amount of debt, they will charge a premium for each additional increase in debt. As the company approaches the point where it can barely meet its interest payments, lenders will charge such high rates and add such restrictive covenants that this form of financing will no longer be a viable option. Accordingly, the perceived level of risk will eventually drive the cost of debt up to the point where it is no longer the least expensive form of funding.

COMMON STOCK

When shareholders purchase shares from a company, the money they pay becomes equity in that organization. This cash can be used for any operational purpose, and is not restricted for a specific use unless so authorized by the board of directors. This type of funding carries with it no immediate payment obligation, because the money does not have to be repaid and there is no obligation to make a continuing or one-time payment to the shareholders. Nonetheless, the shareholders elect all members of the board of directors, which in turn is empowered to authorize periodic dividend payments to the shareholders. Also, the shareholders expect to see the earnings per share increase over time, which increases the value of their shares and allows them to sell their shares for a profit. These are the two ways in which shareholders expect to be paid back for their investments, and this constitutes a hefty performance target for the management team to reach.

An additional expense associated with the use of common stock for public companies is the large quantity of financial reports that must be continually filed with the Securities and Exchange Commission, as well as increased audit expenses, shareholder reports and mailings, and the cost of officer liability insurance that protects the board of directors and managers against the risk of payouts in the event of shareholder lawsuits if the price of the stock drops as a result of management actions. All of these costs will be incurred if a company sells its stock to the public, and so can reasonably be called an added cost of using common stock as a source of funding.

The sale of shares by a company is not to be confused with the sale of shares on one of the stock markets, where shares are traded between buyers and sellers for the going market rate; the company benefits only from the initial sale of its shares, after which it does not profit from increases in the price of its shares, unless it makes a secondary stock offering at the higher prices. A company can wait until the market price of its shares is at a relatively low point and use excess cash to buy back some shares, which will increase the earnings per share for the remaining outstanding shares and thereby increase their value.

Common stock is a useful funding source for three reasons. The first is that it can raise an inordinate amount of money if the public thinks that the company has a strong potential to increase its value in the future (even if it is losing money in the present—witness the astounding valuations of some Internet start-up companies). Another reason is that a company may have borrowed all the money it possibly can from lenders, who are now balking at lending anything more unless the owners match some proportion of the debt load with equity. If the owners do not have the wherewithal to add equity, then the best option left is to sell some portion of the company to the public to bring in funds by that means. The final reason is that the current shareholders—probably a mix of funding entities and management personnel—can liquidate some or all of the shares they already own, which increases their personal net worth, though not that of the company.

Consequently, the strong funding advantages of common stock are offset by its high cost and shareholder expectations of earnings per share performance, which can lead to the ouster of the board of directors and the management team by shareholders if earnings targets are not met.

CONVERTIBLE SECURITIES

A convertible security is a bond that can be converted into common stock. The common stock price at which the bond can be converted is based on the conversion ratio, which is the ratio of the number of shares that can be purchased with each bond. For example, if a $1,000 bond has a conversion ratio of 10, then it can be converted into 10 shares, which translates into a share price of $100. This does not mean that the holder of a bond will immediately convert to shares, however; that will happen only when the market price of the stock equals or exceeds the amount indicated by the conversion ratio. To return to our example, this means that a bondholder will be tempted to make the conversion only when the price of the stock reaches $100 or more. Until then, it makes more sense to retain the bond, because the return is greater. If the market price of the common stock exceeds the price indicated by the conversion ratio, the price of the bond will also rise, because its value, based on its convertibility, is now greater than its price based on the stream of future interest payments from the company in payment for the bond.

A convertible security is worthy of much attention if a company does not want to pay back the underlying principle on its bonds. This is most common in a high-growth situation in which all cash will be needed for the foreseeable future. Also, by converting debt over to equity, a company can improve its debt/equity ratio, which will improve relations with lenders, while also eliminating the need to pay interest on the bonds that no longer exist. Finally, a company can convert a group of existing debtholders into a group of shareholders, which means that it has a (presumably) friendly and long-term group of investors now holding its stock. The only downsides of this approach are that the increased number of shares will reduce the earnings per share, and that control will be spread over a larger group of investors, which may weaken the stake of a majority owner.

PREFERRED STOCK

When a company accepts payment for its preferred stock, its only obligation is to pay a prespecified interest rate on that investment in perpetuity, or until the shares of preferred stock are bought back by the company. Though there is no obligation to pay back the equity invested by the shareholders, this is an expensive option, because the interest payments are considered by the government to be dividend payments, which are not tax deductible. Also, because preferred stock cannot be collateralized with company assets to give the shareholders some degree of protection in the event of a default, the interest rate on the stock is higher than the amount that a lender would charge for collateralized debt. Consequently, a company must pay a premium on top of the current market interest rate, and cannot deduct any of this as an expense on the corporate tax return. In short, this is a financing option whose sole benefit is the elimination of a payback to the shareholders of their initial investment. Because of this one advantage, it is of greatest benefit to companies that are short of cash and cannot pay back the principal on any other kind of financing option.

STOCK RIGHTS

A stock right is an authorization to purchase additional shares of common stock at a set price, with a specified termination date to the offer. It is offered to existing shareholders in the same proportions as their stock holdings in the company. For example, if Mr. Smith holds 40 percent of all common stock, he will be awarded 40 percent of the stock rights. This approach is designed to retain the existing proportions of company ownership, while also raising funds only from existing shareholders, who are assumed to be friendly to the corporation. However, there are several flaws in the underlying logic that make stock rights not quite the perfect way to retain the existing proportions of corporate ownership while still raising funds.

The first problem is that not all recipients of stock rights will choose to use them for the purchase of additional shares. When this happens, the proportional ownership of those common stockholders who *do* purchase shares will increase. This point is illustrated in Exhibit 4.1. In this example, there are five shareholders, with the combined holdings of the Smith and Jones families (shaded in the third column) comprising an absolute majority of 51 percent. The company then issues stock rights to all existing shareholders in exact proportion to their current holdings, with each right giving the holder the option to purchase one half of an additional share. However, the Smith and Jones families do not have the funds to pay for additional shares, and let their stock rights lapse. The three minority shareholders, however, have exercised their purchase rights, which results in a new set of ownership percentages that place the ownership of the three formerly minority owners, when combined, in a majority stock ownership position (as noted by the shading in the last column). Thus, stock rights do not necessarily allow current stockholders to retain their proportion of ownership.

Exhibit 4.1   Changes in Corporate Ownership as a Result of Stock Rights Usage

Stockholder Name	No. Shares Held	Shares Held (%)	Stock Rights Issued*	Stock Rights Used	New Total No. Shares Held	New Total Shares Held (%)
Smith	150,000	15	150,000	0	150,000	12
Jones	360,000	36	360,000	0	360,000	29
Fitch	100,000	10	100,000	100,000	150,000	12
Evans	250,000	25	250,000	250,000	375,000	30
King	140,000	14	140,000	140,000	210,000	17
Totals	1,000,000	100	1,000,000	490,000	1,245,000	100

* Two stock rights are needed to purchase one additional share.

The other problem is that stock rights can be sold to another party. This situation arises when the stock price at which shares can be purchased with stock rights is less than the current market price. The difference between these two amounts is the value of the stock right, and it will trade on the open market at that price differential. Because of the transferability and market for stock rights, the underlying intent to keep new stock ownership within the existing group of shareholders is negated (unless the rights offering stipulates that it is only for current shareholders and states that the rights are not transferable).

Given the problems with control over ownership percentages, rights offerings should be used simply as an alternative means of raising funds, rather than as a surefire way to raise funds while keeping current owners in control of the corporation.

WARRANTS

A warrant is a right to purchase common stock at a fixed price and usually has a distant termination date, if any. It is usually linked to the sale of a debt instrument, such as a bond, for the express purpose of making the purchase of those bonds appear more attractive to bond purchasers. For example, if a warrant allows the holder to buy a share for $10, even though the current market price is $11, then the warrant has a value of $1. Because bond purchasers recognize that such a warrant has value, they will be more willing to purchase a bond from the issuing company at an interest rate that is somewhat lower than the market rate, knowing that the difference will be made up for by the value of the warrant.

A warrant is not a good tool for raising funds by itself, because it is attached to some other debt instrument, but it can be an exceedingly useful tool if the issuing company's objective is to avoid a high interest expense. For example, if ABC Company does not have enough cash flow to adequately cover its interest and principal costs, it can mitigate the situation somewhat by issuing warrants with its bonds and reducing the stated interest rate on the bonds. Investors will still buy the bonds, as long as the value of the warrants offsets the lost interest income.

The risk of using this approach is that the warrants must have a perceived value at the time of the bond sale, or else the bond interest rate will not be accepted by bond buyers. Also, if there are many issued warrants, there is some risk of diluted earnings per share, as well as a control problem if a hostile shareholder uses the outstanding warrants to acquire a controlling interest in the company.

SUMMARY

In this chapter, the most common forms of financing were reviewed, as well as their attendant costs, risks, and control issues. A summary of these options is

Exhibit 4.2   Summary of Financing Option Advantages and Disadvantages

Financing Option	Advantages	Disadvantages
Leasing	Good for replacement of assets that wear out quickly; the sale-and-leaseback option makes available a large amount of cash	Can be very expensive unless all components of the transaction are carefully evaluated and negotiated
Loans	Least expensive form of funding	May require assets as loan collateral, as well as loan covenants, some control over operations, and first call on the results of asset sales in the event of a liquidation
Common stock	Can raise substantial amounts of funds, and there is no need to pay back the capital	Shareholder expectations for returns are very high, and it also gives them the ability to oust the board of directors and (indirectly) the management team if their performance expectations are not met. Also, dividend payments are not tax deductible
Convertible securities	Can avoid paying off bond debt, as well as reducing interest payments and improving the debt/equity ratio	Reduces the earnings per share and weakens the control of current shareholders, but only if conversion to shares occurs
Preferred stock	Can avoid paying back the principal	The interest expense is not tax deductible
Stock rights	Simple way to raise funds from existing shareholders	Will not necessarily retain ownership interests in the same proportions prior to the stock rights offering
Warrants	Can reduce bond interest rates	Dilutes earnings per share and may weaken owner control of the company

listed in Exhibit 4.2. Given the wide array of available financing options, it is evident that a controller must be well aware of a company's current loan covenants, ability to cover debt costs, and the degree to which the current owners want to maintain control of the organization, before making a decision regarding which financing option is the correct one to pursue.

5

Evaluating Cash Flow

This chapter covers the compilation and analysis of a company's cash flows. This information forms the basis for cash forecasting, project analysis, and incremental cash flow analysis, which makes it crucial for many of the most common analyses that a controller is expected to complete. The chapter begins with the most simple form of cash analysis and works up to the most difficult cash flow reporting format; accordingly, it starts with a review of working capital and advances to cash flow models for a capital investment and then to corporate cash forecasts. The chapter concludes with a review of incremental cash flow analysis and the correct interpretation of variations in the flow of cash.

EVALUATING WORKING CAPITAL

The most inexplicable event for a senior-level manager is to see a profit at the bottom of the income statement, and yet field a request from the accounting staff to obtain more cash, because there is not enough on hand to meet all current cash requirements. What happened? There may be large asset purchases, but these normally require the approval of senior management, so everyone is aware of them. The primary remaining reason why there is a cash outflow is that working capital requirements have increased. A controller is frequently called on to review the elements of this key investment area and tell management why increases have occurred and how to reduce them. This section reviews the elements of working capital and how to evaluate them.

There are three components to working capital. The first two, accounts receivable and inventory, represent a net usage of cash. The third component, accounts payable, is a source of cash. Thus, the total amount of working capital is accounts receivable plus inventory, minus accounts payable. To reduce the investment in working capital, then, one must either decrease the amount of accounts receivable or inventory, or increase the amount of accounts payable. However, before taking action to alter the working capital investment, it is best to first understand what caused any increase in working capital that is now the focus of management attention. Accordingly, a controller should review the following most common causes of working capital changes to find the culprit:

Accounts Receivable
- *Credit granting problems.* If the finance staff is doing a poor job of granting credit to new customers, or if there is no process at all for doing so, then it is likely that some customers will take advantage of the situation and purchase more from the company than they can pay for, which will result in an increased company investment in accounts receivable.

- *Credit review problems.* Once a customer has been granted a credit limit by the finance staff, this does not mean that the customer's ability to pay must never be reviewed again. On the contrary, this should be at least a yearly exercise, so that the company can spot any customers who are having difficulty paying on time and reduce their credit. Without this annual review, the financial condition of a few customers will worsen, resulting in their inability to pay on time and an increased company investment in accounts receivable.

- *Credit hold problems.* Even if there is an excellent credit granting and review process, a company is still in danger of shipping to customers with poor credit ratings if the shipping department is not informed of any customers' being on credit hold. When this happens, shipments will go to customers who are not paying on time, which results in an increased company investment in accounts receivable.

- *Collection problems.* Some customers will not pay invoices on time, either because they lack the funds, or because they have a problem with the invoice that must be resolved before they will pay. In either case, it is the job of the collections staff to contact the customers to determine the nature of any problems, correct them, and follow up with the customer to ensure that payment is then made. If this function does not exist or is poorly run, then the company's investment in accounts receivable will increase.

- *Product return problems.* Sometimes, customers will return products and then not pay for the related invoices. Though this is acceptable behavior when the customer obtains a return authorization from the company, it is quite a different matter when the customer simply returns volumes of product that it does not use and refuses to pay the related invoices. This lapse can be solved by creating an effective return authorization program that rejects all other returned goods. Without it, a company's investment in either accounts receivable (because of the unpaid invoices) or inventory (because of the returned product) will increase.

- *Billing problems.* If a company cannot send its customers error-free invoices, then the customers will refuse to pay them until the errors are corrected, which usually involves mailing out either a credit or a new invoice; in either case, the problem is usually not discovered until the invoice is overdue, followed by a few weeks for the revised invoice to reach and be processed by the customer, followed by another week or two for the payment to arrive at the company. Thus, the time lag associated with correcting the problem will result in an increase in the company's investment in accounts receivable.

- *Sales growth.* If company sales increase, then the investment in accounts receivable will inevitably increase alongside it and in the same proportion. For example, if all customers pay in 30 days and sales are $1 million per month, then there should always be a minimum of $1 million in accounts receivable. However, if sales double to $2 million per month, then so too will the accounts receivable investment.

Inventory
- *Production obsolescence problems.* Some inventory will not be used. This may be due to the withdrawal from the market or poor sales of a specific product, for which all related finished goods, work-in-process, and raw materials will now languish. When this happens, the company will have invested an excess amount in inventory.

- *Engineering design change problems.* Some raw materials or work-in-process items will never be added to finished products, because the engineering department switched to a new component prior to using up all available stocks of the old parts. As a result, these old parts will never be used and will stay in the inventory. Since the inventory now includes both the old and replacement parts, the company has increased its investment in inventory.

- *Purchasing overage problems.* The purchasing staff may be tempted to order parts in extra-large quantities, which generally fetches a lower per-unit price, while also reducing the number of orders that the purchasing staff must place. However, this leads to much larger stock of raw material items in inventory, as well as an increased risk of inventory obsolescence, because it may take years to use up all the stock. Thus, the company's investment in inventory is increased.

- *Costing methodology problems.* If the accounting staff chooses to alter the inventory costing method, this can have an impact on the total investment in inventory. For example, if the most recent layers of costing in the inventory costing database are the most expensive, switching to the first in–first out (FIFO) method from the last in–first out (LIFO) method will increase the cost of what is in inventory.

- *Sales forecasting problems.* If the sales staff incorrectly forecasts an excessive quantity of sales, then the production scheduling staff will order the production of an excessive quantity of finished goods, which will increase the company's investment in finished goods inventory until the goods are eventually sold.

- *Production methodology problems.* If a company has difficulty in controlling the flow of production, or is using a production system that tends to require more inventory, then there will be an excess amount of raw materials and work-in-process inventory on hand. For example, if a company uses manufacturing resource planning (MRP), then it will create a forecast of expected production and "push" product through the manufacturing facility, which can result in excess quantities of finished goods inventory. However, if a company uses the just-in-time (JIT) manufacturing system, then it produces only if there are specific customer orders in hand (generally speaking), which "pulls" inventory through the facility only as needed, and tends to reduce the overall level of inventory.

- *Overhead absorption problems.* If the management team is compensated based on the level of company profits, it will be tempted to increase the level of inventory, even if there is no need for the excess amount. The reason for doing so is that overhead costs can be spread over more units of production, which keeps much of the overhead cost from being charged to the cost of goods sold, which in turn increases profits. However, the cost of doing so is that the company's investment in inventory increases.

- *Distribution problems.* If a company has a distribution policy of having inventory as close to the customer as possible for rapid servicing issues, the result will be additional inventory. For example, if a company adds a local warehouse for every new sales territory that it creates, the company's investment in inventory will be significantly greater.

- *Sales growth.* As company sales increase, so too will the inventory needed to support those sales. For example, if a retail chain increases sales by adding new stores, each new store must contain an adequate amount of inventory. Accordingly, inventory will increase in roughly the same proportion to sales as is currently the case, which will increase the company's investment in inventory.

Accounts Payable
- *Changes to new suppliers.* If a company switches to a new supplier that requires short payment terms, the company's access to free credit from that supplier will be reduced. If the supplier is a major one, or if there are many new suppliers, all of whom require rapid payment, then this source of funds will be significantly reduced.

- *New terms with existing suppliers.* If an existing supplier negotiates a shorter payment term from the company, the amount of funds available through accounts payable will be reduced. This circumstance may arise as a result of price negotiations in which the company trades off a shorter payment period for lower unit prices, or perhaps because the supplier has experienced excessively long payment periods from the company and is now tightening its credit.

- *Usage of early payment discount terms.* Another reason for a reduction in accounts payable is that the controller has decided to reduce expenses by taking as many early payment discounts as possible. When this happens, the overall level of expenses will drop, but the amount of available funds from suppliers will also decrease.

- *Incorrect early payments.* If the accounts payable staff is incorrectly managed, it is possible that some payments to suppliers will be made earlier than necessary, which will reduce the amount of funds available from suppliers.

The preceding list detailed 20 ways in which a company's investment in working capital can increase—and these are only the most common reasons. When management asks a controller for advice regarding how to reduce the overall investment in working capital, it is extremely useful to know why it increased in the first place, because the answer (with the exception of sales growth) to the underlying reason is also the correct recommendation to make to management. For example, if the accounts receivable balance has increased due to poor credit granting systems, then the obvious recommendation is to improve those systems. Likewise, an increase in inventory that is attributable to a poor changeover system by the engineering staff to new products should be addressed by a recommendation to improve *that* system.

There are only two cases in which fixing the root cause may not be the best answer. One is when the accounts payable balance has decreased due to new payment terms from suppliers or the accounting staff's taking an early payment discount. In this case, it may be necessary to use the new suppliers with the shorter payment terms, perhaps because they offer the best unit prices or delivery reliability, while taking early payment discounts may result in a reduction in costs. When this happens, the cost reductions should outweigh the reduced supplier funding. The other case is when a company is growing so fast that the associated accounts receivable and inventory must inevitably rise alongside it. In this case, there may not be a reasonable method for reducing the working capital investment, besides a recommendation to keep tight control over all existing systems that have an impact on this investment. In these two cases, a company will have to find alternate sources of funding so that it can invest in a higher level of working capital.

This section has described the components of working capital, why they change, and what a controller can recommend to improve the situation. The next section turns to the next most common cash flow analysis item for a controller—the analysis of cash flows for a project that requires a capital investment.

CREATING A CASH FLOW MODEL FOR A CAPITAL INVESTMENT

The review of capital investments was described in Chapter 3, but the focus in that chapter was on the use of cash flow discounting methods to determine the net present value and rate of return on projects; this section will focus on how to create a cash flow model that correctly describes the timing and extent of all cash inflows and outflows, which can then be used for the analyses noted in Chapter 3.

When creating a cash flow model for a capital investment, it is best to create a time line of at least five years over which cash flow projections of various kinds can be traced. Sometimes, if there are very large cash flows in later years, this is justification for extending the time line out to 10 years. However, because of the large discounting used for present value factors for many years into the future, the discounted value of cash flows many years away tends to be very small. Consequently, very long time lines will not substantially alter the net present value of all discounted cash flows, which can save a controller a great deal of modeling time by keeping the time line relatively short and reviewing cash inflows and outflows only within that time frame.

Once the time line is created, the next step is to itemize all cash outflows. These tend to be grouped at the beginning of a project, because this is when equipment is acquired and installed. However, there are also cases in which one can reasonably predict the need for maintenance or equipment upgrades at set intervals. If so, the cash outflows associated with these expenditures should also be included on the time line. An additional reason for a cash outflow is the need for working capital. For example, if a machine will create a product that is to be sold, then the accounts receivable and inventory needed to support those sales will constitute a cash outflow. An example of these cash outflows is shown in Exhibit 5.1. In this example, we are assuming that XYZ Plastics Company is purchasing an injection molding machine for $250,000. This expenditure appears in Year 0, since the cash outflow will occur before any time has passed. It is estimated that approximately one year will pass before the machine is fully operational, at which point cash will begin to come from the sale of goods molded on the machine. However, there will also be working capital associated with those sales in the form of accounts receivable and inventory, so these are shown as cash outflows for working capital at the end of Year 1. Finally, there is scheduled maintenance every year that will cost $20,000 each time. These expenditures represent cash outflows that will recur for as long as the machine is in use. All these cash outflows are noted in Exhibit 5.1.

However, all the cash inflows noted in Exhibit 5.1 have yet to be explained. The most obvious one is receipts from sales that come from the machine. These are positive cash flows and are summarized for each year. Also, we will assume that the machine will be sold at the end of Year 7, which creates a salvage value of $75,000 at the end of the seventh year. Finally, the working capital will be retrieved when sales are completed at the end of the seventh year, because accounts receivable will disappear after the last sales have been collected and all supporting inventories will have been sold.

Exhibit 5.1   Example of a Cash Flow Model for Capital Investment

Year	Description	Cash Inflow (+) or Outflow (−)	Present Value Factor	Present Value of Line Item	Cumulative Net Present Value
0	Machine purchase	$−250,000	0	$−250,000	$−250,000
1	Working capital	−100,000	.8929	−89,290	−339,290
1	Revenue	+350,000	.8929	+312,515	−26,775
1	Reduction in taxes due to depreciation	+10,000	.8929	+8,929	−17,846
2	Maintenance costs	−20,000	.7972	−15,944	−33,790
2	Revenue	+350,000	.7972	+279,020	+245,230
2	Reduction in taxes due to depreciation	+10,000	.7972	+7,972	+253,202
3	Revenue	+350,000	.7118	+249,130	+502,332
3	Reduction in taxes due to depreciation	+10,000	.7118	+7,118	+509,450
4	Maintenance costs	−20,000	.6355	−12,710	+496,740
4	Revenue	+350,000	.6355	+222,425	+719,165
4	Reduction in taxes due to depreciation	+10,000	.6355	+6,355	+725,520
5	Revenue	+350,000	.5674	+198,590	+924,110
5	Reduction in taxes due to depreciation	+10,000	.5674	+5,674	+929,784
6	Maintenance costs	−20,000	.5066	−10,132	+919,652
6	Revenue	+350,000	.5066	+177,310	+1,096,962
6	Reduction in taxes due to depreciation	+10,000	.5066	+5,066	+1,102,028
7	Revenue	+350,000	.4523	+158,305	+1,260,333
7	Reduction in taxes due to depreciation	+10,000	.4523	+4,523	+1,264,856
7	Working capital recovery	+100,000	.4523	+45,230	+1,310,086
7	Machine salvage value	+75,000	.4523	+33,923	$1,344,009

Note: (a) All revenue line items are net of income taxes paid. (b) The present value factor is based on a discount rate of 12%. (c) The reduction in taxes due to depreciation expense is based on a depreciable asset value of $175,000, straight-line depreciation for seven years, and an incremental corporate tax rate of 40%.

Also, there is a line item in each year of the analysis in Exhibit 5.1— reduction in taxes due to depreciation. This line is inserted in the matrix because the depreciation expense on the machinery, though not an actual cash flow in each year (the only cash flow was when the asset was originally purchased), will reduce the taxable amount of reported income each year by the amount of the tax rate. In the example, the positive cash flow generated by the depreciation expense each year is $10,000. To arrive at that number, the amount of depreciation per year is first determined. Because the asset has a base cost of $250,000 and will be sold for $75,000 at the end of its useful life, there is a net cost of $175,000 to depreciate over seven years. The depreciation needed to eliminate this asset from the books at the end of seven years is $25,000 per year. At a tax rate of 40 percent, the amount of tax savings that the annual depreciation of $25,000 will generate is $10,000. For assets that generate a great deal of depreciation, this is an extremely important line item to include in the cash flow analysis, for it can contribute a significant amount to a project's net present value.

A final issue is that many of the cash flows in or out can be traced to specific dates, such as during the first, second, or third quarter of each year. If so, the model shown in Exhibit 5.1 can be subdivided into a larger range of periods, perhaps by month or quarter. However, this adds a considerable degree of complexity to the net present value calculation for which this model will be used. Also, defining a cash flow down to the precise month of a year that is several years in the future will produce a change in the net present value that is negligible, when compared to just clustering all cash flows by year. It is up to the controller to decide if greater precision in the date ranges in the cash flow model is worth the time to research and report on this information.

Once all of the cash flows have been itemized in the cash flow model, the next step is to include the present value factor for each line item that yields the net present value of the cash flow. In the model in Exhibit 5.1, this factor is included in the fourth column from the left. The present value factor for each year is based on a discount rate of 12 percent, which in this case is the company's cost of capital. The present value of each line item is then calculated by multiplying the present value factor by each cash inflow or outflow, and this information is entered in the fifth column in the model. The final column in the model is used to keep a cumulative total of all cash flows, so that one can quickly determine in what year the net cash flows from the project turn positive. In this case, the project is returning a positive cash flow by the end of the second year.

The cash flow model shown in this section should be sufficient for the bulk of all capital investment projects with which a controller is likely to be involved.

CREATING AND EVALUATING A CASH FORECAST

If there is no chief financial officer (CFO) or treasurer, then the job of determining the projected flow of cash falls on the shoulders of the controller. This means that the controller must maintain a worksheet that estimates the cash inflows and outflows, perhaps as frequently as on a weekly or even daily basis, so that management can tell when there will be a need for either extra financing to obtain cash or extra investing for excess cash.

The basic concept on which the cash forecast is built is that this is *not* accrual accounting—we do not care about accrued revenues or expenses, just actual receipts or payments, from and to all possible sources. For example, if the accrual system is gradually recording an annual property tax payment of $120,000 in monthly $10,000 installments, these installments will not appear in the cash budget, because there is no actual monthly payment. Instead, there will be a single annual cash expenditure of $120,000 that will appear in the forecast when the full amount is due for payment.

The cash forecast format constructed in this section is split into three pieces: one for assumptions, another for cash inflows, and the final piece for cash outflows. In the first section of the budget, as shown in Exhibit 5.2, the underlying data and assumptions needed to compile the remainder of the report are listed. The key data and assumptions are:

- *Sales dollars per period.* The key driver of the entire cash forecast is the amount of sales volume to be expected in each of the measurement periods. This is because the sales figure interacts with the amount of purchases and days of inventory and accounts receivable that are expected to be on hand; and all three of these items are major components of the cash outflow portion of the cash forecast.

- *Production costs as a percentage of sales.* The amount of production costs needed in each period is derived directly from the anticipated sales figure for each reporting period. The controller usually uses historical actual results from the financial statements to determine the percentage of purchases that occur for each dollar of sales. This is typically a reliably steady and easily predicted figure.

- *Days needed to collect accounts receivable.* This assumption interacts with the sales figure from previous months to arrive at the amount of collections from accounts receivable expected in the current month. For example, if an average of 30 days are needed to collect funds, then the entire sales figure from the immediately preceding month can be listed as cash received in the current month. However, if the collection period is 60 days, then the entire sales figure from two months ago can be predicted as cash received in the current month.

- *Days needed to pay accounts payable.* When determining cash outflows, the primary determinant is the average number of days during which a company holds onto its accounts payable before issuing payment to suppliers. This figure can vary over time as the mix of suppliers (who may have differing payment terms) changes, or is based on decisions by management to lengthen payment terms if there will be anticipated cash shortages.

- *Days of inventory on hand.* A major element of working capital that has a strong impact on cash flows is the days of inventory that management chooses to keep on hand. This is not a steady turnover figure, especially for companies with a wide array of new products, because new inventory must be added to support new products. This item in particular is deserving of careful attention to ensure that the correct turnover figure is used.

Exhibit 5.2 Sample Cash Forecast

Cash Flow Line Item	January	February	March
Section I—Assumptions			
Sales dollars per period	$2,000,000	$2,500,000	$3,000,000
Production costs as a percentage of sales	50%	55%	55%
Days needed to collect accounts receivable	45	45	45
Days needed to pay accounts payable	30	30	30
Days of inventory on hand	60	60	60
Sales tax percentage	6%	6%	6%
Sales per employee	$100,000	$100,000	$100,000
Annual average pay per employee	$40,000	$41,000	$41,500
Section II—Cash Inflows			
Collections on accounts receivable*	$2,000,000	$2,000,000	$2,250,000
Collections on notes receivable	5,000	5,000	2,500
Collections from asset sales	0	15,000	0
Collections from equity sales	0	0	100,000
Total Cash Inflows	$2,005,000	$2,020,000	$2,352,500
Section III—Cash Outflows			
Payments for production costs*	$1,000,000	$1,100,000	$1,375,000
Payments for salaries and wages	66,667	85,417	103,750
Payments for general and administrative costs	175,000	175,000	175,000
Payments for capital expenditures	0	150,000	0
Payments for notes payable	25,000	25,000	25,000
Payments for sales taxes	120,000	150,000	180,000
Payments for income taxes	0	0	75,000
Payments for dividends	0	0	200,000
Incremental inventory change	0	750,000	550,000
Total Cash Outflows	$1,386,667	$2,435,417	$2,683,750
Net Cash Flows	**+618,333**	**−415,417**	**−331,250**
Cumulative Net Cash Flows	**+$618,333**	**$202,916**	**−$128,334**

* Sales for each of the two preceding months are assumed to be $2,000,000.

- *Sales tax percentage.* This is the percentage that the company owes the government on sales that occurred in the prior period. This percentage is then multiplied by the sales projection for the preceding period to derive the total sales tax payment for the current month.

- *Sales per employee.* A component of the cash outflow section at the bottom of the cash forecast is the payroll cost, which is partially derived by this line item, which assumes a certain headcount based on the sales volume. This figure must be used with care, because some employees in the overhead category will be on the payroll even if there are no sales. Consequently, a more detailed cash forecast might also include the number of overhead employees based on the budget, rather than tying all personnel to sales volume.

- *Average pay per employee.* The preceding measure determines the number of employees who will be paid in the payroll expense that is noted under the cash outflows section of the cash forecast report, while *this* measure multiplies the total headcount by the average pay per person to determine the actual cash outflow.

In the second section of the cash forecast shown in Exhibit 5.2, all possible sources of cash inflows are included. The primary one by far is collections on accounts receivable, though there are three additional line items for other sorts of discretionary cash inflows. Because these last three are not based on continuing operations and are not driven by formulas from the first section of the cash forecast, they are highlighted with italics, which denotes manual entries in the model. Descriptions of the line items are:

- *Collections on accounts receivable.* This is the primary source of cash inflows, and the only one from continuing operations. It is created by a formula that determines the amount of cash receipts that can be expected from the sales in previous months. The inputs are the "sales dollars per period" and "days needed to collect accounts receivable" line items in the first section of the cash forecast.

- *Collections on notes receivable.* A relatively minor item in most cases is the receipt of cash in payment for funds that the company has lent out to employees or other organizations. This is usually a manual entry in the cash forecast.

- *Collections from asset sales.* A company will sell assets from time to time, which results in a cash inflow. Because the exact period or amount of sale is rarely predictable, this cannot be included in the assumptions section and is a manual entry in the cash forecast.

- *Collections from equity sales.* Another source of funds is the sale of equity. This is done at the company's discretion and is usually timed to take advantage of the highest possible market price of company stock. Due to the timing problems associated with market conditions, this is not a predictable item that can be included in the assumptions section and is thus a manual entry in the cash forecast.

In the final section in Exhibit 5.2, all possible sources of cash outflows are included. There are a number of major contributors to this category (as opposed to the single one—collections from accounts receivable—that was the case for cash inflows). The most important ones (in descending order) are payments for production costs, payroll, general and administrative payments, capital expenditures, and notes payable. These final two items may be switched in priority for highly leveraged companies that make large debt payments. There are several items in this section that are not based on continuing operations or derived from formulas in the first section of the cash forecast, so they are highlighted with italics, which denotes manual entries in the forecasting model. Descriptions of the line items are:

- *Payments for production costs.* These are the costs for materials and associated production supplies that are needed to create products. In essence, this is the cost of goods sold, not including direct labor costs. This is typically the largest cash outflow for most companies, with the exception of service industries.

- *Payments for salaries and wages.* This is usually the second largest cash outflow, save for companies located in services industries, in which it is the largest. In Exhibit 5.2, this cash outflow is derived with a formula that is based on the sales per employee and the average pay per person. However, this formulation assumes that headcount varies directly with the sales level, which may not be the case. An alternative approach is to use the payroll listed in the budget.

- *Payments for general and administrative costs.* These costs are associated with corporate overhead, such as sales, audits, insurance, and rent. The best source of this information is the budget, because it rarely varies with the estimated sales level.

- *Payments for capital expenditures.* Payments for capital expenditures are highly predictable, because they are already listed in the budget and can be determined with some additional precision, since the expenditure authorizations normally come through the accounting department well in advance of any purchase.

- *Payments for notes payable.* Debt payments can be derived from a separate schedule of loan payment dates and amounts. There is no need to separate the interest expense and principal into two separate line items, because the concern here is only with the amount of the cash outflow, and not the exact nature of the outflow.

- *Payments for sales taxes.* Sales taxes can be predicted based on a percentage of the estimated sales. Accordingly, the formula for this is a combination of the estimated sales from the preceding month and the sales tax percentage.

- *Payments for income taxes.* It is difficult to reevaluate the entire budget in order to arrive at an estimate of the net income for the next few periods, so an easier approach is to use the estimated net income tax already located in the budget, adjust for any obvious expected changes in income, and record this expense in the cash forecast as a quarterly payment.

- *Payments for dividends.* Dividends are very predictable, because the board of directors specifies the amount to be paid, usually well in advance of the actual payment, and also because most companies maintain such a consistent level of dividend payments that the amount to be paid is probably very consistent with previous payment amounts.

- *Incremental inventory change.* Projected changes in inventory can be an important reason for both cash inflows and outflows. This is the only line item in the cash outflows section that can show either an inflow or an outflow, because inventory levels may rise or fall. This item is derived from a formula that alters the inventory level based on the assumed number of days of inventory shown in the assumptions section of the cash forecast.

Having described the components of the cash forecast in some detail, the information can now be assembled into a coherent forecasting model, as shown in Exhibit 5.2. In the example, the forecast is limited to three monthly reporting periods. The model could include the previous two periods, because the collections and payments information is based on sales information from previous periods. However, adding historical information can be confusing to the reader, so it will be assumed that this information is located in hidden columns that are not included in the final report. Next, all relevant assumptions are included. Sales are expected to increase through the reported periods, with an increase in the cost of production as a proportion of sales; these are the first two items in the cash forecast, because they have the largest impact on the forecast result. Then the two cash delaying factors are included, which are the standard number of days that will pass before a company can expect to receive cash in payment for previous sales, as well as to make payments for previous purchases. The next item, the days of inventory on hand, is used later in the cash outflows section to determine the amount of inventory that must be maintained to support the current sales level. A sophisticated cash forecasting model might include a provision for inventory to be built up in advance of sales, so that there would be an associated cash outflow some time in advance of sales being generated, because customers will not purchase products unless there is first a stock of inventory on hand from which to purchase. The next two line items, the sales per employee and the average pay per employee, are used later in the cash outflows section of the model to arrive at the payroll cost.

In the second section of the forecast shown in Exhibit 5.2, all cash inflows are shown. The collections on accounts receivable are based on a collection period of 45 days, as was noted under the assumptions in the first section of the forecast. For the months of January and February, collections are drawn in part from preceding months that are not shown in this forecast; it will be assumed that the amount of sales in all previous months is $2 million (as is also stated in the note at the bottom of Exhibit 5.2). Because the sales in previous months are all the same, the collections will also be $2 million per month for the first two months. However, the collections figure for March shows a different amount. The collections total of $2,250,000 is based on a 45-day collection period for months that have different sales totals; in this case, one half of the sales are drawn from January sales and one half from February. Going forward, the same calculation will apply in April, which will include one half of the sales from February and one half from March. The remaining items in the cash outflows section are manually entered, because they are not based on continuing operations and therefore cannot be automatically forecasted.

In the third and final part of the forecast in Exhibit 5.2, the amount of payments for production costs is calculated by taking the total sales figure for the preceding month (since one of the assumptions in the first section is a time lag on payments of 30 days) and multiplying it by the percentage of production costs, which was also noted in the assumptions section. The salaries and wages payment is calculated by multiplying the sales level for the month by the sales per person (which assumes that headcount varies directly with sales volume), and is then multiplied by the average pay rate, which must then be divided by 12 to determine the monthly salary total. The general and administrative expense is taken from the budget, as are the cash flows shown in the following line items for capital expenditures, notes payable, and income taxes. The payment for sales taxes is derived by multiplying the projected sales for each month by the sales tax per dollar of sales. A sophisticated model could include a time-lag feature for the sales tax payment, since remittances to the various governments require a varying number of days delay before payment is due. Finally, the incremental inventory change is calculated by multiplying the percentage of production costs (as noted in the assumptions section) by the sales dollars for the period, which gives us the materials portion of the cost of goods sold. Then, the days of inventory on hand is taken into account, which is 60 days for all three forecasted periods; this translates into having enough inventory on hand to cover the materials portion of the cost of goods sold for two months. Sales are projected to increase substantially for the second two months of the report, so the inventory will correspondingly increase. This turns out to be a very substantial cash amount, because the inventory level required to support sales is considerable.

The last steps are to summarize the cash outflows sections and subtract them from the totals for the cash inflows sections. The last row of the report shows the cumulative cash flow for all reported periods. The cumulative figure is of most use for determining any borrowing or investing needs in the near term. In the example, the increase in sales has sparked a significant increase in the amount of cash needed for inventory, which offsets cash inflows from the increased sales. As a result of the revenue surge, there is less cash than at the beginning of the reporting period.

A generally minor issue in a cash forecast is cash inflows and outflows that are not based on credit. For example, customers may pay for their purchases immediately in cash, as may the company to its suppliers. However, most organizations conduct their business almost entirely on credit, which leaves cash transactions as a vanishingly small portion of the total of all cash inflows and outflows. Thus, it is generally safe to exclude cash transactions from the cash forecasting model. The main exception to this rule is those industries, such as retail food distribution, in which nearly all sales transactions are paid in cash. In these situations, the cash inflows must be divided into cash from sales, with a lag of zero days, and all other sales (probably in the form of credit cards or checks), for which there is a short delay of perhaps 7 to 10 days. This arrangement should be sufficient for those situations in which cash inflows are the norm.

A key issue in the preparation and distribution of the cash forecast is that it must be as accurate as possible—the controller should not just mechanically prepare it based on old assumptions from months before. On the contrary, many of the underlying assumptions that are listed in the first part of the cash budget will change over time and must be updated regularly to ensure the highest possible degree of accuracy in the forecast. If this updating function is not performed, then the cash forecasts will not be as accurate, which will lead to a loss of confidence by users in the report; eventually, it may even fall into disuse if the information it imparts is sufficiently inaccurate. To determine the level of accuracy, it may be useful to retain the last few reporting periods on the report and, for those periods, report the actual cash balance next to the projected balance, with a percentage difference. This extra information reveals the level of accuracy of the reported information.

If the cash forecast is continually inaccurate, one should investigate the underlying causes. For example, there may be a small group of customers who habitually pay later than all other ones. If so, it may be necessary to divide projected sales into two categories, one for those customers and one for all others, and assume different collection periods for each group. Similar levels of detailed refinement may be necessary in other areas as well. If this results in an excessively lengthy cash forecast that is difficult to update, then a controller must weigh the utility of having more accurate information against the work required to obtain it. There is usually some median level of reporting accuracy that is sufficient for a company's practical needs, and this is the point at which no further cash forecast revision work is necessary.

INCREMENTAL CASH FLOW ANALYSIS

A key issue to consider when constructing or reviewing any of the preceding cash flow analyses is that the only cash flow that matters from the perspective of making a decision is incremental cash flow. This is the increase or decrease in cash flows that are specifically attributable to a management action. For example, if the management team is reviewing a proposal to improve the capacity of a machine, the entire cash flow resulting from the use of that machine is *not* the point on which the decision must be made, but rather the incremental cost of improving the machine and the incremental revenue that results from having additional capacity. For example, assume that a machine produces 1,000 cans per hour, and an upgrade to the machinery will result in an increase in the theoretical capacity to 1,500 cans per hour, for an incremental change of 500 cans per hour. The cost of the upgrade is $100,000, and the profit from each can is $.04. The machine runs eight hours a day for five days per week; therefore, the increase in capacity will result in an added cash inflow of $41,600, which is calculated as follows:

$$\text{(500 cans per hour)} \times \$.04 = \$20 \text{ per hour incremental cash inflow}$$
$$= (\$20 \text{ per hour of cash inflow}) \times \text{(40 hours per week)} \times$$
$$\text{(52 weeks per year)} = \$41,600$$

This incremental investment translates into a payback of 2.4 years, which is a reasonable return period for most investments. However, from an incremental perspective, why not run the machine a bit longer each day to obtain the same production that the machine would yield with the enhanced equipment? If the machine operator is paid $10 per hour and the same person stays late to work an extra 4 hours per day to run the machine, the added overtime cost per year will be only $15,600 (4 hours per day × 260 days × $15/hour), which is far less expensive than the equipment option. In addition, there may be no incremental need for the added capacity, since we do not know that the machine must be run at full capacity at all times. By using overtime instead of a fixed investment, the use of the machine can be scaled back on a day-to-day basis to exactly match production to sales. This example shows that one must review the specific cash flows that will change as a result of a specific management decision to see if it will result in a positive incremental change in cash flows.

INTERPRETING VARIATIONS IN THE FLOW OF CASH

When generating a cash forecast similar to the one shown previously in Exhibit 5.2, it may reveal significant changes in the short term that the controller will likely be called on to explain. In many cases, the reason for the change is a seasonal one; that is, the product being sold will experience the bulk of its sales at just one point during the year, so cash flows will center on that period. Examples of products that sell on a seasonal basis are Christmas ornaments (winter), lawn mowers (summer), pool supplies (summer), and ski-mobiles (winter). For products such as these, management will usually begin production some months in advance of the selling season, or even keep the production facility open for the full year, but at a very low level of production. During these production months, cash flows will be decidedly negative, because there will be no sales. Then, sales will explode during the peak selling season, with collections on accounts receivable starting a month or so later, resulting in an enormous cash inflow during a relatively short period, which hopefully more than offsets the cash outflow during the rest of the year. For a controller who is presenting cash flows that are based on seasonal production, it is critical to know the seasonal phase covered by the forecast, so that management can be told that cash outflows are based on the preseason inventory buildup, or that cash inflows are from the postseason collections. Without knowing which part of the season is involved in the forecast, management will not know if cash flows are in line with expectations, or if there is a more serious problem requiring immediate attention.

Another issue that gives rise to significant cash flow variations is the impact of the business cycle on company activities. A business cycle is a long-term change in business that is due to external economic conditions. See Chapter 9 for a complete review of this issue and how it can impact a company.

SUMMARY

This chapter presented a review of the various cash flow reporting formats that can be used for a number of different analysis situations. Though the most complicated models by far are for the corporate-wide analysis of cash forecasts, the most common reviews that a controller will be expected to conduct are the simpler cash flow models used for the analysis of working capital and capital budgeting. The final two sections of the chapter emphasized the need for a detailed review to ensure that only those cash flows specifically related to incremental decisions are included in an analysis, and also to ensure that the controller closely reviews cash flows over time to see if the cause of changes in cash flows may be based on seasonal or cyclical factors, rather than operational ones. Only the most detailed analysis into the root causes of cash flow changes will assist management in determining the specific actions that will result in positive cash flows in the future.

6

Evaluating Acquisition Targets

There are a great many kinds of analysis needed when a company is contemplating an acquisition. For a full acquisition, involving the assumption of all financial, environmental, and legal liabilities, as well as all assets, there are a great many subsets of analysis to perform. However, for a lesser acquisition, such as the purchase of all or specific assets, the number of analyses is substantially less. In this chapter, the types of financial analysis are broken down into a wide range of categories, which makes it easier for a controller to select just those needed for a specific type of acquisition.

This chapter also presents a brief overview of acquisition analysis, the obtainability of information for such analysis, and a series of topics that cover the different types of analysis work that must be conducted. Of special interest is the section on fraud analysis. This topic is of considerable importance, given a controller's complete lack of knowledge of the adequacy of control systems within the acquisition target. The chapter finishes with a set of handy checklists that itemize all the analysis steps noted earlier in the chapter.

Some of the analyses listed here are not strictly financial in nature, since legal issues are also noted. These extra analyses are added for the sake of being comprehensive, though the main focus of the chapter is on the *financial* analysis of acquisition targets.

OVERVIEW OF ACQUISITION ANALYSIS

The analysis of an acquisition is like no other type of financial analysis—not because the analysis itself is different, but because of the logistics of the situation. Typically, a potential acquisition situation arises suddenly, requires the fullest attention of the accounting staff for a short time, and then subsides, either because the acquisition is judged to be not a good one or because the deal is completed, and management takes over the activities of melding the organizations together. In either case, the controller is ensconced in the front end of the process, rendering opinions on any possible corporate purchase that the chief executive officer (CEO) sees fit to investigate.

Because of the suddenness of an acquisition evaluation, the controller must be fully prepared to switch from any current activities and into a full-bore analysis mode. To do so, this chapter includes the bulk of analyses that one should pursue in order to determine if the condition of an acquiree is as its purports to be. However, much more than a checklist is required. A controller and his or her staff have other duties, and cannot let them lie in order to conduct an investigation. Accordingly, the capacity of the accounting department to complete a potentially massive analysis chore may not be possible if the department is still to operate in anything close to a normal and efficient manner. Accordingly, a controller has three choices to make. First, if there are very few acquisition evaluations to make and the potential acquirees are small ones, then it may be possible to accept some degree of disruption in the accounting ranks and perform all the work with the existing staff. A second alternative is to form an acquisition analysis group that does nothing but evaluate potential candidates on a full-time basis. This is an excellent approach if a company is embarked on the path of growth by acquisition, and is willing to buy as many corporations as possible. The third alternative is to hire an outside auditing firm to conduct the financial analysis on behalf of the company. This is a good alternative if the in-house staff does not have the time or training to conduct the work, and if there are not enough acquisitions to justify hiring a full-time team of analysts. However, using outside auditors can be an expensive proposition, and one must be careful to ensure that the audit staff used is of a high enough level of training and experience to conduct a thorough review. Thus, the number of potential acquisitions and the ability of the internal accounting staff to complete acquisition analysis work will dictate the method a controller uses to obtain sufficient analysis assistance.

Having assembled the correct analysis procedures and a competent analysis staff, the question arises: Why analyze acquisition candidates at all? This is not a foolish question, for the answer can then be used to determine the precise types of analysis generated, which is the focus of the rest of this chapter. The primary reason for analyzing an acquisition candidate is to obtain any information that will cause management to change its opinion regarding the financial condition of the acquiree. Thus, all of the financial analyses noted in the remainder of this chapter are oriented toward verifying and interpreting the acquiree's financial information.

Given the preceding reason for using financial analysis, we can then add a follow-on question: What portion of the acquiree is management contemplating purchasing? After all, there is no need to buy an entire organization. If not, then why analyze all of it? Management may be interested only in buying a specific patent, brand, or production facility. Accordingly, a controller must first ascertain the extent of the proposed purchase and reduce the scope of the analysis if the entity to be purchased is only a subset of the entire target company. For example, if the only purchase that management is interested in is a specific production facility, so that it can add to current production capacity, the controller should tailor the analysis to focus on the age of the machinery in that facility, the adequacy of its logistical systems, and the possible obsolescence of inventory that may be acquired along with it.

Once these questions have been answered, a controller can proceed through the remaining sections of this chapter to determine the precise sets of analysis questions to answer, in order to ensure that the type of acquisition being contemplated is fully analyzed, without wasting time on any additional analysis work. The main analysis sections of this chapter, and the reasons why they are listed separately, are:

- *Personnel.* If a company is in need of employees with great experience or skill, it can fill the need by buying a company that employs them. This is a rare circumstance when only a few people are involved, since it is easier to hire them away with employment offers. However, if a potential acquiree has one or more departments that are justly famous for their work, then buying the company may be worthwhile in order to obtain those specific departments. This situation arises most frequently with engineering or research firms. The main analysis needed here is to determine the current compensation levels of the people being acquired, as well as how these pay levels compare to both internal and industry pay standards, as well as the presence of any long-term compensation agreements, and their net present value.

- *Patents.* A target company may possess one or more valuable patents, especially ones that can be used to enhance the value of the acquiring company's products. This approach is most common with research and drug firms. In this case, the primary analysis focuses on the cost of maintaining those patents, the number of years remaining prior to expiration, and (especially) the expected cash flows to be obtained from them prior to their expiration.

- *Brands.* A brand name is immensely valuable if it has been carefully maintained for many years, has been strongly supported with proper marketing, and represents excellent products. This is a good reason to acquire a target company, and is most common in the consumer goods field. The analysis for this type of acquisition focuses on the incremental profits to be gained by use of the brand name in relation to the cost of maintaining the brand.

- *Capacity.* If a company is faced with a long lead time or technological challenges to acquire greater production capacity, it may be worthwhile to purchase a production facility from another company. The analysis for this type of acquisition focuses on the age and usefulness of the machinery and facility purchased.

- *Assets and liabilities.* When an entire company is purchased, the acquiring organization is taking over virtually all assets, as well as all associated risks. In this instance, a comprehensive review of all balance sheet line items is mandatory.

- *Profitability.* A company may be bought because it has a greater percentage of profitability than the acquiring company, which increases the acquiring company's combined profitability. For this acquisition, a close review of the income statement and balance sheet is necessary.

- *Cash flow.* If a company has a large store of cash or continuing cash flows, it is a prime target for purchase by companies that need the cash, possibly to fund further acquisitions. For this type of acquisition, an intensive review of the balance sheet, income statement, and funds flow statement are necessary.

- *Fraud.* A special acquisition topic is the possible presence of fraud. Because a controller rarely has the time, and because the target does not want such an intensive review, the controls that are designed to prevent fraud in the target company may never be found in time, leaving the acquirer to pay for and fix the fraud problems after consummating the acquisition. However, there are some telltale signs that fraud-based analysis can detect.

- *Synergies.* A controller is sometimes asked to review the operations of a target company to spot ways in which operations can be combined to improve the consolidated performance of both companies. The analysis for synergies focuses on the primary expenditure items for both organizations, as well as headcount measures for specific transactions.

The analysis of acquisitions is an absolutely mandatory task, and one that a controller must be well prepared to complete. The task is made easier by knowing what kind and frequency of acquisition is contemplated, which allows for the preparation of a tailored set of analysis questions, as well as the formation of a specialized group of analysis personnel.

OBTAINING INFORMATION FOR AN ACQUISITION ANALYSIS

If a company is involved in a friendly acquisition, then the target company is generally willing to open its accounting books for inspection. The exception to the rule is that, if the target company is a direct competitor to the acquiring organization, then it will resist discussions of trade secrets or processes that will allow it to continue to effectively compete against the acquiring company in case the acquisition does not occur. Also, if an acquisition is of the unfriendly variety, then the opposing company will be quite active in denying access to any information whatever. This is an especially serious problem when a company is privately held, because very little information will be publicly available. In these situations in which information is not readily obtainable, how can a controller find a sufficient amount of information to conduct an analysis?

The first step is to dredge up all possible sources of information. One possibility is the target company's credit report, which may list a recent financial statement (although it is usually supplied by the target company, which may not be interested in publicly displaying its financial health and therefore may not be remotely accurate). Another source is articles in trade journals about the organization, as well as a simple review of the facility. By counting the number of cars in the parking lot, one can make a rough estimate, based on the industry average of sales per employee, of the amount of company sales. It may also be possible to talk to former or current employees about the company, as well as its customers or suppliers. Another option is to talk to local recruiters about the positions for which they have been asked to recruit, which may indicate problems that have resulted in employee turnover. Also, the credit report will list all assets against which lenders have filed security claims, which shows the degree to which the target company is using financial leverage to fund its operations. It may be possible to hire an investigative agency to acquire more information. Finally, reviewing public records about lawsuit filings will reveal whether there is any outstanding litigation against the firm. All of these options should be pursued if an acquiring company is willing to spend the time and money to accumulate the information.

However, if the target company is diligent in blocking attempts at obtaining information about it, and this results in a significant loss of information, the controller will not be able to complete a full analysis of the situation. If so, it is very useful to make a list of what information has not been obtained, and what the risk may be of not obtaining it. For example, if there is no information available about a company's gross margin, then there is a risk of making too large an offer for a company that does not have the margins to support the price. Once all these risks are assembled into a list, the controller should discuss them with the CEO or chief financial officer (CFO) to determine the level of risk the company is willing to bear by not having the information, or in deciding to invest the time and money to obtain the information. This will be an iterative process, as the number of questions posed by the controller gradually decreases, and the cost and time needed to find the answers to the remaining questions goes up. At some point, the CEO will decide that enough information is available to proceed with making an offer, or that the work required is excessive, to stop any further investigative efforts, and to proceed to the investigation of other target companies for whom information is easier to obtain.

Even if there is a sufficient amount of financial information available for a controller to conduct the requisite amount of financial analysis, there may be limited access to information about other issues that could represent significant liabilities or opportunities. Additional outside information sources that may be of use in compiling a comprehensive set of data for a prospective acquisition include:

- *Stock transfer agent.* This entity can verify the target company's outstanding capitalization.

- *Title search company.* These organizations, of which Dun & Bradstreet is the best known, will review all public records for the existence of liens on the assets of the target company. The list of liens should be compared to any outstanding debt schedules provided to the buyer to see if there are any discrepancies.

- *Patent/Trademark search company.* This type of company reviews all legal filings to see if there are infringement lawsuits against the patents or trademarks of the target company, and can also obtain copies of the original patents or trademarks.

- *Appraisal companies.* An appraisal company can provide a list of the appraised value of a target company's assets, though it will not reveal this information without the prior approval of the target company.

PERSONNEL ANALYSIS

If the main reason for acquiring a target company is to hire away a specific person or group of people who are deemed to have valuable skills, a controller has one of two analysis options to pursue. The first is that, if the company has chosen to purchase the entire target company, then a full-blown analysis of all assets, liabilities, controls, and legal issues must be conducted. The analyses for those categories are noted under the following sections of this chapter. However, if the company has persuaded the target company to accept payment in exchange for the transfer of some smaller portion of the company that includes the targeted employees, then the analysis work becomes much more specific.

An example of a partial purchase to obtain employees is a target company's deciding to eliminate one of its lines of business and selling the related customer list and assets to the acquiring company. As part of the transaction, the target company lays off its employees that were associated with the line of business that is being transferred to the new company. The acquiring company obtains a list of these employees from the selling company and contacts them to offer them jobs. Because of the nature of this transaction, there is essentially nothing more than a transfer of assets, which greatly reduces the amount of analysis required of the controller. Only the following analyses should be conducted that are specifically targeted at the employees to be hired, with an emphasis on their quality, cost, and turnover:

- *Investigate employee names listed on patents.* If individual employees are named on patents or patent applications filed by the target company, then it is a good bet that those employees may be in a revenue-sharing agreement with the company employing them. If so, the controller must research further to determine the amounts paid to the employees for use of the patents, such as a fee per unit sold or an annual payment. These patent payments must be added to the employee salaries to determine the true cost of bringing in the new personnel.

- *Interview customers and suppliers about employees.* If there are problems with the desired employees, the target company is almost certainly not going to reveal this information, because it is trying to obtain payment for "selling" them to the acquiring company. Accordingly, it may be necessary to call the target company's suppliers or customers to see if they have had dealings with the people under consideration and what their opinions may be.

- *Compare employee pay levels to industry and internal averages.* Obtain the pay rates for the entire department to be acquired, and determine the distribution of pay through the group to see if there are any inordinately highly paid people. Then, compare these rates not only to the industry average, but also the acquiring company's average, to determine the difference between the pay levels about to be brought in and the existing rates. If there is a major difference between the two pay rates, then an additional cost of the acquisition may be to bring the pay levels of the in-house staff up to match those of the incoming personnel, in order avoid turmoil caused by the pay differential.

- *Determine the current turnover rate in the targeted department.* If there is a high turnover rate in the department being acquired, then the cost of acquisition may not be worthwhile if there is a high risk of losing the entire group. However, this issue can be overcome by proper treatment of the incoming employees.

- *Review long-term compensation agreements.* If a target company has obtained the services of a number of exceptional employees, it is quite possible that it has done so by offering them expensive, long-term employment contracts. The controller should review them not only for the projected payment amounts, increases, and net present value, but also for golden parachute clauses that pay these employees exorbitant amounts if the target company is purchased.

The upshot of what a controller is looking for when reviewing the acquisition of personnel is the actual cost of those employees and the potential impact on their counterparts. The first item is purely financial in nature, whereas the second is a matter for conjecture regarding the impact of a group of higher-paid employees on the existing in-house group that is paid less. The controller can only provide the information regarding pay disparities to the CEO and human resources director, and let them determine what to do to boost the morale of the existing staff when they learn about the higher wages being paid to the newly arriving personnel. An example of the analysis report that the controller should issue for an acquisition based on personnel is shown in Exhibit 6.1.

Note that the cost of acquisition has been converted at the bottom of the example into a cost per employee, which is then compared to the average market rate. The premium to be paid over the market rate gives management

Exhibit 6.1   Analysis Report for Acquisition of Personnel

Description	Additional Information	Summary Costs
Total cost of incoming staff (15 staff)		$1,237,500
Average cost of incoming staff	$82,500	
Average cost of in-house staff	73,000	
Prior year employee turnover level	10%	
Additional cost to match in-house salaries to incoming salaries (13 staff)		123,500
Net present value of projected patent payments to employees		420,000
Cost of employment contract buyouts		250,000
Total cost of employee acquisition		**$2,031,000**
Total cost per employee acquired (15 staff)		**$135,400**
Industry average pay rate per person		$80,000
Percentage premium over market rate		**69%**

its best idea of the true cost of the staff it is acquiring, and whether it is a good idea to proceed with the acquisition.

PATENT ANALYSIS

If a company wants to acquire a patent from another company, it does not usually go to the extreme of buying the whole company. Instead, it negotiates for the patent itself, which makes the analysis work substantially easier for the controller. There are very few measures to investigate, with an emphasis on the existing costs and revenues currently experienced by the holder of the patent. Management may require additional analysis to include the estimated additional revenues and costs that will subsequently be incurred by its use of the patent, which may vary from the use to which it has been put by the current patent owner. The primary analyses are:

- *Determine annual patent renewal costs.* Annual patent costs are quite minimal, but should be included in any patent analysis, such as the one noted in Exhibit 6.2, in order to present a comprehensive set of cost information. This information can be obtained either from the target company or the patent office.

- *Determine current patent-related revenue stream.* This information is needed to determine the amount of money that the company is willing to pay for a patent; however, if the company wants to shift the focus of the patent to a different application, then this number has less use. Without cooperation from the target company, this can be a

Exhibit 6.2   Analysis Report for Patent Acquisition

Description	Additional Information	Summary Revenues and Costs
Years left prior to patent expiration	10	
Net present value of cash inflows		$1,200,000
Discounted cost of remaining filing costs		–42,000
Discounted cost of expected annual legal fees		–375,000
Net present value of patent		**$783,000**

very difficult number to determine, because the only alternative is to contact those companies who are licensed to use the patent and see if they will reveal the per-unit payment they are required to make to the target company for use of their patent. This information is frequently protected by licensing agreements, however, so there may be no way to determine the exact amount. If the target company is willing to reveal this information, then also try to obtain it for the last few years, to see if there is an upward or downward trend line for the revenues; if the trend is downward, then the revenue stream for which the company is paying is worth less money.

- *Ascertain extent of current litigation to support patent.* A major issue for any patent holder is the amount of money it must spend to keep other entities from encroaching on the patent with parallel patents, or just by issuing products that illegally use technology based on the patent. These legal costs can be enormous. If a company wants to take over a patent, it must be aware of the extent of encroachment and the cost of legally pursuing the encroachers.

The bottom line of the patent acquisition analysis report is the net present value of all cash flows, which the CEO and CFO can use as the highest recommended amount to pay for the patent. However, given alternative uses for the patent that they may be contemplating, they may anticipate a higher cash inflow that will allow them to pay a higher price for the patent.

BRAND ANALYSIS

When a company purchases a brand from another company, it can be as simple as the transfer of the name (witness the frequent transfer of the PanAm and Indian motorcycle names), or it can be a more comprehensive transfer of all the factories and personnel who manufacture products under that brand name. More frequently, the purchase covers the entire corporate division that operates under the brand name. However, because such a complete purchase is covered in later sections by the analysis of assets, liabilities, profitability, and cash flows, the analysis in this section will be confined to just the brand name.

The analyses needed to review a brand name are relatively simple from the financial perspective, though somewhat more involved from the legal side, because one must conduct research to ensure that there is a clear title to the trademark, as well as ascertain the extent of possible infringements on the brand name and the extent and recent history of litigation needed to support the brand. The primary analyses are:

- *Determine the amount of annual trademark fees.* This is a very minor item, but can grow to considerable proportions if the trademark is being maintained worldwide, which requires filings and maintenance fees in a multitude of jurisdictions.

- *Determine clear title to the brand name.* This is not just a matter of paying for a small amount of research by a legal firm to determine the existence of any countervailing trademarks, but also requires a search in multiple jurisdictions if the buying company wants to expand the brand to other countries.

- *Ascertain the amount and trend of any current cash inflows from the brand name.* This is a very difficult item to determine, because very few companies establish a brand name and then charge licensing fees for the use of it. A more common approach by far is to build all products sold under the brand name, so that there is tighter control over quality. However, it is nearly impossible to determine the incremental cash inflow that is specifically due to the brand name itself and not just product sales. The two best analysis options here are to either measure just that portion of sales that are specifically due to licensing agreements (and therefore easily traceable) or by measuring the incremental difference in cash flows from all products under the brand name, in comparison to those of the industry average or specific competitors.

- *Note the amount and trend of any legal fees needed to stop encroachment.* A quality brand frequently attracts a number of companies, either in the country or abroad, that build inexpensive knockoffs and illegally sell them for vastly reduced prices. Given the reduced quality and prices, the net impact of these fake goods is to cheapen the brand's image. Consequently, constant legal pursuit of these companies is the only way to keep knockoff products off the market. The controller should estimate the cost of current lawsuits, roughly estimated by reviewing all current lawsuits that are public record, or by asking the target company. If the acquiring company wants to maintain the brand image, it must be willing to continue to use legal alternatives, so the current legal cost can be used as a reasonable benchmark of future costs as well.

- *Note any challenges to use of the brand name.* Yet another legal issue is that there may be lawsuits pending that claim the trademark of another

Exhibit 6.3   Analysis Report for Brand Acquisition

Description	Additional Information	Summary Revenues and Costs
Net present value of current cash inflows		$500,000
Discounted cost of annual trademark fees		–65,000
Cost of trademark search (for clear title)		–175,000
Discounted cost of annual legal fees		–780,000
Cost to purchase competing brand names	See note	–2,250,000
Total net cost of brand name		**$–2,770,000**

Note: A competing trademark has already been filed by company XYZ in all countries of the European Community and Japan. The cost required to purchase this trademark is included in the analysis.

person or corporation supersedes the one about to be purchased. If so, a search of all open lawsuits should reveal this information. Once again, if the company contemplates worldwide usage of the brand name, then a much more extensive search for competing trademarks in other locations is necessary. If there are cases in which someone else has filed for the right to use the brand name in another country, then the controller should calculate the estimated cost of acquiring the rights to that name.

Clearly, there is little in the way of financial analysis and a great of legal analysis required before purchasing a brand name. Nonetheless, the controller must be involved, because of the cost of the legal searches. In Exhibit 6.3, we itemize the financial analysis associated with a brand name acquisition that a controller should expect to issue to management.

Because virtually all of the costs associated with the purchase of a brand name involve the legal department, the controller can expect to work closely with this group in determining the costs of the each line item noted in Exhibit 6.3.

CAPACITY ANALYSIS

When a company purchases a specific manufacturing facility from another company, it is usually doing so to increase its capacity. With this end in mind, the key analyses revolve around the condition and cost of the facility, so that one can determine the amount of replacement machinery to install, as well as the actual production capacity percentage, the cost per percentage of capacity, and the facility's overhead cost. This section outlines the standard analyses to conduct to arrive at a complete set of answers. For many of the analyses, the information the controller assembles must be for three activity levels—minimum, normal, and maximum capacity levels. The reason for the threefold for-

Exhibit 6.4   Analysis Report for Capacity Acquisitions

Description	Costs at Minimum Capacity Usage	Costs at Normal Capacity Usage	Costs at Maximum Capacity Usage
Facility overhead cost	$1,000,000	$3,500,000	$5,000,000
Capital replacement cost*	0	0	400,000
Equipment maintenance cost	0	450,000	600,000
Cost of environmental damage insurance	50,000	50,000	50,000
Cost to investigate possible environmental damage	100,000	100,000	100,000
Facility modification costs	0	0	700,000
Total costs	**$1,150,000**	**$4,100,000**	**$6,850,000**
Percent capacity level	0%	50%	85%
Cost per percentage of capacity	**N/A**	**$82,000**	**$81,000**

* Represents the depreciation on capital replacement items.

mat (as shown in Exhibit 6.4) is that management may not use the facility as much as it anticipates, in which case it must be aware of the minimum costs that will still be incurred, as well as the extra costs that must be covered if the facility runs at the highest possible rate of production. The primary analyses are:

- *Determine the facility overhead cost required for minimum, standard, and maximum capacity.* Any facility requires a minimum cost to maintain, even if it is not running. Such costs include taxes, security, insurance, and building maintenance. Management must know this minimum cost level in case it does not use the facility, but must still pay for the upkeep. Also, current accounting records will reveal the overhead needed to run the facility at a normal level, while the industrial engineering or production personnel can estimate the additional costs needed to run the plant at full capacity.

- *Ascertain the amount of capital replacements needed.* Some machinery will be so worn out or outdated that it must be replaced. This information is beyond the knowledge of a controller, but not of an industrial engineer or production manager, who can walk through the facility and determine the condition of the equipment. If this is not readily apparent, then perusing the maintenance records will reveal which machines require so much continuing work that a complete replacement is a more efficient alternative.

- *Find out the periodic maintenance cost of existing equipment.* Even if equipment does not require replacement, it must still be maintained, which can be a considerable cost. This information should be obtained for the normal run rate and estimated for the maximum capacity level.

- *Determine the maximum production capacity.* The industrial engineering staff must estimate the maximum capacity level at which the facility can run, subject to expenditures for equipment replacements and facility modifications.

- *Investigate any environmental liabilities.* Sometimes, the target company is more than willing to get rid of a facility if it suspects there is environmental damage that must be fixed. This can be an extraordinarily expensive item, and can sometimes exceed the cost of the entire facility. To guard against this problem, a controller should determine the cost of conducting an environmental investigation, as well as the cost of insurance to provide coverage in case such damage is discovered after the purchase date.

- *Determine the cost of modifications needed to increase the capacity of the facility.* Unless a facility has been very carefully laid out in the beginning for the highest possible maximization of throughput, it is likely that it can use a significant overhaul of its layout. To do this, the industrial engineering staff must review the current situation and recommend the shifting of equipment and installation of additional materials movement capabilities, such as conveyor belts.

The preceding analyses are summarized in the sample capacity analysis report shown in Exhibit 6.4. This differs from the examples shown in previous sections, in that there are low, medium, and high categories for costs that are based on projected capacity utilization levels. At the bottom of the example, all costs are converted into a dollar amount for each percentage of capacity used. Note that there is no utilization listed for the minimum level, because the facility is shuttered under this assumption; management must be made aware of the minimum cost of maintaining a facility even when it is not currently being used for any production.

In the example shown in Exhibit 6.4, the facility being purchased is one that requires a significant amount of improvement, since the cost needed to bring it up to full capacity utilization is considerable. According to the last line of the example, the cost per percentage of capacity is nearly the same at the maximum utilization level as it is at the normal level. This is an unusual state of affairs for a modern facility in which the equipment is new enough not to warrant much replacement to attain the highest usage levels. For a modern facility, the cost per percentage of utilization should drop sharply when the plant is running at its highest possible run rate, because existing costs are spread over far more units of production.

ASSET ANALYSIS

A company will sometimes acquire just the assets of another organization. This is most common when there is some risk associated with the liabilities of the target company, such as lawsuits, environmental problems, or an excessive amount of debt. Also, if a company is not experienced in taking over or liquidating a fully operational organization, then a good approach is to just pay for the assets and let the owners of the target company take care of the resolution of liabilities with the proceeds from the asset sale. When assets are purchased, the buyer can be quite selective in buying only those few assets that are of the most value, and leave the remainder for the target company. Some of these assets may be patents, brands, or personnel, as covered in previous sections. In this section, the additional analyses needed to ensure that all other assets are properly reviewed prior to an acquisition are noted. Those analyses are:

- *Conduct a fixed asset audit.* Before paying for an asset, make sure that the asset is there. The fixed-asset records of some companies are in such poor condition that assets still on the books may have been disposed of years before. An appraiser or an internal audit team can conduct this review.

- *Appraise the value of fixed assets.* Even if an asset exists, it may have far less value than the amount listed in the fixed-asset database (which is simply the original purchase price, net of whatever depreciation method is currently in use). To be sure of the current value of all assets, have an appraiser review all assets and determine their value. The final appraisal report should contain two values for each asset: the rush liquidation value and a higher value based on a more careful liquidation approach. These two values can be the focus of a great deal of negotiating between the buyer and the target company, because the buyer will want to pay based on the rush liquidation value, and the target company will prefer to sell at the price indicated by the slower liquidation approach. If there is a significant disagreement over the appraised value, the target company can bring in its own appraiser, who may deliver a different set of asset values.

- *Ascertain the existence of liens against assets.* A company should not purchase an asset if there is a lien against it. This usually occurs when the target company has used the assets as collateral for loans or used leases to finance the purchase of specific assets. The standard procedure in an acquisition is to have lenders remove liens prior to the completion of an acquisition, which frequently requires paying off those lenders with a new "bridge" loan that covers the period of a few weeks or days between the removal of liens and the transfer of payment from the buyer to the target company, which is then used to pay off the bridge loan.

- *Determine the collectibility of accounts receivable.* If the purchase includes all current accounts receivable, then trace the largest invoices back to specific shipments, and confirm them with the customers to whom the invoices were sent. Also, be sure to trace the history of bad debt write-offs to determine an appropriate average amount that will reflect the amount of the current accounts receivable that will become bad debt.

- *Verify the bank reconciliation for all bank accounts.* For any checking or investment account, verify the amount of cash at the bank and reconcile it to the amount listed in the corporate accounting records. Also, investigate any reconciling items to ensure that they are appropriate.

- *Audit the existence and valuation of remaining assets.* There are usually a number of smaller-dollar assets on the books, such as the payoff value of life insurance, deposits on rentals and leases, and loans to employees or officers. All of these items must be audited, both through investigation of the original contracts on which they are based and through confirmations from those entities who owe the target company money.

- *Determine the value of any tax loss carry-forward.* If the buyer is acquiring a tax loss carry-forward from the target company, it can use this to reduce its own tax burden. The controller should use either the corporate tax staff or outside auditors to review the validity of the target company's tax returns to ensure that the reported loss on which the carry-forward is based is valid, as well as to review the (ever changing) tax laws to ensure that the company is qualified to use the loss carry-forward.

The analyses noted in this section require a controller to use the services of a much larger group of people than was the case for any previous type of acquisition. There are tax personnel to review tax loss carry-forwards, auditors to review accounts receivable, lawyers to examine underlying contracts for other assets, and assessors to review fixed assets. Thus, this type of broader-based review requires a much higher degree of coordination skill than was needed for previous types of acquisition analysis.

In the example in Exhibit 6.5, only the appraised rapid liquidation value of the assets to be purchased is listed in the "Valuation Summary" column, whereas two other forms of asset valuation are noted in the "Additional Information" column. The reason for this treatment of asset values is that the controller is presenting to management the lowest possible asset value, which it will use to determine its lowest offering price for the purchase of the target company's assets. The other higher asset values are included as notations, in case management wants to bid a higher dollar amount and needs to determine its upper boundaries for a reasonable offer price. In addition, the value of remaining assets and the tax loss carry-forward are both listed at their net present values. The reason for using discounting for these two items is that they may not be readily liquidated in the short term. For example, other assets may include loans to employees or officers that will take several years to collect, while only a portion of a tax loss carry-forward can usually be used in each year. Accordingly, the discount rate for the net present value calculation for each of these line items is noted in the "Additional Information" column in the example. Also, the bad debt deduction from the accounts receivable is not the one used by the target company, but rather the

Exhibit 6.5   Analysis Report for Assets

Description	Additional Information	Valuation Summary
Appraised value of assets (rapid liquidation)		$16,000,000
Appraised value of assets (slow liquidation)	$18,500,000	
Book value of assets	19,000,000	
Book value of assets with outstanding liens	19,000,000	
Book value of accounts receivable		5,500,000
Recommended bad debt reserve		−150,000
Value of cash and investments		750,000
Net present value of remaining assets	Discount rate is 13%	629,500
Net present value of tax loss carry-forwards	Discount rate is 13%	2,575,000
Total asset valuation		**$25,304,500**

one compiled by the controller's staff, following its review of the history of bad debt write-offs and the risk of bad debt occurrences for the current group of accounts receivable.

LIABILITY ANALYSIS

If a company decides to purchase a target company as a complete entity, rather than buying pieces of it (as was focused on by the previous sections), then the liabilities side of the balance sheet will be part of the purchase, and will require analysis by the controller. In this section, the analyses needed to verify the target company's liabilities are reviewed. The main analyses are:

- *Reconcile unpaid debt to lender balances.* There may be a difference between the amount recorded on the company's books as being the debt liability and the lender's version of the amount still payable. The controller must compare the difference and research the reason for it. If there is some doubt regarding whose version is correct, the controller should always use the amount noted by the lender, because this entity will not release its lien on company assets until it believes itself to be fully paid.

- *Look for unrecorded debt.* A target company may have incorrectly reported a capital lease as an operating lease, or may be recording some other form of debt payment as an expense without recording the underlying debt liability. The internal audit staff can review the target company's stream of payments to see if there are any continuing payments, most likely in the same amount from period to period, that indicate the presence of a debt paydown.

- *Audit accounts payable.* The internal audit staff should also verify that all accounts payable listed on the target company's books are actual expenses and not duplications of earlier payments. Also, the audit staff should investigate the unvouchered accounts payable to see if these are all approved and binding expenses and if there are additional receipts for which there are no existing accounts payable listed in the accounting records.

- *Audit accrued liabilities.* An area that is worthy of considerable analysis is accrued liabilities. A target company that wants to obtain the highest possible selling price will downplay these expenses, so the internal audit staff must be careful to verify the existence of all possible accrued expenses, and then recalculate how the accruals were derived, to ensure that the underlying expenses that these accruals will eventually offset are accurate. The following accruals are among the more common ones that the audit staff should review:

  - Income taxes

  - Payroll taxes

Exhibit 6.6   Analysis Report for Liabilities

Description	Additional Information	Summary Revenues and Costs
Book balance of debt		$3,750,000
Add: Additional lender balance due	a	15,000
Add: Unrecorded capital leases	b	175,000
Book balance of accounts payable		2,200,000
Add: Unrecorded accounts payable	c	28,000
Subtract: Duplicate accounts payable	d	–2,000
Book balance of accrued liabilities		450,000
Add: Additional accrual for property taxes	e	80,000
Add: Accrual for workers' compensation insurance	f	15,000
Total liabilities valuation		**$6,711,000**

[a] Company recorded $15,000 in late interest payments as a debt reduction.

[b] Capital leases for six forklifts recorded as expenses.

[c] No supplier invoice recorded for maintenance supplies received on last day of the month.

[d] Supplier invoices for in-house construction work recorded under both vouchered and unvouchered accounts payable.

[e] Original accrual did not reflect an increase of 2.3% in the tax rate.

[f] Original accrual based on a payroll level that is 15% lower than the actual payroll amount.

- Personal property taxes
- Warranty costs
- Product recalls

All of the above analyses are summarized in the sample analysis report for liabilities (Exhibit 6.6). Of particular interest are the line items for reconciliation problems, such as extra debt and accounts payable, as well as corrections to the accrued expenses. All of these adjustments are used by the CEO and CFO to negotiate a lower price for the target company, because the higher liabilities reduce its net value.

PROFITABILITY ANALYSIS

There are several key methods a controller should use when reviewing the profitability of a target company. One is a significant reliance on the trends in several key variables, because these will indicate worsening profit situations. Also, it is important to segment costs and profits by customer, so that one can see if certain customers are soaking up an inordinate proportion of the expenses. Further, it may be possible (if there is a great deal of cooperation from the target company) to determine the head count associated with each major transaction, so that one can determine the possibility of reducing expenses by imposing transaction-related efficiencies that have worked for the acquiring company. The intent of these analyses is to quickly determine the current state and trend of a target company's profits, as well as to pinpoint those customers and costs that are associated with the majority of profits and losses. The main analyses are:

- *Review a trend line of revenues.* The topmost analysis is to see if there has been a significant change in the level of profits over the last few years. If there has been a decline in the rate of growth or an overall decline in revenues, then review the company's percentage of the total market to see if the cause might be a shrinkage in the overall market. If not, then review sales by product and customer to determine the exact cause of the problem.

- *Review a trend line of bad debt expense.* As a market matures and additional sales are harder to come by, a company's management may loosen its credit terms, which allows it to increase sales, but at the cost of a higher level of bad debt, which may even exceed the additional gross margin earned from the incremental sales that were added. To see if a target company has resorted to this approach to increasing sales, review the trend line of bad debt expense to see if there has been a significant increase. Also, review the current accounts receivable for old invoices that have not yet been written off as bad debt, and also see if there are sales credits that are actually bad debts. The sum of these items constitute the true bad debt expense.

- *Review a trend line of sales discounts.* As a follow-up to the last item, management may offer discounts to customers in advance for additional sales or add customers who are in the habit of taking discounts, whether approved or not. These issues are most common when a company's sales are no longer trending upward and management is looking for a new approach to spur sales, even at the cost of reduced margins due to the discounts. The discounts may be stored in a separate account for sales discounts or mixed in with sales credits of other kinds. Some research may be required of the controller to determine the actual amount of sales discounts.

- *Review a trend line of material costs.* The next item listed in the income statement is usually the material cost. For most organizations outside of the service sector, this is the largest cost, and so requires a reasonable degree of attention. The controller cannot hope to delve into all possible aspects of material costs during a due diligence review, such as variances for scrap, purchase prices, or cycle counting adjustments. However, it is easy to run a trend line of material costs for the last few years, just to see if these costs are changing as a proportion of sales. A small increase in costs here can relate to the entire cost of a department in other areas of the company, due to the large overall cost of materials, so a change of as little as 1 percent in this expense category is cause for concern.

- *Review a trend line of direct labor costs.* A controller should review the trend line of costs for direct labor costs in much the same manner as for material costs. Though this is usually a much smaller cost than for materials, it is still sufficiently large to be a cause for serious concern if there is a significant and continuing trend line of increasing expenses in this area.

- *Review a trend line of gross margins.* All of the preceding analyses are summarized into the gross margin percentage, so this is a summary measure for which greater detail can be gained through a review of the preceding items. This measure is worthy of comparison to industry averages or to the gross margins of specific competitors, so the acquiring company can gain some idea of the production efficiencies of the company it is attempting to purchase. It is not necessarily a bad thing for the target company to have a poor gross margin, because the buyer can view this as an opportunity to enact major improvements.

- *Review a trend line of net margins.* If the gross margin looks reasonable, then proceed to a trend line analysis of net margins. If there is a declining trend here that was not apparent in the preceding gross margin analysis, then the controller can focus on the sales, general and administrative expense areas to see where the cost increase has occurred. If there is no significant change in that area, the remaining culprit is that the interest cost has increased.

- *Ascertain the gross profit by product.* Review the gross profit for each product at the direct cost level to determine which ones have excessively low profit levels and are targets either for withdrawal from the market or a price increase. If possible, also determine the cost of fixed assets that are associated with each product (i.e., product-specific production equipment), so that the buyer can budget for an asset reduction alongside any product terminations.

- *Ascertain the gross profit by customer.* Review the gross profit for each customer at the direct cost level. This means subtracting the standard direct labor and materials cost from the price for every product sold to each customer to derive a gross margin. If there is time and the target company has the available information, then also charge overhead costs to customers with activity-based costing or some other allocation method; however, this information is rarely available. This type of analysis is particularly useful if the management of the acquiring company suspects that the target company has built up an excessive overhead structure to service a large number of customers, of whom only a few are truly profitable. By retaining only the largest customers and dropping the overhead related to the smaller customers, the acquiring company can engineer an immediate increase in profits and cash flow.

- *Review a trend line of overhead personnel per major customer.* To continue along the lines of the last two analyses, the controller wants to know how much overhead is needed to support a profitable base of customers. Having already determined the gross margins by product and customer, it is now time to determine the number of personnel needed to support the customer base. Though one can start with a simple ratio of overhead personnel to the number of major customers, this review can extend much more deeply to determine which customers require inordinate amounts of time by the support staff. Unfortunately, the target company may not be willing to allow sufficient time for this type of in-depth analysis, or else the acquisition time line may not allow for the time investment.

- *Review a trend line of overhead personnel per transaction.* If the acquiring company is an expert in conducting highly efficient transactions, then its main focus in performing acquisitions may be to find target companies that are very inefficient in their handling of transactions, and to focus on improving profits by enhancing the efficiency in this area. Accordingly, the appropriate analysis is to determine the number of personnel involved in all major transactions, such as accounts payable, accounts receivable, receiving, and purchasing, and divide this number into the annual total of all these transactions. If there appears to be an excessive number of employees based on this calculation, then the target may be a worthy acquisition candidate.

The preceding analyses are sufficient for producing a general overview of where a target company is having profitability problems. As part of a due dili-

Exhibit 6.7   Analysis Report for Profitability

Type of Analysis Conducted	Notes
Review a trend line of revenues	Percentage rate of growth has declined in last two years.
Review a trend line of bad debt expense	Bad debt expense has increased, due to relaxation of credit standards.
Review a trend line of sales discounts	80% of the newest customers have all been given sales discounts of 10–15%.
Review a trend line of material costs	No significant change.
Review a trend line of direct labor costs	No significant change.
Review a trend line of gross margins	The gross margin has dropped 13% in the last two years, entirely due to increased bad debts and sales discounts.
Review a trend line of net margins	Slightly worse reduction than indicated by the gross margin trend line analysis.
Ascertain the gross profit by product	All products experienced a reduction in gross profit in the last two years.
Ascertain the gross profit by customer	Sales to older customers have retained their gross margin levels, but newer customers have substantially lower margins.
Review a trend line of overhead personnel per major customer	There has been a slight increase in the collections staffing level in the last two years, due to the difficulty of collecting from newer customers.
Review a trend line of overhead personnel per transaction	No significant change.

Conclusion and recommendations: The target company has experienced flattening sales, and so has shifted new sales efforts to low-end customers who cannot pay on time and will accept only lower-priced products, which also increases the overhead needed to service these accounts. Recommend dropping all low-margin, low-credit customers, as well as all associated overhead costs to increase profits.

gence analysis, these measures and trend lines will tell a controller where to focus the bulk of the analysis team's attention in determining the extent of problem areas and their impact on profitability. In the example analysis report shown in Exhibit 6.7, a verbal review of each analysis area is noted, rather than a cost summary, as was the case for previous analyses. The reason for the change is that this review is intended to find further problems, not to devise a valuation for the target company.

CASH FLOW ANALYSIS

The analysis of a target company's cash flows is a critical item if the entire organization is to be purchased. The reason is that, though a profitability analysis may reveal a corporation to be in healthy condition, a further review of its cash flows may also reveal that it is investing far too heavily in working capital and fixed assets, so that profits are masking a considerable need for cash. If a controller were to miss this key item, the buying company could find itself paying for an organization that must be supported with a massive additional infusion of cash. However, if the buyer has experience in the target company's industry and knows how to implement cost-reducing strategies, it can milk a considerable amount of cash *out of* the target company, possibly enough to even pay for the acquisition. For either reason, it is very important to determine if a target company soaks up or spins off cash, in order to adopt the correct strategy for either proceeding with or terminating any further acquisition planning. The key cash flow analyses to focus on are:

- *Review trend line of net cash flow before debt and interest payments.* The financial statements that are most commonly reviewed for financial purposes are the balance sheet and the income statement. However, for this analysis, we shift to the statement of cash flows, which presents the sources and uses of cash for the reporting period. This report is included in the financial statements of all publicly held companies, though it can be difficult to obtain for a privately held company (as can be all financial information for these entities). For this analysis, we want to see if there is an upward or downward trend in cash flows over the last few years. The impact of debt and interest payments will be ignored, because inordinately high cash flows to pay for these two items may mask a perfectly good underlying business. If there is a pronounced additional requirement for more cash to fund either the acquisition of fixed assets or working capital, then we identify the culprit and then proceed with the remaining analyses noted in this section. This first trend line, then, was to determine the existence of a problem and to more precisely define it.

- *Review trend line of working capital.* Working capital increases are a common reason for a company's cash usage. For example, poor customer credit review policies or inadequate collection efforts will lead to an increased investment in accounts receivable, while excessive production or product obsolescence will increase the inventory investment. Also, a reduction in the days of credit before payments are made to suppliers will reduce the free credit that a company receives from them. To see if there is a problem in this area, add the total accounts receivable to inventory, and subtract the accounts payable balance to arrive at the total working capital amount. Then, plot this information on a trend line that extends back for at least a year. If there is a steady increase in the total of working capital, determine which one (or more) of the three components have caused the problem, and investigate to the lowest level of detail to determine the cause of the problem.

- *Segment working capital investment by customer and product.* From the perspective of the acquiring company, it is especially important to determine if there is a specific customer or product that is causing an increase in working capital. The controller should focus in particular on the accounts receivable and finished goods inventory investments to see if there is a specific customer who is responsible, or review just the inventory investment to see if a specific product is the cause. In either case, this information should be cross-referenced against the analysis for profitability by customer and product that was conducted in the last section to see if there are any combinations of low-profit, high-investment customers or products that are obvious targets for termination in the event of an acquisition.

- *Review trend line of capital purchases.* The final area in which cash can be used is for the acquisition of fixed assets. This is a simple matter to determine by general fixed-asset category, because this information is reported on the balance sheet. However, there may be good reasons for large increases in fixed-asset investments, such as automation, the addition of new facilities, or a general level of competitiveness in the industry that requires constant capital improvements. Only by being certain of the underlying reasons for cash usage in this area can a controller suggest that cash can be saved here by reducing the volume of

Exhibit 6.8   Analysis Report for Cash Flow

Type of Analysis Conducted	Notes
Review trend line of net cash flow before debt and interest payments	The target company is experiencing a massive cash outflow in both the working capital and fixed-assets areas.
Review trend line of working capital	There is a severe cash outflow, due to $2,000,000 in accounts receivable invested in the Gidget Company, as well as a large investment in five distribution warehouses for its Auto-Klean product, each of which requires $1,500,000 in inventory.
Segment working capital investment by customer and product	The main cash outflows are due to the Gidget Company customer and the Auto-Klean product.
Review trend line of capital purchases	Has purchased $10,000,000 of automation equipment to improve margins on its sales to the Gidget Company.

Conclusions and recommendations: There is a major investment in sales to the Gidget Company, which is not justified by the 5% return on sales to that customer. The receivable investment of $2,000,000 can be eliminated by stopping sales to this customer, while $5,000,000 can be realized from the sale of automation equipment used for the production of items for sale to it. Also, the number of distribution warehouses for the Auto-Klean product can be reduced by two, which will decrease the inventory investment by $3,000,000. The amount of cash investment that can be eliminated as a result of these actions is $10,000,000.

asset purchases. Thus, considerable investigation into the reasons behind fixed-asset purchases forms the basis of the underlying analysis.

The report that a controller issues as part of the cash flow analysis is primarily composed of judgments regarding the need for historical cash flows, estimates of future cash flows, and how the acquiring company can alter these flows through specific management actions. A sample of such a report is shown in Exhibit 6.8.

FRAUD ANALYSIS

When acquiring a company, there is always a risk that the target company may contain a significant case of fraud that will have a major adverse impact on the price paid by the acquiring company, and which may even result in a massive drop in the acquiring firm's stock price once the news becomes public, which in turn may result in a series of shareholder lawsuits. Given the severity of the results, a controller must make an attempt to review any target company for evidence of fraud. Unfortunately, fraud is extremely difficult to find, especially if it is being conducted by corporate officers. Nonetheless, there are a few steps to complete that may hint at the possible existence of fraud, and therefore lead to a targeted and more in-depth review:

- *Confirm sales to major customers.* A target company that is trying to improve its financial results will sometimes do so by faking sales to its customers. The controller can take several approaches to see if these sales are legitimate. One step is to send out confirmations to a random sampling of customers to verify that they agree with the target company's list of open accounts receivable for them. Another option is to closely review the sales by customer to see if there is an unusual concentration of sales to one customer, especially at the end of a reporting period, which might indicate the presence of an entity that is not a going concern, but is just used as a shipment delivery destination. Another step is to trace shipments from the billing, back through the shipping log, to the warehouse and production processes to ensure that products were really built and shipped. Yet another (and most expensive) option is to visit a few customer sites to see if they really exist, though this approach is usually used only if the acquiring company strongly suspects fraud at the target company.

- *Review trend line of accounts receivable turnover.* To follow up on the last point, if additional sales are being added to actual sales, then these must be recorded on the accounts receivable listing as uncollected invoices. When this happens, the accounts receivable turnover figure (the proportion of accounts receivable investment to sales) will drop, which is easy to spot on a multiyear trend line. Unfortunately, this is only one of several reasons for a drop in turnover (such as poor collections work or inadequate customer credit reviews), but it is at least an indicator of the possible presence of fraud.

- *Review trend line of inventory turnover.* If a company is falsely increasing its records of on-hand inventory in order to show a reduced cost of goods sold, this will alter the ratio of inventory to cost of goods sold, which is the inventory turnover ratio. This problem will be readily apparent when the ratio is itemized on a multiyear trend line. However, other issues, such as poor purchasing policies, unrecognized inventory obsolescence, and overstocks of finished goods, will also yield the same trend line result. Nonetheless, this measure will sometimes indicate the presence of a fraudulent situation that can then be reviewed in more detail to ascertain the exact problem.

If a controller finds fraud, management is faced with two choices: either continue with the due diligence, but now at a very detailed level, or else back out of the purchase negotiations at once. For a company with limited funds for acquisitions, it is best to back out right away, because the assumption must be made that there is more fraud that has not yet been uncovered and that will be very expensive in the long run to root out and repair. However, for a company that knows precisely what it wants from a target company (perhaps just a patent or two and a few key employees), the existence of fraud may not be a hindrance and may be more of a tool in driving down the purchase price, as well as a way to scare off other suitors from putting in bids.

SYNERGY ANALYSIS

The task of determining possible synergies between the acquiring and target companies is one that should involve the entire management team, because the possible areas of emphasis can cover all functional areas. The controller's role is usually to investigate and make recommendations about synergies that are just related to the accounting role, though the controller of a smaller organization, who has a broader range of responsibility, may also recommend synergy-related changes that involve both the human resources and management information systems areas. This section presents a short list of areas that are prime targets for a controller to analyze for possible synergies in the areas of accounting, human resources, and management information systems:

Accounting
- *Combine transaction operations.* This is the primary synergy to be gained from the perspective of the accounting function. The accounts receivable and payable departments of both companies are merged, as well as the payroll department, so that the transaction volume per person is improved through the use of high-end computerized matching systems and other automation. However, this process will not work if there are major differences in how the underlying documentation is used, and can also present problems if the resulting accounting infor-

mation is recorded in charts of accounts that vary significantly for each of the companies. The situation in which this option works best is the combining companies' being in the same industry and having very similar transaction flows.

- *Combine audits.* An auditor will charge somewhat less to conduct the annual audit for a larger company than for several smaller companies that have the same amount of revenue, because there is less "overhead" work to complete. For example, there is only one set of control points to review, one set of bylaws, one set of corporate minutes, and so on. Also, if the company being acquired represents only a small portion of the total assets or revenues of the combined entity, the auditor may not even bother to review the company, since any problems with its accounting records would have an indiscernible impact on overall reported results.

- *Merge bank accounts.* By consolidating the bank accounts in which cash is received or from which it is paid out or invested, the finance staff can more easily manage the flow of cash into the most profitable investments on a daily basis, which results in an increase in interest income, as well as a modest reduction in bank fees.

Computer Systems
- *Combine software licenses.* If each company has a different type of software to run its operations, it may make sense to merge them both into the same software package, which not only eliminates the annual licensing fees for one of the packages, but also allows for easier sharing of data between the two locations. However, the effort required to convert one of the systems is large, and so should be attempted only if one of the companies has an old software system that is already due for replacement.

- *Combine help desks.* If companies have similar software installations, then they can merge portions of their help desks, so that information about problems and their means of resolution can be stored in and disseminated from a single location.

Human Resources
- *Combine benefit plans.* The cost per person for medical, dental, and life insurance is partially driven by the number of people in the plan, since the providing insurance company must spread administration costs over the total group of participating employees. This administration cost will decrease as the number of participating employees rises, so adding the employees of any acquired company should somewhat reduce the overall cost. However, many companies already have so many employees enrolled in these plans that adding a small acquisition will result in only a small reduction in per-person benefit costs.

General
- *Spread all automation.* In general, if one company has devised a more automated way of completing a transaction, then this innovation should be shared with the other company. For example, if one organization has perfected a method for having employees update their deductions through phone or computer access, then this represents a clear reduction in the number of human resource clerks, and so should be shared with all company divisions.

An analysis report that incorporates many of the preceding analyses is noted in Exhibit 6.9.

One of the most common failings of any acquisition is that management pays a high price for the target company in expectation of creating significant expense reductions or revenue increases through synergies, but they never materialize. To prevent this from happening, the controller should be very careful to clarify all the assumptions that form the basis for every expected synergy, as well as quantifying the reasoning behind every cost reduction or revenue increase. For example, one can determine the number of transactions per year for each accounts payable person before and after an acquisition to see if it is reasonable for the current accounts payable staff to take on

Exhibit 6.9 Analysis Report for Possible Synergies

Description	Additional Information	Summary of Savings[a]
Combine accounting operations	b	$750,000
Eliminate audit at acquired company		100,000
Combine software licenses	c	–450,000
Merge benefit plans		125,000
Merge payroll systems	d	200,000
Switch to payables approval at receiving dock	e	600,000
Total Synergy Savings		**$1,325,000**

[a] All savings are at net present value, discounted at the cost of capital.

[b] The accounts payable and receivable areas will be merged; all other accounting functions remain in their current locations.

[c] The ABC Company's custom-designed software will be replaced by the Oracle software currently used by the XYZ Company. However, the conversion cost far exceeds the savings from using combined systems.

[d] Will switch to the outsourced ADP (Automated Data Processing) solution used by the XYZ Company, which eliminates 12 payroll positions at the ABC company, which is partially offset by increased outsourcing fees.

[e] This modification will eliminate 80% of the accounts payable staff, but will add two positions at both receiving docks.

all the payables work of the other company without an increase in head count. Alternatively, is it really possible for the current sales staff to double its sales per person by selling the products of the current company as well as those of the acquired company? These are basic reasonableness tests that the management group must closely review to see if there is a realistic chance of achieving synergies. Without this kind of detailed review, management will be more likely to base a high purchase price on poorly grounded assumptions that cannot be achieved.

Here is an example of the degree of detailed analysis to which a controller must go to ensure that projected synergies will really occur: The CEO of the Clean Easy Janitorial Supplies Company wants to buy the Clean Sweep Company for its unique line of patented brooms. The reasoning behind the merger is that the Clean Easy sales staff can include the brooms in their sales pitch to customers, thereby selling more product with the same number of sales calls. In addition, the sales staff of Clean Sweep can include the products of Clean Easy in *their* sales calls, with similar results. To see if this reasoning will yield synergies in the sales area, the controller quantifies the projected revenue increases estimated by the sales department. These appear to be reasonable. The controller then goes back to the history of how the company has fared in its penetration of new accounts, however, and finds that it succeeds in only 10 percent of its sales calls, and then only if the company can undercut the prices of its competitors. The sales staff denies that this data is relevant, since all of the projected sales increases will be from the current customers of the two companies. However, the controller returns to the historical records and finds out that prices had to be cut by an average of 15 percent in order to take business away from competitors, which still must be done for the new products about to be sold. When multiplying this percentage by the expected new sales, the controller finds that gross margins will be much worse than the management team initially anticipated. Based on this information, the value of the acquisition will be significantly lower than expected, so the CEO bids a much lower price for the target company. This level of detailed analysis is necessary to ensure that synergy claims can be brought to fruition.

The main issue for any controller who is involved in the analysis of projected synergies is to be as skeptical as possible, and to highlight all possible problems, so that the management team is well aware of the timing, cost, and risks associated with the implementation of any changes.

CONTRACTUAL AND LEGAL ISSUES

Besides purely financial issues, there are a wide array of legal issues that a company's legal staff must peruse. The controller may be tangentially involved in these nonfinancial analysis issues, so they are included here as a reference source. In most cases, the analysis issues noted here are related to various kinds of contracts. When these arise, a key analysis topic for all of them is to see if they can be dissolved in the event of a corporate change of control. Many contracts contain this feature, so that onerous agreements will not cause a potentially high-priced purchase to fall apart. The nonfinancial analysis issues are:

- *Bylaws.* This document will include any "poison pill" provisions that are intended to make a change of control very expensive.

- *Certificate of incorporation, including name changes.* This is used to find the list of all names under which the target company operates, which is needed for real estate title searches.

- *Employment contracts.* Key employees may be guaranteed high pay levels for a number of years, or a "golden parachute" clause that guarantees them a large payment if the company is sold.

- *Engineering reports.* These documents will note any structural weaknesses in corporate buildings that may require expensive repairs.

- *Environmental exposure.* Review all literature received from the Environmental Protection Agency, as well as the Occupational Safety and Health Administration, and conduct environmental hazard testing around all company premises to ascertain the extent of potential environmental litigation.

- *Insurance policies.* Verify that the existing insurance policies cover all significant risks that are not otherwise covered by internal safety policies. Also, compare these policies to those held by the buyer to see if there can be savings by consolidating the policies for both companies.

- *Labor union agreements.* If the target company is a union shop, the union contract may contain unfavorable provisions related to work rules, guaranteed pay increases, payouts or guaranteed retraining funds in the event of a plant closure, or onerous benefit payments.

- *Leases.* Creating a schedule of all current leases tells a buyer the extent of commitments to pay for leased assets, as well as interest rates and any fees for early lease terminations.

- *Licenses.* A license for a target company to do business, usually granted by a local government, but also by another company for whom it is the distributor or franchisee, may not be transferable if there is change of ownership. This can be quite a surprise to a buyer that now finds it cannot use the company it has just bought.

- *Litigation.* This is a broad area that requires a considerable amount of review before legal counsel can be reasonably satisfied as to the extent and potential liability associated with current and potential litigation. This review should encompass an investigation of all civil suits and criminal actions that may include contract disputes, fraud, discrimination, breach of employment contract, wrongful termination, inadequate disclosure issues, deceptive trade practices, antitrust suits, or other issues. It should also include tax claims and notices of potential litigation received from any of the following government agencies:

  - Department of Justice
  - Department of Labor

- Equal Employment Opportunity Commission

- Federal Trade Commission

- Internal Revenue Service

- Securities and Exchange Commission (applies only to a publicly held entity)

- *Marketing materials.* The target company's advertising of its product capabilities can be a source of potential litigation, if the publicized product claims are overstated.

- *Pension plans.* Determine the size of the employer-funded portion of the pension plan. This will require the services of an actuary to verify the current cost of required future funding.

- *Product warranty agreements.* Review the published warranty that is issued alongside each product to verify its term, as well as what specific features it will replace in the event of product failure.

- *Sponsorship agreements.* A target company may have a long-term commitment to sponsor an event that will require a significant expenditure to maintain or terminate.

- *Supplier or customer contracts.* A target company may be locked into a long-term agreement with one or more of its suppliers or customers, possibly guaranteeing unfavorable terms that will noticeably affect profits if the buyer purchases the company.

Though the preceding nonfinancial issues are primarily related to the legal liabilities of a corporate entity, there are a few cases in which the controller may be called on to provide an estimate of possible attendant costs. For example, if the bylaws include a poison pill provision, then the controller can quantify the extra cost required to fulfill the poison pill provisions. Another set of

Exhibit 6.10   Analysis Report for Contractual and Legal Issues

Description	Additional Information	Summary of Costs
Poison pill payout provision	Bylaws section 2, clause 14	$12,500,000
Golden parachute provision	For all officers	3,250,000
Discounted cost of all lease provisions	Copiers, forklifts	320,000
Discounted pension plan funding requirements		4,750,000
Discounted cost of sponsorship agreement		220,000
Termination payment for long-term supplier contracts		540,000
Total cost of contractual and legal issues		**$21,580,000**

cases is to determine the net present value of all employment, labor union, and lease provisions that require a specified minimum set of payments for a designated time period. Other examples of the same situation are minimum guaranteed payments under the terms of pension plans, sponsorship agreements, and supplier contracts. An example of the format one can use to summarize these expenses is shown in Exhibit 6.10.

TABLE OF ANALYSIS TOPICS

This section includes a series of checklists that are based on the analysis topics covered under all of the preceding sections of this chapter. It is intended to be a summary listing of all possible acquisition analyses, for use by someone who is browsing for a specific set of analyses to conduct in regard to a designated type of acquisition. The only topic not included here is the analysis of potential synergies, because it is difficult to anticipate all possible synergies on which a controller can be expected to conduct an analysis. The tables are itemized in their original order by section title in Exhibit 6.11.

Exhibit 6.11   Recommended Analyses by Type of Acquisition

Type of Acquisition/ Analysis	Recommended Analysis
Personnel	Investigate employee names listed on patents.
Personnel	Interview customers and suppliers about employees.
Personnel	Compare employee pay levels to industry and internal averages.
Personnel	Determine the current turnover rate in the targeted department.
Personnel	Review long-term compensation agreements.
Patent	Determine annual patent renewal costs.
Patent	Determine current patent-related revenue stream.
Patent	Ascertain extent of current litigation to support patent.
Brand	Determine the amount of annual trademark fees.
Brand	Determine clear title to the brand name.
Brand	Ascertain the amount and trend of any current cash inflows from the brand name.
Brand	Note the amount and trend of any legal fees needed to stop encroachment.
Brand	Note any challenges to use of the brand name.
Capacity	Determine the facility overhead cost required for minimum, standard, and maximum capacity.
Capacity	Ascertain the amount of capital replacements needed.
Capacity	Find out the periodic maintenance cost of existing equipment.

Continued

Exhibit 6.11   *Continued*

Type of Acquisition/ Analysis	Recommended Analysis
Capacity	Determine the maximum production capacity.
Capacity	Investigate any environmental liabilities.
Capacity	Determine the cost of modifications needed to increase the capacity of the facility.
Assets	Conduct a fixed-asset audit.
Assets	Appraise the value of fixed assets.
Assets	Ascertain the existence of liens against assets.
Assets	Determine the collectibility of accounts receivable.
Assets	Verify the bank reconciliation for all bank accounts.
Assets	Audit the existence and valuation of remaining assets.
Assets	Determine the value of any tax loss carry-forward.
Liabilities	Reconcile unpaid debt to lender balances.
Liabilities	Look for unrecorded debt.
Liabilities	Audit accounts payable.
Liabilities	Audit accrued liabilities.
Profitability	Review a trend line of revenues.
Profitability	Review a trend line of bad debt expense.
Profitability	Review a trend line of sales discounts.
Profitability	Review a trend line of material costs.
Profitability	Review a trend line of direct labor costs.
Profitability	Review a trend line of gross margins.
Profitability	Review a trend line of net margins.
Profitability	Ascertain the gross profit by product.
Profitability	Ascertain the gross profit by customer.
Profitability	Review a trend line of overhead personnel per major customer.
Profitability	Review a trend line of overhead personnel per transaction.
Cash flow	Review trend line of net cash flow before debt and interest payments.
Cash flow	Review trend line of working capital.
Cash flow	Segment working capital investment by customer.
Cash flow	Review trend line of capital purchases.
Fraud	Confirm sales to major customers.
Fraud	Review trend line of accounts receivable turnover.
Fraud	Review trend line of accounts payable turnover.
Fraud	Review trend line of inventory turnover.
Contractual and legal issues	Review bylaws.
Contractual and legal issues	Review the certificate of incorporation, including name changes.

Type of Acquisition/ Analysis	Recommended Analysis
Contractual and legal issues	Review employment contracts.
Contractual and legal issues	Review engineering reports.
Contractual and legal issues	Review environmental exposure.
Contractual and legal issues	Review insurance policies.
Contractual and legal issues	Review labor union agreements.
Contractual and legal issues	Review leases.
Contractual and legal issues	Review licenses.
Contractual and legal issues	Review litigation.
Contractual and legal issues	Review marketing materials.
Contractual and legal issues	Review pension plans.
Contractual and legal issues	Review product warranty agreements.
Contractual and legal issues	Review sponsorship agreements.
Contractual and legal issues	Review supplier or customer contracts.

SUMMARY

This chapter focused on the analyses that must be conducted in order to be assured that an acquisition target is fairly stating its financial condition and results, and that there are no hidden issues that could substantially alter the target's valuation or leave the acquiring company open to an unknown amount of litigation. The information on which these analyses are based is frequently difficult to obtain, and may be required in very short order, so that the deal can either be consummated or dropped. Given the time pressures involved, a controller is usually under a great deal of stress to conduct a fair and in-depth evaluation. Using the detailed analysis information and related checklists contained in this chapter, a controller has the framework on which to base such an analysis.

7

Increasing Shareholder Value

The reason for the existence of a company is ultimately to increase the value of the shares held by stockholders. Given this basic underlying issue, it is reasonable that a controller will be called on from time to time to provide suggestions for how to improve the current value of these shares. This chapter covers the reasoning behind how shareholder value fluctuates, and then discusses the income statement and balance sheet to see how key parts of each one can be modified to enhance cash flow.

LINKING SHAREHOLDER VALUE AND CASH FLOWS

There are several theories regarding how the value of shares can be altered. This section shows how share prices can be changed in the short run by a variety of factors, but how long-term value improvements can be brought about only by improvements in a company's cash flows.

The most recently promulgated approach for improving shareholder value is to grab as much market share as possible at whatever cost on the grounds that the company with the most customers wins. This has been a particularly powerful argument in the world of Internet stocks, where such companies as Amazon, eBay, and Yahoo continue to post enormous losses and burn through large quantities of cash, and yet sport multibillion-dollar valuations. This is a rare situation that applies only to new industries, in which the business model that will ultimately develop is still uncertain and profits are scarce. In such a scenario, investors have little to rely on in making their judgments regarding stock valuations, so they assume that those that have the most customers will eventually win out over those who do not, and will then be able to improve their business models to ensure long-term profitability. This approach can be twisted so far that investors may encourage a company *not* to make money for the first few years of its existence, on the grounds that any profits should have been spent on additional efforts to attract more customers. This approach to improving shareholder value is obviously only a short-term approach that does not allow for corporate survival in the long run, since all cash will eventually be used up, throwing a company into bankruptcy.

Another approach to improving shareholder value is to design a company to be a takeover target, which rewards shareholders when their shares are bought at a premium by the company that eventually buys it. This is a common approach for companies that specialize in research and development (R&D), or those that possess special patents or rights to certain markets. For example, Craig McCaw bought up a number of cellular phone licenses in the markets where AT&T had no access, thereby designing a company that AT&T desperately needed to expand itself into a nationwide presence. For his efforts, McCaw earned more than $1 billion. However, this approach does not allow for long-term share appreciation, because in the long term the company will not be in existence. Once again, only a short-term approach to improving value has been achieved.

Yet another approach is to improve accounting earnings, most commonly known as earnings per share. This is a better approach, because it relates a company's net profit to the number of shares outstanding. As the earnings per share increase, investors should bid up the price of the stock to reflect the increased flow of earnings. Though an essentially sound method for increasing shareholder value, this approach suffers from the potential for manipulation. For example, a company can set up expense reserves during high-profit periods and dole out these reserves to cover losses during less profitable periods, thereby fooling investors into thinking that profits are higher than they really are. Similarly, one can also report large losses in a single period that are really reserves that can then be spread over a number of future periods to make results look better in the future. Also, there can be a temptation to use accruals or shaky accounting methods to improve the amount of reported revenues or reduce the amount of reported expenses in a period. This frequently results in a future reduction in the earnings per share, since "the truth will come out" when the scheme collapses and downward adjustments must be made. Finally, the measure does not take account of any changes in fixed assets or working capital, which can absorb a large amount of cash. If these last areas are not managed properly, a company can find itself out of cash, even though it is consistently reporting a respectable level of earnings per share. Consequently, there are too many ways to twist the earnings per share figure to make it a worthwhile long-term method for increasing shareholder value, while it also does not factor in a company's use of cash.

The only method that provides a consistent view of the true results of a company is the stream of cash flows in and out of a company. When an organization is able to generate large amounts of cash on a consistent basis, a higher valuation results, if only because that cash can theoretically be distributed to shareholders, either in the form of ongoing dividends or as a single final payout in the event of a liquidation. Also, this large store of cash drives up the value of any company in the eyes of potential acquirers, because they can include that cash reserve in their valuation of the company. In addition, a strong cash flow allows a company to pay off its debts and keep from adding on new debt, which eliminates the risk of not being able to pay its interest and principal payments, which in turn results in a steadier and more predictable cash flow. Finally, having access to large amounts of internally generated cash allows a company to grow at a more rapid rate, because it does not have to worry about running out of funds that can be used to pay for new projects. All of these factors mean that a company's ability to not only survive but to prosper in the long run is driven by its ability to spin off large amounts of cash flow. Given that this is the long-term underlying reason for a corporation's health, it naturally follows that strong cash flow is closely tied to share value.

Of all the methods presented here for increasing shareholder value, all but the last are short-term strategies that allow the owners of common stock to enhance their value. However, all but the last will work only under specific and short-term circumstances. The one exception is having a positive cash flow, which is the single method that consistently allows a company to improve the value of its common stock in the long run. Accordingly, the remainder of this chapter covers how to provide analysis to management of the key areas in the income statement and balance sheet that result in significant changes in cash flow.

PRICING

To increase shareholder value by improving cash flow, start at the top of the income statement, where revenue resides. In this area, the focus is on improving the average price point at which each product or service sells. This is more complicated than simply tracking product pricing on a trend line, as is noted in this section.

The trouble many companies face is that they set a price for a product without accounting for a group of deductions that can take a large bite out of the original price, resulting in a price point that is much less than originally anticipated. When this occurs, margins will be less than planned and cash flows will suffer. Some of the deductions that will reduce the net price that customers pay include:

- *Advertising support.* Some customers may demand funding of advertising for a specific product, or a company may offer this approach to customers in order to create brand awareness in the marketplace. This can be total payment of all advertising expenses but is more commonly a split with the customer who does the advertising. This cost is not usually deducted directly from revenues; instead, it is buried in the advertising expense line in the sales expenses part of the income statement.

- *Bad debt deductions.* This expense can be hidden in a variety of locations on the income statement, such as the sales department expense or under general and administrative expense. It is a standard percentage that is used to build up a reserve fund against which uncollectible invoices are charged.

- *Early payment discounts.* Some customers are flush with cash and can afford to pay within a few days of product receipt, though at the price of a 1 or 2 percent discount in the base price.

- *Promotional allowances.* In some industries, it is a common practice to offer discounts at some times of the year in order to move additional product volumes, perhaps in conjunction with a major holiday or the beginning or end of a selling season. When this happens, customers may purchase inordinately large volumes of product at a lower price, which skews downward the overall pricing on the product.

- *Volume discounts.* Larger customers with considerable buying power will demand pricing concessions in exchange for buying large volumes of product. A sales force must carefully consider whether it really wants to sell to this type of customer, since the customer will resell the product at a much lower price, thereby dropping the final price that the ultimate customer pays, and reducing the value of the product in the marketplace as a whole.

As the market in which a product sells gradually matures and becomes more competitive, all of these pricing deductions become proportionally larger, as the sales force struggles to maintain sales volume in the face of increased competition. For example, it may be necessary to sell to a financially less secure group of customers, which results in an increase in bad debts. Alternatively, adding a large retailer may require concessions on pricing in order to sell large product volumes through that entity. These are just costs of doing business, but management does not realize that they result in an increased reduction in the net product price as time goes by.

Accumulating the above information and consolidating it into a set of net prices is more difficult than it may at first appear. Part of the trouble is that the deductions are located in different parts of the income statement, and must be located and assembled. For example, the bad debt expense is most frequently reported in the sales department expense, as is the advertising reimbursement cost, whereas promotional allowances, volume discounts, and early payment discounts are typically listed as direct deductions from revenues. The next problem is that, even with the correct information in hand, the controller must sort it by individual product price to determine which ones are being most severely impacted by deductions, discounts, and promotions. It is most important to report on this information at an individual product level, so that management can take the most informed action possible to correct the situation. If there are many products, it can be quite a chore to assemble pricing information at this level of detail.

Once the fully reduced pricing information is completed, what is the most appropriate way to present it to management? It is most useful and informative if given to management as a trend line, since this allows for comparison of current net pricing against the results of previous periods. By doing this for each product, management can quickly sort through all of the pricing trends, find the ones that are declining, and focus its attention on them. In the example shown in Exhibit 7.1, there are pricing trends for three products, of which only the last shows a significant downward trend over sev-

Exhibit 7.1   Pricing Trend Charts

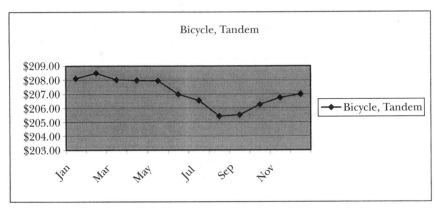

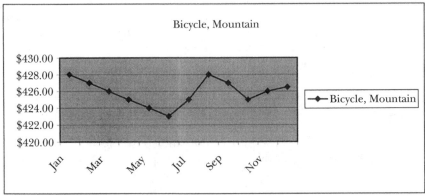

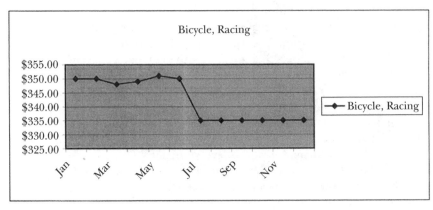

Exhibit 7.2   Detailed Pricing Review Table

Pricing Detail for Racing Bike in September

Customer	Base Price	Quantity Purchased	Promo-tional Allowance	Adver-tising Support	Total Revenue	Net Unit Price
Schwab Racing	$350.00	100	—	—	$35,000	$350.00
Bike Town	350.00	50	—	—	17,500	350.00
Wheels, Inc.	350.00	25	—	—	8,750	350.00
Spokes 'n Stuff	350.00	12	—	—	4,200	350.00
Bikers Villages	350.00	75	—	—	26,250	350.00
Fred's Discount	342.00	500	$5,930	$1,500	163,570	327.14
Totals	—	762	5,930	1,500	255,270	$335.00

eral months. Based on the data, management can focus its attention entirely on the last product.

Once management knows which products are experiencing pricing difficulty, it requires an additional level of detailed information to determine exactly what is causing the trouble. For example, it may be any of the additional expenses noted at the beginning of this section, or it may be the addition of a new customer to whom lower pricing was offered. A good way to present this information to management is shown in Exhibit 7.2, which contains all sales of a specific product for one month, showing the quantity, unit price, and various deductions, resulting in a net price. By presenting the data in this format, it rapidly becomes apparent that the exact reason for the price decline is a combination of large sales volume at a slightly reduced price to a national retailer, as well as promotional allowances and advertising support to that same customer. In light of this information, management needs to determine if the reduced pricing on sales to this customer are worth the reduction in the overall margin percentage that will result.

It is only by rigorously examining pricing at an extremely detailed level, and then properly presenting this information for consumption by management, that a controller can have an impact on a company's responsiveness to pricing issues.

MATERIAL COSTS

The cost of materials used to produce a company's products is the most difficult one to apply financial analysis to, because materials pass through and are used by many different departments and are used in large quantities. As a result, materials can be lost at many points, which makes it difficult to determine exactly how many materials are used by each product. However, rather than throwing up one's hands in frustration and moving on to the analysis of other expenses, several methods that yield approximate margins that are most useful for financial analysis purposes are described in this section.

One of the best ways to determine the material cost of a product is to rely on its bill of materials (BOM). A BOM is a description of the material contents of a product, and is usually created by the engineering staff that designed the product. Though a BOM can be inaccurate and may require some review by the production staff that assembles the product and the purchasing staff that buys the materials in order to improve its accuracy, it remains an excellent source of information about material costs. One way to use the BOM is to compare it to the standard selling price of a product to derive a gross margin (which must also include the labor cost, covered in the next section). The result of this analysis is a report similar to the one shown in Exhibit 7.3, which itemizes the standard gross margins of all company products. In the example, the products are sorted in increasing order of margin, so that the worst product margins appear at the top of the report. The sales staff can use this information to requote product margins to customers, if there is some ability to alter pricing. If not, the report can still be used by the engineering staff to see if material costs can somehow be reduced. Finally, the purchasing staff can use the report to see if material costs can be reduced by sourcing to different suppliers or by purchasing in larger quantities. In short, this simple standard gross margin report can be used by several departments to improve margins. Given the risk of losing profits if low-margin products are sold for too long, it is best to issue this report at least once a month, if not more frequently.

The analysis in Exhibit 7.3 can be extended to include a margin trend line by product, so that any variation in margins can be immediately spotted and acted on by management.

The standard margin comparison should be the baseline report used for all analyses of materials. Once this report is in place, it is possible to use it for several additional comparison reports that provide extra information about material costs. One such comparison is a trend line of total material costs that shows the standard cost, as determined by the bill of materials, at the end of each month. This report reveals if there is a gradual or sudden

Exhibit 7.3   Standard Gross Margins Report

Product	Quantity Sold	Selling Price/Ea	Material Cost/Ea	Labor Cost/Ea	Standard Margin (%)	Standard Margin ($)
Saw	450	22.00	15.00	4.00	14	1,386
Table saw	540	210.00	150.00	28.00	15	17,010
Screwdriver	1,000	5.40	3.00	1.50	17	918
Hammer	500	12.00	6.50	3.50	17	1,020
Drill	890	48.00	31.00	5.00	25	10,680
Wrench	310	15.00	8.00	3.00	27	1,256
Bench	720	41.00	21.00	7.00	32	9,446

costing problem that will interfere with gross margins, such as the addition of a new part to the old bill of materials, or a sudden price increase by a supplier. This report can be more revealing than the one shown in Exhibit 7.3, because management can more easily spot changes in material costs.

Another type of analysis that has the same result is a comparison of current material costs to the original material cost that was determined during the target costing phase of production. Target costing is an approach whereby management creates a target cost that must be attained before production of a new product is allowed to start. In addition, there may be extra cost reductions targeted at set intervals after production has begun that will lead to a gradual and continuous reduction in costs over time. When these baseline material targets are used to compare to current actual material costs, management can quickly determine whether there are products for which cost targets have not been attained, and then focus its attention on achieving those targets.

Once the accounting staff has refined its analysis of standard material costs, it can branch out into the reporting of scrap costs, which can be very significant in size and represent a large proportion of total material costs. The biggest problem with reporting on scrap costs is to create a system that reliably accumulates those costs. Because the production staff is frequently held accountable for any scrap generated, it has a tendency to underreport scrap in order to stay out of trouble. The following approaches can be used to get around this problem:

- *Measure scrap after the production process.* Once scrap has been generated, it has to go somewhere to be disposed of. By intercepting and measuring the scrap at this point, one can determine the exact amount of the scrap without any potential alteration of the information by the production staff. One problem with this approach, however, is that it will not account for any scrap that is still sitting in the production area, which makes it difficult to determine how much of the scrap is associated with a specific production run.

- *Measure scrap indirectly.* If it is not practical to determine the exact quantity of specific materials that are scrapped, it may still be possible to infer this information from other sources. For example, if the scrap is metal, one can periodically weigh the metal scrap recycling bin to ascertain the poundage that was thrown out. Clearly, this is a very inexact approach and should be considered a last resort for scrap measurement.

- *Reinforce the significance of scrap reporting.* There can be some benefit to regularly reinforcing the scrap reporting issue by meeting with and going over this problem with the production staff. However, it is rarely a good idea to pay bonuses for accurate reporting, because the production staff may create extra scrap just to obtain the bonus! A better way is to conduct ongoing audits of the process by the internal audit staff to determine who is (and is not) reporting scrap through the predetermined reporting system.

- *Involve production in BOM accuracy measurements.* If the specific reason for tracking scrap information is to include more accurate scrap information into BOMs, it is possible to include the production staff in the "game" of updating the bills. This is rarely a problem for the production staff, because the engineering staff is ultimately responsible for the accuracy of these documents, not the production staff. Accordingly, they are usually more than willing to assist the engineers (i.e., prove them wrong) in determining the actual amount of scrap used to produce specific products.

Once one or more of these reporting methods have been made operational, a controller can accumulate scrap by product, production process, or machine (or all three) and report this information to management, which can then focus on those processes that result in the largest amount of scrap. An example of such a report is shown in Exhibit 7.4, in which a trend line is shown of the scrap percentage and cost for a series of molds used in a plastic injection molding operation. The report is sorted so that the molds with the largest amounts of scrap are listed at the top of the report, and molds with better operating results are listed further down. This report layout allows management to focus on those molds that require repairs or enhancements to improve their scrap yield.

The trend line component of the scrap report in Exhibit 7.4 is especially useful, because it reveals any scrap trends within the last quarter of operations. Obviously, an increase in the scrap percentage during this period calls for immediate management action.

This section has shown that a controller can effectively use financial analysis to present management with a large quantity of information related to the accuracy and amount of material and scrap costs that a company must undertake in order to produce a product. Key tools in this analysis are the use of standard and target costs, trend lines, margin analysis, and an ongoing review of scrap costs.

Exhibit 7.4   Scrap Report by Mold

Mold No.	Mold Description	January Scrap (%)	February Scrap (%)	March Scrap (%)	Quarterly Scrap Cost
94587	Pail	5.0	5.5	5.6	$4,508
90401	Tray pack	2.0	1.9	1.7	4,001
93214	Litter box	2.9	3.0	2.8	3,801
90207	Golf ball	3.1	3.2	3.5	3,500
92058	Rocket kit	8.0	7.2	6.1	2,508
98765	Storage box	5.3	5.3	4.2	2,008
99061	Alarm panel	18.0	15.2	11.1	721

LABOR COSTS

Labor no longer constitutes the large percentage of product costs that it used to, now that automation has eliminated so much of it. Nonetheless, it can still represent a significant proportion of total costs in selected industries, especially in the service sector. Consequently, it is generally worth the effort to create analyses that will at least monitor the amount of labor, if not assist in reducing it.

There are several trend lines that are useful for determining changes in labor costs. If there is a significant increase in costs based on these trend lines, management can then take action to reverse the trend. For example, the average hourly rate, either for the whole company or for selected product lines or work groups, is an excellent item to track. Once the trend line has been constructed, a controller can delve further into the reasons for changes in the hourly rate, such as union-negotiated rate changes or an alteration in the mix of employee pay rates that comprise the average rate. Another good trend line is the average overtime rate. This can be broken down by department or even by individual, so that one can see where there are continuing problems requiring correction. A key issue for a controller to consider in this area is a recommendation to increase a department's permanent level of staffing if its overtime rate is consistently high. Key to this decision is a determination of whether the department is suffering from a short-term work increase that can be resolved through overtime or whether the underlying workload has increased to the point where extra staff is required. A final trend line that is worthy of review is the total amount of labor cost as a percentage of total sales, which can also be subdivided into individual profit centers. By comparing the overall labor cost to the best overall measure of company activity (sales), it is easy to determine whether a company is efficiently utilizing its labor.

These three trend lines are usually sufficient for spotting the main issues related to labor. However, it is frequently necessary to dig deeply into the underlying reasons for changes in labor costs in order to fully understand how they can be reduced. Several problem areas that can influence the cost of labor are:

- *Production scheduling.* Overtime may increase because the production scheduling staff is scheduling many short-term jobs for production, even though there is plenty of capacity in the long term. Resolving this problem does not require a mandate to slash overtime, but rather a discussion with the scheduling department to shift scheduled work further into the future.

- *Production processes.* Excessive labor costs may not be the fault of the production staff at all, if the production process is laid out in an inefficient manner. When this happens, the production staff cannot possibly manufacture at the targeted levels, so the best approach is to bring in the industrial engineering staff to reconfigure the production process.

- *Employee training.* Some companies make the mistake of hiring low-end, untrained personnel in the belief that they are obtaining labor for the lowest possible price. Though the base pay rate may be low, the inefficiency of this type of person can be considerable, so detailed, prolonged, and repetitive training is needed to bring labor efficiency levels up to targeted levels.

- *Production management.* More times than not, there is nothing wrong with the production personnel, who are doing what they are told in an efficient manner. However, the production manager is not distributing the workload properly among the tasks that need to be completed, resulting in underworked employees in some locations and overworked ones in others. Proper training and evaluation of production managers is the best way to resolve this problem.

The examples shown here are only a small sample of the wide array of problems that can cause labor inefficiencies. Only a detailed review of underlying causes will bring these problems to light, so that management can resolve them. A truly responsible controller will not stop at simply reporting labor cost trends, but will dig deeper to tell the report recipients why problems are occurring.

INTEREST INCOME AND EXPENSE

The typical corporation has a mix of outstanding debt or investment instruments. For example, it may have a line of credit, several leases, and a variety of term loans, as well as a money market account for short-term investments, and a few long-term bonds from various sources for long-term investments. When managed properly, these debts and investments can be modified to improve a company's cash flow. A controller's role in this process is to report on the interest expense or income from each of these items and recommend alterations that will either reduce the interest expense or increase the interest income.

In the area of interest income and expense, the goal is to reduce the cash outflow caused by paying an excessive amount of interest expense. To do so, it is useful to construct a table, such as the one shown in Exhibit 7.5, that lists each debt and investment and its interest cost or return, respectively, net of tax effect. One can then peruse the table and determine where the highest expense is located, and use either excess investments or funds available through a low-cost debt instrument to pay off those debts with the highest interest expense. By reshuffling funds in this manner, the cash outflow due to interest expense can be reduced to the lowest possible level.

In Exhibit 7.5, the key column to review is "interest net of tax (%)." This one tells us the true cost of debt or income from investments after the impact of tax deductions has been factored into the initial interest rate. Based on this information, one can see that the line of credit debt carries the highest interest cost, and so should be the primary target for a paydown. The source of this

Exhibit 7.5   Table Showing Expense and Income from Debts and Investments

Description	Total Amount	Interest Rate (%)	Tax Rate (%)	Interest Net of Tax (%)	Interest Cost or Income
Line of credit	$2,500,000	9.5	35	6.175	$-154,375
Term note	500,000	8.0	35	5.200	-26,000
Term note	750,000	8.3	35	5.395	-40,463
Term note	250,000	9.2	35	5.980	-14,950
Money market	100,000	2.0	35	1.300	+1,300
Municipal bond	300,000	5.2	0	5.200	+15,600
Corporate paper	200,000	7.1	35	4.615	+9,230

money should be the money being invested in the money market fund, the corporate paper, and the municipal bond, in that order (because the money market fund earns only a minimal interest rate, whereas the municipal bond earns the most interest income). Using the example, if all three investments were liquidated and used to pay down the line of credit by an equivalent amount, the company would experience the following net improvement in its annual cash flow:

- Annual cash income from investments that will be lost:

Money market	1,300
Municipal bond	15,600
Corporate paper	9,230
Total	$26,130

- Annual interest expense that will be avoided:

  = Line of credit reduction of $600,000 $\times$ after-tax rate

  = $600,000 $\times$ 6.175%

  = $37,050

- Net reduction in interest expense:

  = Interest expense reduction – interest income reduction

  = $37,050 – $26,130

  = $10,920

Thus, by using low-income investments to pay off more expensive debt, a company can realize a greater level of cash flow, which contributes to an increase in shareholder value.

However, before liquidating all investments and using the resulting funds to offset the line of credit, one must also consider when the investments come due. If there is not a ready market for sale of the investment, a company may take a considerable amount of time to find a buyer and may have to sell at a discount in order to liquidate the investment. Also, if there is a ready market for the investments, but they sell at a discount because the listed interest rate is below the current market rate, the company may not realize the book value of the investment upon liquidation. Also, a company may have a considerable fluctuation in its daily cash needs and prefer to park a cash reserve in a readily accessible investment account, such as the money market fund in the example, rather than continually draw down the funds from a line of credit. To take this last point a step further, if the most expensive debt had been a term note, there would be a greater risk involved than in paying down the line of credit. The reason is that, if a company invests too much money in a line of credit paydown, it can always borrow the money back through the line of credit to meet its operating needs, whereas a paydown of a term note is fixed and cannot be given back to the company. Thus, paying down any term note is riskier than paying down a line of credit. All of these factors must be taken into account before liquidating investments in favor of paying down debts.

If there are many debt instruments with varying debt levels, it may also be worth the trouble to consolidate these loans into a single one that carries a lower interest rate. This situation is most likely when a company has acquired several other corporations, along with all their debts, and finds itself burdened with possibly dozens of different debts. The downside of this approach is that the current market rates or changes in the creditor's perceived risk in lending to the company may result in a *higher* interest expense if all debts are consolidated than the existing blended rate from all the current debt instruments. Consequently, one must first ask lending institutions about expected interest rates prior to initiating the paperwork to consolidate debts.

One can also focus on stringing out debt payments as far into the future as possible, on the grounds that a company can more profitably use the cash internally to create or maintain projects that yield a net increase in cash. Though this is sometimes a worthwhile objective, very long-term debt with small periodic payments tends to carry a higher interest rate than debt that can be recovered by the lender more quickly, because the lender's money is at risk for a longer period of time. Since the interest rate is higher, fewer projects will have an incremental cash flow that exceeds the cost of the debt, which means that there may not be that many internal projects that can be profitably funded in this manner. Instead, it is best to pay off shorter-term debt at regularly scheduled intervals, and to then borrow more money as needed that has similar repayment terms.

RESEARCH AND DEVELOPMENT EFFORTS

For companies that are solely concerned with cash flows, such as those in leveraged buyout situations that need all possible cash to pay off debt, R&D

expenditures are the first thing to go. When a controller recommends such a move, the payoff is an immediate increase in cash flows as the R&D staff is laid off and development funds are curtailed. If a company is doing this to a division that it no longer has an interest in keeping in the forefront of its market, or if it is simply winding down a division and liquidating it, this is a reasonable move. However, there are many situations in which this is not a good way to protect or increase shareholder value at all.

One such situation is a company's being squarely situated in the midst of an exploding market in which product categories are ill defined and market share fluctuates by the minute. In this situation, a company's stock can be bid up to stratospheric levels by investors who are eager to buy into any company that seems to have a slight edge in the new market. In this case, the net increase in shareholder value due to increases in the share price will vastly outpace any improvement in cash flows due to cutting back on R&D expenditures. Accordingly, in this situation, it is wisest to ignore cash flows and throw as much money as possible at the R&D function, in hopes of developing the new wonder product that will take the market by storm. The unbelievable run-up in the price of Internet stocks is a good example of this situation. (For more information about explosive growth companies, see the author's book *Managing Explosive Corporate Growth* [John Wiley & Sons, 1999].)

Explosive growth markets do not explode for long, however. They then settle down into staid industries that obey more common profit and loss criteria to determine shareholder value. In this more common situation, a company still needs some modest degree of R&D expenditures if it wants to continue to be viable in the marketplace, depending on its competitive strategy. For example, if a company like TRW wants to maintain its exceptional edge in aerospace electronics, its must invest an inordinate amount in R&D in order to invent new products that will command a significant edge in pricing over the less sophisticated products of its competitors. If a company is content to adopt a "me too" attitude to R&D and churn out knockoffs of the products made by its more cutting-edge competitors, and then compete on reduced production costs or other efficiencies, it can settle for considerably less R&D funding. However, it is a rare case indeed when a company can completely abandon all R&D funding and still hope to compete in the marketplace with reasonably modern products. Finally, there are industries, such as pharmaceuticals, in which R&D is the foundation of the entire industry and the largest single cost is R&D and will continue to be for the foreseeable future. Such great drug companies as Merck, Upjohn, and Schering-Plough would not be in their enviable competitive positions were it not for their considerable and multiyear funding of R&D efforts. Thus, the level of R&D funding depends largely on the strategy it wishes to pursue or the industry in which it is located.

Given that some R&D expenditures are needed in most cases, what can a controller do to determine if the correct amount is being spent? This is one of the toughest areas in which one can develop a reasonably accurate picture of R&D adequacy, because the results of R&D funding may be separated by years or even decades from the initial funding. Some ways to do so include:

- *Rearview mirror tracking.* One can easily determine the amount of funding in previous periods and compare it to marketable products or patents that were generated based on that funding. This is a classic accounting approach, because it only "looks in the rearview mirror" to see results, without attempting to look ahead to see if the same results can be expected in the future. However, it may be useful to some degree to determine if there is an upward or downward trend in the results achieved through R&D funding, so that a controller will at least have some idea if the current level of spending is achieving anything.

- *Trend of expected products and patents.* It is usually possible to determine the approximate dates when new products are likely to be released to market or when patents are probably going to be granted by the patent office. This gives a company a fairly accurate look in the near future at the results of its R&D expenditures. However, these results are usually good for only one year into the future, and are usually based on R&D expenditures that were largely completed some time in the past. There is no way to determine if current expenditures will continue to relate to the same number of resulting products or patents.

- *Competitor R&D percentages.* If it appears difficult or impossible to determine the correct level of R&D expenditure internally, one can always examine the financial statements of publicly held competitors to determine the size of their R&D expenses, either in straight dollar terms or as a percentage of sales. This can be a very useful approach if the R&D departments of all competitors work with roughly the same levels of efficiency and effectiveness, because the amount of dollars spent should be the deciding factor in determining who will have the largest number of new products and patents.

- *Detailed review.* By far the best approach of all is to regularly visit with the research and engineering staffs to ascertain their views of what projects are most likely to succeed and which should be terminated. The accounting staff is rarely capable of determining which projects should be dropped and which should stay; therefore, this work really requires the efforts of a committee composed of members from many departments, such as marketing, engineering, and production. The opinion of this committee should be the deciding factor in determining the correct amount of R&D funding.

Though the last option noted above was described as the best one, many companies will not have the staff available to conduct such a detailed and ongoing review, usually because of the extreme expense of doing so. If the total amount of R&D expense is small and a company does not place a great deal of emphasis on this item, then the need for a detailed review is greatly reduced. However, if R&D is a key component of the company strategy and a large proportion of its total costs, then there is no excuse for not creating a large and highly experienced group to conduct an ongoing review of R&D expenditures.

Sometimes, there is no way to determine which R&D projects will result in a final product. This is a particular problem in advanced research environments in which there is no guarantee of results, or when pure research is being conducted with little chance of producing an idea that can be developed into a product. In these cases, the correct amount of R&D funding is essentially impossible to predict. Instead, one can create a range of possible expense levels by viewing funding as a series of bets on a range of possible outcomes. For example, if there are 10 current or expected projects in a specific area of research, one can determine the minimum amount of funding required to keep each one running. The decision to supply this funding is essentially a "bet" by the company to keep its hand in an ongoing R&D poker game. If the company decides to "up the ante" in this area of research, it can pour more funds in. Alternatively, it can fold and withdraw some or all funding, thereby eliminating its chances of "winning" by removing the number of prospective "winning hands" from this particular area of research. This betting method should be used only in the most pure research situations, where there is almost no way to predict the outcome of research projects. In most other cases, a detailed review of current and submitted projects by a committee, as previously described, is the preferred way to determine the correct amount of R&D funding.

In this section, it was noted that some degree of R&D funding is needed in all but a rare subset of situations. It is very difficult to determine the correct amount of R&D funding, so a controller should call on the services of other knowledgeable parties in the company to review the likelihood of success of various projects, and to approve funding in accordance with those expectations. The more effort that is put into this review process, the better the chance of arriving at an adequate R&D budget that will result in the maximum level of cash flow.

TAXATION

In many organizations, the tax expense is simply recorded each month as a standard accrual, with management simply accepting the expense and not considering ways to reduce it. Though there is not a great deal that can be done for a very small company that wants to reduce its tax rates, there are a variety of approaches available to larger, multisite corporations. All of these approaches require expert taxation advice, so a controller is well advised to obtain it prior to recommending operational changes to management. If experts are not consulted, a tax avoidance or reduction scheme may well result in an investigation by government authorities that can result in large tax penalties. This section does not aspire to list all tax reduction methods, which are legion, but instead notes these few that are generally available:

- *Geographical differences.* The tax rates in different parts of the country will vary for state and local taxes. If all other site location factors are equal, a company may consider locating in those states that have reduced tax rates. The same method applies at a federal level to those organizations that are willing to relocate and shift their bases of operations outside the country.

- *Negotiated rates.* A company that is large enough to initiate a competition among local governments who want it to move to their districts can sometimes negotiate tax reductions for specified time periods in exchange for building a facility there.

- *Development zones.* Many cities have set up economic development zones. Companies located in these zones pay lower local tax rates.

- *Income deferment.* There are many methods available for shifting the recognition of revenue into future periods. Although this does not eliminate a tax expense, it does move it to a later period, thereby improving cash flows even though reported income will decline in the short term.

- *Tax credits.* There are variety of tax credits available that a company can take advantage of, such as for donating assets to a nonprofit organization, or for certain kinds of capital investments or research. The amount and nature of credits vary with nearly every legislative session, but there are always some available for the discerning corporation to take advantage of.

In addition to the tax reduction methods noted here, there is a nearly infinite array of tax reduction or deferment strategies available to those organizations with sufficient taxation expertise to exploit them. However, when doing so, keep in mind that top-notch taxation advice is mandatory. When in doubt regarding any gray areas of the taxation law, it is best to consult with whichever government entity is in charge of the tax laws to obtain a ruling on the matter. Despite the work required to obtain significant reductions in tax expenses, this is a major area of opportunity that can lead to significant improvements in cash flows.

WORKING CAPITAL

One of the best ways to positively impact the amount of cash flow that a company spins off is to take tight control of its working capital and eliminate much of the investment in this area. Working capital is the funding that a company needs to support its accounts receivable and inventory, and is offset by the amount of funding it obtains from its suppliers through accounts payable. Working capital can have a much greater impact on a company's cash flows than the results of its operations. For example, a company with modest profits of 5 percent on sales of $10 million will achieve cash flows due to profits of $50,000. However, if its controls over inventory collapse and inventory turns worsen from one per month to once every two months, the increase in inventory, assuming a cost of goods sold of 50 percent, will grow by $416,667! In this example, which is by no means an extreme one, management may be patting itself on the back for achieving a profit, only to find that it is running out of money because all of its excess cash has been soaked up by new inventory requirements. Because shareholder value is tied to cash flows, management has just succeeded in reducing the value of the company despite earning a profit. How can a controller spot such working capital problems? This section isolates the potential problem areas and reviews them one at a time.

The area that causes the most trouble is usually inventory. However, a simple increase in inventory tells one nothing about what has caused the increase. To do that, one must delve deeper and look at each of the main categories: raw materials, work-in-process (WIP), and finished goods. In the first category, raw materials, an inventory increase can be caused by overpurchasing by a specific buyer, the elimination of a finished good that used to require specific raw materials, or deliberate overpurchasing by a buyer because of a very low level of inventory accuracy that requires a company to keep excessive stocks on hand in order to avoid stock-out problems. In the first instance, it is a simple matter to track raw material inventory levels by buyer, as long as certain categories of parts are assigned to specific buyers. If so, a daily or weekly graph of total raw material inventories assigned to each buyer can be printed and distributed to management. Any excessive increases will become immediately apparent, possibly leading to the replacement of or additional training for the buyer. This is not a good measure if the product sales for which the buyer is obtaining raw materials is rising at a rapid rate, however, because inventories must increase to some extent to ensure that sales targets are met. If such is the case, an alternative is to graph the daily or weekly inventory turnover alongside the raw material dollar levels to see if inventories are actually being exceeded by an excessive amount.

In the second case, that of finished products no longer being produced, it may be possible to access the computer system and run a "where used" report to identify which raw materials will become obsolete. This report is a common feature of most material requirements planning systems. It accesses the BOM of all products in the company database and identifies those raw materials in stock that are not currently used in any of those products. With this report, management can quickly identify and dispose of any raw materials that are no longer being used. If taken further, management can also use the report to question the sales and engineering departments with regard to why they have discontinued products without first using up all raw materials in the warehouse. The controller's main role in this process is to frequently distribute a listing of all raw materials in stock that are no longer being used and follow up on actions that other departments are supposed to take to eliminate these materials.

The third item is buying too much inventory in order to cover for expected inventory inaccuracy problems. In this situation, the purchasing staff must buy more than it really needs in order to avoid stock-out conditions for which it will be blamed. The best way to avoid this problem is to compile a weekly report on inventory accuracy and present it to management, which can then take action based on the reported results. To do so, the controller can assign a staff person to compare the quantities and locations reported in the inventory database to the actual amounts and locations noted in the warehouse, and then compile this information into a report. Although the controller has no direct control over how to fix inventory issues, the accuracy report is a crucial feedback report that management needs to determine the amount of effort to bear on this problem.

All three of these problems are common ones that lead to excessive increases in the quantity of raw materials inventory. Only by continually addressing them with periodic reports will a controller be able to keep management informed of the key underlying reasons for excessive investments in raw materials.

There are different reasons why WIP inventory can increase. One is improper production scheduling, and another is inefficient downstream production. In the first case, the person who schedules work for each machine in the production facility may be mistakenly scheduling too much production, which results in a buildup of WIP inventory either between machines or facilities. This problem is easily remedied by working with the scheduler to reduce the amount of work scheduled for production, though it will probably have the downside impact of seriously reducing the utilization of the production facility, which must occur until the excess WIP is used up by downstream production facilities. The other problem is inefficient downstream production. The WIP inventory can increase when the correct amount of WIP is produced, but the facilities or machines that use it become bottlenecks due to inefficient production practices, which results in an increase in WIP in front of those operations. Once again, the best solution is to work closely with the production scheduler to ascertain where production bottlenecks are developing, and then schedule reduced production in front of those locations to gradually reduce the amount of WIP. The analysis that a controller can perform to give appropriate feedback to the production scheduler is to issue a daily list of on-hand WIP inventory valuations, as well as a daily graph that shows the current cost of all WIP on hand. Exhibit 7.6 is an example of such a graph. These reports, along with an active production scheduler who is partially compensated based on keeping WIP levels low, are normally sufficient for ensuring that the level of WIP inventory does not increase.

The next inventory problem is finished goods. An excessive amount of this type of inventory can be caused by incorrect forecasting of customer purchasing patterns, an excessive number of product configurations, product obsolescence, the conversion of too much WIP into finished goods, or the capitalization of excessive amounts of overhead by management in order to increase the reported level of profits. In most cases, several of these issues are present. The first problem, incorrectly forecasting customer demand, is the most common one, and can result in a massive oversupply of products. A controller can easily analyze this problem by comparing actual to projected sales

Figure 7.6   Daily WIP Inventory Report

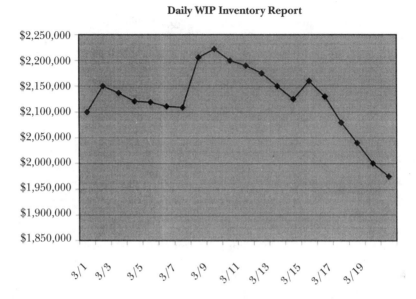

by product line and distributing the report to management. The second problem involves a company producing so many product configurations that it cannot accurately forecast the exact configuration that customers are purchasing. The answer is the same as the last item—to supply management with a complete list of budgeted versus actual sales, but at a greater level of detail than by product line, so management can see that some product configurations are not selling well. The third problem involves not being able to sell finished goods at all. To analyze whether something is obsolete, one can continue to use the same report just described, but also add a column that lists how long it will take to use up the existing inventory of each item, based on current sales rates. A separate analysis can also review how long it has been since anything was purchased for a particular item. The next item, converting too much WIP into finished goods, is a rare and short-term problem, and results from a production scheduler's trying to eliminate an excessive amount of WIP. When this happens, there is a brief surge in the amount of finished goods when the conversion takes place. This is rarely worthy of much analysis, because the problem lasts only as long as it takes to sell off the finished goods. For a really large increase in finished goods inventory, one can graph the amount of WIP and finished goods inventory side-by-side in order to see that the decrease in one led to the increase in the other. The final item, which is the intentional buildup of inventory in order to capitalize expenses, is an excessively common one. In this case, a manager realizes that profits can be artificially enhanced by greatly increasing production, which thereby increases the amount of finished goods inventory and allows the accountants to add overhead costs to inventory rather than expensing it in the current period. This approach is a great drain on cash, and so is anathema to anyone trying to improve shareholder value. Though the analysis is obvious—a simple graph showing the run-up in inventory dollars—the real problem is that the senior manager receiving the report is possibly the same one who authorized the increase in inventory. All of these problems with increases in finished goods inventory are easily analyzed either by graphical comparisons or presentations, or by comparing inventory levels to sales projections. It is very important for a controller to work with other departments, especially the sales department that provides sales forecasts, when distributing this information, so that production levels can be reduced on those finished goods items for which there are excessive amounts already in stock.

A lesser and relatively uncommon inventory issue that can also impact cash flow is the use of consignment inventory. Under this method, a company sends finished goods inventory to the location of a customer, but still owns the inventory until the customer sells it. Under this method, it is important for a company to continue to record the inventory in the balance sheet until a payment for it has been made by customers, thereby signifying the completion of a sale transaction. If this is not done, a company will record a sale transaction even though there has been no payment by the customer, which is a drain on cash, since there will be no payment by the customer that will result in a cash payment. In those rare cases in which a company has such inventory stored at customer locations, especially if large quantities are involved, it is critical for a controller to keep close track of the off-site inventories and to chart this information by location, so that management knows the size of its investment at these locations. It is also useful to include in this analysis a calculation of the inventory turnover rate at each consignment location, in case some customers are not able to sell the product. When this happens, management can see that its inventory investment is languishing at certain customer locations, and can then act to pull back the product and send it to other locations where sales are better.

Another key component of working capital that can have a major impact on cash flow is accounts receivable. If a company does a poor job of granting credit to customers or in collecting money from them, the investment in this category can rapidly become excessive, possibly leading to a large proportion of write-offs or at least a great deal of collection effort to bring the investment in this area back down to size. As noted, the first problem is the granting of credit. If a customer is sold something on credit without a pre-established credit level, or if that level is exceeded, there is a high risk that the customer will not pay its bills. A simple way to analyze this issue is to prepare a summary listing by customer that shows the customer name, maximum credit allowed, current balance owed, and the percentage of credit limit used. The report can be sorted to show those whose current credit levels are close to or being exceeded by actual accounts receivable. An additional column that may be of use is one that lists the proportion of accounts receivable that is currently overdue. An example of the report is shown in Exhibit 7.7. The information presented tells the reader not only if a customer is using up all of its available credit, but also if it is capable of paying off those invoices when they come due.

Exhibit 7.7 Comparison of Customer Credit Levels to Open Accounts
Receivable

Customer Name	Credit Limit	Current Balance	Credit Used(%)	Proportion Overdue (%)
Flower Alley	$100,000	$110,000	110	40
Peonies Inc.	50,000	52,000	104	0
Columbine Co.	80,000	75,000	94	20
Evergreens Plus	20,000	15,000	75	15
Deciduous Delight	10,000	5,000	50	8
Aspens to Go	40,000	15,000	38	12
Lilies Ltd.	60,000	10,000	17	0

In the example, it is readily apparent that the credit granted to Flower Alley is probably excessive, since it cannot pay off the credit currently granted to it. This customer is probably due for a credit review that will lead to a reduction in its credit limit. Alternately, the second customer in the chart, Peonies Inc., has no overdue accounts receivable despite having overreached its preset credit limit, and so may be ready for an increase in its credit line. This is a very useful report for determining if customer credit levels are appropriate.

The second issue related to accounts receivable is a company's ability to collect on payments from customers in a timely manner. If not, the cash absorbed by a large accounts receivable balance can quickly become excessive. The best way to analyze this problem in detail is to print an accounts receivable aging and review each overdue invoice for the specifics of why payments are not being made. One can also measure collection problems by collections person, to see if some collections personnel are better at this work than others. The only key measure that should be tracked at least weekly is the accounts receivable turnover number, which is:

$$\text{Days of accounts receivable} =$$
$$(\text{Accounts receivable} / \text{Annualized sales}) \times 365$$

This measure calculates the proportion of accounts receivable to annualized sales. A good turnover proportion should roughly match the average number of days' credit granted to customers. For example, a turnover rate of 35 days is excellent if the average invoice must be paid in 30 days, but is not good at all if the average invoice must be paid in 10 days. A significant increase in the accounts receivable turnover figure leads to an increased cash investment in this area and should be dealt with immediately.

The various types of analysis and other actions noted in this section are designed to reduce a company's cash investment in working capital, which is one of the most significant sources of cash in a company. A sharp reduction in the cash used in this area has a direct positive impact on shareholder value.

FIXED ASSETS

Company management tends to ignore fixed assets, since this area has no direct impact on the income statement, besides an incremental change in depreciation expense. Though true, a controller must realize that this area has a major impact on corporate cash flow, especially if there are large purchases or sales of fixed assets. When there is a major impact on cash flow, especially of the negative variety, this can be construed by shareholders as an increase in the level of operating risk, which will cause them to drive down the price of the stock unless there is an offsetting increase in the return on equity that offsets the initial reduction in cash flow. Accordingly, this section focuses on the analysis and reporting of these acquisition and sale transactions.

Fixed assets typically go through a double approval process—once when a company includes all expected purchases for the upcoming year in the budget, and again through a capital expenditure approval process once it is time to actually purchase each item. This is not the place to delve into the intricacies of evaluating capital expenditures (that task is covered in Chapter 3), but rather to describe a presentation to management of a reporting structure that reveals the cash impact of these acquisitions. Cash outflows caused by the purchase of fixed assets can easily outpace the cash inflows generated by continuing operations, especially if a company is engaged in a capital-intensive industry that requires large and continuing equipment investments in order to remain competitive. It is very important to relate these offsetting cash flows to management, so that it realizes the extent to which its capital acquisitions can be funded by internal cash flows, and how much of the excess must be funded by other means, such as debt. An example of such a format is the set of graphical displays shown in Exhibit 7.8. The first chart is a bar chart. The negative bars represent the amounts to be paid out each month for capital purchases, while the positive bars show the amount of cash flows expected from continuing operations. If these two bars offset each other by a significant amount, management will realize that there is a cash flow imbalance that must be funded by other means. The second graph shows the same information on an area chart. This variation more clearly shows the extent to which capital expenditure payments can be covered by internal cash flows. No matter what the method of presentation, the point is to make it abundantly clear to management if capital expenditures are causing a net outflow of cash. If management is sitting on a large pile of accumulated cash from previous periods, a single-year cash outflow may not be considered a large problem, so using this presentation method may not be necessary in all cases, even if there appears to be a net cash drain.

So far, the analysis has focused on the initial change in cash flows that result from expending funds on capital items. Though this activity can have a major downward impact on the price of a company's stock, since it reduces cash flows, the analysis so far focuses only on the downside of capital acquisitions. In addition, a controller must continually review the positive cash flows that result from the installation of the new capital items. By doing so, one can determine if projected cash flows are matching actual results. If not, the con-

Exhibit 7.8   Presentation of Cash Flows for Capital Purchases

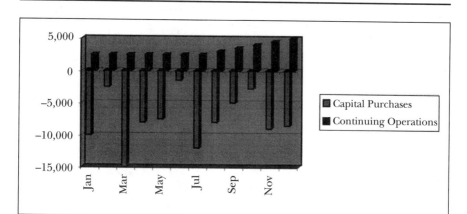

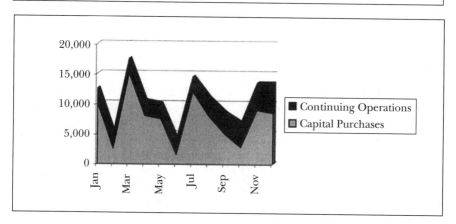

troller should see if there is a pattern of cash flow overestimation by project sponsors (which should be reflected in their job reviews). Also, any project that results in inadequate cash flows may become a candidate for asset disposal, so that some cash can be gleaned from an asset sale and used for other capital purchases that will yield greater cash flows. An example of an analysis table for a project's cash flows is shown in Exhibit 7.9, in which the expected and actual cash flows for a printing press are noted side by side. In this instance, not only is the initial outlay greater than expected, but the resulting cash flows have consistently trended lower than the budgeted amount.

Nearly every corporation has a number of unused assets, perhaps forgotten and left in a distant warehouse. Since there is no use for them in-house, they can become an excellent source of cash by selling them. This also reduces a company's asset base, which has the ancillary benefit of improving its reported return on assets. The best way for a controller to become involved in this activity is to conduct a thorough search of all company premises and quiz all employees regarding the need for assets. This information can be used to compile a list of all unused assets. An example of this report is shown

Exhibit 7.9   Comparison of Actual to Budgeted Cash Flows by Project

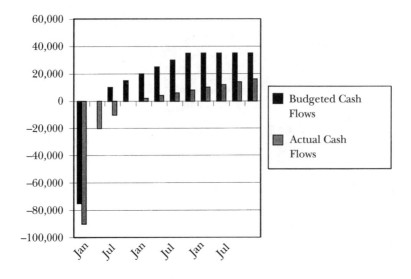

in Exhibit 7.10. An appraiser can then determine a rough market value for each one, which a company can use to determine which items can bring in the most cash. These items should be sold off first, with lesser assets being disposed of later on. This entire approach should be done at least once a year to ensure that any assets that have recently been decommissioned will be rapidly put up for sale. The net result of this method is a rapid conversion of non-performing assets into cash that can be used to fund new activities that will have a better chance of yielding enhanced cash flows.

The main objection to selling off assets is that they may have a book value that is greater than the amount of cash that can be obtained by selling them. In these cases, the traditional accountant's recommendation is to wait until more depreciation has gradually reduced the asset's book value to an amount equal to or less than the amount of cash that will be realized through

Exhibit 7.10   Unused Asset List

Asset No.	Asset Description	Net Book Value	Resale Value	Disposition Notes
1112	55-ton injection press	$35,000	$41,000	On sale consignment
1308	90-ton injection press	52,000	61,000	On sale consignment
1411	Grinder	8,000	7,000	Being advertised
1509	Hyster forklift	10,000	4,500	No action
1616	Warehouse racking	9,500	9,500	Being advertised
1772	Ford flatbed truck	18,500	16,000	No action
1779	CNC Driller	52,000	31,000	On sale consignment

an asset sale. This is a specious argument for two reasons. First, the amount of cash that can be realized will be reduced over time as an asset increases in age, so waiting for deprecation expenses to accumulate will only reduce the amount of cash that will eventually be received, while also stretching out the date at which the cash receipt will take place. Second, if the cash received is less than the book value, this results in a loss on sale of the asset, which can be used to reduce reported income for tax purposes, thereby reducing the amount of income on which taxes must be paid, and consequently reducing the cash outflow required to pay for those taxes. Thus, waiting for an asset's book value to be reduced before selling the asset has a negative impact on cash flows. Accordingly, selling unused assets promptly is always the best alternative when viewed from the perspective of enhancing shareholder value.

DEBT

In larger companies, the management of debt falls on the chief financial officer (CFO). However, smaller companies allow the controller to manage debt in the absence of a CFO. For the purposes of this discussion, we will assume that the controller is either responsible for debt management, or is in a position to present debt expense information to the CFO for further action.

The key factor in improving cash flows in the debt area is to keep track of the interest cost of each type of debt, and to first pay down those debt categories that are the most expensive. Though a simple enough procedure, one must be aware of periodic interest changes that are linked to changes in some underlying interest rate, such as the prime rate or the London Interbank Offer Rate (LIBOR). Consequently, a frequent review of current interest rates on all debt instruments is necessary, unless all forms of debt have locked-in interest rates.

The only additional factor to consider when deciding on which debt to retire first is which types of debt have onerous lender covenants attached to them as well. For example, if a particular debt instrument also requires that a large cash balance be maintained in the checking account at the lending institution, it may make sense to pay off this debt first, even though it may not have the highest interest rate, so that the covenant can be eliminated. Another example of a burdensome covenant is not being able to make capital expenditures without lender approval. Thus, removing attached covenants may take precedence over improving cash flows by paying off the highest-cost debt first.

OWNER'S EQUITY

A very effective, though risky, way to enhance shareholder value is to retire equity by using debt to pay it down. This approach reduces the amount of equity into which earnings are divided, thereby automatically improving the return on equity. Theoretically, this approach can be used to reduce equity to $1, which yields a nearly infinite return on equity. However, there are two problems with this approach. One is that lenders are not pleased with it and may withhold funds unless some matching amount of equity is kept on the books. Lenders do not like a reduced level of equity, because it implies that the owners are not risking any of their funds in the operation of the business, while the lenders have all of their funds at risk. The other problem is that, since debt is usually used to buy back equity, the amount of debt can increase to dangerous levels, making it difficult for a company to make continuing principal and interest payments if cash flows unexpectedly drop. These topics are covered in much greater detail, with supporting tables, in Chapter 16.

The key point here is that shareholder value can be greatly enhanced by manipulating the portions of debt and equity on the balance sheet, but the attendant risks are considerable and require careful analysis before any changes are made.

SUMMARY

In this chapter, we noted that the ultimate foundation of long-term gains in shareholder value lie in improving cash flows. The rest of the chapter was devoted to rooting out ways for a controller to locate untapped sources of enhanced cash flow. These sources ranged from reporting on low-margin products to innovative alterations in the debt/equity structure, and even post-implementation reviews of the cash flows of completed capital projects. The short answer to how to improve shareholder value is that the prospective list of innovations is a long one and is located in every nook and cranny of a corporation.

8

Breakeven Analysis

There is usually a very narrow band of pricing and costs within which a company operates in order to earn a profit. If it does not charge a minimum price to cover its fixed and variable costs, it will quickly burn through its cash reserves and go out of business. During the early stages of development of a new product, when pricing can be very high, it is difficult *not* to cover all possible costs, resulting in easy profits. When competition intensifies, however, prices will drop to the point where they only barely cover costs, and profits are thin or nonexistent. When competition reaches this point of intensity, only those companies with a good understanding of their own breakeven points, and those of their competitors, are likely to make the correct pricing and cost decisions to remain competitive.

This section reviews breakeven analysis, which is also known as the cost–volume–profit relationship. This is one of the most important concepts in financial analysis, so the following sections go into some detail regarding how the methodology works, what happens to the breakeven point when all possible variables are altered, and how to use it in a variety of analysis situations. Breakeven charts are used liberally in this chapter, beginning with the most elementary examples, and later progressing through a variety of additional variables that reveal how complex this topic can be.

BASIC BREAKEVEN FORMULA

The breakeven formula is an exceedingly simple one. To determine a breakeven point, add up all the fixed costs for the company or product being analyzed, and divide it by the associated gross margin percentage. This results in the sales level at which a company will neither lose nor make money—its breakeven point. As an equation the formula is:

Total fixed costs / Gross margin percentage = Breakeven sales level

The uses to which this simple formula can be put are legion. A sample of them, along with examples of how to modify the formula to attain desired results, are shown later in this chapter, in the Case Studies in Breakeven Analysis section.

For those who prefer a graphical layout to a mathematical formula, a breakeven chart can be quite informative. The sample chart in Exhibit 8.1 shows a horizontal line across the chart that represents the fixed costs that must be covered by gross margins, irrespective of the sales level. The fixed-cost level will fluctuate over time and in conjunction with extreme changes in sales volume, as noted in the next section, but we will assume no changes for the purposes of this simplified analysis. Also, there is an upward-sloping line that begins at the left end of the fixed-cost line and extends to the right across the chart. This is the percentage of variable costs, such as direct labor and materials, that are needed to create the product. Once again, the variable-cost rate is assumed not to vary with volume, though this is not always the case, as discussed in a later section, Impact of Variable-Cost Changes in Breakeven. The last major component of the breakeven chart is the sales line, which is based in the lower left corner of the chart and extends to the upper right corner. The amount of the sales volume in dollars is noted on the vertical axis, while the amount of production capacity used to create the sales volume is noted across

Exhibit 8.1   Simplified Breakeven Chart

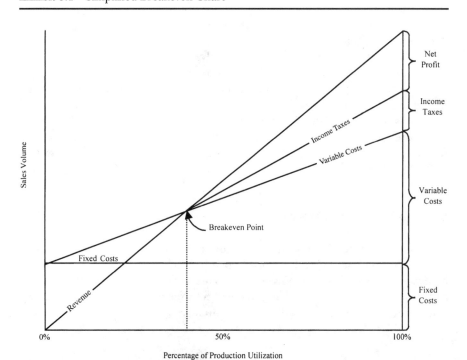

Percentage of Production Utilization

the horizontal axis. Finally, there is a line that extends from the marked breakeven point to the right, which is always between the sales line and the variable cost line. This represents income tax costs. These are the main components of the breakeven chart.

It is also useful to look between the lines on the graph and understand what the volumes represent. For example, as noted in Exhibit 8.1, the area beneath the fixed-cost line is the total fixed cost to be covered by product margins. The area between the fixed-cost line and the variable-cost line is the total variable cost at different volume levels. The area beneath the income line and above the variable-cost line is the income tax expense at various sales levels. Finally, the area beneath the revenue line and above the income tax line is the amount of net profit to be expected at various sales levels.

This section described the simplest version of the breakeven formula, and how to understand a breakeven chart. The following sections explore the vagaries of all three breakeven components—fixed costs, variable costs, and sales volume—to see how special circumstances can further affect this powerful analysis tool.

IMPACT OF FIXED-COST CHANGES ON BREAKEVEN

Although the breakeven chart in Exhibit 8.1 appears quite simplistic, there are additional variables that can make a real-world breakeven analysis a much more complex endeavor to understand. This section looks at one of those variables, which is changes in the level of fixed costs.

A fixed cost is a misnomer, for any cost can vary over time, or outside of a specified set of operating conditions. For example, the overhead costs associated with a team of engineers may be considered a fixed cost if a product line requires continuing improvements and enhancements over time. However, what if management decides to gradually eliminate a product line and milk it for cash flow, rather than keep the features and styling up to date? If so, the engineers are no longer needed, and the associated fixed cost goes down. Any situation in which management is essentially abandoning a product line in the long term will probably result in a decline in overhead costs.

A much more common alteration in fixed costs occurs when additional personnel or equipment are needed in order to support an increased level of sales activity. As noted in the breakeven chart in Exhibit 8.2, the fixed cost will step up to a higher level (an occurrence known as step costing) when a certain capacity level is reached. This situation occurs when a company has maximized the use of a single shift, for example, and must add supervision and other overhead costs, such as electricity and natural gas expenses, in order to run an additional shift. Another example is when a new facility must be brought on line or an additional machine is acquired. Whenever this happens, management must take a close look at the amount of fixed costs that will be incurred, because the net profit level may be less after the fixed costs are added, despite the extra sales volume. In Exhibit 8.2, the maximum amount of profit that a company can attain is at the sales level just *prior to*

Exhibit 8.2   Breakeven Chart Including Impact of Step Costing

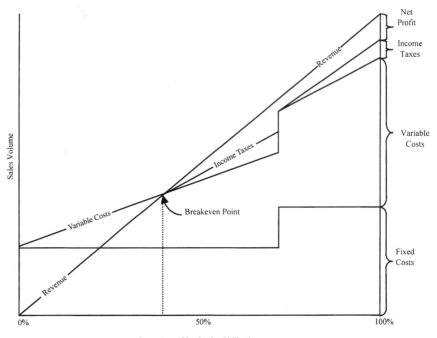

Percentage of Production Utilization

incurring extra fixed costs, because the increase in fixed costs is so high. Although step costing does not always involve such a large increase in costs as noted in Exhibit 8.2, this is certainly a major point to be aware of when increasing capacity to take on additional sales volume. In short, more sales do not necessarily lead to more profits.

IMPACT OF VARIABLE-COST CHANGES ON BREAKEVEN

The next variable in the breakeven formula is the variable-cost line. Though one would think that the variable cost is a simple percentage that is composed of labor and material costs, and which never varies, this is not the case. This percentage can vary considerably, and frequently drops as the sales volume increases. The reason for the change is that the purchasing department can cut better deals with suppliers when it orders in larger volumes. In addition, full truckload or railcar deliveries result in lower freight expenses than would be the case if only small quantities were purchased. The result is shown in Exhibit 8.3, in which the variable-cost percentage is at its highest when sales volume is at its lowest, and gradually decreases in concert with an increase in volume.

Because material and freight costs tend to drop as volume increases, it is apparent that profits will increase at an increasing rate as sales volume goes

Exhibit 8.3   Breakeven Chart Including Impact of Volume Purchases

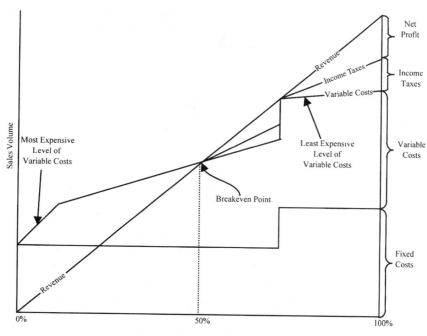

Percentage of Production Utilization

up, though there may be step costing problems at higher capacity levels, as is the case in Exhibit 8.3.

Another point is that the percentage of variable costs will not decline at a steady rate. Instead, and as noted in Exhibit 8.3, there will be specific volume levels at which costs will drop, because the purchasing staff can negotiate price reductions only at specific volume points. Once such a price reduction has been achieved, there will not be another opportunity to reduce prices further until a separate and distinct volume level is reached once again. In short, suppliers do not charge lower prices just because a customer's sales volume goes up incrementally by one unit—they reduce prices only when there are increases in the volume of purchases of thousands of units.

IMPACT OF PRICING CHANGES ON BREAKEVEN

The changes to fixed costs and variable costs in the breakeven analysis are relatively simple and predictable, but now we come to the final variable, sales volume, which can alter for several reasons, making it the most difficult of the three components to predict.

The first reason why the volume line in the breakeven chart can vary is the mix of products sold. A perfectly straight sale volume line, progressing from the lower left to the upper right corners of the chart, assumes that the exact same mix of products will be sold at all volume levels. Unfortunately, it is a rare situation indeed in which this happens, because one product is bound to become more popular with customers, resulting in greater sales and variation in the overall product mix. If the margins for the different products being sold are different, then any change in the product mix will result in a variation, either up or down, in the sales volume achieved, which can have either a positive or negative impact on the resulting profits. It is very difficult to predict how the mix of products sold will vary at different volume levels; therefore, most analysts do not attempt to alter the mix in their projections, thereby accepting the risk that some variation in mix can occur.

The more common problem that impacts the volume line in the breakeven calculation is that unit prices do not remain the same when volume increases. Instead, a company finds that it can charge a high price early on, when the product is new and competes with few other products in a small niche market. Later, when management decides to go after larger unit volume, unit prices drop in order to secure sales to a larger array of customers, or to resellers who have a choice of competing products to resell. For example, the price of a personal computer used to hover around $3,000, and was affordable for less than 10 percent of all households. As of this writing, the price of a personal computer has dropped to as little as $400, resulting in more than 50 percent of all households owning one. Thus, higher volume translates into lower unit prices. The result appears in Exhibit 8.4, in which

Exhibit 8.4   Breakeven Chart Including Impact of Variable Pricing Levels

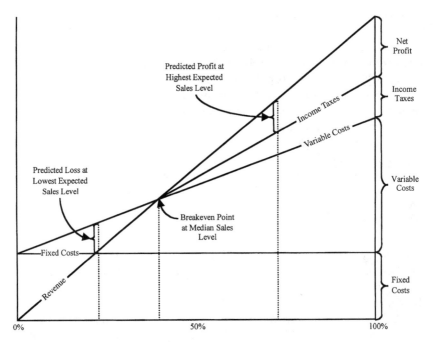

Percentage of Production Utilization

the revenue per unit gradually declines despite a continuing rise in unit volume, which causes a much slower increase in profits than would be the case if revenues rose in a straight, unaltered line.

The breakeven chart in Exhibit 8.4 may make management think twice before pursuing a high-volume sales strategy, because profits will not necessarily increase. The only way to be sure of the size of price discounts would be to begin negotiations with resellers or to sell the product in test markets at a range of lower prices to determine changes in volume. Otherwise, management is operating in a vacuum of relevant data. In some cases, the only way to survive is to keep cutting prices in pursuit of greater volume, since there are no high-priced market niches in which to sell. For example, would anyone buy a color television set for more than a slight price premium? Of course not. This market is so intensely competitive that all competitors must continually pursue a strategy of selling at the smallest possible unit price.

The breakeven chart in Exhibit 8.4 is a good example of what the breakeven analysis really looks like in the marketplace. Fixed costs jump at different capacity levels, variable costs decline at various volume levels, and unit prices drop with increases in volume. Given the fluidity of the model, it is reasonable to periodically revisit it in light of continuing changes in the marketplace in order to update assumptions and make better calculations of breakeven points and projected profit levels.

CASE STUDIES IN BREAKEVEN ANALYSIS

There are many ways an innovative controller can use the breakeven model to yield useful results. This section contains eight examples that are representative of the broad range of situations in which the model can be used. In each case, the situation is described, followed by an analysis of how to use a breakeven calculation to come up with a desired result.

1. *What level of extra revenue is needed to cover the costs of a capital acquisition?* In this case, the Letdown Window Blind Company is considering the purchase of a $100,000 machine that will replace an old one that is still functional but moderately inefficient. The old machine has long since been fully depreciated. To see what impact this decision has on the breakeven point, refer to the modified breakeven chart shown in Exhibit 8.5. Here, the dotted lines show how the original breakeven chart that was developed in Exhibit 8.1 is altered. The fixed-cost line rises, because the new machine cost has been added. Without any other changes to offset the increased cost, the breakeven point has shifted to a much higher level, where company utilization levels are at approximately 70 percent. Because the breakeven point is so much higher, the company can make a profit only at the highest utilization levels, which gives it little chance of making any money, and a significantly higher risk of *not* making one. Therefore, the decision to buy this machine is a bad one, unless management can show that there are other mitigating factors,

Exhibit 8.5   Breakeven Chart Including Impact of Extra Fixed Costs

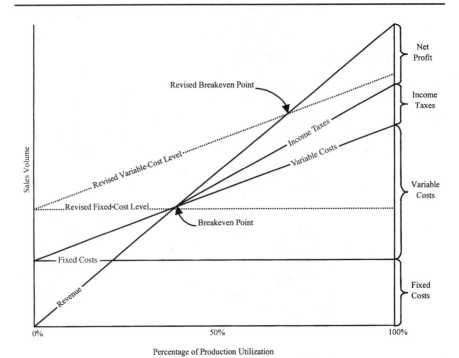

such as an offsetting reduction in variable costs that will keep the breakeven point where it is.

2. *How do I know if a new business forecast is accurate?* When reviewing a business forecast, it is very difficult to extract from the morass of detail the essentials of the forecast, which are the breakeven point and the risk of not achieving it. The breakeven calculation for a forecast follows that of a typical calculation, and has the usual components: volume, fixed costs, and variable costs. As long as these items are listed somewhere in the forecast, it is a simple matter to derive the breakeven point. If not, the forecast should be rejected at once and not reviewed again until the requisite information is supplied. The *real* issue is determining the risk of the forecast. This risk is the range of breakeven points associated with the sales targets that are most likely to be achieved, which are the highest, median, and lowest values. A forecast must contain these ranges of sales values to allow for a risk analysis with the breakeven formula. If any of these values result in a breakeven level that will yield no profit or a loss, then there is some risk in using the business forecast as the basis for running a company. In such a situation, it is up to management to determine the probability that the forecasted scenario will result in the projected loss. An example of this risk analysis is noted in Exhibit 8.6, where three forecasted sales levels are shown. Note that the minimum sales level results in a loss, which may be of concern to management.

Exhibit 8.6   Risk Analysis of a Business Forecast

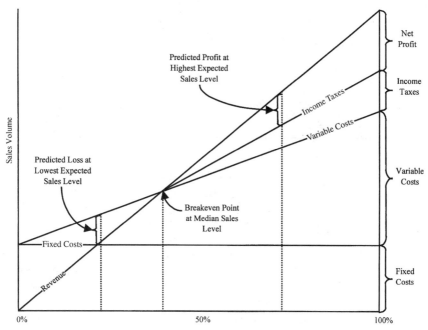

3. *At a specified sales level, what cost reductions are needed to earn a specific profit?* This is an analysis that should be reviewed whenever pricing changes in a commodity market force a company to change its pricing levels, resulting in a modification of profitability. An example of how to calculate this measure is to first set a target sales level. We will use $1,000, and then set a target profit figure of $150. These two numbers will remain constant through the remainder of the calculation. We then progress to the remaining two elements of the breakeven equation, which are variable costs and fixed costs. Either one can be changed to achieve a targeted profit level. Since either or both numbers can be altered, there are theoretically an infinite range of changes that will result in the target profit of $150 at the targeted sales level of $1,000. However, to make the range of alternatives easier to understand, a chart can be used to outline the different costs that will result in the target profit. For our example, such a chart is shown in Exhibit 8.7. The chart notes the expected sales level in the left column, a range of variable-cost percentages in the next column, and a range of fixed costs in the third column that will always result in the target profit, which is located in the final column. Some analysts will assume that fixed costs cannot change in the short term, and so will focus their attention only on changes in variable costs, but fixed costs can be altered over time, so it is more accurate to use both costs as variables in the calculation.

Exhibit 8.7   Table of Cost Variations That Achieve a Specified Profit Level

Target Sales Level	Variable Costs (%)	Fixed Costs	Target Profit Level
$1,000	50	$350	$150
1,000	45	300	150
1,000	40	250	150
1,000	35	200	150
1,000	30	150	150
1,000	25	100	150

4. *What is the effect of change in product mix on overall profits?* Product mix has an enormous impact on corporate profits, except for those very rare cases in which all products happen to have the same profit margins. To determine how the change in mix will impact profits, it is best to construct a chart, such as the one shown in Exhibit 8.8, that contains the number of units sold and the standard margin for each product or product line, and the resulting gross margin dollars. The resulting average margin will affect the denominator in the standard breakeven formula. For example, if the average mix for a month's sales results in a gross margin of 40 percent, and fixed costs for the period were $50,000, the breakeven point would be $50,000/40 percent, or $125,000. If the product mix for the following month were to result in a gross margin of 42 percent, the breakeven point would shift downward to $50,000/42 percent, or $119,048. Thus, changes in product mix will alter the breakeven point by changing the gross margin number that is part of the breakeven formula.

5. *What is the effect on profits of a specific increase in sales?* We can use the breakeven calculation to provide this information. However, when doing so, always remember that there are usually extra fixed costs associated with an increase in sales that will reduce the actual profit level to one that is lower than predicted by the formula. For example, there may be a need for more order entry or sales staff, or perhaps machinery mainte-

Exhibit 8.8   Calculation Table for Margin Changes Due to Product Mix

Product	Unit Sales	Margin (%)	Margin ($)
Flow meter	50,000	25	12,500
Water collector	12,000	32	3,840
Ditch digger	51,000	45	22,950
Evapo-Preventor	30,000	50	15,000
Piping connector	17,000	15	2,550
Totals	160,000	36	56,840

nance or utility costs will go up to reflect the increased use of machinery. If these situations are likely, it is best to factor in a higher level of fixed costs (if the changes will be in the category of cost) or increased variable costs (if these costs are the ones most likely to rise). To calculate the change in profits that will result from a change in sales, multiply the expected sales level times one minus the anticipated variable-cost percentage to obtain the gross margin. Then subtract the expected fixed costs from the gross margin to arrive at the projected profit. To use an example, if sales are expected to increase to $250,000, the variable-cost percentage is 55 percent, and fixed costs are $100,000, the calculation is:

$$(\$250,000) \times (1 - .55) = \$112,500$$
$$\$112,500 - \$100,000 = \$12,500$$

6. *What is the increased volume needed to offset a reduced selling price?* The Kleaner Klothes bleach company is considering a promotion to sell more of its product. The promotion will be a coupon for 50 cents off the retail price of the product, which normally sells for $2. Currently, the company breaks even on this product when sales reach $188,888 per month, which is due to fixed costs of $85,000 and a gross margin of 45 percent. It is currently earning $27,500 on sales of $250,000. The calculation needed to determine the new sales volume that will ensure the identical profit level first requires one to determine the new gross margin, which dropped when the price was reduced. The previous margin was 45 percent on a unit price of $2, so this translates into a cost of goods sold of $1.10 [or $2 × (1 – 45%)]. Because the cost of goods sold is assumed to stay the same even though the price drops, the new gross margin percentage will be 27 percent (or $1.50 – $1.10). The desired profit of $27,500 is then added to the existing fixed costs of $85,000 to sum to $112,500, which is the amount that the gross margins from sale of the product must equal. The final calculation is to divide the new margin of 27 percent into $112,500 to determine that an enormous jump in sales—to $416,667—is needed to ensure that profits from the product will remain the same after the promotion is implemented. Given the size of the sales increase needed, management should perhaps reduce the size of the promotional discount.

7. *What is the range of profits I can expect, given current market conditions?* In some industries, especially the most competitive ones, pricing will vary in the short run within fairly predictable points. For example, crop levels at the time of harvesting will create a glut that drives down prices, while there will be shortages just prior to the harvest, because only remaining stocks from the previous year are being used up. In such cases, a company knows that prices will be variable and that they will travel within a reasonably predictable range of prices. If so, it is useful to know the range of profits to be expected. A breakeven analysis can determine the high–low profit points, but it cannot determine the amounts of time that

market conditions will keep profits at one end of the spectrum or the other—that is for the user to determine. To calculate this measure, determine the lowest expected revenue level, multiply by the gross margin percentage, and subtract the expected fixed costs to determine the minimum profit level. Then, run the same calculation for the highest expected sales level. For example, if the lowest and highest sales levels are expected to be $500,000 and $800,000, the gross margin percentage is 31 percent, and fixed costs are $150,000, the calculation for the range of profits will be:

	Lowest Sales	Highest Sales
Sales level	$500,000	$800,000
Gross margin percentage	× 31%	× 31%
Gross margin	$155,000	$248,000
Fixed costs	$150,000	$150,000
Profit (Loss)	$5,000	98,000

8. *What is the unit cost at different sales levels?* The cost of a product includes both fixed and variable costs. The fixed-cost component will vary with the number of products sold, because the cost can be spread over more or fewer units. For example, a software package with $100,000 of fixed programming costs will have a unit cost of $100,000 if only one copy of the software is sold, but will have a unit cost of only $1 if the cost is spread over 100,000 copies sold. Based on this example, it is obvious that product costing is highly dependent on the volume produced, especially if the proportion of fixed costs to the total product costs is high. To calculate this measure, determine the variable cost first, then divide the total number of units sold by the total fixed cost to determine the per-unit fixed cost, and then add these two costs together to determine the total unit cost. For example, if a product has a variable cost of 62 percent and a unit price of $5.16, the variable cost is:

$$\$5.16 \times .62 = \$3.20$$

If the fixed cost for all production is $275,000 and 75,000 units will be sold, the fixed-cost component is:

$$\$275,000 / 75,000 = \$3.67$$

Thus, the total cost of the product at a sales level of 75,000 units is:

$$(\$3.20 \text{ of variable costs}) + (\$3.67 \text{ of fixed costs}) = \$6.87$$

Exhibit 8.9   Table of Product Cost Changes at Different Volume Levels

Unit Volume	Unit Variable Cost	Unit Fixed Cost	Total Unit Cost
55,000	$3.20	$5.00	$8.20
65,000	3.20	4.23	7.43
75,000	3.20	3.67	6.87
85,000	3.20	3.24	6.44
95,000	3.20	2.89	6.09

To clarify this information for a large range of volume levels, it may be useful to present the information in a chart, such as the one in Exhibit 8.9 that lists a number of unit volumes and the fixed- and total-cost changes that result from those different volumes. In Exhibit 8.9, the same cost and volume assumptions are used that were noted in the costing example.

SUMMARY

This chapter explained how the breakeven analysis works, and gradually built on the basic model by adding explanations and discussions of ways in which the fixed-cost, variable-cost, and volume components of the calculation can be modified to arrive at a variety of real-world breakeven scenarios, several of which were covered in the preceding section. A brief perusal of the breakeven case studies makes it apparent that paying continual attention to this form of analysis in the daily running of a business will yield a better understanding of how and at what volume level a company can be expected to turn a profit.

9

Business Cycle Forecasting

A company's planning and operations can be severely affected by a significant change in the business environment, such as can be caused by the vagaries of a business cycle. This section describes the nature of a business cycle and how it impacts a corporation. Then, the various methods currently used for forecasting business cycles are noted, as well as several theories regarding why business cycles occur. Finally, the areas in which a controller can provide meaningful input to company management regarding the impact of business cycles on a company's specific lines of business are explored.

NATURE OF THE BUSINESS CYCLE

A business cycle is a recurring series of expansions and contractions, involving and driven by a vast number of economic variables, that manifests itself as changes in the level of income, production, and employment. As will be described in the next section, these swings can have a profound impact on a company. A business cycle tends to be long-term in nature, and is very difficult to predict in terms of length or intensity. It is driven by so many variables, most of which interact with each other, that it is excruciatingly difficult to determine the exact causes of previous cycles and the timing of the next one based on those variables.

Although the exact causes of the business cycle are difficult to discern (see the Theories behind Business Cycle Forecasting section), there are essentially two types of variables that cause business cycle changes to occur. The first is an *exogenous variable*. This is a variable that affects the economic system, though it is not an integral component *of* the system. A bad rainy season will affect the crop yields in the farming community, for example, which in turn reduces the amount of purchases by farmers for the next season's crop, which in turn affects the activity of the suppliers of those purchases, and so on. Another exogenous variable is a war, which can wreak enough destruction to entirely shatter an economy. These types of variables can, to some extent, be called "acts of God." The other type of variable is the *endogenous variable.* This is a variable that impacts an economic system from within. For example, over-capacity in the resin production industry causes suppliers to reduce their resin prices to plastic molding companies, which in turn can now reduce the prices of their products, which creates an increase in sales and contributes to an increase in the level of economic activity. Other examples of this type include the demand for products and pricing changes.

With these two types of variables constantly impinging on the economy in hundreds of ways every day, it is amazing that it manages to absorb their impact so well. Due to the sheer size and scope of the economy, even a relatively severe occurrence, such as a Los Angeles earthquake or a major refinery fire that dramatically cuts oil supplies, does not cause a major upturn or downturn of lasting significance. It is only a combination of these events, especially when they continue for some time, that causes a dramatic change in the economy.

However, the typical company operates within a single sector of the economy (we can't *all* be General Electric!), in which a single major shock, of either the endogenous or exogenous variety, can cause immediate and massive changes, because individual sectors are much smaller than the national economy, and so can be severely impacted by smaller events. For example, an increase in the price of jet fuel will cause the airlines to increase their prices, which reduces the number of seats filled, which drives down airline profits and forces them to postpone orders for new jets, which in turn harms the airline manufacturing companies and *their* supporting groups of suppliers—all due to an increase in the price of jet fuel, which is just a single variable.

Consequently, a controller may not be overwhelmingly concerned with the operations of the entire national or international economy, because the typical economic contraction only corresponds to a drop in gross national product (GNP) of a few percentage points. However, industry-specific changes within that larger economy can be truly catastrophic, and it is within this smaller economic environment that a company operates and must make management changes. This leads us to the next section, which covers the specific problems a company faces as a result of changes in the business cycle.

IMPACT OF THE BUSINESS CYCLE ON A CORPORATION

What happens to a company when the business cycle changes to a new phase, either upward or downward? We will begin with the impact of an economic contraction.

When management realizes that sales have declined, it must contract the business. One of the first steps taken is to reduce inventories, so that the company is not stuck with a large investment of products that will be at risk of becoming obsolete before they can be sold. One way to reduce inventories is to sell it off at reduced prices, but this cuts into gross margins and also fills the distribution pipeline, so that no additional sales can be made until the pipeline clears. The more common approach is to reduce the production staff and all related overhead staff with a layoff, the extent of which will be driven by management's perception of the depth of the upcoming cyclical decline. Management will also likely curtail capital expenditures and increase controls over incidental expenses. Further, the controller will be called on to tighten credit to customers and heighten collection activities to ensure that accounts receivable do not include any bad debts and that collections are made as soon as possible. If there are excess funds available, management will likely use them to pay down debt, so that fixed costs are reduced to the bare minimum in anticipation of poor sales conditions at the bottom of the economic cycle.

Also during business downturns, there will be a few adventurous companies that will buck the industry trend and *expand*. They do this because they anticipate a short downturn in the economy, and they want to pick up new business, either by undercutting competitors or (more commonly) by waiting until financially weaker companies begin to fail and then buying them. They may also take advantage of lower real estate and equipment costs during these periods to add to their capacity with inexpensive new production facilities. This strategy is possible only if a company has substantial cash reserves or available debt and an aggressive management team that is willing to take chances.

When the economy begins to turn in an upward direction, management must make several contrary decisions. The first one is to ramp up existing production capacity, which may have been shuttered and now requires refurbishment before production can begin. Then, management must determine the extent to which it wants to rebuild its inventory levels to anticipate renewed sales. This is a critical decision, because overproduction in a weakly rebounding economy will create more inventory than is needed, whereas producing too little in the midst of a strong economic rebound will result in sales being lost to more aggressive competitors. If the rebound is sudden, the company must spend more money on staff overtime and rush equipment deliveries to bring production back up to speed as soon as possible. Credit policies will likely be loosened in order to bring in new business, and management must decide on how much new capital equipment to purchase and the most appropriate time to acquire it.

All of the changes noted here, for either an increase or decrease in the business cycle, call for changes in a company's operations that will certainly have some impact on profits, but even more so on the level of working capital and fixed assets. For example, waiting too long to cut back production will result in an excess investment in inventory, as well as any new capital projects that were not curtailed in time. The reverse problem arises during an economic upswing, when reacting too slowly will result in a cash inflow from the sale of all inventory, followed by the loss of additional profits because *all* of the inventory has been sold and there is none left to sell. Thus, proper management of working capital and fixed assets lies at the heart of management's decisions regarding how to deal with changes in the business cycle.

All of these changes are made by the management team, which needs the best possible information from the controller and outside prediction sources regarding the timing and extent of a change in the business cycle. Before we delve into various theories used to predict business cycles and the precise means for doing so, let us diverge for a moment to review the history of business cycles through a portion of the twentieth century, in order to gain an understanding of the number and potential size of business cycles, which explains why this is such an important item to factor into a company's management decisions.

HISTORY OF BUSINESS CYCLES

The preceding discussion on how a business cycle can affect a company may seem like Chicken Little's warning that the sky is falling, because the United States has not suffered a severe business downturn in many years. To deter the reader from becoming too complacent, however, here are a few facts regarding the 12 business contractions in the period from 1920 to 1982.[1]

- For the Great Depression, the GNP dropped 33 percent.

- For two major depressions, the GNP dropped by 13 percent.

- For nine severe or mild depressions, the GNP dropped by 2 to 3 percent.

Not only are these declines significant, but also look at the number of contractions—12 in a period of 62 years, which works out to one every five years. The dates of these contractions were 1920–21, 1929, 1930, 1931, 1933, 1957–58, 1959–60, 1966, 1969–70, 1973–75, 1980, and 1981–82. Clearly, business downturns are frequent enough to be a constant concern to management. However, do they have a sufficiently large impact to cause a major alteration in a company's financial results?

Let us look again at the amount of reductions in GNP. The average reduction for all 12 business contractions was 6.8 percent. However, if we drop out the impact of the Great Depression, the amount shrinks to 4.4 percent. The median value is closer to a 2.5 percent reduction. If we assume that the mistakes at the root of the Great Depression (tariff increases, bank failures, etc.) can no longer occur, and use only the information from the other contractions, we are still faced with typical GNP reductions in the range of 2.5 to 4.5 percent during every business cycle downturn. Because the typical company usually budgets for a sales increase in the upcoming year and spends accordingly, the real shortfall in financial results that a management team must deal with is the difference between the amount of the sales increase that management expects to achieve and the amount it is reduced to as a result of the business cycle downturn. For example, if the contraction results in a sales decline of 4.4 percent and a company has forecasted a reasonable *increase* in sales for the same period of 5 percent, then the difference is 9.4 percent, which is quite considerable, given the extra investment in fixed assets, working capital, and personnel that the company has committed itself to in order to achieve the higher sales target. This example results in a decline in sales of 9.4 percent from the expected level, which is probably sufficient to throw a company from a gain to a loss situation. So the answer to the earlier question is yes—an average business cycle contraction, based on historical results, is of major interest to a company.

THEORIES BEHIND BUSINESS CYCLE FORECASTING

There are a great many theories regarding why the economy goes through periodic peaks and valleys of business activity. These are based on either conjecture or a lengthy analysis of specific economic indicators that have been compiled over the years. Many of these theories have been based on how well they fit the historical facts, and some do a good job of it, though without any practical reason for doing so. For example, the height of women's skirts tends to rise and fall with the stock market. If this were a true indicator of the economy's condition, then the true path to success would be to enter a career as a fashion designer, and then invest in the stock market in a manner that takes advantage of your latest skirt lengths! Obviously, this is a case in which the correlation between the indicator and actual economic conditions is a false one. Economic researchers spend a great deal of their time trying to find indicators of future economic activity that have a more fundamental linkage to economic conditions, and then fitting these indicators into coherent and defensible theories of how their indicators link together to form a concept for how to predict the rise and fall of business cycles. The following list briefly notes a number of theories that have been raised in the past century regarding the reasons for business cycles:

- *Consumer demand.* One theory states that a rise in consumer demand causes a demand for more production equipment, so that manufacturers can meet the demand. Manufacturers then install an excessive amount of equipment, which leads to overcapacity. The manufacturers then cannot produce enough to pay for the new equipment, which causes debt defaults. Banks then tighten their lending policies, which causes a reduction in consumer demand.

- *Inventory expectations.* Another theory states that inventory is at the core of business cycles. Producers build inventories in expectation of creating new sales volume. The added production increases the number of jobs in the economy, which spins off enough consumer demand to purchase the inventory. Once the inventory levels drop, producers expect more sales, so they hire more people to produce more inventory. Then, when the perception changes that consumers will no longer buy the inventory, producers cut back on production, which reduces the number of jobs, which reduces demand for the inventory.

- *Cost of capacity utilization.* Another theory holds that, as a company enters the late stages of a business expansion, the costs of operating at very high levels of capacity utilization will reduce profits, because the costs of overtime, machine maintenance, and high-demand supplies will rise. Because of the drop in cash flow caused by the reduced profits, businesses will have to curtail their capital spending, which reduces orders in the durable goods industries, which in turn reduces the level of activity in other supporting areas. This eventually cuts the level of activity in the entire economy.

- *Debt accumulation.* Another (and very similar) theory is that companies gradually burden themselves with more and more debt, which they need to build more capacity to fuel additional growth. Eventually, they are unable to pay back the debt, which causes lenders to tighten their credit terms, which in turn reduces lending on new projects until demand "catches up" with the current level of production capacity.

- *Money supply.* Yet another theory says that a moderate, positive growth rate in the money supply will avoid business contractions, while a reduction in the money supply will bring about a recession or depression. The money supply can be affected by government actions, as well as by the retention, investment, or spending of funds by consumers.

- *Innovation basis.* Another theory states that economic growth is founded on bursts of innovation, which tends to be sector specific, and has a trickle-down effect on other parts of the economy. There tends to be immense growth within the sectors experiencing innovation, followed by speculation, overexpansion, and consolidation among the strongest remaining companies. Then there are layoffs as a result of the consolidations, and the economy enters a downward phase.

- *Long-term growth.* A final view is that long-term boom periods will eventually end due to a loss of investor prudence (when they assume that the growth period will go on forever), resulting in increasingly poor and risky investments, growing indebtedness, and a loss of liquidity. There will then be a rising tide of debt restructurings and defaults that drives lenders into tighter credit policies, which in turn reduces consumer demand, which causes an economic downturn.

The last theory, that of long-term growth, appears to be the most likely one as of the time of this writing. There are several reasons why economists believe that we are now in a more stable period, where it is less likely that a severe downturn will arise. One reason is that a larger percentage of the economy has shifted into the hands of the government, which will create and spend money irrespective of the particular phase of the business cycle in which the country finds itself. This institution largely ignores business cycles and also constitutes a large part of the economy, so it stands to reason that it acts as a modifying influence on any business contraction. Another reason is that the government has provided for automatic stabilizers, such as welfare and unemployment payments, that have their greatest impact when the most people are out of work, which results in a cash infusion into the economy during the lowest part of the business cycle, and when it is most needed. Further, the distribution of work in the economy has gradually shifted away from highly cyclical industries, such as manufacturing and construction, and into more stable areas, such as services and finance. An additional item is that federal deposit insurance keeps people from withdrawing their funds from banks when there are rumors of bank closings, which eliminates the risk of bank crashes. Finally, government legislation to spend money during the low end of business cycles may have some marginal impact on the cycle, but tends to occur too late to have a noticeable impact (if anything, it overheats the economy as it starts to expand). All of these factors would lead us to believe that the last theory stated is perhaps the one that best explains the current economic situation.

There is some element of truth in all of the above theories, but no one of them *completely* explains the operations of the national or international economies, nor do any of them accurately predict the timing or extent of business cycles. The problem with each one is that it is based on historical information that does not necessarily reflect the variety of new conditions that are impinging on the present-day economy, such as the nearly instantaneous flow of information, the lack of restrictions on funds flows through most parts of the world, the increasing internationalization of business, or the impact that technology is having on the flow of commerce. Although a new theory will undoubtedly emerge that eventually includes these factors, there will then be new factors affecting the economy of the future that are not anticipated by or included in the latest predictive models. Consequently, it is nearly impossible for any theory to perfectly predict business cycles. Nonetheless, given the enormous value of having such a model, a variety of government and private institutions continue to develop and enhance predictive models that at least yield reasonably accurate expectations of future conditions. However, they are all like the weather forecast—they are fairly accurate for the next few days, and then the accuracy of their predictions drops rapidly.

ELEMENTS OF BUSINESS CYCLE FORECASTING

Now that we know some of the theory and history behind business cycles, it would be useful to determine the methods used by forecasting professionals to predict key business cycle information. This section will review who does forecasting, what information they forecast, and the methods they use for doing so.

Forecasting is conducted not only by various branches of the federal government, such as the Department of Commerce and the Federal Reserve Board, but also by a number of universities and private institutions. The governments and schools do so as a public service, but the private groups do so for an entirely different reason: They create tailored forecasts that churn out estimates on very specific items, such as stock prices or exchange rates, that are requested by top-paying clients. These forecasts commonly cover a series of quarterly periods, which, because of the short time frames involved, are much more difficult to predict with any degree of reliability than the annual forecasts that were more common in the last few decades. The government and universities focus on such macro issues as the GNP or the rate of inflation. The trade group to which most of these organizations belong is the National Association of Business Economists.

There are four primary methods used to arrive at forecasts. Each one is based on different information and may arrive at somewhat different results; therefore, it is common for forecasters to blend the results of two or more methods to arrive at their estimates of future conditions. The methods are:

1. *Anticipation surveys.* These are surveys of key people in the business community. The purpose of these surveys is to collect information about the intentions of the survey participants to engage in capital purchases, acquisitions, changes in headcount, or any other steps that may affect the economy, and then aggregate this information to arrive at general estimates of trends.

2. *Time series models.* These are trend lines that are based on historical information. For a forecast, one finds the trend line that fits a similar set of previous conditions and fits it to the current conditions to arrive at a trend line of future expectations. These can be relatively accurate in the short run, but do not generate good results very far into the future.

3. *Econometric models.* These are highly complex and iterative models that simulate the real economy and are frequently composed of hundreds of variables that interact with each other. These can yield good results over periods longer than those predicted by time series models. However, changes in the results of the models are difficult to explain, given the complexity of the underlying formulas.

4. *Cyclical indicators.* These are the leading, coincident, and lagging indicators that foretell changes in the economy. This method is a good way to confirm the existence of business cycle changes that have been predicted by other forecasting methods. A leading indicator is something that changes in advance of an alteration in a business cycle, such as the number of new business formations, new capital expenditure requests, construction contracts, the length of the average workweek, layoff rate, unemployment insurance claims, profit margins, new orders, investments in residential structures, capacity utilization, and new bond or equity issues. These can change anywhere from a few months to over a year in advance of a related change in the phase of the business cycle. A lagging indicator is something that changes after an alteration in the business cycle has occurred, and is used by forecasters to confirm the business cycle change that was indicated by leading indicators. Examples of lagging indicators are investments in nonresidential structures, unit labor costs, and the amount of consumer credit outstanding.

The exact forecasting method used depends on the person doing the forecasting, and is largely influenced by judgment. The reason why judgment is such a necessary factor in forecasting is that all of the forecasting methods, with the exception of anticipation surveys, are based on the interpretation of historical economic data, which may no longer affect the economy in the same manner as it did when the various models were constructed. Thus, having an in-depth knowledge of the current economic situation, and using their information to adjust the results of quantitatively derived forecasts is the key difference between a quantitative analyst, who does nothing but tweak the numbers, and a great forecaster, who consistently outperforms the outcomes predicted by the various models.

In addition to judgment, forecasters will use numeric weighting schemes, in which they give greater value to the results of certain forecasting models or specific variables, depending on their experience of past forecasting results, or their guesses regarding changes in the economy for the period being predicted. Some forecasters will even combine and average out the predictions of groups of other forecasters, on the grounds that this will create a consensus opinion that has a better chance of being accurate. However, there may be a wide dispersion in the various forecasts being predicted, which makes it difficult to arrive at a time period for forecasted changes in the business cycle based on this approach.

Once the forecasters make their predictions, they also compare their forecasts to the actual results as that information arrives. They will then spend a great deal of time modifying their forecasting methods to make their next set of forecasts more closely match the future results. This is an ongoing process that never ends, because the underlying variables that drive business cycles are constantly altering the degrees of force with which they impact the economy. Also, old variables may eventually have so little impact on business cycles that they are dropped entirely from the forecasting systems, while new variables must be researched and inserted into the models. Thus, the after-the-fact review of forecasting models and their component parts is a major forecasting task.

When reviewing the effectiveness of the variables that comprise a forecast, there are several factors to consider. One is that a small pool of variables may result in an incorrect forecast, because each of them may be adversely impacted by exogenous variables that yield results not truly representing their impact on the business cycle as a whole. However, by using a large number of variables in a forecasting model, one can tolerate a minority of variables that yield incorrect results, while still arriving at an overall forecast that is made accurate by the sheer volume of variables included in the model. Another item to review is the number of months by which leading indicators presage a change in the business cycle. Though there may be historical justification for using a certain number of months in a forecasting model, these periods can change, sometimes to the extent of having a leading indicator turn into a lagging indicator. Also, the selection process for variables needs to be very in-depth before they are added to a forecasting model. For example, a new variable should be thoroughly researched to determine the extent of its linkage to a business cycle, how well it predicts business cycle behavior, how consistently it does so, and also how frequently information about the variable is reported (so that it can be included in the forecast in a timely manner). Only if all these questions receive favorable answers should a new variable be included in a forecasting model.

Having briefly described who creates forecasts, what information they issue, and how they arrive at these forecasts, we now turn to the role of the controller in creating forecasts that are tailored for the use of company management.

BUSINESS CYCLE FORECASTING AT THE CORPORATE LEVEL

Having described what business cycles are, why they can be damaging to a company, and the gyrations that professional forecasters go through to predict them, we now arrive at the central question: What can a controller do in his or her role as a financial analyst to provide business cycle predictions to the management team? There are several possible routes to take.

The main factor a controller must decide on is balancing the time needed for forecasting against the perceived value of the information. For example, if a company has a stable sales base that rarely varies, irrespective of what stage the business cycle is currently in, then there is no reason to track cycles very carefully. Also, if the accounting function is understaffed, the needs of day-to-day activities will probably supersede any demands for forecasting. However, if a controller can prove that the deleterious effects of *not* tracking business cycle conditions will lead to company losses that significantly exceed the cost of having extra staff on hand to perform the analysis, then this second factor disappears.

Let us assume that there is some time available for forecasting work, and that business cycles have a sufficient impact on company conditions to be worthy of review. If so, here are some possible actions to take to obtain, analyze, and report on business cycle forecasts. They are listed in ascending order of difficulty:

- *Report on published forecasts.* There are forecasts published by nearly every major business magazine for the economy at large, which can be easily extracted, reformatted into an internal report, and presented to management, perhaps as part of the monthly financial statements. Several key advantages are that the information is fairly accurate for the entire economy, it is prepared by professional forecasters, and the information is essentially free. The problem is that each company operates in a smaller industry within the national economy, and as such is subject to "mini" business cycles that may not move in lockstep with that of the national economy. For this reason, the reported information may only be generally relevant to a company's specific situation.

- *Subscribe to a forecasting service.* A company can pay a significant fee, probably in the five- to six-figure range, to a forecasting service for more specific reports that relate to the industry in which it operates. This is a good approach for those organizations that do not have the resources to gather, summarize, and interpret economic data by themselves. However, some industries are too small to be serviced by a specialized forecasting service, or the fee charged is considered too high in comparison to the value of the information received.

- *Develop an in-house forecasting model.* In cases in which a company either wants to run its own forecasting model or there are no forecasting services available that can provide the information, and it is deemed relevant, it is time to try some in-house forecasting. This effort can range from a minimalist approach to a comprehensive one, with each level of effort yielding better results. First, go through the steps noted in the preceding section to find the right kinds of data to accumulate and implement a data gathering method that yields reliable data in a timely manner. Then, one must work with management to determine what resulting information is desired (usually a sales estimate), and the controller must arrive at a methodology for translating the underlying data into a forecast. Then, the controller should develop a standard reporting format that imparts the results to management. This report should include the underlying assumptions and data used to arrive at the forecast, so that any changes in the assumptions are clearly laid out. Finally, there should be a methodology for comparing the results against actual data and adjusting the forecasting methodology based on that information. Although this approach is a time-consuming one, it can yield the best results if a carefully developed forecasting system is used.

For example, let us assume that a controller of a sport rack company has elected to use the last of the preceding options for creating forecasting information. Sport racks is a very small niche market that creates and sells racks for skis, snowboards, bicycles, and kayaks that can be attached to the tops of most kinds of automobiles. The controller wants to derive a forecasting system that will give management an estimate of the amount by which projected sales can be expected to vary. She decides to subdivide the market into four categories, one each for skis, snowboards, bicycles, and kayaks. Based on a historical analysis, she finds that 25 percent of ski purchasers, 35 percent of snowboard purchasers, 75 percent of bicycle purchasers, and 30 percent of kayak purchasers will purchase a car-top rack system to hold their new equipment. The typical delay in these purchases from the time when they bought their sports equipment to the time they bought sport racks was six months. The controller finds that she can obtain new sports equipment sales data from industry trade groups every three months. Given the lag time before users purchase car-top racks, this means that she can accumulate the underlying data that predicts sport rack sales and disseminate it to management with three months to go before the resulting sport rack sales will occur. Thus, she concludes that this is usable data. The next task is to determine the company's share of the sport rack market, which is readily obtainable from the industry trade group for sport racks, although this information is at least one year old. Given the stability of sales within the industry, she feels that this information is still accurate. She then prepares the report shown in Exhibit 9.1. It shows total sports equipment sales for the last quarter, uses historical percentages to arrive at the amount of resulting sport rack sales, and then factors in the company's market share percentage to determine the forecasted sales of each type of sport rack. By comparing this information to the previously forecasted sales information, the report reveals that the company should significantly ramp up its production of snowboard sport racks as soon as possible.

The example used was for an extremely limited niche market, but it does point out that a modest amount of forecasting work can yield excellent results that are much more company specific than would be the case if a company relied solely on the forecasts of experts who were concerned with only general national trends. For most companies, there will be a number of additional underlying indicators that should be factored into the forecasting model; however, the work associated with tracking these added data must be compared to the benefit of more accurate results, so that a controller arrives at a reasonable cost–benefit compromise. The level of precision into which a company can delve to arrive at an outstanding forecasting model can be overwhelming. Here, for example, is a quote from a forecasting manual concerning the use of a specific time series trend line analysis:

> . . . consider the autoregressive integrated moving-average modeling, in which the time series are reduced to stationarity by differencing and then their autoregressive and moving-average components are analyzed.[2]

A statistician will know exactly what this quote means, but a controller probably will not, and will not want to delve into this kind of analysis in order to produce a marginally more accurate forecast. Thus, keep the analysis work within the range of knowledge of the accounting staff, and do not try to use complicated statistical methods that cannot be explained to the management team when it asks how the controller came up with a particular forecasted result.

Exhibit 9.1   Industry-Specific Forecasting Model

Description	Sports Equipment Unit Sales	% Buying Sport Racks	Company Market Share	Forecasted Company Unit Sales	Original Company Forecast	Variance
Ski	3,200,000	25	40%	320,000	300,000	+20,000
Snowboard	2,700,000	35	40%	378,000	300,000	+78,000
Bicycle	2,500,000	75	30%	562,500	550,000	+16,500
Kayak	450,000	30	30%	40,500	45,000	−4,500

SUMMARY

Throughout this chapter, the key issues behind business cycles have been rein-
forced—they are caused by a multitude of constantly shifting variables that are
very difficult to interpret or use to affect future business conditions, and their
impact on a company can be terminal if not properly anticipated. The last two
sections of the chapter noted the extreme complexity of the data gathering
and interpretation now being conducted by a variety of organizations in an
effort to predict the future, and why the bulk of this analysis is well beyond the
comprehension and available time of the average controller. However, by seg-
menting a business cycle down into the smallest possible niches and diligently
searching for the key drivers that have an impact on those niches, it is possible
for a controller to report on the key drivers of "mini" business cycles that most
directly affect a company's operations.

ENDNOTES

1. This information comes from Victor Zarnowitz's excellent and in-
depth work, *Business Cycles,* Chicago: University of Chicago Press, 1992,
p. 24.
2. *Id.*, p. 184.

PART THREE

OPERATIONAL
ANALYSIS

10

Evaluating Management Performance

The accounting staff is sometimes called on to not only calculate performance measures on which the management staff is judged and compensated, but also to recommend specific measurements for this purpose. The accounting department is sometimes drawn into the evaluation of manager performance because the accounting staff knows best what measures are easy to calculate and which require significant effort to compile. Also, if the controller is of high standing within the company, with a broad knowledge of company operations, then this person may have well-founded and well-respected reasons for recommending specific performance measurements. No matter what the reasons involved, this chapter is meant to be of assistance in determining which measurements to recommend, how to go about measuring them, and the format to use when reporting results. This chapter also delves into the interesting area of how tying performance to specific measurements can alter the behavior of managers, and not always in a positive manner.

CHOOSING PERFORMANCE REVIEW MEASURES

If asked to provide specific performance measurements for the review of management, a controller must first consider a number of issues. This section covers the reasoning behind linking measurements to corporate strategy and goals, as well as ensuring that measurements do not conflict with each other, and that at least some portion of the measurement orientation is toward cash flow.

The single greatest consideration when assembling a group of performance measurements is that they seamlessly tie into the strategic plan as well as all subsidiary goals that are linked to that plan. If not, then managers will be pursuing performance goals that will not assist in achieving the corporate strategy or even actively keep it from happening. Though this seems like an obvious guideline, all too many companies either have no strategic plan or ignore the one they have. If this is the case, a controller should steer the company back toward the strategic plan, either by recommending a set of measurements that is specifically and pointedly tied to the strategic plan that everyone else is ignoring, by tying to an older strategic plan if it is the most recent one available, or by suggesting that the strategic plan be compiled first before any performance measurements are assembled. If the controller is still being pushed to recommend measurements in the absence of a strategic plan, then the best course to follow is one that at least cannot harm the company, which is a focus on increased profitability and cash flows.

One example of a situation in which not linking measurements to strategy can cause problems is the chief executive officer's having designed a strategic plan that points the company in the direction of entering new lines of business, but the performance measures being all oriented toward improving the existing businesses, which leaves managers with no time to implement the plan. Another case is the strategic plan's specifying a reduction in the number of customers in order to focus on the most profitable ones, but a key measurement is the retention of existing customers. Yet another situation is the strategic plan's being heavily oriented toward improving the speed of delivery to customers, but having a measurement in use that focuses on reducing working capital by shrinking inventories, which makes it harder to fill customer orders on time. All of these are cases in which not tying performance measurements to the strategic plan leads to counterproductive behavior.

Another factor to consider is that too many performance measurements can swamp the management team, because they must pay attention to the underlying factors that drive too many measures. For example, if the sales manager is being compensated based on customer retention, sales per customer, accuracy of order taking by the sales staff, profitability by customer, salesperson retention, and departmental expense reduction, it is probably not possible to achieve all of them. Also, if earning a bonus can be achieved only if all measurement targets are met, then it is likely that the affected managers will simply give up, knowing that there is no way to meet every single goal. Having too many measures can be counterproductive.

Another problem to consider is that many performance measurements conflict with each other. When this happens, managers are forced to decide between them or come up with a compromise level of activity that results in the achievement of no measurements. Another possible behavior change is that a manager suffering from conflicting goals will choose to achieve the one that results in the highest personal monetary gain. An example of this is a production manager's being asked to reduce the number of employee hours worked, while also switching to shorter production runs in order to keep inventory levels lower. Unfortunately, short production runs usually require more direct labor because they are less efficient, which leaves the production manager caught between conflicting goals.

Conflicting measurements do not just have to be within a single department. They can also be between managers, so that the measures that one manager is attempting to improve are conflicting with those of another manager. For example, if the purchasing manager has been asked to order materials in smaller and more frequent quantities in order to keep inventory levels down and reduce the risk of obsolescence, this will have a direct impact on the accounting staff, which may be measured on the number of accounting clerks employed, because the amount of receiving and supplier invoices will increase as a result of the actions taken by the purchasing staff, which will require the addition of more accounting staff.

Given the number of problems involved with recommending specific performance measurements, a controller should fall back on making the smallest number of recommendations, so that any conflicting measures, not only within a department but also between departments, are easily spotted and fixed. In most cases, this means that performance measures should be limited to no more than two per department.

An alternative approach is to tie the performance compensation of all members of the management team to bottom-line profits, since this method has all management personnel focusing on the same goal. The main problem with doing so is that, for many managers, there does not appear to be a direct relationship between their work and the resulting company profits, and so they have little incentive. For example, the controller and engineering manager are not in line positions in which their actions have a direct impact on profits, though there are a few actions they can take that will have a minor impact on profits; for these people, depending on a profit increase in order to receive a raise or bonus is not much of an incentive.

Another possibility for a performance measure is cash flow. As noted in Chapter 7, a company's stock price is very closely tied to increases in its cash flows. Accordingly, the appropriate measure, especially for those companies with an excessive investment in working capital, may be an increase in cash flow. This is an area in which departments that cannot impact profits can effect a change. For example, the accounting and finance departments can have a significant impact on the amount of working capital invested in accounts receivable by tightening customer credit and engaging in more aggressive collection efforts.

The perfect set of performance measures will almost certainly be a mix of the preceding various measures, since all companies are driven by different strategies and different operating environments. A company that suffers from both low profitability *and* an excessive investment in fixed assets may set a combined performance goal of increasing profits and increasing the return on assets, while a company that has already achieved a high return on assets goal may ignore this item and concentrate on profitability. Also, if there is no direct correlation between profitability and a manager's area of responsibility, a solution is to use a combined performance measure of profitability (so that the manager will support those departments that *do* have an impact on profits), and one or two measures that the manager can directly affect.

A final issue to consider when recommending performance measures is allowing for multilevel targets for each goal. This means that a manager can earn a small bonus by achieving a relatively low-end goal, a better bonus by reaching a mid-range goal, and an outstanding bonus by surpassing a "stretch" target. Controllers are in a unique position to make recommendations in this area, based on their ability to analyze the performance of departments in the past and see what they have been able to achieve historically. Also, in the controller's role as a financial analyst, it is possible to create "what if" scenarios for what a manager is capable of achieving, given a likely set of resources. For these reasons, a controller can accompany a recommendation for specific types of performance measurements with detailed, multilevel targets for managers to reach.

Given all the consequences of recommending the wrong set of performance measures for the management team, it is evident that the controller must carefully weigh all possible behavioral factors that will arise prior to suggesting specific measures. The following section contains a few examples of what can happen when the wrong performance measures are used.

BEHAVIORAL CHANGES RESULTING
FROM PERFORMANCE REVIEW MEASURES

Prior to recommending specific performance measures for the management team, a controller should be aware of the unusual changes in behavior that can result when a manager is confronted with a new performance measurement. This section covers several possible management behavior changes, as well as how to guard against counterproductive activities. Because there are quite a few behavioral problems associated with performance measures, they are listed here and sorted by the type of performance measure used.

- *Adding customers/market share.* When a sales manager is asked to increase the number of customers or increase market share, this person may have to do so by taking on low-margin customers. For example, if a company already has most of the customers in the market who are willing to pay high prices for the company's products, then adding any new ones will lower the average margin. Also, if the industry is extremely cost competitive, the only way to lure away those new customers is to offer them rock-bottom pricing or special services that cut into profitability. To avoid this problem, the controller should work with the sales manager in advance to summarize all target customers and determine the expected levels of profitability. Then the performance measure can be changed to target just those new customers who will pay for high-margin products and avoid all others.

- *Increasing profitability.* When a division's management team is required to improve profitability, it may embark on a number of approaches to increase the value of the inventory, which reduces the cost of goods sold and increases profits. For example, they can increase the amount of inventory on hand so that additional overhead costs can be absorbed by the inventory instead of being charged to the cost of goods sold. Another ploy is to book sales in the current period that should be recorded in the next period. Yet another option is to alter the method for recording inventory costs to one that results in higher profits. To avoid these problems, the controller should record a trend line of inventory turnover to see if there is a sudden jump in inventory costs. Another option is to tie a profit goal to another goal for reducing the amount of working capital, which would keep management from shifting costs into the inventory. To keep management from recording future sales in the current period, the internal audit staff should schedule surprise audits of the month-end cutoff to spot any such problems and report exceptions to the audit committee.

- *Increasing sales.* When the sales manager has an incentive to increase sales, a common action is to load up current customers with more orders, even if they will exceed their credit limits by doing so. Then, the sales manager applies pressure to the finance department to increase credit levels, which they sometimes do when the customer orders are already in hand. If the customers are unable to pay on time (which is why those credit limits were established in the first place), the accounts receivable investment will increase. Also, the sales manager may sell to new customers that have poor payment histories, which results in a similar increase in the accounts receivable investment. To counteract this problem, the sales manager's performance should be focused instead on the *profits* of all customers. Also, if there is going to be a performance measure for increasing sales, then a good way to counteract any negative behavior is to work with the sales manager in advance to agree on credit levels for all existing customers as well as the amounts that will be granted to a specific list of prospective new customers, which avoids any subsequent pressure on the finance department to increase credit levels.

- *Increasing sales per salesperson.* If the sales manager must increase the sales per salesperson, which is an efficiency measure, the correct action is to institute an intensive training and prescreening system to increase the quality of the sales staff. However, a negative behavior that sometimes arises is to fire those existing sales staff with poor performance, without attempting to train or replace them. Although this action will certainly improve the reported level of sales per salesperson, the end result will be fewer total sales, because the sales staff has been reduced. This behavior can be counteracted by also requiring a low staff turnover goal, or by focusing instead on the total profitability of each customer, or by ensuring that an adequate sales training system is installed.

- *Increasing the return on assets.* When management is tasked with increasing the return on assets, it may shrink the asset base in some very imaginative ways. One approach is to write off any fully depreciated assets, so that the gross asset balance disappears from the books, even though the asset is still on the premises and being used. Another approach is to avoid the purchase of replacement assets in favor of keeping older ones; although a reasonable approach when used with moderation, this method can eventually result in a decrepit facility. In addition, management may sell off assets that are not being fully utilized, thereby reducing the manufacturing capacity of the facility. To avoid the first and third problems, there should be tight controls over the write-off or sale of assets, while the board of directors can address the second problem by reviewing the average age of assets or any year-to-year reductions in asset purchases and forcing the management team to invest in new assets.

- *Increasing the return on equity.* When managers are reviewed based on the return on equity, it is a common matter for them to place more emphasis on the equity part of the equation than the return part. When this happens, management may incur additional debt in order to buy back stock, which will increase the return on equity, but will also increase the risk that the company cannot pay off the debt. To avoid this issue, all stock buybacks, and the sources of funding for such purchases, must be approved in advance by the board of directors.

- *Reducing bad debt.* When the chief financial officer (CFO) is tasked with reducing the amount of bad debt write-offs, the most common response is to tighten a company's credit granting rules, so that customers must maintain smaller credit balances, and some customers may be converted to cash-only terms. Although this approach will certainly reduce the amount of bad debt, there is also a risk that some customer sales will be lost, as well as some customers. Accordingly, before using this performance measure, it is best to review the current credit situation and see if the current amount of bad debt is being adequately offset by profits from marginal customers. Another approach used to hide bad debt losses is to record them as credits instead of write-offs against the bad debt reserve. To avoid this problem, the controller should prepare a weekly list of all credits granted, and make this information available to senior management, so that there is no possibility of hiding bad debts in this area.

- *Reducing headcount.* If management is asked to reduce headcount, a common response is to offset the reductions with an increase in temporary employees or consultants, which may be much more expensive and less efficient than the people they are replacing. To avoid this problem, the controller can report to senior management regarding the cost and number of temporary and consulting staff being used, as well as the names of the managers to whom they are reporting, and the reasons why they are working for the company.

HOW TO COMPILE PERFORMANCE REVIEW MEASURES

Although it may seem simple to calculate performance review measures, there are some pitfalls to be aware of. The main ones are that all managers whose performance is being reviewed with measurements must be fully cognizant of exactly how their measurements are being compiled, the sources of the information from which the measurements are derived, and the timing of when the completed measures are released.

The reason for the first item, that of managers knowing how measures are compiled, is that any manager whose pay is closely tied to a performance measure will assuredly be trying to guess at the outcome before the final measure is released. If the final measure varies significantly from the informal measure that each manager has been privately compiling, then the controller will be fielding a number of possibly irate requests for explanations of the detail for each calculation. To avoid this problem, it is well worth the controller's time to write up an exact explanation of each measure used, and to go over this with each manager being measured, taking care to clarify any areas of uncertainly. Also, if there is a change to the calculation in the future, the controller should be very clear about the reasons for the change, and once again write down the revised calculation and distribute it. This approach, though tedious, will save time in the long run by making the calculation as clear for all parties as possible.

Similarly, managers should be made aware of the sources of information that are used as inputs to their performance measurements. If this is not done, they will guess at information sources and possibly compile measurements based on the wrong data. If so, the controller will be sure to hear about the managers' displeasure, and must spend extra time explaining why the information sources used by the managers are not the correct ones.

Finally, it is very important to let the managers know when the measurements will be issued to them and senior managers. If this is not done, the entire accounting staff will be bothered in advance by those managers who want to know measurement results. By training everyone to expect measures on a specific day, there will be no duplication of effort in tracking down measurements in advance and possibly giving out inaccurate measurements that have not yet been checked for errors. Even if measures are prepared early, it is best to meet the expectations of managers and release the information on the same day of every month, so that a tradition is built up of issuing data on a specific date.

All of these steps are necessary to ensure that managers are properly informed of the content of performance measure calculations, that they do not second guess the accounting staff who are compiling the final results, and that they do not press for the early release of measurement information.

REPORTING PERFORMANCE REVIEW MEASURES

Despite having just mentioned that managers should be trained to expect the release of performance review measures on a specific day, it may be wise when the measurement results look unusual to release the information early to the affected managers, so that they have a chance to respond. For example, if a measure has an exceptionally poor result, there may be a very good reason that was not incorporated into the measure by the accounting staff, but which the manager is well aware of and would be happy to share with the accounting staff. This is also a good approach from the perspective of corporate politics, because managers prefer to hear about bad news in advance and have a chance to fix the problem before the information is released to their peers or supervisors. This is especially the case when the information is based on incorrect information that the manager could have fixed in advance, resulting in the manager's looking bad in front of the company, when there was really no problem at all.

To take this concept one step further, a controller may consider it useful from the perspective of relations with other managers to allow them to include their explanations for poor measurement results in the measurements report that goes to their peers and senior management. By doing so, senior managers do not have to go to the managers themselves with questions when the answers are listed alongside the measurements. Also, it makes managers think that the controller is really trying to help them by allowing them to add explanations next to any possible bad news that the measurements report may impart; this is a good idea, because the controller must deal with these managers on a plethora of other tasks and needs their cooperation. In addition, in order to give managers enough time to research the causes of poor measurements results, it is useful to set the standard measurement release date far enough down the calendar that they have sufficient time to conduct their research. Accordingly, the release of performance measurement information involves some advance notice to affected managers and time enough for them to prepare their responses to bad measurements.

SUMMARY

The focus of this chapter has been on controlling the behavior of management in order to ensure that the corporate strategy is pursued, with no counterproductive actions occurring. Accordingly, when asked to recommend management performance measurement, a controller should not be quick to reply. Instead, the decision regarding what measures to use for each manager and additional controls over possible adverse behavior, as well as the range of target performance levels to use, is worthy of a great deal of thought, especially with regard to how managers will react to them and interact with each other. Further, the controller must be careful to discuss measurement criteria with the affected managers and to go over adverse measurement results with them in private prior to releasing measurement results to the rest of the company. Successful performance measurement will occur only when due consideration is given not only to the successful pursuit of corporate strategy, but how best to drive the management team in the direction of that strategy.

11

Analyzing Process Cycles

Although many analysts believe that all the major processes, cash flows, and key functions of their companies are fully documented and reviewed with periodic measurements, the majority of them are ignoring a gaping hole in the overall structure of their analysis. This is the process cycle, which has a major impact on the accuracy and speed of information flowing through a company. In the worst possible situation, a poor process cycle can even bring down a company. And yet, because a process cycle is such a low-profile item, few analysts think about it, and rarely try to measure it. This chapter corrects the problem by describing the key process cycles and the ways in which errors can arise through their usage, as well as how one may measure their performance.

DEFINITION OF A PROCESS CYCLE

A process cycle is the complete set of activities needed to complete a task. The typical company has only a few major ones, which are described in the following chapters. One of the most important is the purchasing cycle, in which an item is requested, usually through an internal purchase order system, then ordered by a purchasing agent or some similar method, received at the receiving dock, and paid for through the accounts payable staff. Another is the revenue cycle, during which a product is sent to a customer, the accounting department issues an invoice, collects the cash to pay for the invoice, and clears the payment through the accounting system. The final major cycle is the order fulfillment cycle, in which a customer places an order, the company schedules it, manufactures it, reviews its quality, stores it, and ships it. All of these process cycles are described in more detail in the succeeding sections.

157

It is evident that all three of these process cycles are responsible for the majority of a company's activities and involve nearly all of its paperwork: however, few organizations pay close attention to the flow of information from their beginnings to their ends. The reason is that responsibility for any major activity is set up by department, so that, for example, the production manager is concerned only with the flow of paper through his or her department and does not care about where the information came from before it arrived in production or where it goes after it departs. As a result, there are a number of managers involved in each of the key process cycles, but none of them see the entire picture, and none of them care to do so. Because of the diffuse nature of each process cycle, it is common for a financial analyst or controller to measure only a few small aspects of one, rather than attempting to obtain a complete picture of each one's scope and tackling the entire process. As a result, the typical process cycle is grossly inefficient, contains far too many steps and redundancies, and takes much longer to push a transaction through than would be the case if the process were thoroughly reviewed and streamlined.

The intent of this book is strictly financial analysis, and so the succeeding sections will describe how to *measure* an existing process cycle. For an excellent study of how to completely *redesign* a process cycle, the reader is directed to Michael Hammer's *Reengineering the Corporation* (Harper Business, New York, 1993).

ANALYZING THE PURCHASING CYCLE

The purchasing cycle involves the steps needed to order a product from a supplier, receive it, and pay for it. As noted in Exhibit 11.1, this process typically involves four departments (excluding the supplier).

Given the large number of participants, it is no surprise that this process cycle is subject to a number of errors, mostly caused by the time lag when information passes between departments, or even the complete loss of this information. The most common problems are:

- *Purchase requisition is lost.* When an employee fills out a requisition form and sends it to the purchasing department, it may disappear in transit or be lost by the purchasing department, which is an area that is commonly awash in a sea of paperwork.

- *Purchase order is lost.* When the purchasing staff completes a purchase order, any number of parts of this multipart form may be lost. If the part going to the supplier is lost, there will be no shipment of product to the company. If the part going to the receiving dock is lost, the receiving staff will reject the item when it arrives because it does not appear to be an authorized purchase. Also, the accounting staff will not pay for the supplier's invoice if it has no purchase order as evidence of authorization.

- *Received product is lost.* If the received product is lost somewhere in the company, the person who ordered the item will have to do so again

Exhibit 11.1   Purchasing Cycle

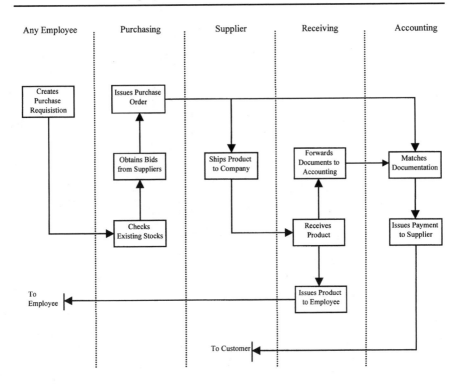

and wait for the usual time period to pass for the transaction to be completed.

- *Receiving documentation is lost.* If the receiving staff loses the bill of lading, or if it is lost in transit to the accounting department, there will be no evidence of receipt, and the accounting staff will not pay for the purchase.

All of these issues are serious ones, and they happen in every corporation, causing a large amount of stress while everyone involved searches for the missing paperwork or product. This extra search effort typically requires far more time than the standardized processing of a purchasing transaction when all the documentation is in order. Unfortunately, because the extra work is spread across many departments instead of with one overworked individual, it is very difficult to determine the extent of problems in this process cycle. This is where the controller comes in.

One of the easiest ways for a controller to determine if there is a problem with the placement or tracking of purchase orders is to run a report from the computer system that shows the proportion of open purchase orders that are overdue. By tracking this information on a trend line, it is an easy matter to see if there is an underlying problem involving either purchase orders being issued with an excessively short lead time, suppliers who are unable to ship parts to the company by their promised delivery dates, or poor paper flow at the receiving dock that prevents a purchase order from being recorded as filled in the computer system in a timely manner. To determine which of these problems is the underlying reason, it is best to trace a sample of overdue purchase orders to determine root causes. This information can then be used by the manager of the purchasing staff to target corrective actions and keep late materials receipts from interfering with the purchasing cycle.

Having a large number of parts in the warehouse with very low usage levels is a clear sign of purchasing or scheduling problems. One way to measure this problem is to run a usage report in the computer system that shows the last date on which a part was used, or (even better) the number of times each part was used in the past year. These measures reveal which parts are stocked in overabundance in the warehouse, and which therefore should be disposed of by a variety of means. A controller should run this report once a month and share it with all managers in the logistics area, so they can determine the reasons why inventory is either being purchased in excessive quantities or used in excessively small quantities.

A truly effective purchasing department retains tight control over the number of suppliers it uses, because more suppliers require more purchasing staff to deal with them and track their performance. A controller can easily measure the number of suppliers by running a computer report that shows the last date on which an order was placed with a supplier. By adding up the number of suppliers used within the past 12 months and tracking this information on a trend line, one can tell if the purchasing staff is effectively managing its pool of suppliers.

One of the best measures of the overall integrity of the purchasing cycle is the proportion of payments to suppliers for which there is no receiving documentation or a purchase order. This measure reveals the number of instances in which purchases were made outside of the approved purchasing system, since there is no purchase order, or when receiving information was lost in transit to the accounting department. By regularly sampling payment packets for this information and delving into the underlying reasons for the missing paperwork, a discerning controller can recommend changes to the purchasing and receiving procedures that will improve the integrity of the entire purchasing cycle.

This section has noted a number of ways in which the performance of the purchasing cycle can be degraded, and how the controller can use simple financial analysis tools to determine the extent of the problems in this area.

ANALYZING THE REVENUE CYCLE

The revenue cycle covers the flow of transactions through four departments that are needed to ensure that a customer order is properly billed, paid for, and cleared through the accounting system. The cycle is shown graphically in Exhibit 11.2, which describes the initial transaction, in which the customer places an order, has an acceptance or rejection of credit, a transfer of ship-

Exhibit 11.2   Revenue Cycle

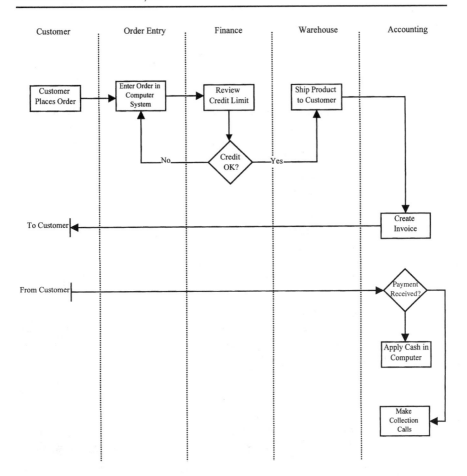

ment documentation to the accounting department for billing, and subsequent collection efforts.

Unfortunately, this seemingly simple process flow hides a plethora of potential system failures. The most common problems are:

- *Customer order is incorrectly entered.* An exceptionally common issue is that the order entry staff does not properly enter the customer's order into the computer system, possibly resulting in the wrong address, part quantities, or part numbers. The results can be orders that are shipped to the wrong location or incorrect parts or wrong quantities shipped, all of which result in an unhappy customer and a very difficult collection job by the accounting staff.

- *Customer orders are entered without a purchase order.* Any customer order that results in a shipment without a corresponding customer authorization in the form of a purchase order results in a possible bad debt, because the customer is under no obligation to pay for the item shipped nor to return it. This is a problem at the point of order entry, where orders should not be accepted without such a form of authorization.

- *Customer credit is incorrectly granted.* A customer may have a terrible credit history and yet be granted an excessively high credit level. This is frequently the result of undue pressure by the sales staff, which has already obtained the customer's order and wants the credit approved in order to earn a commission. Given the undue level of pressure, the finance staff caves in and grants the request. Unfortunately, a really large sale is the one that not only earns the largest commission for a salesperson, but is also the one that can land a customer in the largest amount of credit trouble, because it may have no way to pay the company such a large amount of money.

- *Customer order is shipped without credit approval.* It is entirely possible for a customer order to be entered into the computer system, subject to credit approval, and still have it produced and shipped to the customer—without any credit approval. The usual breakdown in the process is when no "hold" flag is assigned to an order, so that downstream operations within the company do not know that the order is on hold and proceed as though it is a normal order. The worst case of all is if there is no "hold" feature in the computer system at all, in which case the company must rely on a separate, manual system that operates alongside the computer system to track credit hold situations.

- *Wrong product is shipped to customer.* A customer may receive the wrong product due to several breakdowns in the process cycle. One is that the initial order was entered incorrectly; another is that the product that reaches the warehouse for shipment is incorrectly labeled; and a third possibility is that the warehouse simply ships the wrong product. This is a classic process cycle problem, because the error can originate in three separate departments!

- *Invoice is incorrectly prepared or not prepared at all.* Even if the product is correctly shipped, there is still the issue of getting an invoice to the customer for payment, before the revenue cycle can be successfully closed. If there is an incorrect transfer of information between the shipping dock and the billings staff, then it is possible that no invoice will be prepared at all. Another issue is that, if quantities or part numbers listed by the shipping personnel on the bill of lading are incorrect, then this improper data will also be used in the invoice. Further, if a deposit or prepayment was made at the time of order entry and incorrectly accounted for, this information will not be recorded in the invoice. If all of these errors are present, it can be a surprise when the accounting staff issues a *correct* invoice.

- *Cash is incorrectly applied.* If cash is received by the order entry or sales staffs as a prepayment or deposit, it is possible that the money will be lost in transit to the accounting staff, or that it will not be correctly identified when sent there. Also, when cash is received at the mailroom in payment for an invoice, the same problems may apply. In either case, the cash will be incorrectly applied to the customer account, which can result in an incorrect customer account receivable balance and additional and unnecessary collection calls.

- *Collection efforts are not made.* If the preceding cash application process results in incorrect customer balances, the collections staff will not know that it is supposed to undertake collection efforts, resulting in customer nonpayment. Though this may seem like a shortcoming of just the collections staff, the preceding point shows that the underlying issue can originate as far away as the order entry process or the mail room.

- *Accounts receivable are improperly credited.* Any of the preceding problems can result in improper credits to customer accounts. For example, an incorrect entry of a customer order or shipping of the wrong product may result in a credit to the customer's account to eliminate the incorrect shipment, but does not reflect the additional shipment, at no cost to the customer, of the correct product. Whenever there is a secondary shipment to a customer to correct an earlier problem, it is all too common to clear out the customer's original account receivable balance without billing for the new shipment.

A major flaw in the revenue cycle that a controller can easily measure is the proportion of invoices issued for which there is no customer purchase order. This measure reveals the extent to which orders are being taken without appropriate customer approval, and points toward potential difficulties later on, when the collections staff tries to collect payment on the invoice. It is very useful to feed back the details of each case to the order entry manager, so that this person can follow up with the order entry staff to ensure that the problem does not arise again.

Another simple measure is the proportion of customers with open accounts receivable but no assigned credit limit. This measure is useful when a controller suspects that there is a problem with shipping orders without first assigning a credit limit. If the problem appears to be a severe one, a secondary measure is to create a subset of just those customers without assigned credit limits, and to then determine their average levels of accounts receivable—a low average level points toward a minimal problem, but high levels should lead to immediate action to clamp down on what may be a severe credit granting problem. Another measure that is oriented more toward the adequacy of existing credit levels is a comparison of current customer accounts receivable balances to their preassigned credit levels, preferably tracked on a trend line. If this percentage is near 100 percent, it may be time to review credit granting policies and extend more credit, especially if there is little evidence of bad debt or excessive payment periods by customers. All of these measures are designed to give a high-level perspective on any potential credit problems in the revenue cycle.

A difficult measure for a controller to track, but one which requires at least an occasional measurement is the proportion of shipments made that are not billed. Though a problem in this area can have major repercussions, it is difficult to accurately measure. The only way to reliably do so is to compare the shipping log to the invoice register and spot any shipments for which there is not a corresponding invoice. The resulting list of shipments must then be investigated and further reduced by the number of free samples, warranty replacements, or other shipments for which there is a valid reason for not having invoiced. The remaining set of shipments must be reviewed in great detail to ensure that the nonbilling problem does not recur.

Sometimes, revenue cycle problems are very hard to spot and cannot be reliably found through traditional measurement systems. Instead, it is best to obtain clues from customers, who are more than happy to call in with complaints about the revenue cycle. These complaints typically include issues with overbillings, incorrect pricing, incorrect credit hold situations, inappropriate collection calls, or shipments that are incorrect for any number of other reasons. By entering this information into a customer complaints database, one can easily summarize the types of complaints and track them to see if there are improvements in the various kinds of revenue cycle problems. This is frequently the best method for measuring the effectiveness of the overall revenue cycle, and is an excellent way to determine the key problem areas that require more extensive measurement systems.

This section covered a number of problems that can arise in the revenue cycle, as well as the more common types of measures one can use to determine the extent and severity of the problems.

ANALYZING THE ORDER FULFILLMENT CYCLE

The only major process cycle in which the accounting department does not play a role is the order fulfillment cycle. In this one, the customer places an order, which is scheduled for production, is produced, reviewed for quality, sent to the warehouse, and shipped to the customer. A slightly more complicated variation, which is derived from the processes of an injection molding facility, is shown in Exhibit 11.3. This process cycle fits inside of the revenue cycle that was described in the last section, for it *produces* the customer order, whereas the revenue cycle is concerned only with the garnering of cash from revenues.

This is the most complicated of the major process cycles, because it requires the close interaction and integration of nearly all departments. The company that has perfected this process cycle is one with a superior advantage over its competitors, because the result is a smoothly flowing order fulfillment process that yields a rapid and accurate delivery to the customer.

Exhibit 11.3 Order Fulfillment Cycle

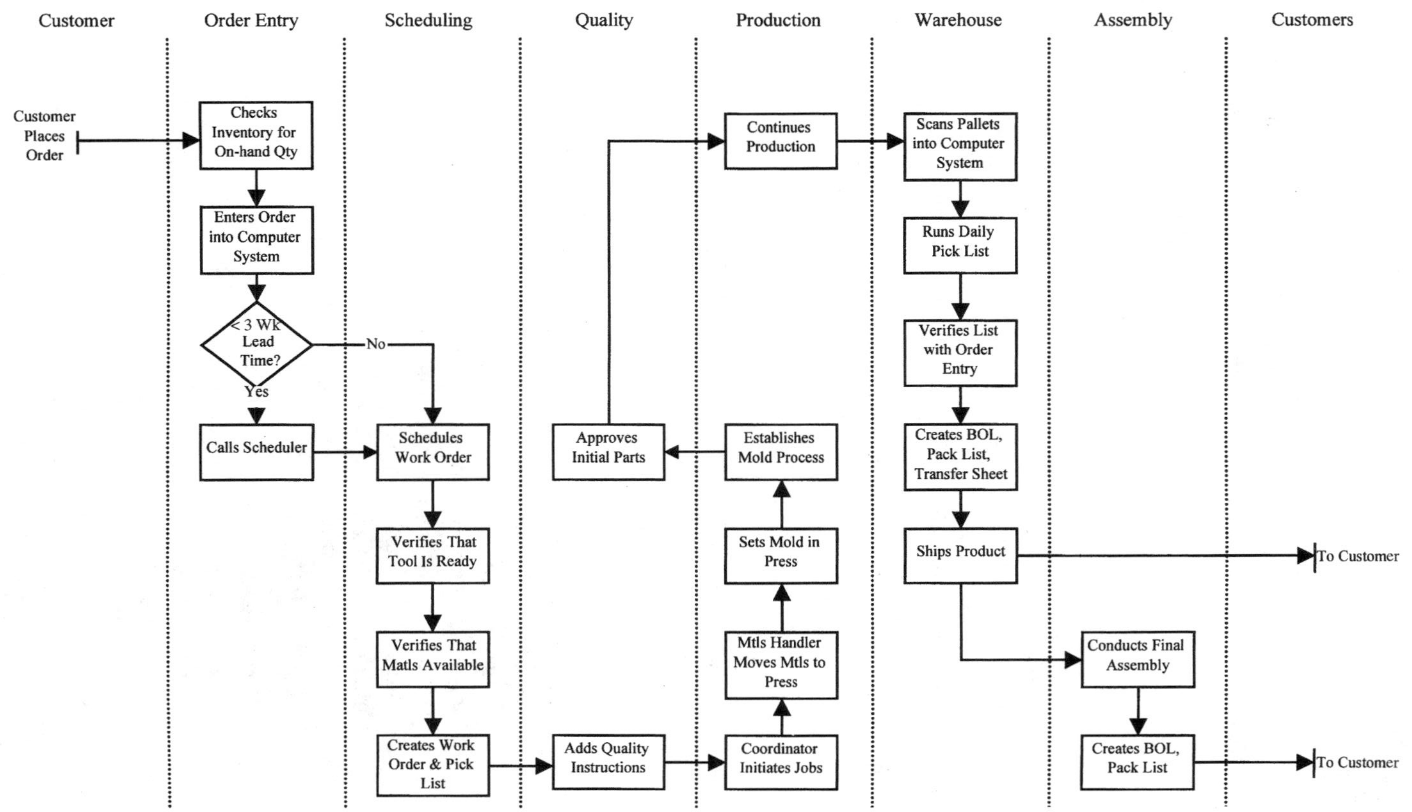

Customer
- Customer Places Order

Order Entry
- Checks Inventory for On-hand Qty
- Enters Order into Computer System
- <3 Wk Lead Time?
  - Yes → Calls Scheduler
  - No → Schedules Work Order

Scheduling
- Schedules Work Order
- Verifies That Tool Is Ready
- Verifies That Matls Available
- Creates Work Order & Pick List

Quality
- Approves Initial Parts
- Adds Quality Instructions

Production
- Continues Production
- Establishes Mold Process
- Sets Mold in Press
- Mtls Handler Moves Mtls to Press
- Coordinator Initiates Jobs

Warehouse
- Scans Pallets into Computer System
- Runs Daily Pick List
- Verifies List with Order Entry
- Creates BOL, Pack List, Transfer Sheet
- Ships Product

Assembly
- Conducts Final Assembly
- Creates BOL, Pack List

Customers
- To Customer
- To Customer

165

However, given the number of handoffs between departments, errors can arise in many areas. The most common problems are:

- *Customer is promised delivery based on nonexistent inventory.* A common problem occurs when the person entering the customer order promises immediate delivery to the customer, even though there is not enough product on hand to fill the order. This is caused by either lack of communication with the warehouse or inaccurate product records in the warehouse database.

- *Delivery date is set too soon.* If there is poor communication between the order entry staff and the production scheduling employees, it is all too common to promise a delivery date to the customer that the production department has no hope of achieving. This can be caused by a multitude of factors, such as missing materials for the required production, a long queue of other jobs to complete first, or capacity constraints. Proper communication among all concerned departments and the order entry staff is the only way to resolve this problem.

- *Materials are not available for production.* If an order is placed and scheduled for production, the production will not happen if materials are not purchased in advance and delivered on time. This requires excellent coordination between the scheduling and purchasing staffs, as well as a good database of material lead times. Once again, proper coordination between departments is the only way to overcome this issue.

- *Work instructions are faulty.* When there are specialized work instructions needed to ensure that a production run is successful (as is commonly the case when there are semicustom jobs), the work instructions must be highly accurate or else the production will not be completed on schedule. This problem may lie with the order entry staff's not telling the scheduling personnel enough details about the work, the scheduling staff's preparing incorrect work instructions, or (most maddening of all) revisions to the previously released work instructions that do not find their way to the shop floor. In all cases, there is the same result—faulty or late production.

- *Warehouse staff does not deliver needed materials.* Production cannot begin if materials are not delivered to the shop floor in a timely manner by the warehouse staff. This may result in miscommunication of the timing of material needs from the scheduling staff to the warehouse, missing materials due to errors by the purchasing staff, or excessively short production lead times by the order entry staff. Many departments may cause this problem.

- *Information system incorrectly records completed production.* If there is an inadequate method for recording completed production, the rest of the company may not know that the production department has successfully completed work on a customer order, resulting in delayed shipments and angry customers. This error is frequently caused by poor materials handling, whereby finished goods are not moved to a data recording station in a timely manner. Another problem may be due to a breakdown in the computer systems that drive automated data reporting or perhaps a dysfunctional paper-based recording system that takes too long to notify other parts of the company.

- *Production is lost in the warehouse.* A shipment will never leave the shipping dock if no one can locate it in the warehouse. This is frequently caused by poor record keeping during the transition period when a product leaves the production area and arrives in the warehouse. If the transition is not handled smoothly, it is easy to mix products or mislabel them, resulting in a very difficult part location problem. The issue is exacerbated when there is an active team of expeditors in the plant, because they will take a product out of the production department as soon as it has been completed, walk it straight to the shipping dock, and put it on a delivery truck—without ever having entered any production or shipment information in the standard information tracking system. This scenario results in missing production, picking, and shipping information that is very difficult to track down and correct.

The preceding list of errors is by no means comprehensive. These are the potential problems that can arise simply because of a poor handoff of information between departments as the order fulfillment process moves from order entry through production to shipping. If there is a failure to communicate during any of these interdepartmental handoffs, the preceding errors are most likely to occur.

The measure that most clearly reveals the existence of problems in the order fulfillment cycle is the percentage of jobs in the production schedule that were completed on time. A low percentage of completion shows that additional investigation is needed to determine which specific areas are causing the poor performance, such as missing materials, capacity problems, or orders without sufficient lead times. A substitute for this measure is the percentage of orders shipped on time, which is a bit more comprehensive—it includes the performance not only of the production department, but also that of the personnel on the shipping dock. This measure should include a detailed analysis of every job that was not completed or shipped on time, so that management can determine where it should focus its efforts to improve the situation.

A lesser measure is to track the proportion of shipments that are made on a rush basis, such as through an overnight freight carrier. This can also be tracked in terms of the dollars spent on rush freight. In either case, it is necessary to determine the exact reasons why each shipment was late and to then backtrack through the involved departments to determine which one was responsible for the problem. This is not as accurate a measure as the percentage of completion of the production schedule, because it ignores any shipments that are late but are not sent out on a rush basis. The customer has agreed to take a late delivery, so those shipments are ignored by the measurement.

Having a large proportion of production orders due to arrive at the customer on the same day that they are scheduled to be completed is another indication of underlying problems. This timing virtually guarantees an expediting situation, in which someone is ready to snatch the job from the production department, run it to the shipping dock, and make a special delivery to the customer—while possibly having avoided all of the record-keeping systems on the way to the customer. When not enough time has been built into the schedule to get a product to the customer, the systems will inevitably break down, so this problem must be identified and avoided.

Shipments will be promised to customers, and materials will be assumed to be ready for production if items are listed as already being in the warehouse. An excellent measure that determines the true accuracy of the inventory is to count a sample of the inventory and compare it to a computer report of what is supposed to be there. If the item description, location, or quantity is wrong, then the item is listed as incorrect. By dividing the number of correct counts by the total number counted, one can get a reasonably accurate picture of the total accuracy of all inventory records. If possible, this information should be tracked by individual warehouse aisle, so that the warehouse manager will know exactly where to concentrate efforts to fix the problem.

A final measure that is most useful for determining the presence of problems in the order fulfillment cycle is the proportion of overdue messages in a manufacturing resource planning (MRP II) system. If a company has such a system, it compares the production schedule to the amount of inventory on hand to see what parts the purchasing staff must buy and issues warning messages if there are parts that can no longer be bought within the usual lead times. If there is a large proportion of these items, the purchasing department will be forced to pay express delivery and rush production charges to bring in the needed parts on time, and may not be able to get the required items on time at all, resulting in production shortages that will inevitably affect customer delivery dates. If there are a large number of these overdue messages, a detailed investigation of each one is the only way to determine why they are present—due to either excessively short production lead times, inaccurate part information in the warehouse, or incorrect part lead times in the computer database. This is a very important measure to review if there appears to be consistent trouble with the timely delivery of parts to the production department.

This section has noted the variety of problems that arise due to the multitude of information handoffs between the many departments involved in the order fulfillment process, as well as several key measures one can use to determine the severity and extent of those problems.

SUMMARY

This chapter has described what a process cycle is, which are the three most important ones and how they function, and the ways in which they can break down. This last point is the most important from the perspective of the controller or financial analyst, because it points toward measures to implement in order to determine the extent of process cycle errors. The measures suggested here are sufficient for determining the most common errors in the main cycles, which management can then use to either create new control points or be the basis for more sweeping changes, such as a complete reengineering of these processes.

12

Financial Analysis of Operational Topics

The majority of this book is concerned with determining the overall financial strength or weakness of a company. However, that type of review does not yield a sufficient degree of information regarding *why* certain financial results have been achieved. The reason is that the performance of individual departments within a company have a great impact on overall results. For example, the failure of the engineering department to charge customers for changes to their product designs can have a serious impact on profitability, while the failure of the logistics department to keep inventory turnover levels to minimum levels can cause a company to run out of cash. A good job of financial analysis, then, must include not only the overall financial results of a company, but also a detailed review of those individual departments that are causing the overall problem. This chapter describes the key areas in which each of the most common departments can affect a company's financial performance, as well as how to calculate those measurements.

ANALYSIS OF ACCOUNTING AND FINANCE

The accounting department, strangely enough, is not as heavily analyzed as other departments, perhaps because the staff doing most corporate review work is based in this department and does not want to measure its own performance. Although many accounting and finance activities are concerned with nothing more than the daily processing of standardized transactions, there are a number of measures that hone in on efficiency problems, error rates, and extraneous expenses that can be eliminated. This section covers the measurement of these areas.

170

It is the job of the accounting staff to collect money from customers. If this is not done well, the repercussions include an unusually high proportion of bad debt write-offs and an excessive amount of cash invested in accounts receivable. Both problems can be attacked with the same activity, which is vigorous exploration of payment problems with customers, resulting in action against customers to collect funds (usually in the minority of cases) and internal actions to improve the underlying problems that are causing receipt problems (usually in the majority of cases), such as incorrect shipments, unauthorized shipments, billing address mistakes, or pricing errors. The starting point for these types of corrective action is to regularly measure the amount of accounts receivable outstanding as a proportion of sales. If the resulting number of days outstanding significantly exceeds the average payment terms on invoices, then enhanced collection activity will be in order. The calculation is:

$$[(\text{Total accounts receivable balance}) / (\text{Annualized sales})] \times 365$$

In addition to tracking the amount of accounts receivable as a proportion, it may also be necessary to track it as a dollar figure. By separating out the amount of funds that are overdue, one can determine the potential payback from an increased level of collections activity, which may be of great use if a company finds itself in a cash-short position. This measure is not easy to calculate if customers have a variety of different payment terms, such as 20, 30, or 45 days. A better measurement environment exists when all payment terms are consistent, such as 30-day payment terms. Also, it is misleading to measure the amount of dollars that are due at 31 days, because there may be a number of transaction processing days that are skewing the resulting figure, such as mail float time, lockbox processing time, and internal check processing time. A better choice is to track the dollars that are 10 days past the average number of due days, which more accurately reflects the amount of overdue funds. When consistently applied and calculated, this yields a good measure of the amount of funds that can potentially be collected through better collection activities.

One area in which the accounting department has a direct impact on company profits is the use of payment discounts when paying suppliers. If regularly taken, this can have a measurable impact on the amount of company profits. The basic measure for determining the ability of the accounting staff to take discounts is to track the dollars of discounts *not* taken. However, this calculation can be very misleading if many of the potential discounts result in a poor use of company funds. For example, if a major supplier offers an early payment discount percentage of one half of a percent within five days of receipt, or 60 days to pay, the result is an interest rate that is probably lower than the company's cost of capital. For most organizations, a discount percentage of anything less than 1 percent is not economically practical. Consequently, it is best to evaluate all discount rates from suppliers beforehand and avoid entering them in the accounts payable system unless they exceed the company's cost of funds. For the remaining early payment discount rates, one can then calculate the amount of discounts lost as a usable performance measurement.

A major issue for a company that sells any kind of product or service is whether the cost accounting staff has issued a final and detailed cost accounting analysis of every product or service prior to its being issued into the marketplace. If this is not done, the margin on the product or service being sold may be too low or even negative. It requires constant interaction with the engineering and marketing departments to ensure that the cost accounting staff is included in all pricing decisions, which may not be part of the existing corporate culture, and which may be something over which the controller has little control. Nonetheless, it is a simple matter to sum up the number of products or services currently on the market and to divide this figure into the number of them for which there are completed costing studies. Sometimes, just presenting the resulting percentage to management and explaining the issue will result in greater future cooperation with the cost accounting staff.

The finance department is in charge of wisely investing corporate funds in such a manner as to maximize earnings on invested funds, while not tying up those funds for an excessive period of time or investing at an excessively high level of risk. Given these constraints, many companies invest in exceedingly safe and liquid securities as a matter of course, without exploring slightly higher-yielding investment options. For those companies with large amounts of cash on hand, this can result in a significant loss in interest earnings. The formula for the average interest rate earned is:

$$\frac{(\text{Total interest receipts}) + (\text{Dividends received}) + (\text{Accrued interest})}{\text{Total amount of cash invested}}$$

This should be tracked on a trend line to show any improvement or worsening of the company's earnings in this area. Also keep in mind that it may not be the fault of the finance staff if the interest rate earned is very low, because the board of directors may have already issued a set of guidelines regarding how all funds are to be invested, in which case altering the earnings rate will require a decision by the board to alter its existing guidelines.

If the accounting or finance departments are responsible for investing cash, then it seems likely that they are also responsible for doing the reverse—securing debt financing. For those organizations with a significant amount of debt, a reasonable measure is to track the weighted average interest rate charged on the debt. The calculation is:

$$\frac{(\text{Interest paid on secured and unsecured debt}) + (\text{Interest paid in leases})}{(\text{Beginning total debt}) + (\text{Ending total debt}) \ / \ 2}$$

If debt levels are not excessively high, this can be a reasonable way to determine the ability of the finance staff to procure low-cost debt financing. However, if debt levels are extremely high as a proportion of equity or assets, each incremental layer of debt will be exceedingly expensive, because the lenders are probably issuing unsecured debt, which carries with it an inherently large amount of risk. In these cases, which are all too common, the finance staff is essentially taking on any debt it can, either to fund an acquisition binge or to ensure corporate survival. In either case, the cost of the debt is not a primary consideration, and should not be the basis of a judgment on the performance of the finance department.

A final key function of the accounting and finance departments is the proportion of net income that must be paid out in taxes. A superior degree of tax planning can have an enormous impact on this percentage, which greatly improves cash flow and is therefore directly tied to an increase in earnings per share. Given the lack of knowledge of all other departments regarding the intricacies of the tax laws, this is an area in which the accounting and finance staffs can really show their worth in enhancing corporate value. The only problem with using this measurement to judge departmental perform- ance is that it requires the approval of other department managers to imple- ment many of the tax-saving changes, such as moving facilities to low-tax regions. Accordingly, the success of the accounting and finance personnel in this area is highly dependent on the cooperation of the rest of the organiza- tion. The calculation is:

$$\frac{\text{(Total cash payments for taxes)} + \text{(Additional accrued tax expenses)}}{\text{Total pretax income}}$$

The accounting and finance departments have a direct impact on the size of selected income and expense items, as well as the working capital category of accounts receivable. The measurements noted in this section can be used to maintain a performance tracking system for these departments.

ANALYSIS OF COMPUTER SERVICES

In most companies, the computer services department is strictly responsible for its own budget, which comprises a small percentage of total company expenses. In these instances, it is usually sufficient to periodically track the department's actual costs against its budget and halt any further financial analysis. However, there are cases in which the computer services department is responsible for very large projects that either have a major impact on avail- able company cash or that must be completed on time in order to give the company a competitive advantage through some technological innovation. The measurements noted in this section can be used in this situation.

The computer services department is, from time to time, responsible for a few very large system implementation projects. It is critical to track the success of these projects in order to ensure that they are completed on time and within the prescribed budget. If not, a company can suffer a severe short- age of cash due to the allocation of extra funds to such a project, or will not have the benefit of the new system until much later than expected. The meas-

Exhibit 12.1   Comparison of Budget to Actual Costs by Milestone

Milestone	Budget	Actual	Total Variance
Storyboards	$175,000	$135,000	–$40,000
Initial coding	572,000	600,000	–12,000
Testing	305,000	300,000	–17,000
Procedures	58,000	65,000	–10,000
Installation	129,000	150,000	11,000

ure to use when tracking such a situation is a continuing comparison of budgeted to actual costs for each major computing project. It is not sufficient to review the current actual cost of an ongoing project to its eventual total cost, because this approach gives the analyst no information about whether the project will be completed on budget. A better method is shown in Exhibit 12.1, in which the budget to actual comparison is conducted for each project on a milestone basis. By breaking down the analysis into smaller pieces, it is easier to determine in advance if a project will probably run over budget. In the example, the project is cumulatively under budget at all milestones until it reaches the installation phase, where it finally incurs a loss relative to the budget. Also, losses are incurred at the initial coding, procedure writing, and installation phases, so all of these work areas should be subject to a review to see if the problems can be avoided for the next computer project.

For those companies in which it is critical that projects be completed on time, a similar analysis based on time, instead of money, can be easily developed. Like the analysis in Exhibit 12.1, it splits a project into milestones and assigns a completion day to each one. By tracking the cumulative variance at each milestone, one can easily determine where variances are arising and roughly when the project should be completed. This analysis is shown in Exhibit 12.2. For both types of analysis, the accuracy of the initial budgeted figures will increase as the computer services staff gains experience in compiling initial budgets, so it is important to go over the final results with them at the conclusion of each project, so that they will receive feedback on their previous estimates.

Besides the tracking of project costs and completion dates, some controllers may feel that the overall costs of the computer services department as a proportion of total company expenses are too high. One way to determine the reasonableness of this cost is to calculate the total computer services cost as a percentage of total revenues, especially on a trend line that reveals any significant changes over time. However, this calculation may yield inaccurate results if a company uses sophisticated computer systems as a linchpin of its overall competitive strategy, which would justify a higher expense level. If computer expenses are treated as a commodity, however, a reasonable way to determine if the cost is excessive is to calculate the computer cost per user and compare this figure to that of other organizations. The calculation is:

Exhibit 12.2   Comparison of Budget to Actual Times by Milestone

Milestone	Budget (days)	Actual (days)	Total Variance (days)
Storyboards	32	29	−3
Initial coding	110	115	+2
Testing	45	40	−3
Procedures	15	20	+2
Installation	30	35	+7

$$\frac{\text{(Total cost of all computer hardware)} + \text{(Computer depreciation expense)} + \text{(Computer outsourcing costs)} + \text{(Allocated personnel and occupancy costs)}}{\text{Number of employees using a computer}}$$

Note: It is very important not to use the total number of company employees in this calculation, because there may be a significant number who do not use computers, such as those on a production assembly line. Including these people in the measurement would significantly skew the cost per user downward. Also, the computer depreciation expense should accurately reflect the actual number of years over which this equipment is used—internal accounting rules may result in depreciation periods that are too long and therefore spread costs over an excessively long period.

This section has focused on only a few key aspects of the computer services department, with a particular emphasis on its ability to efficiently and effectively complete hardware and software creation and installation projects in a timely manner. These are crucial factors in those companies that rely on advanced computer technologies to ensure their competitive survival. The controllers of these organizations should strongly consider the use of the measurements noted in this section to keep close track of computer services activities. Some of these measures can also be duplicated for the engineering department, the subject of the next section, which operates in a similar manner.

ANALYSIS OF ENGINEERING

The engineering department is the key to success in some industries, such as equipment manufacturing, high technology, and product design. In these areas, this department can be the foundation for an enormously profitable company, or one that founders due to cost overruns, poor product designs, or late product introductions. In such situations, it is critical to monitor the engineering department with the appropriate set of measurements. This section discusses those measures.

Measures in the engineering area can be clustered into two categories: those that track effectiveness, which is the department's ability to produce the right product, and those that track efficiency, which is its ability to produce with a minimal amount of resources. The engineering manager must succeed in both categories, not just one, to contribute the greatest possible value to the corporation. For example, the department may produce the most extraordinary product imaginable, but only a year after the market window for it has closed. Alternatively, it could have produced a subpar product, but right on time and under budget. Neither alternative is acceptable. Accordingly, a controller must design a set of measures that track the impact of both types of performance. We will begin with effectiveness measures.

Several effectiveness measures revolve around the concept of reusability. This concept is central to an effective engineering department, because it means that the engineers are designing with economy—they are using the same basic platform or component parts to design multiple products. By doing so, they do not have to "reinvent the wheel" for every new product. The concept can be taken further by tracking the number of product variations that exist for each product (e.g., different colors or other features). By keeping the number of variations to a minimum, there is less engineering work involved, as well as less downstream production work and fewer parts for the logistics group to purchase and track. The first effectiveness measure is the number of products using a common platform. This is defined as the number of discrete products currently sold that are founded on the same mechanical platform or:

$$\frac{\text{Total number of currently marketed products}}{\text{Total number of product platforms}}$$

Note: Do not include old products in the numerator that are no longer being marketed, because adding obsolete or retired products here would artificially inflate the proportion of products per platform.

This can be a difficult measurement to calculate, because what constitutes a mechanical platform is subject to a great deal of interpretation: It can be the presence of a large, commonly used subassembly or perhaps a high preponderance of similar parts in the designs. Whatever definition is used, the key is to be consistent in applying the measure, so that it is consistent and reliable. Also, a company that defines a common platform as only a few small, common parts is only fooling itself, for the measure is not to hoodwink anyone else—it is for management's own use and should therefore be rigorously defined and consistently applied.

If a controller finds, as a result of this analysis, that there is a platform supporting only a few product configurations, there may be grounds for a recommendation to either expand the number of configurations, or, as a cost-cutting measure, to eliminate the platform entirely and concentrate on fewer platforms, thereby reducing the amount of ongoing engineering work needed.

Another effectiveness measure is the number of product configurations, or options, that are associated with each product. For example, a car can have attachments for a driver-side rearview mirror, an extra air bag, racing suspension, and wood paneling. All of these features require extra engineering work, and the extra fees from having them may not offset the cost and extra time required for the design work. Also, the number of product options has downstream ramifications, because the production department must deal with the complexity of installing extra options, while the logistics and customer service teams must stock extra parts and be knowledgeable in the repair of the extra features. To calculate the maximum number of product options, add up all possible options currently offered and then multiply the number of options together in sequence. For example, if there are five options, the total number of possible product configurations is 120, which is calculated as:

$$5 \text{ product options} = (5 \times 4 \times 3 \times 2 \times 1) = \\ 120 \text{ possible product configurations}$$

The large number of possible configurations is caused by the multitude of combinations that can result. If there had been six options, the total number of configurations would have risen to 720! Though it clearly requires extra work by the engineering staff to design the extra options, which impacts its effectiveness, it is dealing with only the total number of options, *not* the total number of configurations, which is much higher. The *real* reduction in effectiveness and efficiency, as noted earlier, appears in the production department, in which the full range of product configurations, as noted in the example, comes into play.

Another key effectiveness measure is the trend line of warranty costs associated with each product line. If the engineering staff has done a thorough job of both designing and testing a new product, there should be few subsequent problems in the marketplace; if not, there will be a continuing stream of warranty claims. If the problems are significant, there may even be additional costs related to a complete product recall. If the engineering department is a large one, this is a good way to determine which design team is not effective in its work, because the warranty costs will be highly product specific. The one problem to be aware of here is that warranty costs are not always caused by the engineering staff. They may be the fault of the purchasing staff, which bought parts of an excessively low quality, or it may be caused by the production staff, which botched the assembly of the product. Consequently, it is very important to determine the exact cause of a warranty claim before tagging the engineering department with the blame.

Even if there are few warranty claims, there may be internal problems with manufacturing the product. This may be because the design uses excessively expensive parts or because it is difficult to manufacture, both of which are problems that the engineers should have recognized and fixed during the initial design work. The evidence of this problem will be a continuing stream of design changes that go into effect after a product has been released to the market. These changes are easy to spot, because there is documentation going from the engineering staff to the production, purchasing, and warehouse staffs regarding when there will be a switch to a new part, which requires an alteration of the bill of materials (BOM), both for changing to the new part and for any possible labor changes associated with the alteration. There is a significant cost to these changes that can be tracked through activity-based costing; there are costs associated with the paperwork for each change, revising the BOM, throwing out parts that are being replaced, and altering the product instruction sheets that are shipped with the product. Although the time needed to derive this measure is greater than for other analyses, a controller who suspects that this is a problem area should invest the time.

When a company is designing products for its customers, the key to overall corporate profitability is to do so with a minimal number of design changes, because extra iterations cost engineering time and will soak up all potential profits. The one situation under which this measure does not work occurs when customers are billed for the extra iterations, in which case the extra work hours will result in more profits, not less. This is an exceptionally difficult measure to determine, because the controller does not normally have any idea of how many design iterations the engineering staff is going through. Also, many changes reflect poorly on the performance of the engineering manager, so it is doubtful that this person will volunteer the information. Consequently, it may be more efficient for the controller to keep close track of which phases of a design project are running over budget, and ask if any of the excess time being used can be billed to customers. If not, then it is time to bring in the internal audit team to investigate the issue.

Efficiency measures for the engineering function are related to completing work on time and within the assigned cost budget. The first of these measures is comparing a project's actual completion time to the time that was originally budgeted. In industries in which time to market is critical, this measure may be more important than any cost overruns, because the company that brings a product to market first will acquire a disproportionate share of the products sold. When this measure is used, it is not of much use to determine that there was a problem after an entire project is complete. Instead, each project should be subdivided into a cluster of stages, with a milestone at the end of each one that is assigned a target date. One can then create a chart, as shown in Exhibit 12.3, that highlights due dates not being met at each project stage. This format is similar to the one used early in this chapter for computer programming projects, because there are many similarities in project management in the computer services and engineering departments. By using this approach, management can intervene before a project is over to bring the completion date back into line with the original targeted date.

Exhibit 12.3 Comparison of Actual to Budgeted Target Times by Milestone

Milestone	Budget (days)	Actual (days)	Total Variance (days)
Design criteria	120	125	+5
Modeling	52	57	+10
Final specifications	83	90	+17
Testing	40	55	+32
Pilot production	100	120	+52

Exhibit 12.3 illustrates a common engineering budgeting problem, which is running over budget at all phases of the project, rather than just in one area. This can be caused by poor management, bad initial budgeting, or the use of advanced and unproved technology in the design. To keep this from happening, it is very important to conduct a postproject review to discuss the reasons for these variances, and to incorporate resulting suggested changes into new projects so that this does not happen again.

Unfortunately, the upshot of a continual review of project problems is that more and more buffer time will be built into the next projects undertaken by the engineering staff so that there is no way it can possibly experience a negative variance. This is not a good situation when time to market is of the essence. Accordingly, tracking the time needed to complete projects on a trend line is an important way to determine if the engineering department is gradually improving its ability to complete projects in a shorter time frame. Exhibit 12.4, which shows the time line needed to create new car designs, is a good format for this analysis. When such a chart is created, it is important to measure only comparable projects on the same time line; for example, if the trend line contains the successive design times of several automobiles, including the much shorter design time for a lawn mower in the same graph would be highly misleading.

A final effectiveness measure is the cost to complete a design project. The primary cost of design work is the salaries of the engineers assigned to do the work, so this measure should have roughly the same result as the previous measure for tracking the time required to complete an engineering project— that is, if the project time runs over, then so too will the cost, and vice versa.

Exhibit 12.4   Trend Line of Project Duration for Comparable Projects

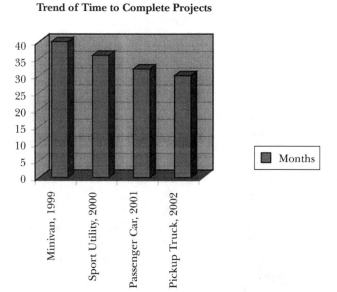

Trend of Time to Complete Projects

Exhibit 12.5 Comparison of Budget to Actual Costs by Milestone

Milestone	Budget	Actual	Total Variance
Design criteria	$350,000	$375,000	$25,000
Modeling	120,000	135,000	40,000
Final specifications	275,000	300,000	65,000
Testing	95,000	110,000	80,000
Pilot production	450,000	525,000	155,000

In addition to this basic relationship, there may be additional costs for travel or the services of outside engineering or testing consultants. Once again, the measurement mechanism is very similar to the one used earlier in this chapter for computer services projects, and is noted in Exhibit 12.5.

Of particular concern in the costing review is the cost of any pilot production process, because this sometimes includes some very leading-edge technology and is highly prone to error and iterative changes until the process works properly. This is an area in which the budgeted amounts can be grossly exceeded.

For some companies, engineering drives the overall level of company success and therefore requires close monitoring. The measures presented in this section were designed to track the efficiency and effectiveness of the engineering staff, so that management can quickly determine if there is a problem in this area and spotlight the specific areas requiring correction.

ANALYSIS OF HUMAN RESOURCES

The human resources department tends to have the least direct impact on a company's financial performance in the short term, because it controls a relatively small number of expenses. However, there are two instances in which it can have a significant impact. One occurs when the revenue per employee is relatively small, so that any changes in per-employee costs will have a significant impact on overall corporate profitability. In this instance, any significant change in the cost of benefits per employee will have a major impact on profits. The other instance occurs when a company is on a fast growth path. The human resources staff can reduce the rate of growth through its failure to locate a sufficient number of new employees to support the additional sales. Accordingly, the remainder of this section clusters measurements around benefit costs and recruiting success.

In the area of benefit costs, the key measurement is the trend of benefit costs per employee, broken out for each benefit. It is also useful to include the employee participation percentage in the same chart, along with the grand total cost of each benefit. By presenting this information in such a format, it becomes a simple matter to determine where costs are rising, whether or not employees care to use them, and the total cost impact of each one. The information should be updated on a rolling basis once a month in order to spot and correct sudden cost increases. An example of this chart is shown in Exhibit 12.6.

A key factor to consider when reviewing this chart is that total benefit costs may go up, but the fault does not lie with the management of costs by the human resources department—instead, the employee participation rate has increased, resulting in more costs. Consequently, it is important to compare the cost per person and participation percentages to determine the true reason for an overall benefit cost increase. Also, notice the jump in per person costs in medical expenses as the participation rate drops in the previous example. This is a common problem for the financial analyst to see, and is caused by an increase in per-person prices by the health insurance company because the company has dropped below a minimum number of participants. Thus, human resources costs can jump outside of expected ranges if the participation levels drop or increase beyond historical rates.

The 401k cost per person can be difficult to estimate for small groups, since there may be a few participants who will invest disproportionately small or large amounts, resulting in wide swings in the cost a company invests in matching programs. However, for larger groups of participants, these variations tend to average out, resulting in highly predictable expenses. Nonetheless, this cost is also subject to wide variation if management decides to alter the terms of the plan, such as automatically enrolling all new employees in it, unless they specifically request to be left out. In this case, the administration cost will increase, because there are more participants, and the matching cost will increase, because there are more people investing in the plan. Accordingly,

Exhibit 12.6 Trend Line of Benefit Costs and Participation Rates

Benefit Type	Month 1	Month 2	Month 3	Month 4	Month 5	Month 6
Medical cost each	$300	$300	$300	$300	$300	$325
Participation	99%	95%	93%	92%	91%	90%
Total medical cost	$59,400	$55,575	$53,010	$51,060	$49,140	$51,188
Dental cost each	$20	$20	$20	$20	$20	$20
Participation	80%	83%	85%	88%	91%	92%
Total dental cost	$4,000	$3,237	$3,230	$3,256	$3,276	$3,220
Life insurance cost each	$10	$10	$10	$10	$10	$10
Participation	10%	9%	14%	18%	21%	22%
Total life insurance cost	$200	$176	$266	$333	$378	$385
401k cost each	$42	$43	$47	$49	$50	$55
Participation	32%	33%	38%	42%	51%	53%
Total 401k cost each	$2,688	$2,767	$3,393	$3,807	$4,590	$5,101
Total No. Employees	**200**	**195**	**190**	**185**	**180**	**175**

any large change in investment costs should lead an analyst to suspect that there has been some change in the plan rules that has caused the variation.

A company's success in its recruiting efforts is of paramount importance to those companies that are on a steep growth path, because they are in dire need of large staff increases to help support their growth. If these recruiting needs are not met, a company can find itself pursuing a much slower growth curve than would normally be the case, which has a major impact on profitability. Accordingly, a financial analyst in such a company should always spend considerable time reviewing the success of the human resources department in attracting new talent. The four key analyses are:

- *Employee turnover.* The human resources department has a direct impact on the percentage of employees who leave a company each year, because it controls the benefits. If the benefit levels are poor, the turnover rate will be higher than would normally be the case. The turnover calculation is:

$$\frac{\text{Number of employees leaving the company in a month}}{(\text{Employee head count at start of month} + \text{Head count at end of month}) / 2}$$

- *Recruiting cost by method.* The recruiting cost per hired employee can be very excessive if the wrong methods are used, such as exclusive reliance on recruiting firms, who typically charge 30 percent of each recruit's first-year pay as their fee. A broader mix of recruiting methods, such as referral bonuses, Web sites, newspaper ads, and trade journal ads, will result in a lower total recruiting cost. If there are many new employees being added, this can be an annual difference in recruiting costs of millions of dollars. An important issue here is that a human resources department may be forced into more expensive recruiting methods as the local pool of talent dries up, possibly due to competition from other firms, a lack of local colleges, or the high growth rate of the company. Thus, the recruiting cost may, to some extent, be beyond the control of the company. This calculation is:

$$\frac{\text{Number of employees hired}}{\text{Cost by recruiting method}}$$

Note: This calculation is designed to yield a recruiting cost per person, which can then be tracked on the table in Exhibit 12.7 to determine changes in costs by recruiting method over time.

- *Recruiting success by method.* Some recruiting methods may work better than others, depending on the geographic region or the type of person being recruited. For example, Web site advertisements will not work well if a company is hiring manual laborers, because these people are highly unlikely to own computers for browsing the Web. Accordingly, it is necessary to trace the success of each recruiting method to

Exhibit 12.7   Historical Tracking of Recruiting Costs by Method per Person Hired

Method	Month 1	Month 2	Month 3	Month 4
Search firms	$25,000	$27,000	$31,000	$28,500
Newspapers	1,000	1,000	1,250	1,500
Trade journals	3,000	3,000	3,000	3,000
Employee bonuses	1,500	3,000	5,000	4,000
Web site	0	0	0	0

determine where the human resources staff should focus its efforts. A formula for this measure is:

$$\frac{\text{Number of people accepting offers based on each recruiting method}}{\substack{\text{Number of people initially contacted by the company} \\ \text{based on each recruiting method}}}$$

Note: It is best to use this measure for no less than quarterly time periods, since the recruiting period needed to hire anyone can easily take this long. A shorter time period might not accurately reflect the number of people actually hired.

- *Training cost per hour.* Even if a sufficient number of employees are brought into a company, they may not be effective if they are not sufficiently trained for assigned tasks, resulting in low levels of efficiency and high employee turnover rates, which will still result in lower-than-expected sales. This is a particular problem for high-growth companies in the retail industry, in which the majority of incoming recruits are severely undertrained. Alternatively, this is not a relevant issue in the high-tech industry, where all recruits are expected to be fully trained prior to hiring. The training cost per hour calculation is:

$$\frac{\text{Total training cost related to employees hired within past 90 days}}{\text{Number of hours of training devoted to employees hired within past 90 days}}$$

Note: The total training cost may require an allocation of training overhead charges to the training devoted to new employees. If so, add overhead costs based on the proportion of training hours for new employees to the total amount of training hours offered by the company during the period.

ANALYSIS OF LOGISTICS

Despite a recent emphasis on improving a company's supply chain, the entire logistics area appears to be cloaked in mystery, at least from the perspective of senior managers, who have typically ascended to their positions from other parts of the company. This is unfortunate, for opportunities in this area to improve profits and (especially) reduce the amount of working capital needed to manufacture, store, and distribute products can be greatly enhanced. This section covers the key measurements that a controller should use to determine if there are opportunities for improvement in this area, as well as to monitor the existing situation to ensure that there is no backsliding in any key performance areas.

The first measurement against which any logistics manager is measured is the turnover of all types of inventory. At its simplest, this is the number of times that inventory is "used up" in proportion to the total cost of goods sold for the entire year. An appropriate turnover ratio can vary widely by industry, ranging from just a few turns in the replacement parts retail industry, where companies compete by having every possible replacement part on hand, to 70 or more turns at the most highly competent of the automobile manufacturers. A discerning controller will take the initial inventory turnover figure and break it down by type of inventory, such as raw materials, work-in-process (WIP), or finished goods, and track the ratio on a trend line to determine in which of these categories problems are arising. A decline in turns calls for an immediate review of the usage patterns of individual stock items within the offending inventory category, which management can then use to either return stock to suppliers (in the case of raw materials), sell to customers (if a finished good is the root problem), or complete WIP assembly to create a salable finished product. This concept is also quite useful when extended to the analysis of all company storage and distribution points; any outlying warehouse that shows a poor inventory turnover figure is ripe for consolidation with some other warehouse, in order to eliminate working capital that is currently invested in the inventory in the warehouse. Given the large number of uses for the inventory turnover measure, it is no wonder that this is the primary tool used to reflect on the performance of the entire logistics function. Two variations on the inventory turnover calculation are:

$$\frac{\text{Annualized cost of goods sold}}{\text{(including all direct labor, materials, and overhead costs)}}$$
$$\text{Total ending inventory}$$

Note: A variation on this measurement is the days of inventory currently on hand, which some managers find more understandable than the turnover figure. The calculation for days of inventory on hand is:

$$[(\text{Total ending inventory}) \, / \, (\text{Annualized cost of goods sold})] \times 365$$

Another measure that is a fine indicator of logistics performance is the accuracy of inventory records. A highly accurate inventory database is of great use to a manufacturing operation in particular, because the production process will operate most smoothly if all parts needed for production runs are stored in the proper locations in the warehouse, and are in the correct quantities in those locations. Without this high degree of record accuracy, the production operation will be halted repeatedly due to stock shortages. This will have a major impact on company production volumes, which can reduce profits by a significant amount. Because of the severe impact of this problem on downstream operations, the accuracy of inventory is accorded nearly as high a level of attention as the inventory turnover measure that was just covered. The inventory accuracy measure is:

$$\frac{\text{Number of inaccurate inventory records counted}}{\text{Total number of inventory records counted}}$$

Note: An inaccurate inventory record is defined as one includes either an inaccurate product description, bin location, or quantity.

Any accuracy level less than 95 percent is unacceptable, since it results in an excessive degree of production stoppages. Truly world class operations strive for accuracy levels that exceed 99 percent.

Inventory obsolescence is a very important way to measure the logistics department, because it verifies the ability of the logistics staff to keep track of the usage levels of inventory, and to eliminate from stock those items that are no longer needed. This can be a very difficult task, for it involves ordering only those parts that are needed for current production levels, which keeps excess parts from being stored in stock. It also requires an excellent inventory tracking system, so that existing parts are not "lost" in the warehouse. Furthermore, it requires close attention to the turnover levels of every part located in the warehouse, so that constant attention is paid to those items that are no longer being used. Since all of these activities require a great deal of continual attention, it is no surprise that few logistics departments do a good job of keeping obsolete inventory to a minimum. Sometimes, the fault for this does not lie with the logistics manager, however; the engineering staff also has some responsibility. Whenever the engineers decide to change a product component in the production process, they should first use up all existing parts in the warehouse before switching to the new part. Otherwise, the old part will never be used. However, when this switchover is initiated due to the old part's being faulty, it is acceptable to leave the remaining quantity in the warehouse, at which point the logistics staff should scrap the part. The measure for inventory obsolescence is:

$$\frac{\text{Dollar value of all inventory that has not been used in xxxx days}}{\text{Dollar value of entire inventory}}$$

Note: The number of days during which there has been no usage is the defining factor for this measure, and will vary greatly by industry. In the case of personal computers, obsolescence may be defined as no usage in just one month, whereas a seasonally oriented industry may find that parts left on the shelf from the previous year can still be used for the following year's production.

Another key factor for the logistics staff to research is the cost of any internal transportation equipment, as opposed to the same cost that the company could have obtained if all shipments had been made by a third party. This measure is applicable only if a company has its own fleet of trucks, barges, ships, or railroads. If the internal transport structure is a large and diversified one, as can be the case for large companies with far-flung subsidiaries, the comparison calculation can be an exceedingly difficult one. However, it may be well worth the effort, because a poorly utilized transport fleet may represent a significant investment in capital that is not yielding a perceptible return on investment. The comparison needed is to review all shipments made by the company, not only to suppliers and customers, but also between company locations, and research a significant sample of these items to determine what the freight cost would have been if a third party had charged for the service. It is important to determine the correct shipping volumes that would have been used with each freight carrier, because this can result in significant volume discounts. One must also determine if outside carriers can ship to some locations, or if higher-priced local transport must be used to reach outlying locations. Further, an internal freight transport system can be used at any time of the day or night to make rush or unscheduled deliveries; when making the comparison, it is necessary to factor in the rush freight costs that were formerly hidden by using the internal system. Once these costs have been compiled, one can accumulate a number of offsetting savings, including:

- *Eliminated depreciation expenses.* This can be from any number of types of transportation equipment that are part of the company fleet.

- *Eliminated fuel costs.* No matter what the type of transport, fuel is a major cost that will now be shifted to the transport suppliers.

- *Eliminated staff positions.* The cost of the wages, salaries, and associated benefits for all fleet drivers and associated support staff represent a sizeable expense that can be completely eliminated, except for the cost of any transport scheduling personnel who must still be used to monitor the activities of third-party carriers.

- *Incidental taxes.* There are significant fees charged at various government levels for road usage, usually through vehicle licensing. There are also onerous and complicated record-keeping tasks required to ensure that all company drivers are certified and have complete trip records. All of these expenses can be eliminated, along with the fleet.

- *Insurance and claims costs.* All types of transport carry with them large fees to insure not only the equipment but all contents carried. These fees can be shifted to third parties.

- *Interest on invested capital.* This is the interest that can be earned if the fleet is liquidated and the proceeds invested. Be sure to use the company's existing investment guidelines, so that only the returns from realistic investments are included in the assumed earnings.

- *Replacement cost of equipment.* When considering whether to eliminate transportation equipment, it is not sufficient to assume that equipment will be replaced at the same price as the old equipment. Instead, one must examine current market prices, which may diverge significantly from the old price levels.

In short, a large number of expenses can be stopped by switching to third-party carriers. The key factor that usually creates the greatest influence over the decision to switch to or from third-party carriers is the utilization level of the in-house transportation equipment. If it is low, the cost of all the equipment is spread over a relatively small number of shipments, which results in a high per-shipment cost. Alternatively, a high level of utilization allows a company to achieve extremely low shipment costs by keeping its transportation function internal. In short, equipment utilization is the key to an analysis of a company's internal transportation costs.

If the analysis shows that a company should keep its existing internal transportation system, then another set of measurements come into play. One of the best is a trend line of maintenance costs by machine. By tracking the costs required to maintain each element of the transportation system, it becomes quite obvious when something requires replacement, because its maintenance costs begin to increase dramatically. It is also useful to cluster together the maintenance trend lines of all similar pieces of equipment by age, because the graph will show which items of equipment are costing more to maintain than other, similar pieces of equipment. It may also be useful to note the age of the equipment and the manufacturer's recommended replacement date alongside the trend lines, so that one can quickly scan the information provided and obtain a sufficient degree of information at a glance to determine which equipment must be replaced. An example of such a chart is shown in Exhibit 12.8, in which the maintenance costs of three tractors are listed.

Exhibit 12.8   Trend Line of Equipment Maintenance Costs

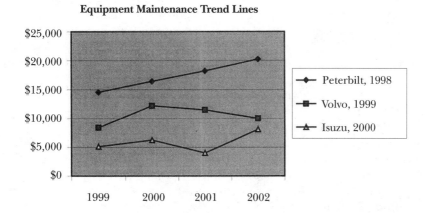

Even if a company's transportation systems have already been closely compared to those of outside services, there still remains the issue of what the correct cost should be for each of a company's most commonly used transportation routes. Though many analysts will calculate a company's average freight cost per shipment, this is at an excessively macro level to give management an idea of what it can do to further reduce freight costs. For example, there may have been an exhaustive analysis of whether to outsource the entire transportation function, yet no one has any idea if the cost to transport goods to a specific point can be improved. The best way to analyze this issue is to first compile all transport charges to and from the company, along with the points to which goods are being shipped from the company, and the points from which they are being sent to the company. These should also include all transportation charges for which the company is being compensated, such as freight charges that are billed to customers (the reason being that the company presumably charges its customers a flat fee for freight, so any reduction in its own freight costs will still have an impact on overall profitability). Once the list is compiled, summarize it by transportation segment to determine the set of segments with the greatest total freight cost. Then, divide the total cost for each segment for the time period being reviewed by the total number of shipments to determine the average cost per shipment. It is then possible to conduct an analysis, using standard freight rates for each available freight company, to determine if there is a less expensive freight rate available for the most frequently used transportation segments. Since most companies ship to a multitude of locations, it is very important to concentrate the analysis effort on only the most commonly used transport segments, so that the cost of the analysis work will be more than compensated by the savings that will be gleaned by lowering costs on the largest possible number of shipments.

Another aspect of the logistics function is purchasing. In this key area, there are several measurements that an analyst should regularly compile and review. One is the number of purchase orders that the average purchasing agent handles. This is an important way to determine the efficiency of the purchasing staff, because a small number of purchase orders per person is probably linked to cumbersome purchasing procedures (common enough in this paperwork-intensive department), such as obtaining multiple supplier quotes for even the least expensive items, not allowing employees to purchase minor office supplies, or using an excessive number of suppliers. This last item is an excellent one to track, especially since companies are trending in the direction of reducing their supplier bases to focus on more integrated supply chain management. Rather than just compiling the total number of current suppliers, it is even better to present this information to management on a trend line, so it can see if a continuing reduction is occurring. Still better, one can break down this information by type of commodity purchased, to see if individual purchasing agents are doing an adequate job of concentrating their purchases with the smallest possible number of suppliers.

A final measure for tracking the performance of the purchasing staff is the proportion of suppliers who offer early payment discounts. It is the

responsibility of the purchasing staff to negotiate the best possible early payment discount terms from the suppliers from whom they purchase. To be
most effective, the measure should include only those discount deals that
exceed a company's cost of capital. Any lower discount deals are not usable
and do not reflect an adequate degree of negotiation by the purchasing staff.
However, some excellent suppliers will not allow discounts under any circumstances, or prefer to give overall price reductions instead of discounts. In
these cases, the purchasing staff should not be penalized for failing to obtain
a discount percentage, as long as the overall purchasing deal is a good one.

   The logistics function encompasses a broad range of activities and
requires a large number of measures to track all possible activities. This section has covered a number of the most important ones involving inventory,
transportation services, and purchasing. Others may be appropriate in special situations, but the measures described here are needed in the majority of
situations. For the controller who is attempting to discern profitability or
operational issues in this area, the measurements described here are an excellent starting point and will serve as the foundation for any additional analysis.

ANALYSIS OF PRODUCTION

In a traditional production environment, the controller usually calculates a
few overhead variances that include some production costs, compares other
production costs to budget, and stops any further analysis. Given that the production department is usually the largest part of the company, both in terms
of head count and overall expenditures, it seems that a bit more analysis may
be in order to obtain a better grasp of the problems that can arise in this area.
This section covers additional measures, such as scrap, capital costs, maintenance expenses, employee turnover rates, and more. Not all of these measures are necessary in all situations; however, a controller should sort through
the ones presented here and select those that are most relevant to individual
situations.

   A measurement that should be used with some care is the scrap percentage. The blame for scrap rates is usually placed squarely on the production
staff, even though there may be other perpetrators outside that department.
For example, the engineering staff may have designed a product that is difficult to assemble, resulting in broken parts. Also, the industrial engineering
staff may have designed a production process that makes it easy to accidentally
break a part. Further, the purchasing staff may have purchased raw materials
that are inadequate for the stresses applied to those parts during the manufacturing process, resulting in breakage when being produced. Clearly, there
are many departments that can be responsible for the scrap that arises during
the production phase. As long as one is diligent in investigating the true reasons for scrap and laying the problems at the doors of the correct departments
for corrective action, measuring scrap can be a very useful analysis to undertake. The measurement for it is:

$$\frac{(\text{Scrap units reported by production workstation}) \times (\text{Standard cost of each part reported})}{\text{Total production quantity for the period}}$$

Note: It is more accurate to use the total production quantity in the denominator, rather than the cost of goods sold, since the cost of goods sold during the period may not accurately reflect the actual volume of production.

Note that the measurement itemizes specific scrap as reported by each manufacturing workstation; the reported quantity should also include a description of what caused the scrap, so that remedial action can be taken as soon as possible. If there is no record of where or why the scrap occurred, then the scrap measurement is only a means for recording the total scrap expense and cannot be used to fix the underlying problem, because there is no way to identify it.

If a manufacturing facility is operating at or near full capacity, it becomes very important to ensure that all machinery is operating at all times. A well-run facility will have a team of maintenance technicians who operate on a preventive maintenance schedule to take a small number of machines out of service on a regularly scheduled basis for preventive repairs that will keep that equipment from going down when least expected (or wanted). A poorly run facility will have no such preventive maintenance schedule, however, resulting in the periodic halt of production work due to broken machinery. In such a situation, a controller is well advised to measure the amount of unscheduled machine downtime. By regularly presenting this information to management, one can convey the fact that the company is losing significant sales volume due to the lack of preventive maintenance. However, this measure is useful only when a facility is operating at or near full capacity, since unscheduled machine downtime has no impact on sales volume if there are many idle machines that can readily take over the work. The calculation is:

$$\frac{(\text{Number of machines down}) \times (\text{Average down time per machine})}{(\text{Total number of machines}) \times (\text{Maximum run time per machine})}$$

Note: The maximum run time per machine is based on the number of shifts that the facility runs. For example, if there are two shifts, a machine can theoretically run for 16 hours. However, some facilities run certain machinery only during one shift (frequently because of the lack of skilled operators), so the maximum run time for this machinery is less than for other equipment that is run for additional shifts.

Some production facilities are located in areas where the facility rental cost per square foot is quite high. In these cases, there can be significant advantages to shrinking the amount of square footage used by the production facility in order to save on rental costs. However, a controller should consider several additional factors before spending time generating this measurement. One is that the company may be locked into a long-term rental agreement that does not allow for subleasing any space, so the company will be stuck with the full facility, no matter how expensive it may be. Another problem is that, even if there are possible sublessees available, any reduced configuration of the plant will require extensive construction, such as wall partitions and air conditioning, to fit them in; accordingly, the savings from reducing rental payments will be more than offset by the cost of setting up a new tenant. Further, a facility that has very large machines in place will require very high expenditures to shift into a smaller space, and the rental savings from doing so may not counterbalance the cost of moving the equipment. This measure is most useful when the existing building lease is close to running out, if the space is easily partitioned for subleasing purposes, and if a reconfiguration would be relatively inexpensive. The most simple measurement is to calculate the number of square feet devoted to production, and use this as the basis for an argument to reconfigure the facility to shrink the used space. A better measure is to bring in an industrial engineer who can draw up a reconfiguration plan that clearly shows the amount of square footage that can be saved. With this extra information in hand, it is much easier to present a convincing argument to the management team to make changes.

Preventive maintenance may not be enough to ensure that a company's equipment stays on line at all times. Some of the machinery may be so old that no amount of maintenance will keep it operational at the high levels needed by a facility that is operating at or near its maximum capacity levels. Other machinery may not be of high quality to begin with, resulting in similar problems. No matter what the case, if a controller spots an increasing trend of machine maintenance costs, it may be a good idea to track those costs by machine, to see which equipment is responsible for the costs. When this information is reported to management, a common response is to stop using the offending equipment to the greatest extent possible (unless it is bottleneck equipment, in which case there is no way to *avoid* using it). When this happens, maintenance costs will drop, but so will the utilization of the equipment that is causing the trouble. If the equipment that is in poor condition is ever used again, maintenance costs will surely increase when that happens. The best way to track this problem is to compare the maintenance cost of each machine to the number of hours it is in operation during a specified time period. The comparison will then yield the maintenance cost per hour of operation, which can then be tracked on a trend line to determine if the situation is worsening. This measure is:

$$\frac{\text{Total period maintenance cost for the period}}{\text{Total hours of machine utilization for the period}}$$

Note: Maintenance costs tend to lag hours of machine usage, because repairs will be conducted after the machine breaks down, and the expense may not be recorded for several days after that, so it is best to aggregate this information into at least monthly, and preferably quarterly, time blocks.

Some companies rely on product pricing that requires production to be completed at or near 100 percent of the originally estimated efficiency levels.

If those levels are not reached, profit levels will be severely affected by the extra labor costs required to complete production. A major determining factor in the achievement of targeted production efficiency levels is the retention of the production workforce, on the grounds that more experienced personnel will complete work more rapidly. Thus, tracking the turnover of the production workforce becomes critical to overall company profitability. This is particularly important in industries in which profit margins are thin to begin with and largely unskilled labor is used in the production process, usually for the assembly of relatively simple products. The calculation is:.

$$\frac{\text{Number of production employees who left during the reporting period}}{\text{(Beginning staff head count)} + \text{(Ending staff head count)} / 2}$$

A production process that operates perfectly requires very little WIP inventory, because unfinished products flow smoothly from machine to machine; there is no bunching up of products in front of bottleneck operations, scrapped products lying about in piles, or overproduction of parts that cannot be used. Unfortunately, the perfect production operation is a rare find. In reality, most production facilities contain a considerable amount of WIP inventory. This represents a significant investment of funds, which cuts into the amount of cash or available debt that a company can use for other purposes. Accordingly, a controller should review the amount of WIP inventory as part of the standard monthly review package. However, it is not sufficient to just report on the total amount of this inventory, because it will fluctuate with the overall level of production activity. A better approach is to report on a ratio of the amount of WIP inventory as a proportion of the total production volume for the period. Do not use the volume of goods sold for the period as the denominator in this ratio, because the amount sold may vary significantly from the amount produced, which is the more accurate activity measure. The formula is:

$$\frac{\text{(Beginning WIP inventory)} + \text{(Ending WIP inventory)} / 2}{\text{Total dollar volume of production during the period}}$$

The production operation can soak up an excessive amount of cash not only through the use of too much WIP, but also by spending an excessive amount on capital investments. This is a particular concern for those companies that rely on automation to reduce the amount of direct labor, or for operations that purchase very large equipment, such as printing presses, to complete their products. There are a number of ways to determine if the capital investment is too high. One is to conduct a trade-off analysis between the additional cost of the capital items versus the savings from a reduction in direct labor costs (or other expected savings). Another approach is to prepare a ratio of capital costs to production volume and track this information over time on a trend line to see if there is a disproportionate increase in the amount of capital required to run the production operation. This ratio can also be benchmarked against other companies for reasonableness. Yet another approach is to track the utilization levels of each piece of major equipment to see if the level of usage justifies the capital cost. Finally, a detailed activity-based costing analysis of each machine will yield a cost per machine that can be used to compile the cost of products produced, both before and after the equipment was installed; this last approach reveals whether a company has achieved a lower product cost as a result of installing the equipment, or if the reverse has occurred. The controller of a company that has a significant asset base in the production facility will probably adopt a blend of several of these measures to determine what level of capital investment is correct.

Finally, it is necessary to review the effectiveness of the production department. This does not relate to the amount of scrap, employee turnover, inventory levels, or machinery maintenance levels, but rather the ability of the department to produce what it originally committed to produce. The original commitment is embodied by the production schedule, which lists the quantities and types of products to be created during the period. If the production department is capable of exactly matching the production schedule, irrespective of other problems, it is being very effective. If it does so at great cost, it is not producing in an efficient manner, though this problem is addressed by most of the other measures in this section. The calculation of production schedule fulfillment is:

$$\frac{\text{Number of production schedule line items completed on time}}{\substack{\text{Total number of production schedule line items} \\ \text{scheduled for completion in the period}}}$$

The production department is usually the largest part of most companies in the manufacturing sector, yet the controller frequently limits the review of this area to a few overhead application and volume variances. This section described a number of additional measures that are very useful for more precisely determining the true efficiency and effectiveness of this department.

ANALYSIS OF SALES

An efficiently operated sales department with top-notch sales personnel can have a large impact on overall company profitability. Alternatively, an inadequate sales staff or one without proper direction can have a disastrous impact on revenue volumes and product mix, leading to significant losses. Accordingly, there are several excellent measures one can use to determine the efficiency and effectiveness of this department. The only case in which there is no need to employ these measures is when a company has structured itself to avoid the need for a sales department, for example, when a company has a captive set of customers (e.g., a monopoly) or when sales are automated, such as through a Web portal. In most other cases, however, some or all of the measures described in this section should be used periodically.

One of the key areas to measure is the cost of the sales staff. One way to do so is to measure the proportion of sales staff compensation that fluctuates based on the sales volume they generate (e.g., commissions). Generally speaking, a high proportion of pay that is directly tied to sales will act as a spur to sales growth, but sometimes at the risk of alienating customers who are being excessively pressured by the sales staff. A low proportion of variable pay usually leads to the reverse results—less energetic pursuit of sales, but possibly with better customer service. The calculation for the proportion of variable sales pay is:

$$\frac{\text{Total commissions paid in the period}}{\text{Total sales salaries in the period}}$$

Note: This measure should be tracked over time periods of more than a month, because commissions paid in one month are usually based on sales in a previous period. The measure can also be skewed by quarterly or year-end bonuses.

Another key sales cost that is rarely tracked is the cost required to send a salesperson to a customer to make a sales call. When there is air travel involved, or an overnight stay, this can be a very high cost per sales visit. This is a particular problem for those companies that sell a customized product that may require numerous visits to the customer before the product specifications are complete. If the initial product margin is not that high, then adding the cost of the sales call may result in a negative margin. This calculation is:

$$\frac{(\text{Total gross margin by customer}) - (\text{Cost of sales calls to that customer})}{\text{Total sales to that customer}}$$

Note: This calculation should be made at the customer level, not by product for each customer, since it is difficult to apportion the cost of a sales call to individual products sold.

Beyond the cost of the sales department staff and its travel, one must also measure its sales performance. One of the most common such measures is the volume of sales per salesperson. This yields a rough idea of how many dollars are being sold by person, and is best tracked on a trend line to determine if there is a long-run problem with salesperson performance. However, this measure has several underlying problems. One is that the sales staff may be doing an excellent sales job but be bringing in less sales volume over time. This is caused by pricing reductions that the company institutes as its markets mature and competition increases. It is not the sales staff's fault, but the measure will make them look bad. Another problem with this measure is that a few poor performers can drag down the overall average. To avoid this problem, it is best to track the measure by salesperson and to sort the report so that the worst performers are clearly highlighted. This format allows one to quickly spot and replace those sales staff who are not meeting minimum sales criteria.

Sales by salesperson is the crudest measure of sales staff performance, because it does not give any evidence of the sales staff's contribution to overall profitability. A much better measure is to determine the standard gross margin for the products sold, and to divide this figure by the number of sales staff, resulting in a gross margin per salesperson. This measure shows if the sales staff is selling large quantities of those products with the best margins, which has a much more direct impact on profits than the volumes of sales dollars obtained. This measure can also be broken down by individual salesperson to see if some individuals are not meeting gross margin expectations. The calculation for this measure is:

$$\frac{\text{(Total revenue)} - \text{(Standard materials, direct labor, and overhead)} - \text{(Commissions)}}{\text{Total number of sales personnel}}$$

Note: This calculation should not include any manufacturing variances, because the sales staff should not be held responsible for them. Accordingly, standard costs are a better choice.

A significant sales measure that should be a major weapon in every controller's analysis arsenal is a trend line of margins by product group. This information is invaluable for determining changes in margin percentages (especially of the downward variety), which are the signposts for further decisions to either alter product pricing, go after more market share, or to enhance the product group's features in order to justify an increase in prices that will recapture lost margin. Consequently, this information should be produced for and distributed to the management team with great regularity. The measurement is:

$$\frac{\text{(Revenues for product group)} - \text{(Product costs)} - \text{(Related sales costs)}}{\text{Revenues for product group}}$$

Note: The margin for this calculation should not include allocated overhead costs that do not have a clearly identifiable and rational basis of being assigned as a cost. Otherwise, the margin will appear too low. Accordingly, this is a good situation in which to use activity-based costing to identify the correct overhead costs.

The other primary sales analysis that one should regularly track is the trend of sales dollars for each product group. Although the preceding calculation does an excellent job of revealing the margin trends of each product group, it yields no information about volumes—only margins. The two measures can be effectively combined into a single table that itemizes total margin dollars (as noted in Exhibit 12.9), with a subsidiary table that itemizes the gross sales dollars, margin percentages, and total margin dollars for each product grouping noted in the lead table (as shown in Exhibit 12.10). In these two figures, notice the decrease in margins on road bikes over time, which is explained in the detailed analysis, which reveals that the margin drop is caused by a reduced margin percentage, despite continuing growth in the overall revenues of the product line. This is a good example of why one

Exhibit 12.9   Summary Review of Margins by Product Group

Product Group	Month 1	Month 2	Month 3	Month 4	Month 5	Month 6
Road bikes	$12,500	$12,400	$12,300	$12,200	$12,100	$12,000
Mountain bikes	10,000	10,500	10,600	10,700	11,500	12,000
Bike accessories	2,500	3,000	2,500	3,000	3,500	2,750
Unicycles	1,000	1,250	1,500	1,750	2,100	1,550
Totals	$26,000	$27,150	$26,900	$27,650	$29,200	$28,300

should not focus solely on gross revenue dollars—the underlying margins are more important.

A lesser issue involves the retention of customers. There are many reasons why a customer leaves, such as excessively high pricing, poor customer service, or a reduced need for the company's products. Given the number of influencing factors, it is not entirely the fault of the sales staff if a customer does not continue to place orders. Nonetheless, there are special cases, such as the credit card business, in which a customer will call the company to discontinue service. If the customer is routed to a salesperson who can convince the customer not to discontinue service, there is a chance that persuasion will lead to continued retention of that customer. If a company finds itself in one of these special cases, it may be useful to track the percentage of customers retained following their initial notice to the company to stop service. If this percentage can be improved, there is a direct relationship between it and increased sales volume that is brought about entirely by the efforts of the sales staff. Thus, in the few situations in which a company has the opportunity to present a case to departing customers, the retention of those customers can be a useful measurement to calculate.

This section has dwelt most persistently on the need to verify and track the margins on sales. This is a much more effective way to review the performance of the sales department, rather than spending needless time on gross sales dollars, because a company will make no money if there is no margin associated with sales, no matter how large those sales may be. Do not be diverted from the main issue here—the sales department must be rated on the total margins it delivers to a company, *not* the gross revenue dollars.

Exhibit 12.10   Detailed Review of Margins by Product Group

Road Bike	Month 1	Month 2	Month 3	Month 4	Month 5	Month 6
Gross sales	$25,000	$25,306	$25,625	$25,957	$26,304	$26,667
Margin (%)	50	49	48	47	46	45
Total margin	$12,500	$12,400	$12,300	$12,200	$12,100	$12,000

ANALYSIS OF OUTSOURCING

There is a growing trend toward outsourcing more corporate functions. This may involve handing over an entire function to another company or just a few tasks. The reason for doing so may be that a company wants to concentrate its efforts on a small number of core competencies, the outsourced cost is less than the internal cost, or perhaps the supplier has better management. Whatever the reason, the controller must treat these suppliers as an extension of the company, because they are providing a service at a specified cost, much as an internal department would. This means that they must be regularly measured to ensure that they are performing up to standard, and that their costs are in line with expectations.

In all cases, the measurements will be the same as those used if the work had been done internally. For example, there will still be concerns in the engineering area about completing projects on time, in accounting if the payroll is not completed on the correct dates, or in logistics if the freight cost per order is excessive. The format of the measurements does not change. However, the manner in which the measures are taken will alter somewhat. One variation is that most activities with an outsourcer are controlled by the legal agreement with the two entities, so that any information provided to the controller must be listed as part of the supplier's set of services; in short, the measurements to be used must be part of the initial outsourcing agreement. Another issue is that the controller can no longer just walk down the hall and measure a function, since it may now be located at the supplier's facility. Instead, there may need to be a relationship with a contact person at the supplier, who does the measurements on behalf of the controller. Further, the emphasis on any cost-related measures will be a comparison of expected costs, as defined in the outsourcing agreement, with actual costs. By doing so, the controller is verifying that the supplier is billing the company for only those services it agreed to bill for, and that the billing rates are in line with the agreement. Any variations from these figures could result in a large change in company expenses, which would give rise to a management investigation of the supplier's billing practices. A controller must be mindful of these changes when measuring the performance of an outsourcing supplier.

REPORTING RESULTS TO TARGET DEPARTMENTS

At least a few of the measurements noted in this chapter will result in unfavorable results for every department in a company—no department is run perfectly, so there is always some measure that will cast it in a bad light. When bad news is revealed through financial analysis, there can be a violent reaction on the part of department heads, and it is usually targeted at the bearer of the bad news—the controller. The measures may be entirely justified and the results highly accurate, but any controller who wants to maintain a reasonable degree of peace with other department heads must find a humane way to reveal the results of these measures to them.

The worst possible way to unveil new measures is to quietly assemble them and abruptly thrust the lot at the entire corporate hierarchy at once. By doing so, a controller has blindsided the very people whom he or she must later work with on other projects; needless to say, these people will be less than enthusiastic about helping someone in the future who most certainly has not done anything to help them (especially if the measurements went to *their* bosses before they had a chance to see the measures first!). At a minimum, a controller who follows this approach will rapidly discover the meaning of the term *corporate pariah*, because no one will be willing to even communicate about anything more than the most basic daily civilities.

The best way to deal with this situation is to constantly remember that the purpose of any new measure is not to report on some new problem, but to *fix* that problem. This means that a controller should take a measurement issue straight to the department head who is most responsible for *improving* the results of that measure and quietly discuss how to fix the underlying problem. The department manager should be given a short period of time in which to validate the calculation of the measurement, as well as to fix the problem. Once these steps have been completed, a controller will have achieved a more humane approach to dealing with another department manager—the issue was dealt with quietly, and the affected person was given a chance to make changes before the issue was broadcast to the rest of the organization.

The only case in which this "kinder and gentler" approach will not work is in a company that is in dire financial difficulty. In this instance, a controller cannot afford to waste any time giving department managers extra time to quietly fix problems. Instead, top management must see all feasible measurements as soon as possible in order to make rapid decisions regarding how to prune expenses and make strategic changes that will save the company. In this case, bruising the egos of managers becomes secondary to overall corporate survival. However, even in this case, one should at least broadcast a message to all managers explaining in advance the reason for going over their heads with the results of measurements, so that they will understand the reason for doing so.

SUMMARY

This chapter dealt with the specific measurements needed to determine the performance of each key functional area of a company. With these measurement tools, one can rapidly determine the underlying problems that are impacting overall corporate profitability. Given the large number of measures in this chapter, it would be an overwhelming task to generate all of them every month; instead, one should carefully review each measure and decide if it applies to the unique circumstances of the company under analysis. Only if there are reasonable grounds for believing that a measure will result in the discovery of some significant departmental problem should it be used. By keeping the number of usable measures down to a minimum, a controller can still assemble a financial reporting package that reveals the innermost issues of each department, while doing so in a minimum amount of time.

13

Capacity Utilization Analysis

Although capacity analysis is a relatively simple review to perform, most controllers do not attempt it, perhaps because it lies so far from the more financial applications in which accounting personnel are traditionally trained. Nonetheless, a proper application of capacity utilization analysis will reveal an abundance of information that leads directly to not only better utilization of equipment and processes, but also capital cost savings and improved profits. Thus, although the beginning analysis may seem far away from the realms of financial analysis, the end result is squarely on the bottom line of the income statement.

RELATIONSHIP BETWEEN PROFITS AND CAPACITY UTILIZATION

Capacity utilization? Isn't that the province of the production scheduling crew, and what could that possibly have to do with the duties of a controller? This section reviews the reasons why paying proper attention to capacity utilization has a very direct impact on both profits and cash flow, both of which are primary responsibilities of the modern controller.

Capacity is made up of either human or machine resources. If those resources are not used to a sufficient degree, there are immediate grounds for eliminating them, either by a layoff (in the case of human capacity) or selling equipment (in the case of machines). In the first case, a layoff usually has a short-term loss associated with it, which covers severance costs, followed by an upturn in profits, since there is no longer a long-term obligation to pay salaries. In the second case, the sale of a machine does not have much of an impact on profits, unless there is a gain or loss on sale of the asset, but it will result in an improvement in cash flow as sale proceeds come in; these funds can be used for a variety of purposes to increase corporate value, such as reinvestment in new machines, a loan payoff, a buyback of equity, and so on. Consequently, a controller who keeps a close eye on capacity levels throughout a company, and who makes recommendations to keep capacity utilization close to current capacity levels, will have a significant impact on both profits and cash flows.

When making such analyses, the main issue to be aware of is that controllers tend to be conservative—they want to maximize the use of current capacity and get rid of everything not being used. This may not be a good thing when activity levels are projected to increase markedly in the near term. If management had followed a controller's recommendation to eliminate excess capacity just prior to a large increase in production volumes, it would require some exceptional scrambling, possibly at high cost, to bring the newly necessary capacity back in house. This would probably result in a major drop in management confidence in the controller, and correspondingly less attention paid to future recommendations of any kind. Consequently, a controller must work with the sales staff to determine future sales (and therefore production) trends before recommending any cuts in capacity.

Capacity utilization also reveals the specific spots in a production process in which work is being held up. These bottleneck operations prevent a production line from attaining its true potential amount of revenue production. A controller can use information about bottlenecks in two ways. One is to recommend improvements to bottleneck operations in order to increase the potential amount of revenue generation. The other is to point out that any capital improvements to other segments of a production operation are essentially a waste of money (from the perspective of increasing the flow of production), since all production is still going to create a logjam in front of the bottleneck operation. Of course, there may be other valid reasons for improving a nonbottleneck operation, such as using automation to eliminate direct labor costs, but at least any projects based on a proposed improvement in production flow through nonbottleneck operations could be canceled to save cash.

Another useful way for a controller to use capacity utilization information is in the determination of pricing levels. For example, if a company has a large amount of surplus excess capacity and does not intend to sell it off in the near term, it makes sense (and cents) to offer pricing deals on incremental sales that result in only small margins. This is because there is no other use for the equipment or production personnel. If low-margin jobs are not produced, the only alternative is no jobs at all, for which there is no margin at all. However, if a controller knows that a production facility is running at maximum capacity, it is time to be choosy on incremental sales, so that only those sales involving large margins are accepted. It may also be possible to stop taking orders for low-margin products in the future, thereby flushing low-margin products out of the current production mix, in favor of newer, higher-margin sales. Although a highly profitable approach, this can also irritate customers who are faced with "take it or leave it" answers by a company that refuses new orders unless higher prices are accepted by the customer. Consequently, incremental pricing for new sales is closely tied not only to how much production capacity a company has left, but also to its long-term strategy for how it wants to treat its customers.

A final area in which capacity analysis can be used to alter profit levels is in mergers and acquisitions. If an acquisition team is looking at buying another company, but can justify it only if there are significant synergies (a rare occurrence), then a hard look at the target company's capacity utilization may provide the needed profit increase. For example, if the target organization has a large amount of excess capacity, the acquiring company can assume that a large part of the excess equipment or production lines can be sold off, thereby garnering additional cash flow. Another approach is to purchase a company in order to make immediate use of its excess capacity. For example, if a company has acquired new customers but does not expect to have the capacity on hand to service those customers for a long time (perhaps delayed by a long backlog at an equipment manufacturer or tight local labor markets), it can buy a competitor solely on the grounds that it needs that company's capacity. This approach has the added benefit of allowing a company to closely review the product margins on sales by both companies, eliminate those customers yielding meager profit margins, and keep the remaining high-margin accounts from both organizations, along with a repositioning of the needed capacity to match the requirements of these most desireable customers. Yet another reason for using capacity as the focus of a merger or acquisition is that building the needed capacity from scratch may be more expensive than acquiring a company that already has not only the facilities but also the expertise to run them. For all of these reasons, capacity utilization analysis should be a key part of any merger or acquisition strategy.

This section has revealed that a controller should be deeply interested in capacity utilization analysis, because it affects gross margins, profits, and cash flows, and can even justify the purchase of or merger with another company. The following section reviews how this analysis can be used to track specific kinds of capacity.

USES FOR CAPACITY PLANNING

A company has a variety of activities that may be important enough to track their capacity utilization. The area most commonly measured is machine utilization, because management teams are always interested in keeping expensive machinery running for as long as possible, so that the invested cost is not put to waste. Thus, capacity tracking for *expensive assets* is certainly a common activity. However, another factor that many organizations miss is the capacity utilization measurement for any *bottleneck operation*. This has nothing to do with a costly asset, but rather with determining whether a key operation in a process is interfering with the successful processing of a transaction. For example, if a number of production lines feed their products to a single person who must box and ship them, and this person cannot keep up with the volume of production arriving at her work station, then she is a bottleneck operation that is interfering with the timely completion of the production schedule. Because she is a bottleneck, her capacity utilization should be tracked most carefully. This worker is not an expensive machine, and may in fact be paid very little, but she is potentially holding up the realization of a great deal of revenue that cannot be shipped to customers. Consequently, using a capacity utilization measure makes a great deal of sense in this situation.

To amplify on the concept of capacity planning for bottleneck operations, it is not sufficient to track the utilization of a single bottleneck operation, because the bottleneck will move to different steps in the production process as improvements are made to the system. For example, the key principle of the just-in-time concept is that management works to identify bottleneck operations and fix them. As a result, each specific bottleneck will be eliminated, but now the second most constrictive operation comes to the fore for review and improvement, which in turn will be followed by a third operation, and so on. Consequently, it is better to identify *every* work center and track the utilization of them all. By using this more comprehensive approach, management can spot upcoming bottleneck problems and address them before they become serious problems.

In the case of machinery, the tracking of utilization for virtually all of them is also useful, not just because they are also potential bottleneck operations, but because of the reverse problem—a machine that is *not* being used is a waste of invested capital, and should be sold off if possible. A detailed capacity utilization report will note those machines that are not being used, which tells management what can potentially be eliminated. This information is especially useful when machines are clustered on the report by type, so that a subtotal of capacity utilization is noted for each group of machines. If the machines within each cluster can be used interchangeably to complete similar work, management can then determine the total amount of work required of each cluster, and add or delete machines to meet that demand, which results in a very efficient use of capital. Exhibit 13.1 is an example of such a report, and we note how it can be used to make decisions regarding the number of machines that are really required in an operation.

In short, capacity utilization can be used to either track bottleneck operations or the usage of machinery, resulting in better information that management can use to either streamline a process flow or reallocate scarce capital among different types of machines.

CAPACITY BASELINE

A company frequently thinks of its production capacity only in terms of the current number of shifts being operated and tracks its capacity utilization accordingly. For example, a production facility that operates for one eight-hour shift and uses all machinery during that time appears operating at 100 percent capacity utilization. In fact, it is using only one third of the available hours in a day, which leaves lots of room for additional production. Accordingly, when developing a utilization measurement, one should always use the maximum amount of theoretical capacity as the baseline, rather than the

Exhibit 13.1 Capacity Utilization Report

Machine ID	Machine Description	Run Hrs	Run Hrs	5/9–5/15 Run Hrs	5/2–5/8 Run Hrs	Month of Apr. Run Hrs	Mar. Run Hrs	Feb. Run Hrs
B1100/BM04	Blow Mold			139	132	112	122	104
B2000/BM03	Blow Mold			137	152	114	154	119
		0%	0%	82%	85%	67%	82%	66%
01-25	25 Ton			126	132	138	125	111
02-90/TO11	90 Ton			152	137	117	132	144
03-90/TO10	90 Ton			164	129	126	111	120
04-90/TO09	90 Ton			94	138	142	167	147
16-55/AG01	55 Ton			163	59	125	109	102
		0%	0%	83%	71%	61%	62%	61%
05-150/TO08	150 Ton			147	162	133	139	133
06-150/TO07	150 Ton			137	152	122	124	127
07-198/TO06	198 Ton			133	77	114	132	54
08-200/TO05	200 Ton			124	141	117	101	113
17-190/TA05	190 Ton			127	116	97	106	91
		0%	0%	80%	77%	69%	72%	62%
09-300/TO04	300 Ton			168	133	148	125	148
10-300/TO03	300 Ton			79	143	135	142	129
11-330/TO02	330 Ton			129	136	93	125	100
20-390/TA04	390 Ton			121	158	128	136	154
21-375/CI06	375 Ton			102	84	78	77	102
26-400/TO01	400 Ton			124	116	101	78	120
		0%	0%	72%	76%	68%	68%	75%
12-500/CI05	500 Ton			166	137	113	62	50
14-500/CI04	500 Ton			100	96	107	142	96
18-450/VN02	450 Ton			163	164	103	111	119
24-500/VN01	500 Ton			167	163	161	96	106
25-500/TA03	500 Ton			145	162	146	128	89
		0%	0%	88%	86%	75%	64%	55%
13-700/CI03	700 Ton			146	142	106	78	60
15-700/VN03	700 Ton			107	152	133	118	118
19-720/TA02	720 Ton			115	161	115	58	113
22-700/CI01	700 Ton			74	154	74	76	144
23-950/TA01	950 Ton			126	159	110	91	112
		0%	0%	68%	91%	64%	50%	65%
		0%	0%	78%	80%	71%	66%	66%
		0%	0%	78%	81%	70%	67%	66%

amount of time during the day that is currently being used. For a single day, this means 24 hours, and for a week, it is 168 hours. On a monthly basis, the total number of hours will vary, because the number of days in a month can vary from 28 to 31. To get around this problem, it is easier to track capacity on a weekly basis, and use either four or five full weeks for individual months, depending on where the final month-end dates fall, so that all months of the year (except the last) on the capacity report show full-week results for either four or five weeks.

Some companies will reduce the amount of available capacity due to holiday shutdowns, such as for Thanksgiving or Christmas. Although these may be legal holidays, production capacity is still available during these periods, and can be used if a company can find any staff willing to work on those days. Consequently, though tradition says that these hours are not available, they can be if a company is willing to force staff to work them, and so they should still be included in the baseline capacity for all utilization measurements.

PRESENTING CAPACITY INFORMATION

Once the decision is made to create a capacity utilization analysis, what format should be used to present it? This section reviews a report used by an injection molding facility to determine individual, machine group, and total machine capacity usage.

Exhibit 13.1 lists the utilization hours of 28 plastic injection and blow molding machines. The identification number of each machine is listed down the left column, with the tonnage of each machine noted in the next column. The next cluster of five columns shows the weekly utilization in hours for each machine. The final three columns show the average weekly utilization by machine for the preceding three months. In addition, there are subtotals for all blow molding machines, and for five clusters of injection molding machines, grouped by tonnage size.

This report format allows management to look across the report from left to right and determine any trends in capacity utilization, while also being able to look down the page and determine usage by clusters of machines. This second factor is of extreme importance in the molding business, because each machine is very expensive and must be eliminated if it is not being used to a sufficient degree. For example, look at the tonnage range of 300 to 400 tons, located midway through the report. A cluster of six machines is consistently showing between 68 and 76 percent of usage. Is it possible to eliminate one machine, thereby spreading the work over fewer machines and raising the overall usage percentage for all the machines? To determine the answer using data for the highest utilization reporting period, which is for the first week of May, at 76 percent, add up all the reported hours of usage for that cluster of machines, which is 770, and divide the total number of hours that the machine cluster has available, assuming that one machine has been removed. The total number of hours available for production will be 168 (which is seven days multiplied by 24 hours per day) times five machines, which is 840. The result is a utilization of 92 percent for the maximum amount of work that has appeared in the last quarter of a year. Consequently, the answer is that it is theoretically possible to remove one machine from the 300- to 400-ton range of machines and still be able to complete all work.

However, when using a capacity report to arrive at such conclusions, there are several additional factors to consider. One is the reliability of the machines. If they have a history of failures, then a standard number of hours per operating period for repair work must be factored into the utilization formula, which will reduce the theoretical capacity of the machine. Another problem is that eliminating a machine is usually done in order to realize a cash inflow from sale of the machine—but what if the machines most likely to be sold will fetch only a minor amount in the marketplace? If so, it may make more sense to retain equipment, even if unused, so that it can take on additional work in the event of an increase in sales volume. Yet another issue is that there may be some difficulty in obtaining a sufficient number of staff to maintain or run a machine during all theoretical operating hours. For example, it is common for those organizations with a reduced number of maintenance personnel to cluster those staff on the day shift for maximum efficiency, which means that any machine failures during other hours will result in a shut-down machine until the maintenance staff arrives the next day. Finally, the preceding example shows management taking actual capacity utilization of its machinery to 92 percent. Is this wise if management has essentially removed all remaining available capacity by selling off the excess machine? What if an existing customer suddenly increases an order and finds that the company cannot accommodate the work because all machines are booked? Not only lost revenues will result, but maybe even a lost customer.

In short, a capacity utilization report similar to the one discussed in this section is of great use to most companies. However, management must use the information on this report with great care, being sure to factor in extra information, such as machine age, staff availability, and desired capacity levels, prior to altering the existing theoretical capacity by changing the number of machines or personnel. The additional information is needed to ensure that correct decisions are made to alter a company's productive power.

PROBLEMS WITH CAPACITY ANALYSIS

Although capacity reporting may seem straightforward enough, based on the last section, there are a few twists on the concept that can result in significant differences in the results of such an analysis.

One problem is that the capacity of a machine or bottleneck operation can vary significantly over time, which means that the reported level of capacity utilization can stay the same for a long time, even though the amount of production running through the process has been significantly altered, either up or down. For example, to continue to use the injection molding machines described earlier in Exhibit 13.1, suppose that such a machine produces one plastic part every 10 seconds, resulting in six completed parts per minute, which is 360 per hour and 8,640 per day. If the machine ran all day, every day, the capacity report would show that the machine was running at 100 percent of capacity, and that the maximum product it could produce was 8,640 per day. However, suppose that a clever engineer figures out how to improve the process, so that each product only takes nine seconds to produce. This translates into the ability to produce 9,600 units per day, which is an improvement of 11 percent, even though the reported capacity utilization remains the same. When this problem arises (though hardly a problem, since the amount of machine capacity has essentially risen!), one can alter the capacity calculation to include the price of the products produced, which not only accounts for the additional number of products produced, but also reveals the best mix of products that will result in the largest sales volume per time period of production. This approach can be taken one step further to report on the gross margin of the products produced per time period, which is the best way to determine the profitability of a production run on a specific machine. Unfortunately, there is not normally an easy way to connect product revenues and costs to units of production. For those companies with the computing resources, this may be worth a try, since it reveals the best combination of production and machinery that will result in the highest level of profit.

Another way in which a capacity analysis can be skewed is if there are either a large number of small jobs running through a process, each of which requires a small amount of down time to switch over to the new job, or else a small number of jobs that require a very lengthy changeover process. In either case, the amount of reported capacity will never reach 100 percent, because the required setup time will take up the amount of capacity that is supposedly available. One action that management can take to alleviate this problem is to work on reducing the changeover time needed to switch to a new job. This typically involves videotaping the changeover process and then reviewing the tape with the changeover team to identify and implement process alterations that will result in reduced setup times—in some cases, vastly reduced setup times. Reducing the changeover time for setups is an improvement that falls under the just-in-time theory of corporate improvement. (For a good review of the entire concept, read *The Just-in-Time Breakthrough* by Edward Hay [John Wiley & Sons, 1988]).

A revenue-related problem that arises when setup times eat up a large portion of total capacity is that the sales department may promise customers that work will begin very soon on their orders, because the capacity utilization report appears to reveal that there is lots of excess capacity. When it turns out that excessive changeover times do not leave any time for additional customer orders, it is possible that customers will take their business elsewhere, resulting in fewer sales and reduced margins. To counteract this problem, it is necessary to determine the amount of *practical capacity,* which is the total capacity, less the average amount of changeover time. If the setup reduction effort noted in the preceding paragraph is implemented, the practical capacity number will increase, because the time available for production will increase as changeover times go down. Consequently, a review of the practical capacity should be made fairly often, to ensure that the correct figure is used.

A problem with using practical capacity as the standard measure of how much work can still be loaded into the production system is that it is based on an average of actual capacity information over several weeks or months. However, if there are one or more jobs scheduled for a changeover that require inordinate amounts of time to complete, the reported practical capacity measure will not reflect reality. Similarly, if the actual changeover times are quite small, the true capacity will be higher than the reported practical capacity. Because practical capacity is a historical average, the actual capacity will be somewhat higher or lower than this average nearly all of the time. Although a company with lots of excess capacity might call this hair-splitting, a company that is running at maximum production levels may find itself blindsided by a lack of available time or some amount of unplanned downtime. In either case, there is a cost to having inaccurate capacity information. Those companies with well-maintained manufacturing resource planning (MRP II) software can avoid this problem by accurately scheduling jobs and changeover times, and updating the data as soon as changes are made.

SUMMARY

This section noted how capacity utilization analysis has a direct impact on both cash flow and profitability, which makes it a necessary tool for every controller. We then covered the two main applications to which capacity analysis is put—the utilization of expensive assets and the monitoring of bottleneck processes. If a controller wants to monitor either of these items, then continuing on through the remainder of the chapter, which covers the proper baseline for capacity calculations, report presentation, and problems with capacity calculations, is of the utmost importance.

PART FOUR

OTHER ANALYSIS TOPICS

14

Financial Analysis with an Electronic Spreadsheet

There are several tools a controller uses to conduct a financial analysis. One is certainly the database of accounting information, in which one can roam for days, tracking down the details regarding when specific transactions have taken place, why they occurred, and the likelihood of their happening again. However, a controller rarely descends straight into the depths of the accounting database without first using some more simple means for determining what problem has arisen, which yields clues regarding where in the database to search. This higher-level information is obtained by using ratio and trend analysis to pinpoint the issue. To get this information, a calculator, pencil, and paper are sufficient, but also very time consuming and prone to error. Instead, an electronic spreadsheet is the best method. This chapter reviews how to use such a spreadsheet—in this case, the Microsoft Excel spreadsheet, version 97.

The formulas presented in this chapter are by no means difficult. The discussion is confined to the simplest and most understandable spreadsheet commands and avoids the use of complicated macros. The discussion focuses on using spreadsheets for four types of analysis: financial statements, project analysis, investment analysis, and risk analysis. In each case, we note how Excel can be used to solve a problem, and then do so with a sample situation.

A key issue that is noted throughout this chapter is the difference between a spreadsheet and a worksheet. In Excel, a spreadsheet can have a number of interlinked layers known as worksheets. When an entry is made in one worksheet, it can be referenced by other worksheets in the same spreadsheet. This is a preferable approach to using Excel for financial analysis, because one can separate the data being analyzed in one worksheet, ratios in another, and graphics in yet another, but with formulas linking all of them together. In the examples used in the first few sections of this chapter, nearly all of the analysis is done on one spreadsheet that contains a half-dozen worksheets.

FINANCIAL STATEMENT PROPORTIONAL ANALYSIS

Proportional analysis is simply converting all of the numbers in an income statement and balance sheet into percentages, so that they can be compared over time to see what differences arise. By conducting this analysis, one can see if there are trends in revenues, costs, assets, or liabilities that may require further analysis or investigation.

When using Excel to conduct a proportional analysis of a financial statement, one must first input the income statement for each period into the worksheet, so that the proportional analysis calculation will appear below it or on a separate worksheet. In the example shown in Exhibit 14.1, a simplified income statement has been entered in the cells at the top of the worksheet. For each line item in this top section, there is a formula entered in the replicated income statement at the bottom of the screen that divides each expense line item by the revenue figure, resulting in a percentage of sales for each item. For example, the materials cost proportion for the month of January is calculated with the following formula, which is entered in cell B15:

$$= B5/B\$4$$

Because the spreadsheet contains the income statement for multiple months, the resulting proportional analysis becomes very useful for finding any trends in the expenses being incurred over the course of the year.

The income statement proportional analysis used in Exhibit 14.1 would be of great use to management in determining why its profits are not increasing along with its evident sales growth. In the example, sales increase from $1,200 in January to $1,400 in August, but profits drop by $9. Why? By perusing the proportional analysis, it is an easy matter to see that the cost of materials has *dropped* as a percentage of sales, which may reflect excellent purchasing, design, or production work to lower these costs. For the answer to why profits have dropped, one must look lower in the spreadsheet. The direct labor cost as a proportion of sales has risen, so this is an obvious target area for further analysis. However, the overall gross margin percentage has dropped by only 1 percent over the time period being analyzed, so there must be more trouble further down in the income statement. Sure enough, the administrative expenses line item reveals a 3 percent jump in costs. Accordingly, a controller using this analysis would conclude that the trouble has arisen in the direct labor and administrative areas, and that the materials expense requires no further analysis.

This type of analysis is an excellent way to hone in on key areas, but it is rarely the final analysis conducted, since it does not reveal enough information. Also, it is not sufficient if there are many operating divisions rolled into the income statement. In these cases, it is best to create a number of separate

Exhibit 14.1   Proportional Analysis of an Income Statement

	A	B	C	D	E	F	G	H	I
	X Microsoft Excel								
	File Edit View Insert Format Tools Data Window Help								
1	Proportional Income Statement Analysis								
2									
3	**Dollars**	Jan	Feb	Mar	Apr	May	Jun	Jul	Aug
4	Revenue	1,200	1,250	1,300	1,250	1,350	1,400	1,450	1,400
5	Materials Cost	550	575	595	565	605	610	635	620
6	Direct Labor Cost	120	120	145	140	150	160	170	180
7	Gross Margin	530	555	560	545	595	630	645	600
8	Administrative Expenses	280	290	340	335	330	350	360	365
9	Profit Before Taxes	250	265	220	210	265	280	285	235
10	Taxes	100	106	88	84	106	112	114	94
11	Net Profit	150	159	132	126	159	168	171	141
12									
13	**Proportions**								
14	Revenue	100%	100%	100%	100%	100%	100%	100%	100%
15	Materials Cost	46%	46%	46%	45%	45%	44%	44%	44%
16	Direct Labor Cost	10%	10%	11%	11%	11%	11%	12%	13%
17	Gross Margin	44%	44%	43%	44%	44%	45%	44%	43%
18	Administrative Expenses	23%	23%	26%	27%	24%	25%	25%	26%
19	Profit Before Taxes	21%	21%	17%	17%	20%	20%	20%	17%
20	Taxes	8%	8%	7%	7%	8%	8%	8%	7%
21	Net Profit	13%	13%	10%	10%	12%	12%	12%	10%
22									
23									
24									
	Sheet1 / Sheet2 / Sheet3 /								

spreadsheets, one for each division, and conduct the analysis on each one, thereby yielding a greater level of detail regarding problem areas.

The same proportional analysis can be applied to the balance sheet. As noted in the example in Exhibit 14.2, the controller can manually enter a simplified version of the balance sheet at the top of the spreadsheet, which produces a set of percentages at the bottom. The asset percentages sum to the grand total of all assets, while the percentages for liabilities and equity sum to the total for those two categories.

As was the case for the proportional analysis of the income statement, the cell formula is extremely simple. To use the example in Exhibit 14.2, the percentage for accounts payable in April is calculated by dividing the total accounts payable dollars, located in cell E10, by the total of all liabilities and equity for that month, which is located in cell E14.

What does the proportional analysis of the balance sheet tell us? To use the example, there is a clear increase in the fixed-asset investment, which requires the use of all cash, as well as an increased debt load, which reaches its height in May, after which cash flow from operations is used to gradually draw down the level of debt. The only other trend of note is that inventory levels are declining, which indicates either excellent logistics practices or a decline in sales that no longer requires such a large supporting base of inven-

Exhibit 14.2   Proportional Analysis of a Balance Sheet

	A	B	C	D	E	F	G	H	I
1	Proportional Balance Sheet Analysis								
3	**Dollars**	Jan	Feb	Mar	Apr	May	Jun	Jul	Aug
4	Cash	152	138	72	31	17	0	0	0
5	Accounts Receivable	375	400	410	415	425	435	442	440
6	Inventory	400	398	396	394	392	390	388	378
7	Fixed Assets	598	603	729	841	900	902	908	911
8	*Total Assets*	1,525	1,539	1,607	1,681	1,734	1,727	1,738	1,729
10	Accounts Payable	450	475	485	490	500	510	517	515
11	Accrued Liabilities	83	83	83	81	81	81	80	80
12	Debt	92	71	119	180	213	186	181	164
13	Equity	900	910	920	930	940	950	960	970
14	*Total Liabilities*	1,525	1,539	1,607	1,681	1,734	1,727	1,738	1,729
16	**Proportions**								
17	Cash	10%	9%	4%	2%	1%	0%	0%	0%
18	Accounts Receivable	25%	26%	26%	25%	25%	25%	25%	25%
19	Inventory	26%	26%	25%	23%	23%	23%	22%	22%
20	Fixed Assets	39%	39%	45%	50%	52%	52%	52%	53%
21	*Total Assets*	100%	100%	100%	100%	100%	100%	100%	100%
23	Accounts Payable	30%	31%	30%	29%	29%	30%	30%	30%
24	Accrued Liabilities	5%	5%	5%	5%	5%	5%	5%	5%
25	Debt	6%	5%	7%	11%	12%	11%	10%	9%
26	Equity	59%	59%	57%	55%	54%	55%	55%	56%
27	*Total Liabilities*	100%	100%	100%	100%	100%	100%	100%	100%

tory. Consequently, a great deal can be discerned by reviewing a proportional balance sheet analysis.

FINANCIAL STATEMENT RATIO ANALYSIS

Perhaps the most common use of an electronic spreadsheet is to conduct a ratio analysis of the income statement and balance sheets. Typically, a summary form of the income statement and balance sheet are located at the top of the worksheet, with ratios located at the bottom that are derived from these two reports. By using this approach, a controller can quickly enter the summary-level financial information for the current reporting period and then see the related ratios appear at the bottom of the worksheet. In a very few moments, the controller has access to a rough analysis of company operations. If there are entries for the financial results of previous months, then one can also see trend lines in ratio results that extend through to the current reporting period.

As an example of the types of ratio analysis one can use in a worksheet, we will use the income statement and balance sheet shown, in Exhibits 14.1 and 14.2. A series of ratios are noted in Exhibit 14.3 that are derived from those statements.

Exhibit 14.3   Ratio Analysis Based on an Income Statement and Balance Sheet

	A	B	C	D	E	F	G	H	I
1	Ratio Analysis								
2									
3		Jan	Feb	Mar	Apr	May	Jun	Jul	Aug
4	Balance Sheet Ratios:								
5	Quick Ratio	1.0	1.0	0.8	0.8	0.8	0.7	0.7	0.7
6	Current Ratio	1.7	1.7	1.5	1.5	1.4	1.4	1.4	1.4
7	Debt/Equity Ratio	0.1	0.1	0.1	0.2	0.2	0.2	0.2	0.2
8									
9									
10	Income Statement Ratios:								
11	Gross Margin	44%	44%	43%	44%	44%	45%	44%	43%
12	Return on Sales	13%	13%	10%	10%	12%	12%	12%	10%
13	Breakeven Point	$634	$653	$789	$768	$749	$778	$809	$852
14									
15									
16	Mixed Ratios:								
17	Fixed Asset Turnover	79%	81%	81%	74%	78%	81%	83%	81%
18	Inventory Turnover	20	21	22	21	23	24	25	25
19	Receivables Turnover	38	38	38	36	38	39	39	38
20	Return on Assets	10%	10%	8%	7%	9%	10%	10%	8%
21	Return on Equity	17%	17%	14%	14%	17%	18%	18%	15%
22									
23									
24									

Trend \ Ratios

In Exhibit 14.3, there are several tabs itemized at the bottom of the worksheet. Each one represents another spreadsheet that is clustered into the same workbook. The first tab, "IS," contains a spreadsheet version of the income statement. The second tab, "BS," contains a spreadsheet version of the balance sheet. The ratios shown in the exhibit are compiled by referencing the cell locations in these two spreadsheets and listing the result on the current "Ratios" spreadsheet. The formulas behind the ratios in Exhibit 14.3 are not shown, so the same spreadsheet is laid out differently in Exhibit 14.4 to provide this information. In this example, we have eliminated the formulas for all but the month of January and then listed each formula in full. For example, the first ratio is the Quick Ratio, which compares easily liquidated assets to current liabilities. To obtain this information, the cell entry goes to the BS spreadsheet and adds together cells B4 and B5, which contain the cash and accounts receivable figures for the month of January. The formula then divides the sum by the accounts payable and accrued liabilities amounts, which are located on the same spreadsheet in cells B10 and B11. Further down in the list of ratios are ones that are built on the income statement. For example, the Return on Sales percentage is derived by referencing the profit figure for January, which is located in cell B11 in the IS spreadsheet and dividing by total sales, which is located in cell B4 in the same spreadsheet. Finally, we can mix references to both the IS and BS spreadsheets in the same ratio formula. For example, to arrive at the return on equity, the formula takes

Exhibit 14.4   Formulas for Previous Ratio Analysis

	A	B	C	D	E	F
1	Ratio Analysis					
2						
3		Jan				
4	*Balance Sheet Ratios:*					
5	Quick Ratio	=(BS!B4+BS!B5)/(BS!B10+BS!B11)				
6	Current Ratio	=(BS!B4+BS!B5+BS!B6)/(BS!B10+BS!B11)				
7	Debt/Equity Ratio	=BS!B12/BS!B13				
8						
9						
10	*Income Statement Ratios:*					
11	Gross Margin	=IS!B7/IS!B4				
12	Return on Sales	=IS!B11/IS!B4				
13	Breakeven Point	=(IS!B8)/(IS!B7/IS!B4)				
14						
15						
16	*Mixed Ratios:*					
17	Fixed Asset Turnover	=(IS!B4*12)/BS!B8				
18	Inventory Turnover	=((IS!B5+IS!B6)*12)/BS!B6				
19	Receivables Turnover	=(IS!B4*12)/BS!B5				
20	Return on Assets	=(IS!B11*12)/BS!B8				
21	Return on Equity	=(IS!B11*12)/BS!B13				
22						
23						
24						

the profit for January, which is located in cell B11 in the IS spreadsheet, annualizes it by multiplying by 12, and divides it by the equity figure, which is located in cell B13 in the BS spreadsheet. Thus, we can mix cell references from a variety of spreadsheets in order to arrive at a centralized set of ratios that can be stored in a single spreadsheet location.

AUTOMATED RATIO RESULT ANALYSIS

If there are a great many ratios linked to a set of financial statements, a controller may want to save time in reviewing them by having the spreadsheet issue a warning message for those ratios that fall outside a preset parameter. Another reason for using this approach is a lending institution's placing constraints on a company by requiring minimum levels for certain ratios, such as a current ratio of at least 2:1, or a debt/equity ratio of no higher than 30 percent. In either case, a formula that presents a "YES/NO" or "GOOD/BAD" result can save some time.

A simple IF formula will create an automated ratio result. To continue with the example used previously in Exhibit 14.4, three rows will be added to the analysis. Under the "Balance Sheet Ratios" section, a row entitled "Meets Quick Ratio Covenant?" will be added. This is a "YES/NO" determination based on the quick ratio's being greater than .9, and will appear in row 8. The formula for the month of January will be:

$$IF(B5 > .9, \text{"Yes"}, \text{"No"})$$

Under the "Income Statement Ratios" section, a row entitled "Meets Gross Margin Covenant?" will be added. This is a "YES/NO" determination based on the gross margin's being greater than 43 percent, and will appear in row 14. The formula for the month of January will be:

$$IF(B11 > .43, \text{"Yes"}, \text{"No"})$$

Under the "Mixed Ratios" section, a row entitled "Meets Inventory Turnover Covenant?" will be added. This is a "YES/NO" determination based on the inventory turnover level being greater than 21, and will appear in row 22. The formula for the month of January will be:

$$IF(B18 > 21, \text{"Yes"}, \text{"No"})$$

All of these new formulations are shown in Exhibit 14.5. In the exhibit, one can quickly skim through the various months of results to determine the occa-

Exhibit 14.5   Automated Ratio Results Analysis

	A	B	C	D	E	F	G	H
1	Ratio Analysis							
2								
3		Jan	Feb	Mar	Apr	May	Jun	
4	Balance Sheet Ratios:							
5	Quick Ratio	1.0	1.0	0.8	0.8	0.8	0.7	
6	Current Ratio	1.7	1.7	1.5	1.5	1.4	1.4	
7	Debt/Equity Ratio	0.1	0.1	0.1	0.2	0.2	0.2	
8	Meets Quick Ratio Covenant?	Yes	Yes	No	No	No	No	
9								
10	Income Statement Ratios:							
11	Gross Margin	44%	44%	43.1%	44%	44%	45%	
12	Return on Sales	13%	13%	10%	10%	12%	12%	
13	Breakeven Point	$634	$653	$789	$768	$749	$778	
14	Meets Gross Margin Covenant?	Yes	Yes	Yes	Yes	Yes	Yes	
15								
16	Mixed Ratios:							
17	Fixed Asset Turnover	79%	81%	81%	74%	78%	81%	
18	Inventory Turnover	20	21	22	21	23	24	
19	Receivables Turnover	38	38	38	36	38	39	
20	Return on Assets	10%	10%	8%	7%	9%	10%	
21	Return on Equity	17%	17%	14%	14%	17%	18%	
22	Meets Inventory Turnover Covenant?	No	No	Yes	Yes	Yes	Yes	
23								
24								

sions when covenants have been violated. Setting up the IF statements that drive these automated ratio results are quite simple, and can help to some extent in the task of sorting through large quantities of ratios.

LEVERAGE ANALYSIS

An additional concept that can be added on to the preceding discussion of ratios is leverage analysis. There are several types of leverage analysis, all of which can be converted into formulas and added to a ratio analysis, as will be shown in this section.

The first type of analysis is of *operating leverage*. Under this concept, the extent to which a percentage change in sales results in a different percentage change in profits is determined. For example, if all costs were totally variable, there would be a percentage change in profits that would exactly match the change in sales, which would result in an operating leverage ratio of 1:1. However, if the bulk of costs are fixed, and will therefore not change when there are changes in sales, then an increase in sales will result in a more rapid increase in profits. For example, if a 10 percent increase in sales results in a 20 percent increase in profits, then the operating leverage ratio is 2:1. This is a wonderful condition to have when sales are on the increase, since large profit jumps will occur. However, the inverse situation arises if sales decline, because fixed costs must still be paid even when sales drop, which results in inordinate profit decreases. Thus, a large operating leverage ratio is a two-edged sword that cuts deeply in a declining sales situation. To measure this, we can create a measurement for the degree of operating leverage, which is calculated by dividing the percentage change in profits (before interest and taxes) by the percentage change in sales. The reason for excluding interest and tax costs is that we are determining the amount of leverage based only on operations, and neither of these expenses are related to operations. This measure has been added to the ratio analysis previously shown in Exhibit 14.3 and is now listed in an expanded format in Exhibit 14.6.

Exhibit 14.6 also includes another ratio. This measures the same concept, but this time it is the relationship between earnings per share and profits. The measure divides the percentage change in earnings per share by the percentage change in earnings before interest and taxes. Since the earnings per share figure includes interest and taxes, as well as changes in the number of shares outstanding, while the earnings figure does not include any of these variables, any differences in the percentages of change between the two measures can be caused only by interest, taxes, or the number of shares. Because all of these items are finance-related issues, we call this the *financial leverage ratio*. In short, any leverage indicated by this ratio is caused by financial manipulation, rather than changes in a company's operational structure.

The leverage measures outlined here are only general measures and yield no more than a high-level understanding of the reasons for changes in profitability levels. Much more detailed analysis is needed to gain a true

Exhibit 14.6   Leverage Ratios

	A	B	C	D	E	F	G	H	I
1	Ratio Analysis								
2		Jan	Feb	Mar	Apr	May	Jun	Jul	
3	*Balance Sheet Ratios:*								
4	Quick Ratio	1.0	1.0	0.8	0.8	0.8	0.7	0.7	
5	Current Ratio	1.7	1.7	1.5	1.5	1.4	1.4	1.4	
6	Debt/Equity Ratio	0.1	0.1	0.1	0.2	0.2	0.2	0.2	
7									
8	*Income Statement Ratios:*								
9	Gross Margin	44%	44%	43%	44%	44%	45%	44%	
10	Return on Sales	13%	13%	10%	10%	12%	12%	12%	
11	Breakeven Point	$634	$653	$789	$768	$749	$778	$809	
12									
13	*Mixed Ratios:*								
14	Fixed Asset Turnover	79%	81%	81%	74%	78%	81%	83%	
15	Inventory Turnover	20	21	22	21	23	24	25	
16	Receivables Turnover	38	38	38	36	38	39	39	
17	Return on Assets	10%	10%	8%	7%	9%	10%	10%	
18	Return on Equity	17%	17%	14%	14%	17%	18%	18%	
19									
20	*Leverage Ratios:*								
21	**Operating Leverage**		1.4	-4.2	1.2	3.3	1.5	0.5	
22	**Financial Leverage**		1.0	1.0	1.0	1.0	1.0	1.0	
23	**Earnings per Share (1,000)**	0.15	0.16	0.13	0.13	0.16	0.17	0.17	
24									

understanding of the specific types of costs and other factors that drive operating and financial leverage.

TREND ANALYSIS

An electronic spreadsheet is one of the best tools to use for the analysis of trends, because one can enter a list of time-sequenced data in a spreadsheet and generate a graphical trend line from it in a few moments. Virtually any type of revenue or cost can be itemized and graphed on a spreadsheet, so trend analysis becomes one of the simplest functions with this tool. To continue with the income statement example shown earlier in Exhibit 14.1, we will select the sales, gross margin, and net income figures for trend analysis on three different graphs, all of which will be located on a new spreadsheet called "Graphs." They are shown in Exhibit 14.7.

All of the graphs shown in Exhibit 14.7 were created using the same set of steps in Excel, which are:

1. Go to the "IS" worksheet in the example and highlight the range of numbers to be graphed on a trend line.

Exhibit 14.7   Graphical Presentation of Trend Lines

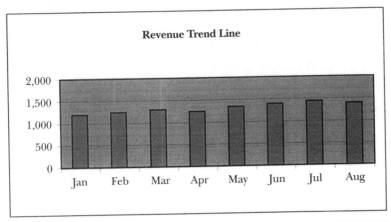

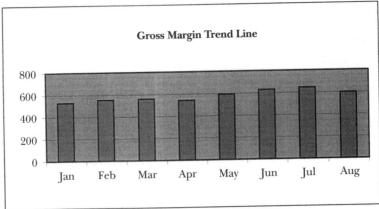

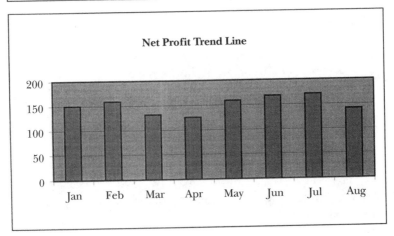

2. Click on the Chart Wizard icon.

3. At the Chart Type prompt select column.

4. Enter the name of the graph in the Chart Title field.

5. Set the Legend option to Off.

The Chart Wizard also gives the option of storing the finished graph on any worksheet within the current spreadsheet, or on a different spreadsheet entirely. It is generally best not to store the graph on the current worksheet, because printouts may inadvertently include the underlying data. In the example, all three graphs draw their data from the IS worksheet and store the finished product in the Graphs worksheet.

The Chart Wizard function is an exceptionally simple guide to creating trend analysis and is an excellent supporting tool for the controller who is not only creating a trend analysis, but also presenting the information in a tasteful format for presentation purposes.

FORECASTING

A controller is sometimes called on to make sales forecasts or verify those made by the sales and marketing departments. One of the better approaches for doing this is to extend the past history of sales volume forward into the periods being projected. Though this method of prediction is like trying to drive a car by looking in the rearview mirror, it is still one of the best tools available, as long as it is supplemented by detailed conversations with the sales staff to see what is really happening in the marketplace.

There are two formulas provided by Excel that result in forecast information. The first—and simplest—is the TREND command. This one superimposes a trend line on an existing set of time-sequenced data points to arrive at an expected sales level for a specified future period. To illustrate the command, we return once again to the income statement shown earlier in Exhibit 14.1. We will use a new worksheet within the same spreadsheet, called "Trend," and reference in it all of the monthly sales figures from the previous income statement. This is shown in Exhibit 14.8, along with a graph that shows the added trend line.

In the worksheet in Exhibit 14.8, we already know all sales data points from January through August, and want to calculate a trend line that extends an additional month to give us a prediction for September sales. Accordingly, in the table of months and historical sales figures noted in the Trend worksheet, there is an additional cell next to the August sales period. In that cell, we enter the following formula:

TREND(B4:B11,A4:A11,A12)

Though it looks complicated, this is a relatively simple command. The trend line is based on the data points contained in cells B4 through B11, for the

Exhibit 14.8   Trend Line Analysis

Sales Trend Analysis

Month	Revenue
Jan	1,200
Feb	1,250
Mar	1,300
Apr	1,250
May	1,350
Jun	1,400
Jul	1,450
Aug	1,400
Sep	**1,475**

Revenue Trend Line

Regression Analysis

Period	Data Item
1	43
2	79
3	12
4	18
5	59
6	114
7	3
8	82
9	55
10	31
11	94
12	14
13	87
14	51
15	82
16	23
17	21
18	94
19	11
20	79

Regression Analysis

date ranges contained in cells A4 through A11. The date for the period to be forecast is noted in cell A12. The formula generates a number that is the extension of the trend shown by the previous data elements, and will deposit this number in the B12 cell. Another way to state the formula is to ignore the dates and just ask for the next number in sequence. The formula, based on the previous example, looks like this:

TREND(B4:B11, ,{9})

Under this variation, the same set of data points are used, but the dates are ignored (hence the two commas in the formula with no data in between) as well as a number in brackets which represents the trend for the ninth number in the sequence of data elements. Because the original set of data included only eight data elements, this will be the next revenue figure after the last month of actual data. If the requested trend were for the month of December, the number in brackets would change to {12}, because this would represent the twelfth data point in the series.

In order to show this information in a graph, use the same series of steps noted for the graphs previously presented for Exhibit 14.7. However, to add a trend line overlay to the presented data, click on the completed graph, move the cursor to the revenue line on the chart, and press the right mouse button. Then click on the "Add Trendline" option, and pick from six available types of trend lines that can be added to the graph.

The second type of forecasting tool provided by Excel is regression analysis. This is a powerful tool for determining the trend line that best fits a disparate set of data, and is most useful when dealing with a set of numbers that are widely scattered and show no apparent pattern. In essence, the method determines the trend line that minimizes the sum of all squared errors between all data points and the line. Rather than delve into the formula for this method, it is easiest to plot the data elements and proceed immediately to a graph, on which Excel will superimpose a regression trend line. In Exhibit 14.8, the second half of the presentation includes the regression analysis. In it, we have plotted 20 data items for 20 periods that are wildly different from each other and have no apparent pattern. The first step in the analysis is to create a graph, using the same methods noted earlier for Exhibit 14.7. Then, use the same steps just described for the TREND analysis to add a trend line to the chart. The result is shown in the bottom half of Exhibit 14.8, where we find that there is a slight upward trend line to the data used to compile the regression trend line.

Of the two methods presented, the TREND formula is more useful, because a controller will find that most data being analyzed in the financial arena has a lengthy and steady trend line of data. Only for the most unusual analyses, involving wildly disparate data items, will the regression analysis be necessary. So far in this chapter, we have dealt with a variety of analyses that are used primarily for financial statement reviews or budget projections. We now move to other Excel functions that are primarily used for the evaluation of capital projects, investments, and risk analysis.

CASH FLOW ANALYSIS

There are many factors to review when evaluating a capital asset proposal, such as expected market conditions, sales estimates, salvage values, and maintenance costs. After all of these items have been reviewed and substantiated, they must all be input into a cash flow projection model to see if the project returns an adequate amount of cash. Excel supplies a formula that makes this an easy task, once the stream of all cash flows has been entered into a spreadsheet. A sample of such an analysis is shown in Exhibit 14.9, where we have simulated a typical cash-generating project that involves a significant up-front expenditure to purchase and set up equipment, five years of progressively larger positive cash flows as more equipment capacity is used, and then addi-

Exhibit 14.9   Net Present Value Calculation

Net Present Value Analysis [All figures in thousands]

Period	Equipment Purchases	Equipment Installation	Testing Costs	Maintenance Costs	Personal Property Taxes	Revenue	Net Cash Flows
1	(1,200)	(400)	(250)	(50)	(48)	300	(1,648)
2				(55)	(48)	600	497
3				(60)	(48)	650	542
4				(65)	(48)	700	587
5				(70)	(48)	750	632
6	120	(75)			(48)		(3)

Cost of Capital: 13%   Net Present Value: $8

Notes:

(1) Assumes a 10% salvage value at the end of the project.

(2) Assumes that positive cash flows will commence halfway into the first year.

(3) Assumes that personal property taxes will still be owed in the final year of operations, despite a projected disposal sometime during that year.

tional costs at the end of the project to dismantle the equipment, which is net of salvage value.

Once this information is stored in a spreadsheet, the net present value formula is added, which is derived as:

NPV(Interest Rate, Range of Cash Flow Values)

The interest rate used in the formula should be the incremental cost of capital. (For more information on that concept, see Chapter 16). The range of cash flow values listed in the second part of the formula represent the net cash flows for each period of the analysis. The formula then determines the current value of the expected future cash flows for each future period, using the cost of capital as the discounting factor, and summarizes all of the separate discounted cash flows into a single dollar value of all cash flows for the project. In the example, the formula uses a cost of capital of 13 percent, which results in the following formula:

NPV(.13,I6:I11)

The NPV formula is a powerful tool for determining the discounted cash flows of projects, but one must keep in mind that the cash flows used in these models are highly subjective in nature (depending on the extent of previous analysis work), which results in net present values that appear to be accurate to the nearest penny but do not have solid quantitative underpinnings, which yields inaccurate results. For example, the cash flow analysis shown in Exhibit 14.9 listed a large percentage of cash inflows in the later years of the project, which contributed to the small positive cash flow anticipated for the project; unfortunately, cash flows several years into the future are more uncertain and unpredictable than those likely to arrive in the near term, so these long-term estimates should be closely reviewed. In short, a controller should spend lots of time questioning the expected cash flows used in a net present value analysis in order to be sure of the outcome.

Cash flow assumptions are not the only factor involved in the net present value calculation. The other factor is the cost of capital used to discount the stream of cash flows. If this factor is incorrect by even a small amount, then the net present value will be incorrect, which can lead to an incorrect decision regarding the acceptance or rejection of a project. The simplest way to determine the potential severity of an error with the cost of capital is to recalculate the net present value using a cost of capital that is incrementally higher than the original interest rate. If the net present value drops below zero, then it may be necessary to review the accuracy of the cost of capital to ensure that it is correct. A slightly more elaborate approach, as shown in Exhibit 14.10, is to plot a comparison of the net present value to the cost of capital to see at what discount rate the net present value drops to zero. Using

Exhibit 14.10   NPV to Discount Rate Comparison

	Cost of Capital	Net Present Value	Formula Text
17	Cost of Capital	Net Present Value	Formula Text
18	1%	$544	=NPV($C18,NPV!$H$6:NPV!$H$11)
19	3%	$429	=NPV($C19,NPV!$H$6:NPV!$H$11)
20	5%	$325	=NPV($C20,NPV!$H$6:NPV!$H$11)
21	7%	$233	=NPV($C21,NPV!$H$6:NPV!$H$11)
22	9%	$150	=NPV($C22,NPV!$H$6:NPV!$H$11)
23	11%	$75	=NPV($C23,NPV!$H$6:NPV!$H$11)
24	13%	$8	=NPV($C24,NPV!$H$6:NPV!$H$11)
25	15%	($52)	=NPV($C25,NPV!$H$6:NPV!$H$11)

this graphical approach, we can see that, if the cost of capital increases by just 1 percent from the 13 percent used in Exhibit 14.9, the net present value will turn negative. Consequently, though the original calculation shows a positive return, it is so small that a reexamination of the cost of capital may be in order to verify that the discount rate used is the correct one.

The calculations used to create the graph in Exhibit 14.10 are shown at the bottom of the exhibit, with the text of all formulas noted in the lower right corner. Each net present value formula references the cost of capital immediately to its right, while also referencing the time-sequenced series of cash flows noted on the NPV worksheet that was shown in Exhibit 14.9.

CAPITAL ASSET ANALYSIS

The preceding section dealt with the main capital asset issue with which Excel can provide assistance, which is in calculating a project's net present value. This section deals with only one additional item related to the analysis of a capital asset investment decision. For a more complete review of the entire capital asset analysis process, refer back to Chapter 3.

A key issue that factors into the cash flow from a project is its depreciation rate. Though depreciation does not directly involve cash flow (since it is only the amortization of the original cash outlay for the capital asset), it has an indirect impact because the depreciation expense in each period will reduce the amount of taxes paid—and that *is* a real cash outflow. There are a variety of depreciation methods available that Excel can translate into period-by-period depreciation rates that can then be inserted into a cash flow model to derive the ultimate impact on cash flows. The following list illustrates the formulas for each one and briefly explains how each depreciation method works:

- *Double-declining balance depreciation.* This method computes depreciation at a highly accelerated rate, generally resulting in the greatest first-period depreciation of all the methods described here. The formula detail is DDB(Cost, Salvage, Life, Period). The Cost part of the equation is the initial cost of the asset. The Salvage part of the equation is the end-of-project salvage value (if any) of the equipment. The Life part of the equation is the number of periods during which the asset is being depreciated, which is assumed to be in years. The Period part of the equation is the period for which you want to determine the depreciation rate. For example, if you want to calculate the depreciation for 10 consecutive years, you will need to run the formula 10 times, while changing the Period part of the equation each time to reflect the desired year's result.

- *Fixed-declining balance depreciation.* This method also computes depreciation at an accelerated rate. The formula detail is DB(Cost, Salvage, Life, Period). The descriptions for all of the inputs to the equation are identical to those for the double-declining balance method.

- *Straight-line depreciation.* This method computes depreciation at the same rate for all periods, resulting in a smooth and easily calculated depreciation amount for all periods. However, it does not assist in accelerating cash flows by aggressively reducing taxes. The formula detail is SLN(Cost, Salvage, Life). The descriptions for all of the inputs to the equation are identical to those for the double-declining balance method. However, there is no Period entry, because the result will be the same, irrespective of the specific period for which you are calculating the depreciation.

- *Sum of the years' digits depreciation.* This method provides accelerated depreciation, though not as rapid as provided under the double-declining balance method. The formula detail is SYD(Cost, Salvage, Life, Period). Once again, the descriptions for all of the inputs to the equation are identical to those for the double-declining balance method.

- *Variable-declining balance depreciation.* This method is essentially the same as the double-declining balance method, but you can alter the depreciation rate, as well as convert over to straight-line depreciation at the point where accelerated depreciation results in a lower depreciation expense. The formula detail is VDB(Cost, Salvage, Life, Start Period, End Period, Depreciation Factor, Switch to Straight Line). The descriptions for the first three inputs to the equation are the same as those used for the double-declining balance method. The Start Period part of the equation specifies the beginning period for which you want to calculate depreciation. The End Period part of the equation specifies the ending period for which you want to calculate depreciation. The Depreciation factor part of the equation specifies the rate at which depreciation is calculated. For example, entering a "2" results in 200 percent double-declining depreciation, whereas entering a 1.5 results in 150 percent depreciation, which is a less rapid form of accelerated depreciation. Finally, the Switch to Straight Line part of the equation allows you to enter TRUE to use declining balance depreciation for all depreciation periods, or enter FALSE to have the formula automatically switch to straight-line depreciation at the point where straight-line results in a higher depreciation expense.

It is evident that the bulk of data inputted into all of these depreciation formulas is nearly identical. Only the underlying formulas will alter the calculated depreciation expense.

The type of depreciation method used matters a great deal, because the most aggressive one, which depreciates the largest amount in the first few periods, will result in reduced taxes in the near term, which results in increased short-term cash flow. Increased cash flow now is worth more than cash flow at the end of a project, so an aggressive depreciation method will yield greater project cash flows.

COMPOUNDING ANALYSIS

A controller is sometimes called on to calculate the results of a variety of payment or receipt scenarios that involve streams of cash flows over multiple periods. This section reviews several of the most common ones, as well as how to use Excel formulas to create accurate answers for each scenario. They are:

- *Future value.* If a company is investing money at a consistent rate for a fixed time period, the controller may want to know how much that investment stream will be worth at a specified future date. To determine the future value of such an investment stream, use the FV formula. The details of the formula are FV(Interest Rate, Number of Periods, Payment Amount). The Interest Rate component is the expected earnings rate on the investment. The Number of Periods component is the number of periods over which a fixed amount is being invested. The Payment Amount component is the fixed amount being paid during each period. For example, if a company were to invest $4,000 per period for 128 months at an annual interest rate of 8 percent, the formula would be FV(8%/12,128,–4000).

- *Interest rate on an annuity.* If a company is offered a specific set of regular payments (i.e., an annuity), it is useful to see if this results in an adequate rate of return. To determine the interest rate on such an annuity, use the RATE formula. The details of the formula are RATE(Number of Periods, Payment Amount, Present Value of Payments). The Number of Periods component specifies the number of periods over which fixed payments will be made. The Payment Amount component shows the amount of each payment. The Present Value of Payments component notes the current cash value of the investment for which payments are being made. For example, if an investor wishes to purchase a bond with a current value of $100,000 and will pay for it with monthly payments of $1,500 for 10 years, the formula would be RATE(10,–1500,100000). The resulting interest rate will be on a monthly basis and must be multiplied by 12 to arrive at an annual interest rate.

- *Loan payment.* One of the most common calculations a controller makes is the determination of loan payments for a specified amount of borrowing at a set interest rate. This calculation can also be used to verify the same information that has been supplied by the lender. To determine the amount of a loan payment, use the PMT formula. The details of the formula are PMT(Interest Rate, Number of Payments, Present Value of Loan). The Interest Rate component is the interest rate per period and is assumed not to vary. The Number of Payments component represents the number of periods over which fixed payments are to be made. The Present Value of Loan component is the original amount of the loan that must now be paid off. For example, to determine the payment amount for a loan of $355,000 at an interest rate of 7 percent, and which will be paid off in 120 periods (e.g., 10 years), the formula would be PMT(7%/12,120,355000).

- *Number of periods.* If there is an obligation to pay a set amount with a standard number of periodic payments, it may be necessary to determine how long those payments will last before the obligation to pay has been fulfilled. To determine the number of required payments, use the NPER formula. The details of the formula are NPER(Interest Rate, Payment Amount, Present Value). The Interest Rate component is the interest rate per period, and is assumed not to vary. The Payment Amount component is the amount paid per period, and is also assumed not to vary. Finally, the Present Value component is the current value of the obligation being paid off. For example, to determine the number of payment periods required to pay off an investment of $150,000 at an annual interest rate of 12 percent, and with periodic payments of $28,134, the formula is NPER(12%,–28134, 150000).

- *Present value.* If a company anticipates receiving a string of payments in future periods, it may be useful to determine their present value, because this information can be used to compare the payment stream to the value of other sources of income to see which is more valuable. Such an analysis may result in the sale of whatever investment is resulting in a payment stream that is considered to have a less-than-stellar present value. To determine an investment's present value, use the PV formula. The details of the formula are PV(Interest Rate, Number of Payment Periods, Total Payment Made per Period). The Interest Rate component is the interest rate per period, and is assumed not to vary. The Number of Payment Periods component is the number of periods during which payments are expected to arrive. The Total Payment Made per Period component is the payment made in each period, and is assumed to be the same in every period. For example, to determine the present value of a stream of $10,000 payments at a 6.5 percent interest rate over 20 years, the formula would be PV(6.5%,20,10000).

- *Principal payment.* A company sometimes makes a fixed payment without a clear delineation of what portion is interest and what is principal. This is especially common for capital leases, in which the lessor is under no legal obligation to reveal how much of either payment component is being paid. To determine the amount of principal within such a payment, use the PPMT formula. The details of the formula are PPMT(Interest Rate, Period, Total Number of Payment Periods, Present Value). The Interest Rate component is the interest rate per period. The Period component is the specific period for which you want to determine the principal payment. The Total Number of Payment Periods component is the number of payment periods for the term of the entire loan. Finally, the Present Value component is the amount of the loan at the beginning of the transaction. For example, if you want to determine the total principal payment in the seventh year of a 12-year, $50,000 loan that bears a 9 percent interest rate, the formula would be PPMT(9%,7,12,50000).

Given the number of available Excel formulas, it is evident that the majority of queries that a controller will receive regarding the time value of money can be answered by a short formula entry in Excel.

INVESTMENT ANALYSIS

Excel contains a large number of formulas that can be used to determine the interest rate on a variety of investments. This section covers the key interest rate formulas, including a brief explanation of each one, the components of each formula, and how the formula is used in an example. The definitions of the components of the various formulas are summarized in a set of definitions at the end of this section. The formulas are:

- *Calculate the accrued interest on a security that pays interest at maturity.* For this calculation, use the ACCRINTM formula. The details of the formula are ACCRINTM(Issue Date, Maturity Date, Annual Coupon Rate, Par Value). For example, if the issue date is 12/12/99 and the maturity date is 5/15/04 on a 9.5 percent coupon rate bond with a par value of $1,000, the formula would be ACCRINTM("12/12/99", "5/15/04",9.5%,1000).

- *Calculate the accrued interest on a security that pays periodic interest.* This formula is used to accrue the amount of interest earned from a stream of regular interest payments from an investment. For this calculation, use the ACCRINT formula. The details of the formula are ACCRINT(Issue Date, First Interest Date, Settlement Date, Annual Coupon Rate, Par Value, No. of Payments per Year). For example, if the issue date is 3/31/01, the first interest date is 4/15/01, the settlement date is 4/10/01, the annual coupon rate is 11 percent, the par value is $1,000, and there are four payments per year, then the formula will be ACCRINT("3/31/01","4/15/01","4/10/01",11%, 1000,4).

- *Calculate the annual yield for a discounted security.* If a company purchases a security at a discounted rate (usually because the stated interest rate is lower than the prevailing market rate), the controller should use the YIELDDISC formula to determine its annual yield. The details of the formula are YIELDDISC(Settlement Date, Maturity Date, Price per $100 Face Value, Redemption Value). For example, if the settlement date is 9/9/05, the maturity date is 12/31/15, the price is $101, and the redemption value is $100, then the formula will be YIELDDISC("9/9/05","12/31/15",101,100).

- *Calculate the yield for a Treasury bill.* To calculate this yield, use the TBILLYIELD formula. The details of the formula are TBILLYIELD (Settlement Date, Maturity Date, Price per $100 Face Value). For example, if the settlement date is 4/13/05, the maturity date is 6/15/12, and the price per $100 face value is $94.30, then the formula will be TBILLYIELD("4/14/05","6/15/12",94.3).

- *Calculate the yield on a security that has a short or long* first *period.* A security that was purchased in between its coupon payment dates will still earn the owner the full amount of the next coupon, even though the security was not held for the full period, which results in a higher-than-normal interest rate earned for the first period. To calculate the full-term yield with the odd-length first period, use the ODDFYIELD formula. The details of the formula are ODDFYIELD(Settlement Date, Maturity Date, Issue Date, First Coupon Date, Annual Coupon Rate, Price per $100 Face Value, Redemption Value, No. of Payments per Year). For example, if the settlement date is 5/2/03, the maturity date is 11/11/08, the issue date is 6/6/01, the first coupon date is 7/7/03, the interest rate is 8.5 percent, the price is $98.25, the redemption value is $100, and four coupon payments are made per year, then the formula will be ODDFYIELD ("5/2/03","11/11/08", "6/6/01","7/7/03",8.5%,98.25,100,4).

- *Calculate the yield on a security that has a short or long* last *period.* This is the same type of situation as just described in the preceding scenario, except that we are now selling a security prior to the next scheduled coupon date. The formula now changes to ODDLYIELD, for which the formula detail is ODDLYIELD(Settlement Date, Maturity Date, Last Coupon Date, Annual Coupon Rate, Price per $100 Face Value, Redemption Value, No. of Payments per Year). To use part of the preceding example, if the settlement date is 5/2/03, the maturity date is 11/11/08, the last coupon date is 8/11/08, the interest rate is 8.5 percent, the price is $98.25, the redemption value is $100, and four coupon payments are made per year, then the formula will be ODD-FYIELD("5/2/03","11/11/08","8/11/08",8.5%,98.25,100,4).

- *Calculate the yield on a security that pays interest at maturity.* Some securities pay all interest at the redemption date, rather than as regular coupon payments. To calculate the yield on these types of securities, use the YIELDMAT formula. The detail for this formula is YIELD-MAT(Settlement Date, Maturity Date, Issue Date, Annual Coupon Rate, Price per $100 Face Value). For example, if the settlement date is 2/15/02, the maturity date is 4/15/11, the issue date is 10/5/01, the interest rate is 8.2 percent, and the price is $101.125, then the formula will be YIELDMAT("2/15/02","4/15/11","10/5/01",8.2%, 101.125).

- *Calculate the yield on a security that pays periodic interest.* This is the standard formula for a basic bond purchase that has no unusual variations in terms of purchase or sale dates, and for which coupon payments are made in standard amounts and on regularly scheduled dates. For this situation, use the YIELD formula. The detail of the formula is YIELD(Settlement Date, Maturity Date, Annual Coupon Rate, Price per $100 Face Value, Redemption Value, No. of Payments per Year). For example, if the settlement date is 1/8/01, the maturity date is 5/15/07, the annual coupon rate is 7.5%, the price is $100.50, the redemption value is $100, and there are two coupon payments per year, then the formula will be YIELD ("1/8/01","5/15/07",7.5%, 100.50,100,2).

Most of the components of the above formulas are identical. To keep from repeating the definitions of each component for every formula listed above, they are summarized below:

- *Annual coupon rate.* The listed coupon rate on a security.

- *First interest date.* The first date on which interest is earned on a security.

- *Issue date.* The date on which a security is issued.

- *Last coupon date.* The last coupon date for a security prior to its redemption date.

- *Maturity date.* The date on which a security expires.

- *No. of payments per year.* The number of coupon payments per year.

- *Par value.* The listed price on a security.

- *Price per $100 face value.* The actual price paid for a security can be higher or lower than the face value, depending on the discount or premium paid to acquire the stated interest to be paid on the security.

- *Redemption value.* The amount paid at the termination date of the security per $100 of face value.

- *Settlement date.* The date when the security is issued to the buyer.

The formulas described here should be sufficient for calculating the interest rates or accrued interest for the majority of investment situations for which a controller will need to calculate interest earnings.

RISK ANALYSIS

When constructing a financial analysis of the likely results of a set of projected cash flows, a controller must always remember that these cash flows are projected—they are not facts, and may vary considerably from reality. Given the level of uncertainty involved, it may be useful to determine the spread of possible outcomes. By doing so, a controller can see if all expected outcomes are grouped tightly about a single estimate, which relates to a low level of risk, or if there is a significant spread of possible outcomes, which greatly increases the risk of meeting the targeted outcome. Excel provides a wide array of statistical tools for determining the level of risk, of which this section describes six that are easy to understand and use.

The first step when using the following statistical tools is to generate a list of possible outcomes for whatever the analysis may be. For example, if there is a capital project under discussion, try to obtain a number of possible outcomes, either by polling several experts in the company or industry, or by personal knowledge of previous actual outcomes for similar types of projects. Then, the first step in the risk analysis work is to determine the highest, lowest, and median values in the list of possible outcomes. These are shown in Exhibit 14.11, in which a dozen possible annual cash inflows from a project have been itemized. All possible variations are noted at the top of the work-

Exhibit 14.11   Risk Analysis for a Capital Project

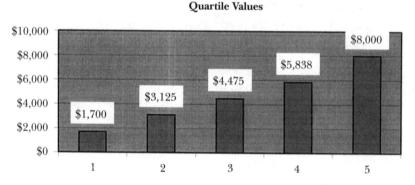

Projected Outcome	Projected Cash Inflow		Result	Text of Formula
1	$5,400	Minimum Value of all Outcomes	$1,700	=MIN($C$5:$C$16)
2	$3,200	Maximum Value of all Outcomes	$8,000	=MAX($C$5:$C$16)
3	$1,700	Median Value of all Outcomes	$4,475	=MEDIAN($C$5:$C$16)
4	$6,100			
5	$2,900	Minimum Value	$1,700	=QUARTILE($C$5:$C$16,0)
6	$4,700	Value of 25th Percentile	$3,125	=QUARTILE($C$5:$C$16,1)
7	$5,800	Value of 50th Percentile	$4,475	=QUARTILE($C$5:$C$16,2)
8	$8,000	Value of 75th Percentile	$5,838	=QUARTILE($C$5:$C$16,3)
9	$3,900	Maximum Value	$8,000	=QUARTILE($C$5:$C$16,4)
10	$4,250			
11	$5,950	Degree of Skew	0.24	=SKEW($C$5:$C$16)
12	$2,500	Standard Deviation	$1,808	=STDEV($C$5:$C$16)

sheet. Below them are the Excel formulas to find the minimum, maximum, and median values from among the list, alongside a listing of the formulas used. However, these are not very precise measures and do not give a sufficiently accurate view of the level of risk.

To provide us with a more detailed idea of the spread of possible outcomes, we can use the Excel QUARTILE formula to generate the average outcome for the first, second, third, and fourth quartiles of all possible outcomes, which we have also converted into a graph with the Excel Chart Wizard icon.

A formula that tells us if the bulk of the data is above or below the median is the SKEW formula. This formula determines the presence of skew toward the higher end of the possible outcomes (which is positive skew) or a skew toward the lower end of the outcomes (which is a negative skew). A skew of zero indicates no skew in either direction. Finally, the standard deviation is an extremely useful tool for determining the dispersion of possible outcomes about the median of all outcomes. The larger the standard deviation of the sample, the larger the dispersion about the median, and the greater the degree of risk that the average outcome will not be attained.

The detail of the formulas shown in Exhibit 14.11 are very simple. All of the formulas reference the range of projected cash inflows, which are noted in cells C5 through C16. The only variation from this pattern is for the quartile formulas, which also require the addition of the quartile number at the end of the formula.

The analysis shown in Exhibit 14.11 tells us that the project has an extremely wide range of possible outcomes, with a maximum value that is more than four times higher than the minimum value. The range of possible outcomes has a positive skew of .24, which tells us that those people providing the estimates have generally guessed that the actual outcome should be higher than the projected average. Finally, the standard deviation from the mean is $1,808, which is slightly more than a 40 percent variation from the median. With such a large dispersion of possible outcomes, the underlying data requires a great deal more validation before the project can be approved. Also, given the higher degree of risk, the cost of capital used to discount the cash flows from the project may be set higher, thereby making it more difficult to obtain approval for the project.

For a more detailed discussion of how to determine the presence of risk, factor it into an analysis, and include it in an analysis summarization, see Chapter 17.

SUMMARY

This chapter described how to use the Excel electronic spreadsheet to review a company's financial statements with proportional, ratio, leverage, and trend analysis. All of these analyses require inputting a simplified form of a company's financial statements into a spreadsheet, after which a number of built-in formulas churn out a variety of percentages, ratios, and trends that are most useful as a starting point for more in-depth analysis. Of some note is that all the analyses presented in this section of the chapter were derived by using multilayered spreadsheets, all of them referencing the data in just two worksheets that contained data for the income statement and balance sheet. This is the preferred method for conducting financial analysis, since data need only be entered once in order to derive from it a great deal of analysis, while also avoiding the danger of arriving at different analysis results because several different sets of data are being referenced by the analysis formulas.

The chapter went on to show how the Excel spreadsheet could also be used to determine the accuracy or likelihood of forecasts and cash flows associated with capital projects, as well as how to use compounding analysis to determine the current value of future cash flows associated with those projects. An associated set of analyses was the use of compounding and investment analysis to determine the current value of other investments besides capital projects. Finally, there was a short discussion of the uses of an electronic spreadsheet for determining the likely risk level of any type of investment.

The analysis examples presented here are by no means the only ways in which an electronic spreadsheet can be used—they are merely the most common and easiest to use. With a more extensive use of modeling, macros, and add-on software, one can achieve an exquisite degree of financial analysis with an electronic spreadsheet. However, do not fall in love with the concept of complete analysis automation with this tool. Although it represents a great leap forward in the ability of a controller to analyze a company's financial results, investment opportunities, and risk, it is still no match for the careful, reasoned review of the results of this analysis, and making thoughtful judgments based on that review.

15

Financial Analysis Reports

Although a controller may be judged by his or her peers and managers on many fronts, such as personal integrity, communication skills, or technical knowledge, it is the controller's reports that have the greatest impact of all. This is because there is constant, daily reinforcement of the controller's reporting skills with all these people, since reports are issued constantly from the controller's department and distributed all over the company. As far as the nonaccounting part of a company is concerned, financial analysis reports are the primary work product of the accounting department, and the controller is judged in accordance with the quality and layout of them.

This chapter reviews the layout, presentation, and accompanying explanations required for financial analysis reports.

TYPES OF FINANCIAL ANALYSIS REPORTS

Previous chapters in this book have focused on using the correct financial analysis to arrive at conclusions in various operating situations. Now it is time to put that information into a report format that is not only easily understood by the managers at whom they are targeted, but also provides them with the right information for making key changes in response to the information noted in the reports.

There are several considerations to make when summarizing a financial analysis into a report. One is the *timing* of the report. If the information to be presented is in response to a one-time request by a manager, then there is less need to spend lots of time creating a special report format. Instead, the desired information may be sent to the requestor via a short e-mail, or some similar, informal method of communication. Examples of such reports would be a response to a request for the amount of depreciation left on a specific machine that the production manager wants to sell, or the trend in sales for a single customer for the last quarter, or the amount of outstanding accounts receivable owed by a customer against which the legal department is considering filing a lawsuit. However, if a report is one that will be presented to management on a regular basis, such as a list of overtime worked by each employee, month by month for the past 12 months, it makes much more sense to spend a large amount of time polishing the format to ensure that the information presented is thoroughly understandable, and reflects well on the efforts of the accounting department in compiling and presenting the information.

Another consideration is the *audience*. It is a rare event for a report to be read by an entire company. Instead, each report is targeted at just a few employees. For example, the overtime report goes to department managers, while the capacity utilization report goes to the production scheduler and the production staff, while the investments report goes solely to the chief financial officer (CFO). Given the variety of audiences that receive accounting reports, it is very important to tailor the presented information to the level of financial knowledge of the recipient. For example, a capacity utilization report may be going to a production manager with no formal accounting training, so a simple bar chart that shows a trend line for utilization is probably going to be the most understandable. Alternatively, an investments report that goes to the CFO can be as detailed as possible, because the CFO is highly educated in financial matters, and certainly needs no summarization or graphs to see where money is being invested and how much interest the company is earning from those investments.

Another consideration is *confidentiality*. Some information will cause a great deal of trouble among employees if it is released to everyone. The most obvious example is employee pay levels. There is an annualized pay report shown in the Labor Reports section later in this chapter that details the exact amount paid to every employee in the company. If the wrong person were to obtain access to this report, there could be a flood of employee requests for pay raises so that their pay matches that of someone else listed on the report. This can also be an issue if a company is trying to avoid employees' becoming unionized. Accordingly, the best way to handle such information is to strictly guard the distribution of the information, as well as to partition such reports into smaller pieces, so that managers receive only the information that applies directly to them. To use the same example, it is much less hazardous to split the annualized pay report by department and to give the information for each department only to the manager of that department. Thus, it may be necessary to create a number of subreports, depending on the confidentiality of the information being distributed.

A final consideration is the *mode of transmission*. For example, if a report is issued to employees in a number of widely separated locations, the best mode of distribution may be by overnight mail or e-mail, which requires short file sizes to ensure the lowest possible transmission costs. If the main form of transmission is e-mail, the use of graphics files may not be practical, given the time required to download large bit-mapped files. In such situations, only the simplest text messages are cost effective. Thus, the mode of transmission affects of the cost of issuing reports, which in turn impacts the types of reports that can be cost-effectively issued.

Once all of the previous points have been considered, one can finally create the report layout. The key issue when doing so is to generate a report that clearly communicates the result of the financial analysis to the reader. One of the best ways to do this when the information being presented is relatively simple is a graphic. Some of the most common forms of graphics are:

- *Bar.* A bar chart shows each data point in analysis as a bar that extends either vertically or horizontally next to a measurement indicator. Several bars side by side or stacked on top of each other can give a clear indication of the comparative amounts of the data points being compared. This format is best used either to show trend lines for a single data item over time or to compare the sizes of related data items for a single time period.

- *High–low.* The data in an analysis may range within set boundaries on a trend line. For example, a company's stock price may reach a high of $102 and a low of $93 in the same day, and generally stay within this range for a long time. If so, it is useful to present the high–low data for each time period to see if there is a trend at the high, low, or median points of the data. This format is also useful for quality analyses, in which the output of a production process can be measured within a high or low tolerance range.

- *Pie.* When the information being presented is for a single time period and is meant to show the proportion of a total that each data item represents, a pie chart is the best form of presentation. As an example, a pie chart can be used to show the proportion of a company's revenues that are composed of sales from each of a number of subsidiaries.

- *Scatter.* Sometimes the point of an analysis is to show either how widely scattered or tightly clumped the data items may be. For example, if the point of an analysis is to show that there is no clustering of safety incidents on certain days of the month, a scatter diagram could show that the wide distribution of incidents on all days of the month eliminates this hypothesis as a reason for safety issues. Alternatively, the same format could be used to prove the reverse conclusion if there are indeed a few cases in which safety problems tend to arise on certain days.

- *Trend.* A line chart is best used to show a trend in the amount of a single data item or a comparison in the trends of a small number of related data items. When presenting a trend analysis, an alternative to the line chart is a bar chart (as discussed earlier), but this format is not usable when one is trying to compare trends in multiple data items on the same chart.

Despite their ease of presentation, graphs are not always the best way to present the results of a financial analysis. The main case in which they cannot be used, or used without supporting detail, is when the analysis is complex or there are large amounts of unrelated information being presented. In the first case, an analysis of the reasoning behind a recommendation to build a new facility certainly cannot be contained in a single graph. Instead, the analysis should include an executive summary, a detailed analysis, and supporting tables and charts. In the later case, a good example of a presentation of mixed data is a weekly management report on the condition of the company, which may encompass such diverse information as the cash balance, the percentage of nonconforming parts produced, and the size of the sales backlog. Given the diverse range of data presented, it is much easier to use a numerical layout than a large number of graphs—not only because the information is more understandable, but also because a very large number of graphs would be needed to convey the same information that would otherwise be itemized on a single page.

Thus, there are many factors to consider when constructing the proper report layout for a financial analysis, including the type of audience, mode of report distribution, confidentiality of the information presented, and the frequency of the report, not to mention the use of graphs, executive summaries, and supporting data. Accordingly, a controller who wants to present a persuasive financial analysis will spend a considerable amount of time devising the appropriate form for communicating the information.

GENERAL MANAGEMENT REPORTS

Every company needs a report card that itemizes its performance. Without this information, management has no way of knowing how it is performing in a variety of key operating areas. Even if management relies on the monthly financial statements for this information, it will know only if there has been a profit or loss and the size of revenues and expenses as compared to those of previous months. From an operational perspective, this is not a sufficient amount of information, not only because no operating information is presented in the financial statements, but also because the statements are not forward looking—they reveal only what has already happened, not what is likely to happen in the future. Accordingly, an additional report is needed to inform management of the status of operations throughout the company.

A controller is frequently called on to generate this report, an example of which is shown in Exhibit 15.1. This report clusters a group of key measures into categories. In the example, there are three measures related to cash, two more for working capital, two for financial issues, four for sales, four for production, and five for the warehouse. A key point here is that, of the 20 measurements found in this report, only two can be found in the financial statements; all of the others are derived from other sources and are more directly related to the day-to-day operations of the company.

Exhibit 15.1 Key Company Measurements Report

	Current Month							
	Week 5	Week 4	Week 3	Week 2	Week 1	Apr.	Mar.	Feb.
Cash								
Available Debt (000s)					$1,500	$1,400	$1,300	$1,200
Overdue Accounts Receivable (000s)					$388	$315	$312	$269
Overdue Accounts Payable (000s)					$114	$276	$312	$401
Working Capital								
Days Accounts Receivable					46	43	41	51
Days Total Inventory					49	61	52	46
Financial								
Breakeven, 2 Mo. Rolling (000s)	—	—			—	$1,430	$1,440	$1,450
Net Profits before Tax (000s)	—	—			—	$30	($33)	($60)
Sales								
Backlog for Next Month					$1,724	$1,922	$1,708	$1,651
Backlog for Month after Next					$461	$652	$505	$491
Backlog for Two Months after Next					$9	$296	$202	$358
Backlog, Total (000s)					$2,194	$2,870	$2,415	$2,500
Production								
Machine Utilization					80%	70%	67%	66%
% Order Line Items Shipped on Time					83%	79%	73%	64%
% Actual Labor Hrs over Standard					17%	23%	40%	25%
Scrap Dollars (000s)					—	$46	$51	$54
Warehouse								
$$$ of Total Inventory (000s)					$2,604	$2,644	$2,352	$2,273
$$$ of Finished Goods (000s)					$536	$496	$454	$668
$$$ of Work-in-Process (000s)					$566	$680	$555	$362
$$$ of Raw Materials (000s)					$1,502	$1,468	$1,343	$1,243
Inventory Accuracy					56%	68%	80%	71%

By avoiding an overabundance of financial measures, management's attention is drawn to alternative operational measures that are the underlying basis for good financial results. These measures will vary widely by industry, and even by company within each industry, but there should always be some attention paid to the use of working capital, because it can consume so much of a company's cash, as well as to the primary drivers of production efficiency. Furthermore, there should always be some forward-looking measures that are indicative of what management can expect company performance to be in the short term, such as the order backlog for the next few months, or a trend line of customer retention rates. With this report in hand, the management team's attention will be much more closely focused on the specific activities that require continual attention in order for a company to succeed.

The report format shown in Exhibit 15.1 is certainly a good starting point for a company's key measures; however, it is designed for a manufacturing organization, and many of the measures in it would not be relevant to, for example, an insurance company or a bank. Because of the wide variety of situations in which such a report can be used, it is important to carefully structure the report to meet the needs of the specific industry and market niche in which a company operates. Furthermore, the measures in this report can be expected to change quite regularly. For example, a company that has just gone through a number of acquisitions may decide that a key measure is the number of checking accounts it now has control over, because each acquisition had several of these accounts, and each one is a location in which cash will languish without earning interest. Accordingly, the measure is an important one, but only until the accounts can be consolidated into a smaller number for cash utilization purposes, after which the measure is meaningless. Because of the increased attention that a measurement system brings to certain activities, it is common to see the performance of these areas increase to a much higher level, after which the measure is not as necessary to maintain. At this point, a controller should review a company's measurement needs again and derive a few replacement measures that will lead to greater improvements.

The measures in the management report can also be derived from the corporate strategic direction. For example, if a company's strategy is to acquire at least one company per month, a simple measure is the cumulative number of acquisitions for the year-to-date. If the direction is to vastly improve customer service, then the results of a monthly customer satisfaction survey should appear on the report. Thus, the general management report should be composed of a wide range of measurements, based on not only financial information, but also operational information and measures that track the success of a company's competitive strategy. The resulting report will be successful if it leads to clear improvements in operations and financial results, and gives feedback on the ability of the organization to achieve its goals.

REVENUE REPORTS

When a company compiles its annual budget, it usually begins with a detailed set of estimates regarding the sales that can be expected from various customers, possibly including detailed estimates of which products each customer will purchase. In the majority of cases, once the budget is completed, the sales estimates are put away until the budget process begins again the following year. This approach does not encourage the sales staff to generate accurate sales forecasts, because there is no mechanism for them to see the results of their estimates, customer by customer. To alleviate this problem and put direct attention on not only the accuracy of sales estimates but also the ability of the sales staff to deliver on their estimates by managing the purchases of their customers, the revenue report shown in Exhibit 15.2 is most useful.

This report is drawn from the annual and monthly sales that were budgeted for each customer; that information is summarized in the year-to-date forecast column and the month forecast column. The actual sales figure for each customer is extracted from the accounting database at the end of each reporting period, resulting in variance columns for both year-to-date and monthly sales that management can use to determine which customers are purchasing at levels below expectations and which are buying so much that additional corporate resources should be turned their way in order to encourage a long-term relationship. Though exceedingly simple, this is an excellent feedback report that a controller can use to not only verify the accuracy of sales forecasts, but also how customer orders are comparing to those estimates.

MATERIAL COST REPORTS

The largest cost of many companies, especially those in the manufacturing field, is the cost of materials that go into finished goods. Surprisingly, few organizations track the changes in these costs against any kind of standard. Instead, they simply accept supplier costs as a matter of course. An alternative is to use the cost comparison noted in Exhibit 15.3.

In Exhibit 15.3, the suppliers from whom parts are purchased are noted down the left side of the page. Next to them are the company's purchase order numbers on which material cost variances have been detected, followed by the identifying numbers and descriptions of those parts. On the far right side of the report is listed the difference between the standard price of each part and the new price that was listed on the purchase order to the supplier, as well as the extrapolated variance between the two costs. This report shows how costs are varying from expectations, and the total cost of such variances. The report can also be sorted so that the largest variances are at the top, where managers can see them more easily.

The report is most useful for active purchasing managers who are determined to pursue and negotiate with those suppliers who have raised prices, with the intention of driving prices back to standard cost levels, thereby keep-

Exhibit 15.2   Forecasted versus Actual Sales Report

[Thru 4/01]

Customer Name	YTD Forecast	YTD Actual	Variance	Month Forecast	Month Actual	Variance
AB Farriars	58,000	73,506	15,506	21,000	8,417	−12,583
Addison Meyers	285,000	738,205	453,205	85,000	178,489	93,489
Best Eastern Corp.	32,000	45,886	13,886	15,000	13,041	−1,959
Bonakemi	48,000	44,453	−3,547	8,000	10,868	2,868
Brittle Designs	30,000	29,230	−770	11,000		−11,000
Brush Mat	15,000	5,281	−9,719	15,000	2,651	−12,349
Case Logic, Inc.	26,000	74,513	48,513	8,000	13,147	5,147
Champion Systems	24,000	24,493	493	0	11,480	11,480
Easy Care, Inc.	45,000	45,589	589	15,000	17,548	2,548
Engaging Systems	1,779,396	2,488,239	708,843	723,878	1,094,675	370,797
Engineered Data Products	47,000	58,800	11,800	25,000	18,074	−6,926
Estes Industries	26,000	83,858	57,858	12,000	26,539	14,539
Gates Rubber	40,000	42,630	2,630	14,000	12,395	−1,605
Great Plains Mfg. Co.	6,600	2,854	−3,746	2,200		−2,200
Green Thumb Foods	0	25,678	25,678	0	25,678	25,678
Hudson Bay Products	525,000	409,968	−115,032	300,000	91,459	−208,541
Hunter Supply	9,000	38,139	29,139	3,000	6,983	3,983
Innovative Solutions	22,000	44,970	22,970	14,000	15,001	1,001
Inovonics	9,000	30,173	21,173	3,000	8,386	5,386
International Diverse Foods	72,000	83,417	11,417	24,000	13,920	−10,080
Kart Designs	350,265	371,051	20,786	138,795	66,964	−71,831
Magnalab	0	4,620	4,620	0	4,620	4,620
Martin & Sons	9,000	11,647	2,647	3,000	3,975	975
Mile High Equipment	80,000	116,002	36,002	30,000	36,457	6,457
Miscellaneous	75,000	2,160	−72,840	25,000		−25,000
Optimum Corp.	390,000	423,465	33,465	120,000	100,274	−19,726
Polymedica	27,000	28,063	1,063	5,000	7,244	2,244
Primary Colors	3,600	1,000	−2,600	1,200	1,000	−200
Product Architects	5,000	12,348	7,348	5,000	4,020	−980
Progressive Specialty Glass	25,000	6,402	−18,598	0	5,561	5,561
Ryco Packaging	0	7,387	7,387	0	3,381	3,381
Scott Systems	30,000	58,475	28,475	0	36,468	36,468
Sensormedics Corp.	0	810	810	0	810	810
Superior Designs	210,000	183,743	−26,257	60,000	49,493	−10,507
T. Marzetti Company	8,000	17,197	9,197	0	3,839	3,839
Temporary Artifacts	0	2,500	2,500	0	2,500	2,500
Tenere	0	431	431	0	431	431
Toxonics	4,000	8,348	4,348	0		0
Tranex	9,000		−9,000	3,000		−3,000
Trimetal Corp.	60,000	10,831	−49,169	20,000	8,244	−11,756
Ventura Foods	41,000	177,399	136,399	20,000	99,641	79,641
Very Fine Foods	46,000	118,023	72,023	14,000	27,947	13,947
Weston Oil	0	2,889	2,889	0	1,445	1,445
Totals	4,471,861	5,954,673	1,482,812	1,744,073	2,033,065	288,992

Exhibit 15.3 Purchase Price Variance Report

Supplier No.	Supplier Name	Purchase Order PO No.	Item Number	Description	Quantity Received	Purchase Order Price	Actual Total $$$ Received	Standard Cost	Purchase Price Variance
001421	M.A. HANNA RESIN	PO13800	10021	PREVAIL 3150 NTL	4,409	2.140	9,435.26	2.330	(837.71)
001447	BF GOODRICH	PO13883	10029	ESTALOC 59104 NATURAL	2,000	2.930	5,860.00	3.960	(2,060.00)
001421	M.A. HANNA RESIN	PO13942	10036.501	K RESIN KR01	2,000	0.960	1,920.00	0.800	320.00
001936	MONTELL USA INC	PO13506	10039.108	PP SB786	42,013	0.380	15,964.94	0.350	1,260.39
002054	M.A. HANNA COLOR	PO13847	10271	LQ OPTIMA RED TL300404XLNP 1.5%	150	10.050	1,507.50	10.950	(135.00)
002390	COZ PLASTICS, INC	PO13904	10294.1	CC CPU1840 BLUE 4%	50	10.120	506.00	11.244	(56.22)
002326	DETROIT TUBULAR RIVET, INC.	PO13636	10315	HINGE PIN RIVET 1-07-4-9005 COMFORT	17,770	0.058	1,036.88	0.060	(29.32)
002324	KENDALE INDUSTRIED INC.	PO13502	10318	WASHER AMM9009 1-07-3-9009 COMFORT	16,680	0.022	371.96	0.035	(211.84)
002329	FORTRESS FORMS	PO13634	10320	RECLINING PIN - M9710	10,000	0.116	1,160.00	0.123	(70.00)
002224	MARTIN MACHINE WORKS, INC.	PO13654	10346	ROLLER PIN (ADM9167) JPC0016	70,000	0.077	5,390.00	0.081	(280.00)
002344	SOUTHERN PRECISION SPRING CO.	PO13671	10347	LOCK SPRING (M9169) JPC0018	500	0.045	22.55	0.045	0.05
002327	INDUSTRIAL FASTENERS COPR.	PO13684	10350	FASTENER JPC0024	5,100	0.028	141.27	0.002	132.09
002248	SAWTELLE PRINTING	PO13869	10366	INSTRUCTION BOOK 1-11-2-8204-000	1,010	0.592	597.52	0.710	(119.58)
002372	FASTENATION, INC.	PO13436	10375.11	VELCRO STRIPS - CRADLE ROCKER 1X3	4,200	0.062	259.01	0.062	(1.39)
002276	PSC FABRICATING (TUB FOAM)	PO13703	10379	STAY WARM BATH FOAM #2	5,000	0.400	2,000.00	0.411	(55.00)
002304	IMR, INC.	PO13690	10387.1	DBL UP SEAT PAD TOP & BOTTOM	400	4.000	1,600.00	6.730	(1,092.00)
002372	FASTENATION, INC.	PO13792	10387.117	DBL UP 1BLUE VELCO H/L 53051746/7	2,000	0.600	1,200.00	0.000	1,200.00
002276	PSC FABRICATING (TUB FOAM)	PO13703	10388	DELUXE BATH FOAM PAD 79326-2029	15,000	0.820	12,300.00	0.880	(900.00)
002278	SYRACUSE LABEL	PO13747	10389	BATH WARNING LABEL 79326-0310	50,000	0.030	1,486.50	0.030	(13.50)
001639	FASTNERS, INC.	PO13823	10452.03	X-MAS TREE CLIP 354-190001-00	20,000	0.039	770.00	0.043	(90.00)
002410	KATZKE PAPER CO	PO13877	10652.01	BUBBLE PACK 12X24 MED	9,000	0.068	612.00	0.000	612.00
002048	LENERTZ INDUSTRIAL SUPPLY	PO13881A	10673	BOX 24X12X12 R-45	4,080	0.000	0.00	0.520	(2,121.60)
002228	JEFFERSON SMURFIT CORP.	PO13700	10683.01	BOX LITHO DOUBLE UP JPC0091	5,850	1.569	9,178.65	1.575	(35.10)
001608	AMERICAN DATAPRINT, INC.	PO13572	10688.02	INSTRUCTION SHEET SURE FOOT GATE	100	0.052	5.18	0.000	5.18
001483	SOFTWARE LABELS CORPORATION	PO13949	10688.03	LABEL - WARNING - SURE FOOT GATE	12,000	0.085	1,014.00	0.019	786.00
001469	DUNWIDDIE ASSOCIATES	PO13431	10689	BOX SIMPLE POTTY MASTER CARTON	720	0.945	680.40	0.855	64.80
001483	SOFTWARE LABELS CORPORATION	PO13832	10689.2	LABEL - FP LOGO - SIMPLE POTTY	15,000	0.030	445.50	0.011	280.50
002410	KATZKE PAPER CO	PO13877	10995.3	1/2X 72YD FILAMENT TAPE ST101	12,960	0.005	68.69	0.000	68.69
002304	IMR, INC.	PO13645	12231	TAKATA COMFORT BOLSTER ARM COVER	400	0.800	320.00	0.930	(52.00)
									(3,430.57)

ing material costs in line with original expectations. Another use for this report is to judge purchasing managers with it, perhaps issuing bonuses to those who can best keep costs in line with expectations.

Another variation on this report is to run a comparison between the amount of the monthly purchase price variance and any changes in the amount of inventory turnover. The reason for this comparison is to spot any increases in inventory that may be caused by a purchasing manager who buys too much stock in exchange for obtaining a lower price from a supplier for buying in bulk. This is frequently a bad trade-off, since a company has now invested extra funds in inventory that may never even be used. This comparison may also be a valuable tool for judging the performance of the purchasing staff.

Yet another variation on this report is to track cost changes on a trend line for only a few of the highest-volume and most expensive parts (tracking all parts on trend lines results only in an enormous report that no one will have the time or inclination to examine). This information reveals whether a few key costs are increasing or dropping, which may lead management to design new products that use more or less of each key material, depending on how prices are moving.

Finally, if a company sets up target costs that it expects the purchasing (or engineering) staffs to achieve for specific parts by targeted dates, it may be possible to itemize the current cost alongside the dates when the targeted cost levels are expected to be reached. An example of such a report is shown in Exhibit 15.4, in which a product's key components are listed, along with the current cost of each item and the targeted percentage reductions to be achieved by specified dates in the future. When creating such a chart, it is useful to determine the preplanned termination date of the product, after which it is assumed that the engineering staff will issue a new product to replace it that will command either better margins or a higher percentage of the market, on the assumption that the current product will eventually fall prey to increased competition by the products of other companies.

Exhibit 15.4   Target Cost Report

Part Description	Current Cost	Target Date	Target Cost Reduction	Target Date	Target Cost Reduction	Target Date	Target Cost Reduction
Headrest	$12.32	02/01	2.5%	08/01	3.0%	02/02	2.0%
Molded seat	10.41	02/01	4.0%	08/01	8.0%	02/02	5.0%
Seat cushion	5.05	02/01	1.0%	08/01	5.0%	02/02	4.0%
Rocker bar	4.21	02/01	5.0%	08/01	3.0%	02/02	8.0%
Seat belt	3.33	02/01	2.5%	08/01	6.0%	02/02	1.0%
Side panel	1.09	02/01	8.0%	08/01	4.0%	02/02	3.0%
Foam pad	.79	02/01	7.0%	08/01	1.0%	02/02	6.0%

LABOR REPORTS

For some organizations, especially in the service industry, labor costs are the largest expense on the income statement. For any companies of this sort, it is usual to provide management with detailed reports regarding the utilization of labor, its cost, and how the current labor mix matches the budgeted mix that was agreed on at the beginning of the year. These reports are discussed in this section.

A good starting point for labor analysis is a simple comparison of the head count in each department as compared to the budgeted head count. In the example shown in Exhibit 15.5, all company departments are listed down the left side of the page, along with all job titles within each department. The next two columns then compare the budgeted head count for each job title to the actual number of employees currently employed. In case there is any question about precisely who is included in each job title, their names are listed in the far right column. This information is extremely useful for determining which department managers are overstaffing their departments, as well as those who are having trouble filling budgeted positions. Also, if there is a cost overrun in the labor area, this is a good starting point for determining what may be the nature of the cost.

Once a controller has analyzed the company head count, it is still necessary to determine the usage of employees, which means the overtime costs they are incurring. This is an especially important piece of information if the bulk of employees are paid on an hourly basis, and if there is little control over the amount of overtime hours worked. In such cases, the overtime cost can reach disproportionate levels, resulting in a significant reduction in profitability. An example of a report that clearly delineates overtime issues is shown in Exhibit 15.6. It lists all employees in each department who are paid on an hourly basis, along with their overtime percentages by pay period. A quick glance at this report reveals to all department managers the names of those people who are abusing their rights to work overtime. It is also useful for determining which departments habitually work large amounts of overtime, which is frequently a clue that an additional person should be hired in those areas. In the example, the logistics department is consistently using large amounts of overtime, and thus may require additional hires.

Though the head count and overtime reports are sufficient for determining the key labor issues in most cases, there is still a hole left in the labor analysis, which is the annualized pay per person. If managers are giving raises or bonuses to employees without authorization, there is no way for senior management to know this without the reporting tool shown in Exhibit 15.7. This annualized pay report is extracted from the periodic payroll reports, showing the most recent annualized pay for employees, based on their pay during the most recent month. Management can use this report to determine average pay levels by category, determine how well pay levels are matching budgeted amounts, whether or not there are unfilled budgeted positions, the last date on which specific employees received pay raises, and when employees started or ended their employment. Given the range of inquiries that can

Exhibit 15.5   Headcount by Position Report

	Budget	Actual	
Engineering			
Engineer	4	3	Meyer, Nelson, Ruggiero
Assembly			
Inspectors	2	1	Williams
Manager	1	1	Zeltman
Supervisor	1	1	Manners
Planner/Scheduler	1	1	Zweifel
Warehouse Staff	2	3	Bowden, Chavira, Jackson
Maintenance			
Maintenance Lead	1	1	Strathmore
Maintenance	3	3	Delatore, Hansen, Lage
Mold			
Mold Coordinator	1	1	Ruybal
Mold Tech	2	3	Davidson, Miller, Stallsworth
Process Tech			
Process Engineer	1	1	Coomes
Process Tech	5	11	Allen, Barron, Estrada, Gergely, Graham, Michels, Pham, Reynolds, Sherman, Tietzel, White
Production			
VP/General Mgr.	1	1	Souders
Plant Manager	1	1	Horton
Shift Coordinator	4	4	Lawrence, Rhoads, Roybal, Schumann
Quality			
Quality Engineer	2	1	Miller
Quality Staff	4	5	Bell, McDonald, Perez, Reidenbach, Smith
Selling, Gen., Admin.			
Accounting Staff	1	1	Martel
Admin. Assistant	1	1	Courtney
Controller	1	1	Manson
Customer Service	2	2	Geurink, Newton
Human Resources	1	1	Nelson
MIS Coordinator	1	1	Hanson
President	1	1	Anderson
Sales Manager	1	1	Miller
Logistics			
Warehouse Coordinator	1	1	Espinoza
Materials Manager	1	1	Rosenthal
Scheduler	2	2	Berlener, Garcia
Warehouse Staff	6	9	Chhoeung, Gage, Jacques, Lowrey, Stewart, Tucker, Warnke, Washington, Webber
Totals	55	64	

Exhibit 15.6 Overtime by Employee Report

	1/4	1/18	2/1	2/15	3/01	3/15	3/29	4/12	4/26
Engineering									
Nelson, Mark	23%	6%	15%	10%	18%	15%	0%	6%	18%
Maintenance									
Delatore, Alex	31%	15%	13%	24%	16%	26%	8%	15%	36%
Hansen, Erik	0%	11%	16%	41%	39%	32%	31%	28%	41%
Lage, Laurence	15%	19%	13%	26%	39%	21%	24%	4%	
Strasheim, Dave	24%	33%	31%	39%	35%	30%	34%	33%	31%
Mold Shop									
Davidson, Raymond	0%	5%	0%	5%	13%	6%	10%	8%	18%
Miller, Jerry	11%	31%	10%	9%	20%	25%	16%	25%	11%
Ruybal, Tim	1%	0%	36%	10%	9%	34%	55%	35%	46%
Stallsworth, Delbert	25%	23%	19%	34%	14%	30%	28%	26%	30%
Process Technicians									
Allen, Aaron	8%	13%	28%	21%	40%	30%	0%	21%	11%
Barron, Alejandro					14%	54%	44%	0%	15%
Estrada, Steve	15%	15%	11%	11%	8%	11%	10%	9%	11%
Gergely, Mark							11%	11%	11%
Graham, Carl							13%	26%	
Michels, Shayne					36%	25%	33%	11%	34%
Pham, Hung								11%	6%
Reynolds, Mike	0%	0%	11%	0%	11%	34%	11%	14%	10%
Sherman, William					11%	11%	5%	0%	11%
Quality Assurance									
Bell, Vellia Mae					13%	30%	0%	0%	0%
McDonald, Theresa	11%	0%	14%	0%	25%	6%	13%	0%	10%
Perez, Yvonne	25%	13%	0%	20%	0%	25%	0%	0%	0%
Reidenbach, Donna	10%	14%	8%	28%	30%	9%	19%	25%	24%
Smith, Jacqueline	0%	13%	13%	13%	13%	13%	13%	0%	13%
Logistics									
Berlener, Kara	24%	23%	29%	19%	24%	25%	8%	25%	19%
Chhoeung, Lin					0%	0%	0%	0%	13%
Gage, Clarence							39%	9%	41%
Garcia, Rebecca	8%	21%	39%	33%	18%	18%	10%	25%	21%
Jacques, Kum	10%	0%	33%	45%	20%	23%	51%	29%	30%
Lowrey, Jim	23%	29%	24%	25%	24%	20%	25%	28%	24%
Stewart, Loretha							26%	53%	46%
Tucker, Dwan					1%	0%	0%	0%	28%
Warnke, Tom	3%	30%	26%	23%	21%	36%	19%	28%	24%
Webber, Ricky							0%	1%	0%

	1/4	1/18	2/1	2/15	3/01	3/15	3/29	4/12	4/26
SG&A									
Courtney, Debbie	8%	9%	6%	13%	5%	13%	6%	13%	8%
Martel, Kim	3%	1%	14%	6%	4%	0%	3%	0%	0%
Newton, Merrie	4%	9%	6%	9%	11%	10%	9%	9%	15%
Assembly									
Bowden, Greg				13%	5%	3%	23%	29%	40%
Chavira, Elvia				6%	0%	1%	6%	15%	29%
Jackson, Mike				18%	16%	8%	21%	6%	33%
Williams, Rosa				8%	3%	11%	20%	0%	74%
Zweifel, Alan	11%	25%	20%	20%	0%	28%	20%	25%	28%
Average of all Overtime	12%	14%	17%	18%	16%	19%	17%	15%	22%

be answered with this simple report format, a controller should strongly consider creating it for the use of senior management.

The only problem with the annualized pay report is that it contains highly confidential information and could cause trouble among employees if a stray copy reaches disgruntled employees who can then compare their pay to that of other employees in the company. Consequently, this must be a password-protected file, and distribution should be severely limited.

When the head count, overtime, and annualized pay reports are compiled on a regular basis and regularly distributed to the proper management personnel, a controller will find that nearly all management inquiries in this area will be answered, or can be quickly answered by reshuffling the information on these reports.

STANDARD MARGIN REPORTS

One of the most important reports that controllers should issue is the standard margin report. This is a listing that offsets the standard cost of a product against its most commonly charged price to arrive at a standard margin. Although not as accurate as an activity-based costing review or an analysis that incorporates a variety of material and labor variances, it is usually very easy to compile and therefore can be issued to management regularly and with little effort. The main benefit of this report is that management can quickly peruse it to determine which products have low profit margins. Management can then take such steps as requoting the product to increase prices, reviewing the product costs to see if some costs can be reduced, or even terminating the product. The report can be sorted by increasing margin percentage to show those products with the worst margins at the top, so management does not have to look further than the first page to spot the most troublesome products.

Exhibit 15.7 Annualized Pay Report

Name	Department	Budget	Jan	Feb	Mar	Apr	May	Jun
Bowery, Dan	Assembly	28,752	19,524	19,524	19,524	20,267	20,267	20,216
Johnson, Gregory	Assembly	28,752	33,052	33,052	33,052	34,944	32,968	32,272
Monfort, Pat	Assembly	43,260	46,521	46,521	46,521	47,060	47,060	47,060
Zwinger, Dave	Assembly	85,488	82,992	82,992	82,992	82,992	82,992	83,000
Zwonter, Steve	Assembly	39,996	47,788	47,788	47,788	47,788	45,019	36,078
Mayes, Dennis	Engineering	48,456	36,504	36,504	36,504	36,504	36,504	38,000
Stewart, Shayne	Engineering	48,456	50,842	50,842	50,842	51,986	51,986	51,986
Open	Engineering	48,456	0	0	0	0	0	0
Esther, Howard	Logistics	49,920	48,321	48,321	50,388	50,388	50,388	50,400
Haun, Alonzo	Logistics	25,392	21,294	21,294	21,294	21,294	21,294	23,320
Linger, Lowell	Logistics	25,392	39,750	39,250	39,500	39,000	36,595	41,550
Rose, Jim	Logistics	55,116	53,200	54,990	54,990	54,990	54,990	55,000
Stewart, Thomas	Logistics	25,392	33,058	31,954	32,058	34,359	30,888	29,571
Wallace, Loretha	Logistics	25,392	30,966	30,966	30,966	30,966	24,115	23,870
Delany, Eric	Maintenance	35,880	29,500	29,500	34,320	33,839	34,320	32,020
Henderson, Alex	Maintenance	35,880	49,321	50,721	49,384	51,155	49,348	29,264
Norris, Aaron	Maintenance	35,880	50,960	50,960	50,960	50,960	54,379	67,227
Allen, Mark	Process Tech	40,992	38,972	39,067	38,555	41,574	33,618	44,630
Boris, Shayne	Process Tech	40,992	31,525	31,525	31,525	31,525	35,152	37,301
Masterson, Jill	Process Tech	50,004	44,642	44,642	44,642	44,642	44,642	45,657

Name	Department							
Phorest, Michael	Process Tech	**40,992**	30,555	30,706	30,541	29,185	31,434	30,145
Reynold, William	Process Tech	**None**	35,000	35,000	37,140	37,141	39,156	45,319
Short, Bob	Process Tech	**None**	30,000	32,000	32,000	32,877	32,071	26,018
Anderson, Carl	Production Mgmt	**110,000**	110,000	110,000	110,000	110,006	110,006	110,000
Graham, Lee	Production Mgmt	**42,996**	32,000	32,000	34,996	34,996	34,996	35,000
Honest, Darrell	Production Mgmt	**70,800**	70,798	70,798	70,798	70,798	70,798	70,799
Lawrence, Michael	Production Mgmt	**42,996**	47,996	47,996	47,996	47,996	47,996	48,000
Summers, Theresa	Production Mgmt	**42,996**	36,010	36,010	36,010	36,010	36,010	36,000
Bella, Donna	Quality Assurance	**24,996**	24,031	24,258	24,258	23,465	24,258	22,381
McDonald, Robert	Quality Assurance	**24,996**	25,386	25,971	25,069	24,063	30,069	27,585
Mills, Alan	Quality Assurance	**50,004**	49,998	49,998	49,998	49,998	49,998	50,000
Reider, Jo	Quality Assurance	**50,004**	30,776	36,521	34,058	35,113	33,436	32,877
Smith, George	Quality Assurance	**24,996**	18,538	18,538	18,538	18,538	18,528	18,538
Walmsley-Dunnet, Al	Quality Assurance	**None**	26,000	26,000	26,000	26,000	26,000	26,000
Bossy, Frank	S, G & A	**84,456**	82,004	82,004	82,004	82,004	82,004	82,000
Gainer, George	S, G & A	**124,992**	125,008	125,008	125,008	125,008	125,008	125,000
Hammit, Robert	S, G & A	**46,056**	45,240	45,240	45,240	45,240	45,916	46,000
Nelson, Andrew	S, G & A	**27,996**	26,754	26,754	26,754	26,754	26,754	26,750
Spudsit, Jeffrey	S, G & A	**75,000**	82,550	82,550	82,550	82,550	82,550	89,196
Torrance, David	S, G & A	**None**	51,000	51,000	51,000	51,000	51,000	51,000
		1,702,124	1,768,376	1,778,765	1,785,763	1,794,975	1,784,513	1,787,030

An example of the standard margin by product report is shown in Exhibit 15.8. This report can be compiled on an electronic spreadsheet or created with a more sophisticated report writing tool that works with an in-house accounting and engineering software package. In the report, the product number, description, and average price are copied or extracted from a month-end sales report from the accounting database. The standard material and labor costs come from the bill of materials, which should be stored in the engineering database. Then, the report subtracts the standard material and labor costs from the price to arrive at a direct gross margin. This report does not attempt to allocate overhead costs to a product—it is simply showing management the clearest and most nondebatable margins for each product. If a product has a poor margin *prior to* any additional overhead costs, then management must immediately address the problem. If overhead costs are added to this report, a common management response is that the overhead costs are not accurate (because they can be directly applied only to a specific product with an allocation method that may be debatable), and the report is quickly returned to the accounting department with a request for a review, because "the numbers must be wrong."

An excellent follow-up report to the standard margin report is one that clusters margins together by customer, such as the report shown in Exhibit 15.9. In this report, we have taken the same information in the standard margin report and added an additional column next to each product to list the customer to whom each product is sold. If each product sells to multiple customers, then there will have to be additional rows in the report to differentiate this information. With this more detailed report format, one can re-sort the report by customer, which yields the margin for each one. In addition, the report in Exhibit 15.9 lists overhead allocations for machine usage as well as a separate assembly operation, which are derived from a separate activity-based costing analysis. In order to differentiate between the margin from direct costs (i.e., materials and labor) and the margin from both direct and overhead costs, the report also includes these two margins side by side on the right side of the report. This report format is highly effective for determining the major costs and margins associated with a company's products.

An excellent way to present the customer margin information in Exhibit 15.9 is to construct the matrix format shown in Exhibit 15.10, in which customers are grouped into one of four areas on the matrix. In the example, those customers with a combination of the lowest sales volume and the lowest margins are located in the lower left quadrant, while those with the highest margins and greatest volume appear in the upper right quadrant. Those customers with low volume but high margins are grouped into the upper left quadrant, and those with a combination of low margins and high volume go into the lower right quadrant. This arrangement is a very effective way for management to see at a glance which customers yield the largest profits and which ones do not. The obvious management actions based on this information are to either attempt to shift as many customers as possible into the upper right quadrant, which results in high-volume, high-profit customers, or to drop those customers with excessively low margins.

Exhibit 15.8 Standard Margin by Product Report

					Standard Cost of Goods Sold Sorted by Margin %					
Item No.	Item Description	Qty Sold	Unit Price	Total Revenue	Unit Cost Material	Unit Cost Labor	Total Cost Material	Total Cost Labor	Margin %	Total Margin $
14003.221	Light Diffuser	3,500	0.025	88	0.002	0.032	9	113	–38.5%	–34
12231	Bolster Arm Cover	3,016	0.8	2,413	0.930	—	2,805	—	–16.3%	–392
12350.001	Cradle Rocker	643	15.64	10,057	14.364	1.077	9,236	692	1.3%	128
12200.7	Baby Bath	65,000	0.141	9,165	0.110	0.024	7,119	1,555	5.4%	491
13250.2	Mophead	18,480	0.907	16,761	0.444	0.318	8,207	5,873	16.0%	2,682
14003.501	Magnet Cover	5,000	0.116	580	0.066	0.027	329	136	19.8%	115
11706	Pail, 5 Gallon	96	1.5	144	1.032	0.109	99	10	24.0%	34
14003.201	Key Pad	7,000	0.075	525	0.023	0.032	158	225	26.9%	141
12320.001	Baby Potty	1,710	7.95	13,595	4.304	1.357	7,360	2,321	28.8%	3,914
13222.2	Ski Tip	5,000	0.605	3,025	0.293	0.135	1,466	674	29.2%	885
12300.001	Diaper Pail	13,992	6.219	87,016	3.472	0.900	48,577	12,589	29.7%	25,851
14039.02	Ruler, 6"	1,741	0.217	378	0.093	0.054	162	95	32.1%	121
14003.352	Terminal Block	20,000	0.1	2,000	0.040	0.026	795	522	34.1%	683
13207	Ski Tail	4,899	0.275	1,347	0.150	0.023	735	113	37.1%	500
12006	Food Storage Tray	332,640	0.135	44,906	0.067	0.015	22,230	5,064	39.2%	17,612
14037.01	Remote Control Case	1,150	0.317	365	0.104	0.061	120	70	47.9%	175
14026.1	Medicine Spoon	5,000	0.092	460	0.033	0.015	166	72	48.1%	221

Exhibit 15.8 *Continued*

Standard Cost of Goods Sold Sorted by Margin %

Item No.	Item Description	Qty Sold	Unit Price	Total Revenue	Unit Cost Material	Unit Cost Labor	Total Cost Material	Total Cost Labor	Margin %	Total Margin $
14052.021	Water Bottle	20,000	0.105	2,100	0.034	0.017	684	337	51.4%	1,079
14026.07	Key Case	56,000	0.084	4,704	0.014	0.027	790	1,492	51.5%	2,422
14003.64	Battery Holder	2,500	0.123	308	0.018	0.039	44	98	53.7%	165
14001.03	Battery Case	4,320	2.009	8,679	0.722	0.106	3,120	457	58.8%	5,103
14003.76	Light Pipe	21,000	0.145	3,045	0.015	0.037	316	776	64.1%	1,953
14052.01	Water Bottle Cap	22,000	0.093	2,046	0.024	0.008	529	179	65.4%	1,337
14025.046	Gasket, 23 mm	106	0.179	19	0.017	0.044	2	5	66.0%	13
14010.096	Retaining Strip	3,000	0.412	1,236	0.054	0.057	161	170	73.3%	905
14025.02	Coin Holder	25,872	0.271	7,011	0.041	0.031	1,063	788	73.6%	5,161
14003.28	Gasket, 35 mm	2,500	0.09	225	0.006	0.017	16	44	73.6%	166
14003.77	LCD Support Bracket	21,000	0.244	5,124	0.023	0.025	481	525	80.4%	4,118
				1,763,913			861,868	231,180	38.0%	670,866

Additional information can go into each quadrant of the report, such as the number of customers located in each quadrant, the percentage of sales that each quadrant accounts for, and the average margin for all sales in each quadrant.

Because this is such an important report—one that management may grow to rely on a great deal for making decisions about keeping or dropping customers—it may make sense to improve the accuracy of the underlying margin analysis from one that relies only on direct costs to one that includes a detailed overhead cost allocation, perhaps through an activity-based costing review. With this additional data, one can more precisely determine the margins for each customer, thereby ensuring that each one falls into the correct revenue/profitability quadrant.

The two reports shown in this section are among the most important that a controller can produce, since decisions based on them can directly affect company profitability. Consequently, one should take extra time to ensure the accuracy of the underlying information that comprises these reports.

BUDGET REPORTS

When financial statements are produced, a controller should release an additional report that shows the actual and budgeted expense line items, along with the amounts by which actual costs are over or under expected levels. Those managers who are responsible for each expense item can then use this information to control costs to keep them within budgeted levels. An example of this report is shown in Exhibit 15.11.

The expense control report lists two departments, administration and manufacturing, and all of the general ledger accounts in which costs are accumulated for each one. Next to these cost accounts are the names of the people who are directly responsible for expenditures. These should be the people who sign purchase orders authorizing expenses in each area. The report then shows the budgeted and actual costs for the month, as well as the variance between the two. This information is repeated for year-to-date information, and concludes with a listing of the full-year budget for each expense line item. This report presentation tells a manager how much money has already been spent and what is still available. A controller can also modify this report to sort by the largest expense variances, so that senior management can quickly ascertain the amounts of the largest variances and question the responsible managers regarding why expenses are so high. The report can also be sorted in the opposite direction to determine which budgeted expenses are not being used, which can be factored into the next budget revision by reducing those budgeted expenses.

This relatively simple report format is a mandatory report that should be distributed to all managers immediately after monthly financial statements are released. It is generally not necessary to also release a list of notes regarding why expenses are not in line with budgeted amounts, because these expla-

Exhibit 15.9 Standard Margin by Customer Report

Item No.	Item Description	Customer Name	YTD Units	Unit Price	Std Material Cost	Std Labor Cost	Std Machine Cost	Assembly Overhead Cost	Total Revenue	Total Expense	Total Margin	Direct Std % Margin	Total All-Inclusive Margin %
14003	Light Diffuser	Early Winters	2,762	24.830	18.1537	2.0184	3.198	1.457	68,580	68,575	6	19%	0%
12231	Bolster Arm Cover	Early Winters	4,327	25.070	18.1019	2.0184	0.661	1.457	108,478	96,225	12,253	20%	11%
12350	Cradle Rocker	Early Winters	20	0.350	0.0255	0.0435	0.015	0.000	7	2	5	80%	76%
12201	Baby Bath	Early Winters	25	0.250	0.0113	0.0435	0.015	0.000	6	2	4	78%	72%
13250	Mophead	Early Winters	378	56.680	33.2162	5.7876	5.012	4.162	21,425	18,211	3,214	31%	15%
14004	Magnet Cover	Early Winters	17,800	43.600	27.5402	5.7876	5.012	4.162	776,080	756,524	19,556	24%	3%
11706	Pail, 5 Gallon	Anterior Designs	320,869	0.141	0.1095	0.0239	0.052	0.000	45,243	59,446	(14,203)	5%	-31%
14003	Key Pad	Anterior Designs	45,000	0.230	0.0424	0.0283	0.042	0.000	10,350	5,074	5,276	69%	51%
12320	Baby Potty	Anterior Designs	53,500	0.250	0.0505	0.0381	0.057	0.000	13,375	7,769	5,606	65%	42%
13222	Ski Tip	Anterior Designs	3,146	25.670	11.8078	8.1774	2.516	0.202	80,758	71,427	9,331	22%	12%
12300	Diaper Pail	Backman Services	1,022	13.870	7.8078	0.5974	2.516	0.202	14,175	11,369	2,806	39%	20%
14039	Ruler, 6"	Backman Services	3,016	3.970	3.9700	0.0000	—	—	11,974	11,974	—	0%	0%
14003	Terminal Block	Backman Services	3,016	0.800	0.9300	0.0000	—	—	2,413	2,805	(392)	-16%	-16%
13207	Ski Tail	Backman Services	84,090	6.396	3.4643	0.9171	1.769	0.227	537,840	536,270	1,569	31%	0%
12006	Food Storage Tray	Backman Services	10	0.500	0.0671	0.0544	0.019	0.000	5	1	4	76%	72%
14037	Remote Control Case	Backman Services	127,737	6.019	3.6483	0.6593	1.687	0.328	768,849	807,653	(38,804)	28%	-5%
14025	Gasket, 23 mm	Engineered Solutions	32,142	7.976	4.6375	0.9292	2.842	0.263	256,365	278,748	(22,383)	30%	-9%
14010	Retaining Strip	Engineered Solutions	42,571	5.984	4.4709	0.6200	1.768	0.381	254,753	308,191	(53,438)	15%	-21%
14025	Coin Holder	Engineered Solutions	11,881	1.951	0.6697	0.2208	0.431	0.000	23,180	15,703	7,477	54%	32%
14003	Gasket, 35 mm	Engineered Solutions	1	13.748	9.3296	1.5807	0.309	0.972	14	12	2	21%	11%
14004	LCD Support Bracket	Engineered Solutions	3,026	3.017	1.5511	0.3698	0.525	0.000	9,128	7,400	1,728	36%	19%
									3,002,998	3,063,381	-60,383		-2%

nations are the responsibility of the managers who originally authorized the purchases in their departments.

INVESTMENT REPORTS

The finance department has a great interest in the amount of interest it earns on a company's invested funds, as well as any offsetting expenses that will reduce the net interest rate earned. For this group, the simple reporting format shown in Exhibit 15.12 is an adequate way to present the required information. It itemizes the type and amount of each investment, the interest rate earned, maturity date, and notations regarding risk and liquidity issues. Unless there is an enormous array of investments, this format is sufficient for reducing a company's entire investment activity onto a single page. There are already notations on one side of the report, so there is rarely a reason for attaching an additional explanatory page.

An additional report that shows changes in investment returns over time is the same information just presented, but tracked on a trend line for multiple periods. This report tells the finance staff if there are investments that are no longer generating returns at previous levels, which may be grounds for shifting into some other type of investment.

CASH FLOW REPORTS

Cash flow is the lifeblood of any organization. Without a consistent flow of cash, there is no way to fund operations, and a company will quickly find itself out of business. Given the severity of the consequences if cash does not arrive on time, this is clearly an area in which analysis must be very frequent—it will not do to wait until the end of the month to determine that the company ran out of cash three weeks ago! Accordingly, the following reports should be calculated and distributed to management at least weekly, and perhaps even daily, for those organizations that have little in the way of cash reserves, and for whom any cash shortfall would be disastrous.

The first cash report to compile is the working capital report. An example of this report is shown in Exhibit 15.13. It lists the three components of working capital, which are accounts receivable, inventory, and accounts payable. When combined, these reveal a company's investment in short-term business activities. When accounts receivable increase, this is an added investment of company funds in shipments to customers for which payments have not been received. The reverse occurs for accounts payable, because suppliers are funding the company with their billings, for which the company has not yet issued a payment. Finally, the inventory figure shows a company's investment in the level of inventory considered necessary for current sales levels. This is a critical report, because a company can easily experience a dramatic surge in its working capital needs, perhaps because of a large unpaid accounts

Exhibit 15.10   Customer Margin Analysis, Matrix Format

	No. Customers = 30 Percent of Sales = 5% Annual Sales = $531K Annual Margin = 47%		No. Customers = 10 Percent of Sales =42% Annual Sales = $4,313K Annual Margin = 37%		
				Margin %	Annual Dollars
	AMI Industries	Innovative Brick	Acme	33%	$607,600
	At Last Gourmet	Inovonics	Best Western	39%	$134,200
	Audubon Park	Mann's International	Champion Auto	43%	$154,900
	Bolder Tech	Mark VII Equipment	Estes Paints	38%	$340,400
High	Broncorp	Martin Gillet	Gates Plastics	39%	$129,800
Margin	Buckeye	Melco Indus.	Hudson Bay Products	35%	$1,586,200
	Bush Hog Turf	Peak Indus.	International Diversified	39%	$964,400
	Chem Source	Product Architects	Monster Equipment	32%	$423,300
	CMS Inc.	Progressive Spec.	Sudden Coffee	41%	$440,100
	Conversion Tech	Ryco Packaging	Venture Home Foods	41%	$139,500
	Denver Instrument	Scientech			$4,312,800
	French Made	Spraying Systems			
	Great Plains	Toxonomics			
	Grecian Delight	Wave Sports			
	Hunter Douglas	Sensormedics			
30%					
	No. Customers = 19 Percent of Sales = 5% Annual Sales = $493K Annual Margin = 11%		No. Customers = 9 Percent of Sales = 48% Annual Sales = $4,871K Annual Margin = 22%		
				Margin %	Annual Dollars
	Aspen Products	Polymedica	Anterior Designs	29%	$204,000
	Backman Services	Primealert	Bombproof Draperies	14%	$130,900
	Brush Mat	Rocky Mtn Oil	Early Research Corp.	24%	$925,000
Low	Case Logic	Scott Systems	Engineered Solutions	25%	$256,400
Margin	CMS Inc.	Sun Co.	Highland Scots	26%	$146,500
	Crowder Supply	T. Marzetti Co.	Kanberra Koala	19%	$1,559,500
	Eastco Interior	Tranex	Optimum Energy	22%	$904,500
	Easy Care	Weston Oil	Trimetal	16%	$548,300
	Halston Oil	Z-Tech	Waverly Sports	24%	$196,000
	Hotsy				$4,871,100

Low Revenue	$100K	High Revenue

Exhibit 15.11 Expense Control Report

Department	Description	Responsible	April Expense	April Budget	April Variance	YTD Expense	YTD Budget	YTD Variance	Full Year Budget
ADMINISTRATION									
Admin	Accounting & Tax	Underhill, David	2,500	2,500	—	11,832	10,000	(1,832)	30,000
Admin	Advertising	Morris, William	1,680	833	(847)	4,959	3,332	(1,627)	9,996
Admin	Auto Expense	Morris, William	1,435	4,316	2,881	7,823	17,264	9,441	51,792
Admin	Bad Debt	Underhill, David	3,000	1,000	(2,000)	6,849	4,000	(2,849)	12,000
Admin	Charitable	Morris, William	—	1,250	1,250	179	5,000	4,821	15,000
Admin	Consultants	Underhill, David	6,363	2,000	(4,363)	17,415	8,000	(9,415)	24,000
Admin	Keyman Insurance	Morris, William	1,337	1,333	(4)	4,659	5,332	673	15,996
Admin	Legal	Morris, William	688	666	(22)	982	2,664	1,682	7,992
Admin	Liability Insurance	Underhill, David	3,500	3,500	—	13,001	14,000	999	42,000
Admin	Maintenance	Underhill, David	256	2,812	2,556	5,406	11,248	5,842	33,744
Admin	Other Expense	Underhill, David	161	1,500	1,339	3,881	6,000	2,119	18,000
Admin	Phones	Underhill, David	6,341	4,750	(1,591)	25,854	19,000	(6,854)	57,000
Admin	Postage	Underhill, David	740	1,270	530	3,719	5,080	1,361	15,240
Admin	Salaries	Underhill, David	48,803	39,215	(9,588)	151,656	156,860	5,204	470,580
Admin	Supplies	Underhill, David	1,668	3,541	1,873	1,749	7,082	5,333	42,492
Admin	Taxes	Underhill, David	(465)	166	631	(1,399)	664	2,063	1,992
Admin	Training	Underhill, David	1,437	291	(1,146)	6,215	1,164	(5,051)	3,492
Admin	Travel	Morris, William	259	3,750	3,491	5,205	15,000	9,795	45,000
	Grand Total		**79,703**	**74,693**	**(5,010)**	**269,985**	**291,690**	**21,705**	**896,316**

259

Exhibit 15.11 *Continued*

Department	Description	Responsible	April Expense	April Budget	April Variance	YTD Expense	YTD Budget	YTD Variance	Full Year Budget
MANUFACTURING									
Assembly	Building Maintenance	Monahan, Delaney	2,434	—	(2,434)	5,284	—	(5,284)	—
Assembly	Building Rent	Monahan, Delaney	17,100	17,100	—	57,670	57,000	(670)	205,200
Assembly	Liability Insurance	Monahan, Delaney	500	500	—	2,000	2,000	—	6,000
Assembly	Maintenance	Monahan, Delaney	1,235	1,200	(35)	3,122	4,400	1,278	14,400
Assembly	Other Expenses	Monahan, Delaney	144	—	(144)	402	—	(402)	—
Assembly	Rentals	Monahan, Delaney	1,767	1,400	(367)	7,430	4,600	(2,830)	16,800
Assembly	Salaries	Monahan, Delaney	33,445	23,197	(10,248)	97,245	92,788	(4,457)	278,364
Assembly	Supplies	Monahan, Delaney	2,303	200	(2,103)	9,182	5,700	(3,482)	2,400
Assembly	Training	Monahan, Delaney	—	116	116	—	116	116	1,392
Assembly	Travel	Monahan, Delaney	3,117	200	(2,917)	4,261	800	(3,461)	2,400
	Grand Total		**62,045**	**43,913**	**(18,132)**	**186,596**	**167,404**	**(19,192)**	**526,956**

receivable or inventory that is not selling well, that vastly exceeds any cash drain that the income statement might reveal if there is a loss from continuing operations. Also, a change in working capital is not normally a sudden occurrence. There is a trend line, as accounts receivable or inventory gradually worsen, so it is important to graph this trend and report it to management, along with an explanatory statement regarding why there are changes in the report.

An example of the information that should accompany this report is:

> The company's investment in working capital has increased by $1 million in the last three months. This is caused by two problems. One is that customer ABC Corporation has recently bought out one of its founders for a large sum, which leaves it cash poor. To fund the cash difference, it is arbitrarily lengthening its payment terms to its suppliers, one of whom is us. The increase in accounts receivable to this customer now stands at $350,000. This is a highly profitable account, with margins of 47 percent, so we do not recommend drastic action in collecting the overdue funds. In addition, the new assembly operation is not completing and shipping products as rapidly as scheduled, which has resulted in an increase in inventory of $650,000 that has been ordered in anticipation of immediate assembly and sale. To correct this problem, we recommend that the

Exhibit 15.12   Investment Summary Report

Investment Description	Amount of Investment	Interest Rate Earned	Maturity Date	Notes
3M Bond	$1,500,000	7.2%	4/05/05	Retain to maturity date
Emerson Electric Bond	2,500,000	6.6%	5/15/12	None
GE Commercial Paper	3,000,000	5.8%	11/15/04	None
Money Market	500,000	2.2%	None	Double this investment to increase amount of operating funds on hand
Motorola Bond	750,000	7.2%	3/15/09	Risk level increased due to iridium failure
U.S. Government Security	2,250,000	5.1%	7/01/19	Sell for higher rates on commercial paper
Totals	**$10,500,000**	**5.7%**	—	—

industrial engineering department conduct an immediate review of the assembly operation to determine why the assembly schedule is not being met.

In addition to the working capital report, it is nearly always necessary to determine the daily cash position. This is a simple report—perhaps just an e-mail to a few financial executives—that notes the book balance that the company has recorded for its current cash position, offset against the bank's collected cash balance, with a variance between the two that signifies the amount of funds that have been paid out, but which have not yet cleared the bank. This information is most useful for determining the amount of cash that must be added to the checking account each day to fund cash requirements, or the amount that can be extracted and added to investments or used to draw down debt balances. From an analysis perspective, this information can also be used

Exhibit 15.13   Working Capital Report

Total Working Capital

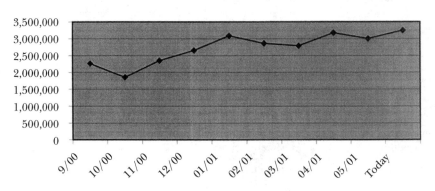

Working Capital Trend Line

	Accounts Receivable		Inventory		Accounts Payable		Total Working Capital
9/00	2,028,000	9/00	1,839,000	9/00	1,604,000	9/00	2,263,000
10/00	1,663,000	10/00	1,614,000	10/00	1,423,000	10/00	1,854,000
11/00	1,498,000	11/00	1,784,000	11/00	933,000	11/00	2,349,000
12/00	1,664,000	12/00	1,932,000	12/00	942,000	12/00	2,654,000
01/01	2,234,000	01/01	2,007,000	01/01	1,152,000	01/01	3,089,000
02/01	2,450,000	02/01	2,273,000	02/01	1,862,000	02/01	2,861,000
03/01	2,042,000	03/01	2,419,000	03/01	1,671,000	03/01	2,790,000
04/01	3,036,000	04/01	2,715,000	04/01	2,575,000	04/01	3,176,000
05/01	2,998,000	05/01	2,588,000	05/01	2,585,000	05/01	3,001,000
Today	2,875,000	Today	2,976,000	Today	2,606,000	Today	3,245,000

to spot patterns in cash flows, perhaps of the seasonal variety, that can be used to predict future cash flows. This information can be used for cash budgeting purposes.

Further, it is necessary to generate a cash forecast, usually for at least the next month, if not the next quarter. This information is based on cash receipts from expected sales, as well as cash disbursements to fund expenses from continuing operations, plus cash from other sources such as borrowings or equity placements, less cash outflows for capital expenditures. A very simple version of this report is shown in Exhibit 15.14. The report is used to determine if there are unusual cash shortfalls coming up in the near future that require special borrowing or equity increases, or cash inflows for which new cash investments must be planned.

Exhibit 15.14   Cash Forecast

Long-Range Cash Forecast
06/03/01
[All Numbers Are in Thousands]

	This Month	Jun-01	Jul-01	Aug-01	Sep-01
Debt Right Now	**4,434**				
Cash In: Revenues—Product Sales	—	1,571	1,640	973	615
Cash In: Revenues—Service	—	175	175	175	175
Cash In: Revenues—Parts	—	150	150	150	150
Cash In: Revenues—Rentals	—	33	33	33	33
Accounts Receivable Receipts	185	—	—	—	—
Total Cash In	185	1,929	1,998	1,331	973
Cash Out:					
Materials	—	1,037	1,082	642	406
Total Nonmaterial Expenses	—	517	517	517	517
Capital Expenditures	—	85	85	85	85
Less: Depreciation	—	-30	-30	-30	-30
Accounts Payable	285	—	—	—	—
Total Payroll	30	—	—	—	—
Total Cash Out	315	1,609	1,654	1,214	978
Net Change in Cash	-130	320	344	117	-5
Ending Debt	**4,564**	**4,244**	**3,900**	**3,783**	**3,788**

Assumptions: All payables paid in 30 days. All receivable collected in 30 days.

Once the cash forecast is compiled and issued, it is very useful to compare cash predictions to what later transpired, so that the finance staff can correct its assumptions to more accurately predict cash flows the next time around. This type of report is a simple two-column comparison of the actual cash balance on a specific date and the predicted cash balance, as well as a variance column and space on the right side for notations regarding why the original cash forecast was incorrect. An example of this report is shown in Exhibit 15.15. It is not necessary to include an explanatory set of notes, because the report already includes this information.

Exhibit 15.15   Cash Forecast Accuracy Report

		[Explanatory Notes Included if Variance Greater than 5%]			
Week	Actual Cash Balance	Forecast 1 Mo. Ago	Variance	Percentage Variance	Explanatory Notes
7-Jan	2,275	2,075	200	9%	DEF customer paid early
14-Jan	2,150	2,109	41	2%	
21-Jan	2,425	2,581	−156	−6%	ABC customer paid late
28-Jan	2,725	2,843	−118	−4%	
4-Feb	3,125	3,000	125	4%	
11-Feb	3,225	3,305	−80	−2%	
18-Feb	3,495	3,450	45	1%	
25-Feb	3,445	2,942	503	15%	Bank error in recording check
4-Mar	3,645	3,751	−106	−3%	
11-Mar	3,555	3,500	55	2%	
18-Mar	3,604	3,209	395	11%	Paid for capital expenditures
25-Mar	3,704	3,589	115	3%	
1-Apr	3,754	3,604	150	4%	
8-Apr	3,879	3,802	77	2%	
15-Apr	3,939	3,921	18	0%	
22-Apr	3,864	3,900	−36	−1%	
29-Apr	4,264	3,781	483	11%	Customers took 2% early payment discount
6-May	4,464	4,351	113	3%	
13-May	4,434	4,031	403	9%	Customers took 2% early payment discount
20-May	4,188	4,000	188	4%	
27-May	4,339	4,503	−164	−4%	

BREAKEVEN REPORTS

If a controller works for a start-up company, perhaps the most important report of all is the breakeven report. This is because such companies are newly organized, possibly in a brand-new market, and have no operating history that allows them to determine the correct mix of sales, margins, and costs that will allow them to turn a profit. In such situations, management should be intensely interested in the exact revenue level at which it no longer loses money. If this breakeven point is excessively high, management will realize that it must alter its cost structure or business plan in order to pursue a more attractive course of action that leads to more profits at a lower sales level. This report is also necessary for any company that has been in existence for some time, but which is having trouble consistently attaining a reasonable level of profit. For these organizations as well, knowing their breakeven point and managing sales and expenses to beat that point are a critical part of management goals.

There is a comprehensive explanation of the breakeven analysis, as well as a number of presentation methods, shown in Chapter 8. This chapter will note only the most common breakeven report format (as shown in Exhibit 15.16), and then describe the method of calculation and how it should be presented with accompanying notes to ensure that management understands the report layout.

To create the breakeven analysis shown in Exhibit 15.16, set up a series of relatively small revenue steps, which are placed in the first column of the analysis. These should cover the entire range of revenues that a company can reasonably expect to achieve in the near term, and each one should be spaced sufficiently far apart to keep from resulting in more than a few dozen data points, thereby keeping the report readable. To arrive at the gross margin, as shown in the second column, divide the direct gross margin (just revenues minus direct labor and materials—do not include any overhead costs) by total revenues. The third column is derived by multiplying the gross margin percentage by the total revenues shown in the second and first columns. To compile the fixed costs shown in the fourth column, add up all overhead; sales, general and administrative; and interest costs. The fifth column is a calculation that subtracts the fixed costs in the fourth column from the gross margin in the third column to arrive at the expected profit at various revenue levels. By completing this analysis and including it with the financial reports issued to management each month, one can easily convey the point at which a company can expect to start turning a profit, as well as roughly how much money it can expect to earn at different revenue levels.

It is best to use at least a two-month average for the gross margin and fixed cost information in this analysis, because this tends to smooth out any inaccuracies that may creep into the financial statements from which this report is derived. For example, if the previous month's financial statements showed an artificially high profit because some inventory was received and used, but the expense to the supplier was not recorded in time, the following

Exhibit 15.16   Breakeven Report

Breakeven Analysis (2-Month Average)

Revenue	Margin	Gross Margin	Fixed Cost	Net Profit (Loss)
950,000	34.0%	323,124	545,000	–221,877
1,000,000	34.0%	340,130	545,000	–204,870
1,050,000	34.0%	357,137	545,000	–187,864
1,100,000	34.0%	374,143	545,000	–170,857
1,150,000	34.0%	391,150	545,000	–153,851
1,200,000	34.0%	408,156	545,000	–136,844
1,250,000	34.0%	425,163	545,000	–119,838
1,300,000	34.0%	442,169	545,000	–102,831
1,350,000	34.0%	459,176	545,000	–85,825
1,400,000	34.0%	476,182	545,000	–68,818
1,450,000	34.0%	493,189	545,000	–51,812
1,500,000	34.0%	510,195	545,000	–34,805
1,550,000	34.0%	527,202	545,000	–17,799
1,600,000	34.0%	544,208	545,000	–792
1,650,000	34.0%	561,215	545,000	16,215
1,700,000	34.0%	578,221	545,000	33,221
1,750,000	34.0%	595,228	545,000	50,228
1,800,000	34.0%	612,234	545,000	67,234
1,850,000	34.0%	629,241	545,000	84,241
1,900,000	34.0%	646,247	545,000	101,247
1,950,000	34.0%	663,254	545,000	118,254
2,000,000	34.0%	680,260	545,000	135,260
2,050,000	34.0%	697,267	545,000	152,267
2,100,000	34.0%	714,273	545,000	169,273
2,150,000	34.0%	731,280	545,000	186,280
2,200,000	34.0%	748,286	545,000	203,286
2,250,000	34.0%	765,293	545,000	220,293
2,300,000	34.0%	782,299	545,000	237,299
2,350,000	34.0%	799,306	545,000	254,306
2,400,000	34.0%	816,312	545,000	271,312

month will show an artificially low profit because the expense is now recognized. This type of error occurs all too frequently but is usually canceled out when correcting adjustments are made in the following month. Consequently, using an average of the results of two consecutive months of activity is the best way to arrive at the information in a breakeven analysis report.

When a breakeven analysis is presented to management, it may be useful to also include a trend line that shows changes in the breakeven level over the last few years or quarters. By presenting this information, management will realize if there is a problem when there is a steady upward trend in the breakeven point. To take this concept a step further, it is most useful to attach a few notes to the charts that itemize precisely why there is a change in the breakeven point. Here is an example of what such a commentary might contain:

> The breakeven point has increased to $1,600,000 from the previous year's average breakeven point of $1,490,000. The reason is that gross margins on the medical sensor line have decreased by five percent, due to pricing pressure that arose when competitor ABC Corporation entered the market with a competing product three months ago. In addition, sales of the company's highest-margin product, the blood test kit, have been on a continual decline for the last two years because of a shift in the market from doctor-administered blood tests, which our product is targeted at, and toward home tests, for which we do not have a competitive product at this time. Further, general and administrative costs have increased because of the extra staff needed to repair deficiencies recently discovered in the kidney dialysis product line. We expect that the field repairs will be completed within the next two months, which will then result in a reduction in the breakeven point to $1,545,000. However, the remaining incremental increase in the breakeven point appears to be permanent and may worsen, unless new, higher-margin products are shipped soon.

Such a clear statement of the causes of changes in the breakeven level are far better than simply issuing a breakeven report without any commentary, which requires management to compare breakeven results to those of prior periods to see if there is a problem, and without any evidence regarding what problems are causing the change in the breakeven level.

CAPACITY REPORTS

Capacity utilization is dealt with in Chapter 13, where there is a full explanation and review of the standard capacity utilization report. Rather than duplicate that discussion here, we will only note a simpler, and more easily readable bar chart that takes the place of the more comprehensive report shown in the other chapter. In this format, shown in Exhibit 15.17, the utilization of each type of equipment is shown on its own separate bar chart. While highly readable, this can be a bulky form of presentation if there are

Exhibit 15.17   Capacity Utilization Bar Chart Report

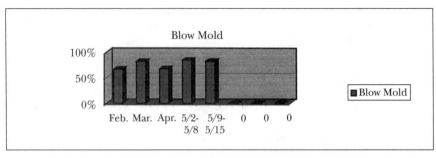

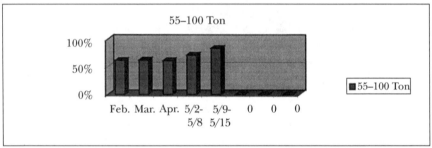

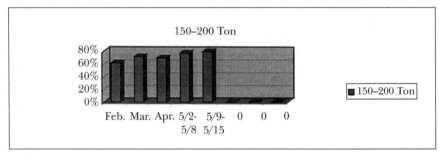

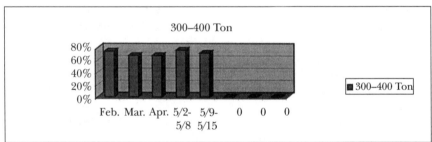

many types of equipment being measured. Also, if utilization differences of a few percent between one period and another are critical, the bar chart format does not readily show such detail. However, for less detailed presentations of the results for just a few types of equipment, or for clusters of equipment, the bar chart report is a reasonable alternative to use.

SUMMARY

This chapter explored the general kinds of reports that can be issued, such as graphical bar or pie charts, as well as the types of report layouts and accompanying notes that should be attached to this information. The chapter went on to cover a variety of report layouts that can be used in a broad array of accounting topics, such as revenue, margins, investments, cash flow, and collections. By showing such a large variety of reports here, controllers can sort through the reporting options and have a good chance of discovering a report format that is likely to meet their needs in presenting almost any type of financial analysis.

16

Determining the Cost of Capital

Many companies make decisions to build new facilities, invest in new machinery, or expend sums for other large projects without any idea of whether the return to be expected from these projects will exceed the cost of capital needed to fund them. As a result, a company may find that it is working furiously on any number of new projects but seeing its ability to generate cash flow to repay debt or pay stockholders decline over time. To avoid this situation, it is necessary to calculate the return on investment, which was covered in Chapters 3 through 5. This chapter discusses the second part of the investment decision, which is the calculation of the cost of capital against which investment decisions must be compared. The chapter describes the primary components of a company's capital, how the cost of each kind is combined to form a weighted cost of capital, and how this information should be most appropriately used when evaluating the return on new projects that require funding, as well as for discounting the cash flows from existing projects.

COMPONENTS OF THE COST OF CAPITAL

Before determining the amount of a company's cost of capital, it is necessary to determine its components. The following two sections describe in detail how to arrive at the cost of capital for these components. The weighted average calculation that brings together all the elements of the cost of capital is then described in the section that follows these.

The first component of the cost of capital is debt. This is a company's commitment to return to a lender both the interest and principal on an initial or series of payments to the company by the lender. This can be short-term debt, which is typically paid back in full within one year, or long-term debt, which can be repaid over many years, either with continual principal repayments, large repayments at set intervals, or a large payment when the entire debt is due, which is called a *balloon* payment. All these forms of repayment can be combined in an infinite number of ways to arrive at a repayment plan that is uniquely structured to fit the needs of the individual corporation.

The second component of the cost of capital is preferred stock. This is a form of equity that is issued to stockholders and carries a specific interest rate. The company is obligated to pay only the stated interest rate to shareholders at stated intervals, but not the initial payment of funds to the company, which it may keep in perpetuity, unless it chooses to buy back the stock. There may also be conversion options, so that a shareholder can convert the preferred stock to common stock in some predetermined proportion. This type of stock is attractive to those companies that do not want to dilute earnings per share with additional common stock or to incur the burden of principal repayments. Although there is an obligation to pay shareholders the stated interest rate, it is usually possible to delay payment if the funds are not available; however, the interest will accumulate and must be paid when cash is available.

The third and final component of the cost of capital is common stock. A company is not required to pay anything to its shareholders in exchange for the stock, which makes this the least risky form of funding available. Instead, shareholders rely on a combination of dividend payments, as authorized by the board of directors (and which are entirely at the option of the board—authorization is not required by law), and appreciation in the value of the shares. However, because shareholders indirectly control the corporation through the board of directors, actions by management that depress the stock price or lead to a reduction in the dividend payment can lead to the firing of management by the board of directors. Also, since shareholders typically expect a high return on investment in exchange for their money, the actual cost of these funds is the highest of all the components of the cost of capital.

As will be discussed in the next two sections, the least expensive of the three forms of funding is debt, followed by preferred stock and common stock. The main reason for the differences between the costs of the three components is the impact of taxes on various kinds of interest payments. This is of particular concern when discussing debt, which is covered in the next section.

CALCULATING THE COST OF DEBT

This section covers the main factors to consider when calculating the cost of debt and also notes how these factors must be incorporated into the final cost calculation. We also note how the net result of these calculations is a form of funding that is less expensive than the cost of equity, which is covered in the next section.

When one is calculating the cost of debt, it is important to remember that the interest expense is tax deductible. This means that the tax paid by the company is reduced by the tax rate multiplied by the interest expense. An example is shown in Exhibit 16.1, where it is assumed that $1 million of debt has a basic interest rate of 9.5 percent, and the corporate tax rate is 35 percent.

Exhibit 16.1 clearly shows that the impact of taxes on the cost of debt significantly reduces the overall debt cost, thereby making this a most desirable form of funding.

If a company is not currently turning a profit, and therefore not in a position to pay taxes, one may question whether the company should factor the impact of taxes into the interest calculation. The answer is still yes, because any net loss will carry forward to the next reporting period, when the company can offset future earnings against the accumulated loss to avoid paying taxes at that time. Thus, the reduction in interest costs caused by the tax deductibility of interest is still applicable even if a company is not currently in a position to pay income taxes.

Another issue is the cost of acquiring debt and how this cost should be factored into the overall cost of debt calculation. When obtaining debt, either through a private placement or simply through a local bank, there are usually extra fees involved, which may include placement or brokerage fees, documentation fees, or the price of a bank audit. In the case of a private placement, the company may set a fixed percentage interest payment on the debt but find that prospective borrowers will not purchase the debt instruments unless they can do so at a discount, thereby effectively increasing the interest rate they will earn on the debt. In both cases, the company is receiving less cash than initially expected but must still pay out the same amount of interest expense. In effect, this raises the cost of the debt. To carry forward the example in Exhibit 16.1 to Exhibit 16.2, it is assumed that the interest payments are the same but that brokerage fees were $25,000 and that the debt was sold at a 2 percent discount. The result is an increase in the actual interest rate.

When compared to the cost of equity that is discussed in the following section, it becomes apparent that debt is a much less expensive form of fund-

Exhibit 16.1   Calculating the Interest Cost of Debt, Net of Taxes

$$\frac{(\text{Interest expense}) \times (1 - \text{tax rate})}{\text{Amount of debt}} = \text{Net after-tax interest expense}$$

Or

$$\frac{\$95,000 \times (1 - .35)}{\$1,000,000} = \text{Net after-tax interest expense}$$

$$\frac{\$61,750}{\$1,000,000} = 6.175\%$$

Exhibit 16.2   Calculating the Interest Cost of Debt, Net of Taxes, Fees, and Discounts

---

$$\frac{(\text{Interest expense}) \times (1 - \text{tax rate})}{(\text{Amount of debt}) - (\text{Fees}) - (\text{Discount on sale of debt})} = \text{Net after-tax interest expense}$$

Or

$$\frac{\$95,000 \times (1 - .35)}{\$1,000,000 - \$25,000 - \$20,000} = \text{Net after-tax interest expense}$$

$$\frac{\$61,750}{\$955,000} = 6.466\%$$

Note: There can also be a premium on sale of debt instead of a discount, if investors are willing to pay extra for the interest rate offered. This usually occurs when the rate offered is higher than the current market rate or if the risk of nonpayment is so low that this is perceived as an extra benefit by investors.

---

ing than equity. However, though it may be tempting to alter a company's capital structure to increase the proportion of debt, thereby reducing the overall cost of capital, there are dangers involved in incurring a large interest expense. These dangers are discussed in a later section of this chapter (see Modifying the Cost of Capital to Enhance Shareholder Value).

CALCULATING THE COST OF EQUITY

This section shows how to calculate the cost of the two main forms of equity: preferred stock and common stock. These calculations, as well as those from the preceding section on the cost of debt, are then combined in the following section to determine the weighted cost of capital.

Preferred stock stands at a midway point between debt and common stock. It requires an interest payment to the holder of each share of preferred stock but does not require repayment to the shareholder of the amount paid for each share. There are a few special cases in which the terms underlying the issuance of a particular set of preferred shares will require an additional payment to shareholders if company earnings exceed a specified level, but this is a rare situation. Also, some preferred shares carry provisions that allow delayed interest payments to be cumulative, so that they must all be paid before dividends can be paid out to holders of common stock. The main feature shared by all kinds of preferred stock is that, under the tax laws, interest payments are treated as dividends instead of interest expense, which means that these payments are not tax deductible. This is a key issue, because it greatly increases the cost of funds for any company using this funding source. By way of comparison, if a company has a choice between issuing debt or preferred stock at the same rate, the difference in cost will be the tax savings on the debt. In the following example, a company issues $1 million of debt and $1 million of preferred stock, both at 9 percent interest rates, with an assumed 35 percent tax rate.

$$\text{Debt cost} = \text{Principal} \times (\text{Interest rate} \times (1 - \text{Tax rate}))$$
$$\text{Debt cost} = \$1,000,000 \times (9\% \times (1 - .35))$$
$$\$58,500 = \$1,000,000 \times (9\% \times .65)$$

If the same information is used to calculate the cost of payments using preferred stock, the result is:

$$\text{Preferred stock interest cost} = \text{Principal} \times \text{interest rate}$$
$$\text{Preferred stock interest cost} = \$1,000,000 \times 9\%$$
$$\$90,000 = \$1,000,000 \times 9\%$$

The above example shows that the differential caused by the applicability of taxes to debt payments makes preferred stock a much more expensive alternative. This being the case, why does anyone use preferred stock? The main reason is that there is no requirement to repay the stockholder for the initial investment, whereas debt requires either a periodic or balloon payment of principal to eventually pay back the original amount. Companies can also eliminate the preferred stock interest payments if they include a convertibility feature into the stock agreement that allows for a conversion to common stock at some preset price point for the common stock. Thus, in cases in which a company does not want to repay principal any time soon, but does not want to increase the amount of common shares outstanding, preferred stock provides a convenient but expensive alternative.

The most difficult cost of funding to calculate by far is common stock, because there is no preset payment from which to derive a cost. Instead, it appears to be free money, because investors hand over cash without any predetermined payment or even any expectation of having the company eventually pay them back for the stock. Unfortunately, the opposite is the case. Because holders of common stock have the most at risk (they are the last ones paid off in the event of bankruptcy), they are the ones who want the most in return. Any management team that ignores its common stockholders and does nothing to give them a return on their investments will find that these people will either vote in a new board of directors that will find a new management team, or else they will sell off their shares at a loss to new investors, thereby driving down the value of the stock and opening up the company to the attention of a corporate raider who will also remove the management team.

One way to determine the cost of common stock is to make a guess at the amount of future dividend payments to stockholders and discount this stream of payments back into a net present value. The problem with this approach is that the amount of dividends paid out is problematic, because they are declared at the discretion of the board of directors. Also, there is no provision in this calculation for changes in the underlying value of the stock; for some companies that do not pay any dividends, this is the only way in which a stockholder will be compensated.

A better method is called the capital asset pricing model (CAPM). Without going into the very considerable theoretical detail behind this system, it essentially derives the cost of capital by determining the relative risk of holding the stock of a specific company as compared to a mix of all stocks in the market. This risk is composed of three elements. The first is the return that any investor can expect from a risk-free investment, which is usually defined as the return on a U.S. government security. The second element is the return from a set of securities considered to have an average level of risk. This can be the average return on a large "market basket" of stocks, such as the Standard & Poor's 500, the Dow Jones Industrials, or some other large cluster of stocks. The final element is a company's beta, which defines the amount by which a specific stock's returns vary from the returns of stocks with an average risk level. This information is provided by several of the major investment services, such as Value Line. A beta of 1.0 means that a specific stock is exactly as risky as the average stock, while a beta of .8 would represent a lower level of risk and a beta of 1.4 would be higher. When combined, this information yields the baseline return to be expected on any investment (the risk-free return), plus an added return that is based on the level of risk that an investor is assuming by purchasing a specific stock. This methodology is totally based on the assumption that the level of risk equates directly to the level of return, which a vast amount of additional research has determined to be a reasonably accurate way to determine the cost of equity capital. The main problem with this approach is that a company's beta will vary over time, since it may add or subtract subsidiaries that are more or less risky, resulting in an altered degree of risk. Because of the likelihood of change, one must regularly recompute the equity cost of capital to determine the most recent cost.

The calculation of the equity cost of capital using the CAPM methodology is relatively simple, once one has accumulated all the components of the equation. For example, if the risk-free cost of capital is 5 percent, the return on the Dow Jones Industrials is 12 percent, and ABC Company's beta is 1.5, the cost of equity for ABC Company would be:

$$
\begin{aligned}
\text{Cost of equity capital} &= \text{Risk-free return} + \text{Beta} \\
&\quad \times (\text{Average stock return} - \text{Risk-free return}) \\
\text{Cost of equity capital} &= 5\% + 1.5\,(12\% - 5\%) \\
\text{Cost of equity capital} &= 5\% + 1.5 \times 7\% \\
\text{Cost of equity capital} &= 5\% + 10.5\% \\
\text{Cost of equity capital} &= 15.5\%
\end{aligned}
$$

Although the example uses a rather high beta that increases the cost of the stock, it is evident that, far from being an inexpensive form of funding, common stock is actually the *most* expensive, given the size of returns that investors demand in exchange for putting their money at risk with a company. Accordingly, this form of funding should be used the most sparingly in order to keep the cost of capital at a lower level.

CALCULATING THE WEIGHTED COST OF CAPITAL

Now that we have derived the costs of debt, preferred stock, and common stock, it is time to assemble all three costs into a weighted cost of capital. This section is structured in an example format, showing the method by which the weighted cost of capital of the Canary Corporation is calculated. Following that, there is a short discussion of how the cost of capital can be used.

The chief financial officer of the Canary Corporation, Mr. Birdsong, is interested in determining the company's weighted cost of capital, to be used to ensure that projects have a sufficient return on investment, which will keep the company from going to seed. There are two debt offerings on the books. The first is $1 million that was sold below par value, which garnered $980,000 in cash proceeds. The company must pay interest of 8.5 percent on this debt. The second is for $3 million and was sold at par but included legal fees of $25,000. The interest rate on this debt is 10 percent. There is also $2,500,000 of preferred stock on the books, which requires annual interest (or dividend) payments amounting to 9 percent of the amount contributed to the company by investors. Finally, there is $4 million of common stock on the books. The risk-free rate of interest, as defined by the return on current U.S. government securities, is 6 percent, while the return expected from a typical market basket of related stocks is 12 percent. The company's beta is 1.2, and it currently pays income taxes at a marginal rate of 35 percent. What is the Canary Company's weighted cost of capital?

The method we will use is to separately compile the percentage cost of each form of funding, and then calculate the weighted cost of capital, based on the amount of funding and percentage cost of each of the above forms of funding. We begin with the first debt item, which was $1 million of debt that was sold for $20,000 less than par value, at 8.5 percent debt. The marginal income tax rate is 35 percent. The calculation is as follows.

$$\text{Net after-tax interest percent} = \frac{((\text{Interest expense}) \times (1 - \text{tax rate})) \times \text{Amount of debt}}{(\text{Amount of debt}) - (\text{Discount on sale of debt})}$$

$$\text{Net after-tax interest percent} = \frac{((8.5\%) \times (1 - .35)) \times \$1,000,000}{\$1,000,000 - \$20,000}$$

$$\text{Net after-tax interest percent} = 5.638\%$$

We employ the same method for the second debt instrument, for which there is $3 million of debt that was sold at par. Legal fees of $25,000 were incurred to place the debt, which pays 10 percent interest. The marginal income tax rate remains at 35 percent. The calculation is:

$$\text{Net after-tax interest percent} = \frac{((\text{Interest expense}) \times (1 - \text{tax rate})) \times \text{Amount of debt}}{(\text{Amount of debt}) - (\text{Discount on sale of debt})}$$

$$\text{Net after-tax interest percent} = \frac{((10\%) \times (1 - .35)) \times \$3,000,000}{\$3,000,000 - \$25,000}$$

$$\text{Net after-tax interest percent} = 7.091\%$$

Having completed the interest expense for the two debt offerings, we move on to the cost of the preferred stock. As noted above, there is $2,500,000 of preferred stock on the books, with an interest rate of 9 percent. The marginal corporate income tax does not apply, because the interest payments are treated like dividends, and are not deductible. The calculation is the simplest of all, for the answer is 9 percent, since there is no income tax to confuse the issue.

To arrive at the cost of equity capital, we take from the example a return on risk-free securities of 6 percent, a return of 12 percent that is expected from a typical market basket of related stocks, and a beta of 1.2. This information is plugged into the following formula to arrive at the cost of equity capital:

$$\text{Cost of equity capital} = \text{Risk-free return} + \text{Beta} \times (\text{Average stock return} - \text{Risk-free return})$$
$$\text{Cost of equity capital} = 6\% + 1.2\,(12\% - 6\%)$$
$$\text{Cost of equity capital} = 13.2\%$$

Now that we know the cost of each type of funding, it is a simple matter to construct a table such as the one shown in Exhibit 16.3 that lists the amount of each type of funding and its related cost, which we can quickly sum to arrive at a weighted cost of capital.

Exhibit 16.3 Weighted Cost of Capital Calculation

Type of Funding	Amount of Funding	Percentage Cost	Dollar Cost
Debt number 1	$980,000	5.638%	$55,252
Debt number 2	2,975,000	7.091%	210,957
Preferred stock	2,500,000	9.000%	225,000
Common stock	4,000,000	13.200%	528,000
Totals	$10,455,000	9.75%	$1,019,209

When combined into the weighted average calculation shown in Exhibit 16.3, we see that the weighted cost of capital is 9.75 percent. Though there is some considerably less expensive debt on the books, the majority of the funding is comprised of more expensive common and preferred stock, which drives up the overall cost of capital.

Thus far, we have discussed the components of the cost of capital, how each one is calculated, and how to combine all the various kinds of capital costs into a single weighted cost of capital. Now that we have it, what do we use it for? That is the subject of the next section.

INCREMENTAL COST OF CAPITAL

Having gone to the effort of calculating a company's weighted cost of capital, we must ask ourselves if this information is of any use. Certainly, we now know the cost of all corporate funding, but this is the cost of funding that has already been incurred. How does this relate to the cost of capital for any upcoming funding that has not yet been obtained? What if a company wants to change its blend of funding sources, and how will this impact the cost of capital? What about using it to discount the cash flows from existing projects?

The trouble with the existing weighted cost of capital is that it reflects the cost of debt and equity only at the time the company obtained it. For example, if a company obtained debt at a fixed interest rate during a period in the past when the prime rate offered by banks for new debt was very high, the resulting cost of capital, that still includes this debt, will be higher than the cost of capital if that debt had been retired and re-funded by new debt that was obtained at current market rates, which are lower. The same issue applies to equity, because the cost of equity can change if the underlying return on risk-free debt has changed, which it does continually (just observe daily or monthly swings in the cost of U.S. government securities, which are considered to be risk free). Similarly, a company's beta will change over time as its overall risk profile changes, possibly due to changes in its markets, or internal changes that alter its mix of business. Accordingly, a company may find that its carefully calculated weighted cost of capital does not bear even a slight resemblance to what the same cost would be if recalculated based on current market conditions.

Where does this disturbing news leave us? If there is no point in using the weighted cost of capital that is recorded on the books, there is no reason why we cannot calculate the incremental weighted cost of capital based on current market conditions and use that as a hurdle rate instead. By doing so, a company recognizes that it will obtain funds at the current market rates, and use the cost of this blended rate to pay for new projects. For example, if a company intends to retain the same proportions of debt and equity, and finds that the new weighted cost of capital is 2 percent higher at current market rates than the old rates recorded on the company books, then the hurdle rate used for evaluating new projects should use the new, higher rate.

It is also important to determine management's intentions in regard to the new blend of debt and equity, for changes in the proportions of the two will alter the weighted cost of capital. If a significant alteration in the current mix is anticipated, the new proportion should be factored into the weighted cost of capital calculation. For example, management may be forced by creditor or owners to alter the existing proportion of debt and equity. This is most common when a company is closely held, and the owners do not want to invest any more equity in the company, thereby forcing it to resort to debt financing. Alternatively, if the debt to equity ratio is very high, lenders may force the addition of additional equity in order to reduce the risk of default, which goes up when there is a large amount of interest and principal to pay out of current cash flow. In short, the incremental cost of capital is the most relevant hurdle rate figure when using new funds to pay for new projects.

The concept of incremental funds costs can be taken too far, however. If a company is initiating only one project in the upcoming year and needs to borrow funds at a specific rate to pay for it, then a good case can be made for designating the cost of that funding as the hurdle rate for the single project under consideration, since the two are inextricably intertwined. However, such a direct relationship is rarely the case. Instead, there are many projects being implemented, which are spread out over a long time frame, with funds being acquired at intervals that do not necessarily match those of the funds requirements of individual projects. For example, a chief financial officer may hold off on an equity offering in the public markets until there is a significant upswing in the stock market, or borrow funds a few months early if a favorably low, long-term fixed rate can be obtained. When this happens, there is no way to tie a specific funding cost to a specific project, so it is better to calculate the blended cost of capital for the period and apply it as a hurdle rate to all of the projects currently under consideration.

All this discussion of the incremental cost of capital does not mean that the cost of capital that is derived from the book cost of existing funding is totally irrelevant—far from it. Many companies finance all new projects out of their existing cash flow and have no reason to go to outside lenders or equity markets to obtain new funding. For these organizations, the true cost of debt is indeed the same as the amount recorded on their books, because they are obligated to pay that exact amount of debt, irrespective of what current market interest rates may be. However, the weighted cost of capital does not just include debt—it also includes equity, and this cost *does* change over time. Even if a company has no need for additional equity, the cost of its existing equity will change, because the earnings expectations of investors will change over time, as well as the company's beta. For example, the underlying risk-free interest rate can and will change as the inflation rate varies, so that there is some return to investors that exceeds the rate of inflation. Similarly, the average market rate of return on equity will change over time as investor expectations change. Further, the mix of businesses and markets in which a company is involved will inevitably lead to variation in its beta over time, as the variability of its cash flows becomes greater or lower. All three of these factors will result in alterations to the weighted cost of capital that will continue to change over time, even if there is no new equity that a company sells to investors. Consequently, the book cost of debt is still a valid part of the weighted cost of capital as long as no new debt is added, whereas the cost of equity *will* change as the expectation for higher or lower returns by investors changes, which results in a weighted cost of capital that can blend the book and market costs of funding in some situations.

So far, the discussion in this chapter has assumed that the reader is interested only in using the weighted cost of capital as a hurdle rate for determining the viability of new projects that will generate a stream of cash flows. It can also be used as the discounting factor when arriving at the net present value of cash flows from existing projects, as discussed at length in Chapter 3. When this is the case, the cost of capital based on the book value of debt is more appropriate than using the current market rates for new debt, since the cash flows being discounted are for existing projects that were already funded by debt and equity that are already recorded on the books.

This section noted how the incremental market cost of capital is the more accurate way to arrive at a hurdle rate for new projects when new funding must be secured to pay for the projects. If a company can fund all cash flows for new projects internally, however, a company can use the book cost of debt and the market-based return on equity to derive the weighted cost of capital that is most accurately used to judge the acceptability of cash flows from prospective new projects. This later version is also most appropriate for discounting the cash flows from existing and previously funded projects.

USING THE COST OF CAPITAL IN SPECIAL SITUATIONS

There are a few situations in which companies frequently modify the cost of capital for special purposes. This section notes two of the more common cases and how to handle them.

When management is considering whether to authorize a project through the capital request process, it should give some thought to the risk of not achieving the estimated returns for it. For example, if management is considering funding two projects with identical cash flows, where one is in an established industry in which returns are relatively certain and another is in a "high-technology" field in which product obsolescence is the norm, it is a fair bet that the cash flow considerations will not form the basis of its decision— the project in the high-technology area will almost certainly be eliminated from consideration on the grounds that the risk of not achieving the projected cash flow is too high. How can one quantify this risk? The short answer is—not easily. Many organizations simply assign a higher cost of capital hurdle rate to risky projects. Unfortunately, it is very difficult to reliably determine what this higher hurdle rate should be. Is a premium of 1 percent over the cost of capital sufficient, or is 5 percent closer to the desired level? The problem is that the increase in the cost of capital cannot be reliably calculated to reflect the exact increase in risk. Instead, this is more a matter of management determining its own comfort level with the risk, and making a decision at that point. To do so, management will need additional information to supplement the cost of capital hurdle rate, such as:

- *Timing of cash flows.* If the positive cash flows from a proposed project are clustered toward the end of a project, perhaps five years away, this sort of project is riskier than one that returns positive cash flows right away.

- *Payback period.* The sooner a project pays back its projected cash outflows, the less risky the project is perceived to be, even if the chance of having large positive cash flows is relatively small. The point here is that the risk of loss is reduced with a quick payback.

- *Level of expected competition.* If a number of competitors are clustering their efforts in the same area, it is a fair bet that there will be price competition when everyone's projects are completed and start to spew new products into the marketplace, resulting in reduced profits for all competitors. One can quantify this risk somewhat by modeling a range of profit scenarios based on a number of different product price points. A further degree of sophistication is to include in the cash flow analysis the estimated dates at which product pricing is anticipated to drop, based on when competing projects are estimated to be completed, resulting in higher competition.

- *History of previous projects in this area.* If a company has funded a number of projects in the same area and the majority of them have not done well, this is certainly a consideration in determining the level of project risk. Unless management thinks it can improve the situation by bringing in new project managers or doing something else to improve the probability of success, a project with this type of history should be assigned a higher degree of risk.

Thus, it is not necessary to blindly increase the hurdle rate, as defined by the cost of capital, to evaluate a new capital project, since a higher hurdle rate does not sufficiently define the level of risk. Instead, it is better to provide management with a range of supplemental data, as noted above, that provide more information about the likely level of project riskiness.

Another special situation in which the cost of capital can be modified is when it is used in a large corporation with multiple divisions that bear no close relationship to each other in terms of the markets they serve, the products they sell, or their methods of obtaining funding. The most common example of this is a conglomerate, which is an assemblage of unrelated businesses that are frequently brought together under one corporate umbrella because they have uniformly high returns on investment, or because they have offsetting cash flows—in other words, one subsidiary may have strong cash flows that match swings in the business cycle, while a fellow subsidiary has cash flows that track the inverse of the business cycle. When combined, the cash flows of the two entities theoretically result in even cash flow at all times and a reduced level of risk for the conglomerate as a whole. In such situations, the conglomerate is the entity that obtains financing, and this results in a specific cost of capital. However, the levels of risk of all the component subsidiaries may diverge wildly from the overall level of risk, resulting in the application of a conglomerate-wide hurdle rate to all subsidiaries that is either too high or too low for each individual subsidiary. For example, a subsidiary with a very high risk of return on its projects will be subject to a hurdle rate that is compiled from the conglomerate as a whole, which may have been assembled for the express purpose of achieving a very low level of variability in cash flows, which of course results in a low cost of equity, and consequently a low cost of capital. When this happens, nearly all the projects of the risky subsidiary will be approved, since the hurdle rate is so low, without any consideration for the high degree of risk. A probable outcome is that the cash flows from many of these projects will be substandard, resulting in low future performance by this subsidiary. Alternatively, using the same hurdle rate for a different subsidiary with extremely low-risk projects will result in the rejection of some projects that are quite capable of generating an adequate return on investment. Thus, using an average hurdle rate for subsidiaries is not a good idea.

Instead, one can determine an average hurdle rate from information about the competitors in each subsidiary's industry, which is available from public sources such as 10-K or 10-Q reports, or the investment analyses of any of the major brokerage firms. By doing so, one can compile the cost of capital of the industry or of selected competitors within each industry and use that as the hurdle rate for applicable subsidiaries. Though not as accurate as determining the specific cost of capital of the subsidiary (which is not possible, since it has not equity or debt of its own—that is held by the corporate parent), it is still much more accurate than the overall cost of capital of the entire organization. This is the preferred method for calculating the cost of capital of a corporate subsidiary.

MODIFYING THE COST OF CAPITAL
TO ENHANCE SHAREHOLDER VALUE

The preceding sections make it quite clear that shareholders can expect a higher return on their investment if the bulk of a company's funding is obtained through debt instead of equity, since debt costs are partially offset by tax-deductible interest expenses. This section covers the extent to which shareholders can increase their returns by this means, as well as the risks of following this approach to an excessive degree.

When company management or owners examine ways to improve the return on equity, one relatively easy method that stands out is buying back some portion of the equity from stockholders with borrowed funds, which reduces the amount of equity that is divided into the earnings, resulting in a greater amount of earnings per share. Exhibit 16.4 shows what happens when

Exhibit 16.4   Itemization of Changes in Return on Equity with Stock Buyback

Predebt Earnings	Predebt Equity	Amount of Buyback	Amount of Post-Tax Interest Expense	Net Earnings	Return on Equity (%)
$150,000	$500,000	$25,000	$2,000	$148,000	31.2
150,000	500,000	50,000	4,000	146,000	32.4
150,000	500,000	75,000	6,000	144,000	33.8
150,000	500,000	100,000	8,000	142,000	35.5
150,000	500,000	125,000	10,000	140,000	37.3
150,000	500,000	150,000	12,000	138,000	39.4
150,000	500,000	175,000	14,000	136,000	41.8
150,000	500,000	200,000	16,000	134,000	44.7
150,000	500,000	225,000	18,000	132,000	48.0

XYZ Company, with $150,000 in earnings, $500,000 in equity, and no debt, decides to buy back shares with funds that are obtained by borrowing funds. The net after-tax cost of the new debt is assumed to be 8 percent, which reduces the amount of reported earnings somewhat.

As Exhibit 16.4 shows, there are major benefits to be had by introducing some debt into the capital structure in order to reduce the amount of equity. The example could be continued to the point where only one share of stock is outstanding, which can yield an extraordinarily high return on equity figure. The method is especially appealing for those companies whose shares are held by a small group of owners who cannot or will not invest additional equity in the business, and who prefer to strip out equity for their own uses as frequently as possible. Accordingly, if the return on equity percentage is considered important, altering the cost of capital by buying back stock is one of the easiest ways to do so.

However, there is a great risk that this strategy can backfire. The problem with shifting the capital structure strongly in the direction of debt and away from equity is that debt requires repayment, whereas equity does not. Because of this, a company's cash flow is impeded by the required debt and principal repayments to lenders, which can be a dangerous situation whenever the business cycle declines or company cash flow drops for other reasons, such as increased competition. When this happens, a company may not be able to meet the payment demands of its lenders, possibly resulting in bankruptcy and the loss of all owner equity.

Management can anticipate this problem by examining the variability of both existing and projected cash flows, and determining the likelihood and extent of potential drops in cash flow. This is obviously a highly judgmental process, since it is only the opinion of management (which may vary considerably by manager) as to how far down cash flow can go during lean times. Nonetheless, the consensus minimum cash flow should be agreed upon. Then the controller or chief financial officer can use this information to determine the amount of debt that can safely be added to the balance sheet while still ensuring that all debt payments can be made. A key factor in this calculation is determining management's level of comfort with the proportion of debt payments that will take up the minimum level of cash flow. For example, many managers are not at all comfortable with the thought of having virtually all of the minimum cash flow being allocated to debt payments, because there is no room left for capital or working capital additions that may be needed to improve the business. Consequently, some reduced proportion of the minimum cash flow level is normally used when determining the level of debt that can be taken on. An example of how this maximum debt level is determined is shown in Exhibit 16.5, in which the minimum cash flow level is assumed to be $50,000. The rest of the table determines the return on equity using a range of debt levels taken from Exhibit 16.4 that fall within this minimum cash flow level. Management can then review the table and select the combination of earnings level, return on equity, and risk that it feels most comfortable with, and then proceed to attain that level by using debt to buy back stock.

In Exhibit 16.5, it would be very unwise to increase the amount of debt to anything beyond the minimum possible cash flow level, even though it is possible to increase the return on equity to stratospheric levels by doing so. A better option is to adopt one of the lower debt levels that still leaves room in the minimum amount of cash flow to cover other operating needs.

For those industries, such as amusement parks, in which cash flow varies widely from month to month, or the airlines, in which it varies in longer cycles, it is generally not a good idea to increase the proportion of debt to excessive levels. The reason is that cash flows are more likely to bottom out

Exhibit 16.5   Table of Cash Usage versus Return on Equity

Minimum Cash Flow	Debt Level	Debt-Related Payments (Principal and Interest)	Proportion of Cash Flow Used by Debt Payments (%)	Return on Equity (%)
$50,000	$25,000	$8,000	16	31.2
50,000	50,000	16,000	32	32.4
50,000	75,000	24,000	48	33.8
50,000	100,000	32,000	64	35.5
50,000	125,000	40,000	80	37.3
50,000	150,000	48,000	96	39.4
50,000	175,000	56,000	112	41.8
50,000	200,000	64,000	128	44.7
50,000	225,000	72,000	144	48.0

during slow periods at extremely low levels, quite possibly requiring that more debt be incurred just to keep operations running. When this happens, a large amount of cash flow that is tied up in the servicing of debt makes it extremely likely that a company will have difficulty in meeting its debt payment obligations, which raises the specter of bankruptcy. Alternatively, if there is an exceptionally steady and predictable level of cash flow that is minimally impacted by long business cycles, the company fortunate enough to experience this situation is ideally positioned to take advantage of an increased degree of leverage and a correspondingly higher return on equity. The key is to be sensitive to swings in cash flow, and to model the appropriate mix of debt and capital to match these swings. The issue is covered in more detail in Chapter 7.

SUMMARY

This chapter reviewed the various components of the weighted cost of capital and how the cost components vary due to the applicability (or inapplicability) of taxes. Because of taxes, there is a strong incentive to use debt instead of equity, but this can lead to considerable additional risk if a company is unable to cover the principal or interest payments on that debt. We also noted how the current market cost of capital is superior to the book method when using the cost of capital to evaluate new projects. When used with a full knowledge of the consequences of miscalculation or misuse, the weighted average cost of capital is an excellent benchmark for determining the ability of a proposed new project to provide positive cash flow to a corporation, as well as the discounted cash flows from existing projects.

17

Analyzing Risk

Now that an abundance of topics related to financial analysis have been reviewed, it may have occurred to the reader that some of those analyses may have incorrect outcomes because the data used as input is incorrect. Not only does this lead to misleading management recommendations, but the controller also does not exactly earn a reputation for precise analysis work! To counteract this problem, the following sections delve into the specific cases in which risk must be factored into the analysis, the many ways in which risk can be measured, and how to report the resulting information to management in a form that it will understand.

In addition to the discussion of risk in this chapter, it may also be useful to review the section on risk at the end of Chapter 14. That discussion centers on the various formulas that are available through the Microsoft Excel electronic spreadsheet. The information in that chapter is supplemental to this one, with the primary emphasis on the tools one can use to measure the concepts noted here.

INCORPORATING RISK INTO FINANCIAL ANALYSIS

Some of the financial analysis that a controller conducts deals with "hard" numbers, which are based on historical data. These data are completely verifiable, and so there is no reason for anyone to mistrust an analysis based on such data. Examples of this kind of financial analysis are ratios based on an income statement, inventory turnover figures based on an inventory report, or customer turnover figures that are based on customers not having ordered from a company in the past year. These are not measurements that contain any risk of being incorrect.

However, a controller is sometimes called on to issue opinions based on *projected* information. This happens whenever a business forecast or sales projection is issued. In particular, it is a primary element of any cash flow projection for a capital expenditure. If there is even a small difference between actual and projected cash flows from a project, it may result in a negative net present value, which means that an implemented project should not have been initially approved. To avoid this problem, a controller must have a good knowledge of the risk of any projection, which is essentially the chance that the actual value will vary significantly from the expected value. Once the controller has interpreted the level of risk, it is also necessary to clearly report this information to management alongside the projections, so that management understands the attendant risks. Consequently, for all situations involving projected (i.e., not historical) information, a controller must know how to measure risk and report this information to management in a clear and understandable manner.

To begin the study of risk, one should first determine the mode of data collection for any projection, which is the subject of the next section.

DATA COLLECTION

When we attempt to quantify the risk of a projected value, we are basing it on the dispersion of estimates regarding the probable outcome. In other words, if we have 10 estimates of an outcome, and they are tightly grouped around a single outcome, then the risk is relatively low that the true outcome will vary much from that figure. Alternatively, if the same 10 estimates vary wildly from each other, then the risk of having an outcome that varies drastically from the median value is very high. Since we are basing the level of risk on a group of estimated outcomes, several questions should arise regarding the data used as input: Where do we obtain these estimates? How accurate are they? Can we use statistical measures to interpret them? This section reviews all these questions.

The first question is: Where do we obtain these estimates? In most cases, the controller is evaluating a cash flow analysis that accompanies a request for a capital expenditure, so there is already a forecast in hand from the project sponsor. This projection is, according to the project sponsor, the most likely result. This person may already have provided additional estimated outcomes for the best and worst cases. However, these outcomes are still the opinions of one person who has a certain set of preconceived notions regarding the probable outcome, based on his or her view of the situation. A controller needs more opinions, especially when the issue being analyzed involves the commitment of a large amount of funds, to ensure that the estimates given have minimal risk of being achieved. One source of this information is to bring in a consultant who can review the information and give an opposing estimate. However, this only provides one more estimate, can be very expensive, and the consultant may not have a very good knowledge of the industry or equipment under consideration. A better alternative is to set up a review board of analysts and managers within the company who give their own estimates. Because these people know the company's operations, the industry in which it operates, and the equipment it uses, they can make much better estimates. From this group, it should be possible to obtain an additional four or five projections that are of good quality.

The next question is: how good are these estimates? To refer to a key term in the realm of computer science, we can use GIGO, which stands for "Garbage In, Garbage Out." In other words, if the estimated outcomes we are using are not well-founded, then all the risk analysis work in the world will not give us a reasonable estimate of risk. To avoid this problem, anyone providing an estimate should be able to back up the estimate with detailed information, and not just a "gut feel" for the outcome. By focusing on why participants are projecting a specific outcome, a controller can also get around the "group think" trap. This condition arises when a group of estimators, especially those who have worked together for a long time, tend to arrive at identical estimates, because they all think the same way. To avoid this problem, the members of the board of analysts and managers should be replaced frequently by new members with new viewpoints. Nonetheless, a controller will find that all internally generated estimates will be based on the company-wide view of marketplace conditions, which may not reflect reality. To avoid this problem, a member of the sales staff (the group with the best knowledge of market conditions) should be part of the review board, so that some fresh views of actual conditions can be injected into the projections discussion. Having noted several ways to improve the quality of these inputs, the fact remains that sometimes all these people will still project outcomes that turn out to be far from the actual outcome. Further options to keep this from happening are to give the group feedback about how their previous estimates stacked up against reality, and to bring in an industry "guru" from time to time to discuss industry trends with this group.

A crucial issue is whether we can use statistical measurement techniques to review the group of projected outcomes to arrive at statistically valid information. Any statistician will answer that the outcome will be much more accurate if the sample size is quite large, preferably in the thousands or millions. In a controller's situation, in which he or she will be lucky to obtain five estimates of projections to compare, and frequently less, a statistician would be very unhappy. Due to the extremely small sample size, the risk of predicting an incorrect outcome is very high. Or, to put the matter in statistical terms, there would be a low degree of confidence in achieving the predicted outcome. Accordingly, why do we bother to measure risk, given the small pool of data on which we must rely? Because, given the high cost of failure for some projects that require very large investments, we must *try* to analyze the data as best we can. Avoiding the topic entirely is not the answer.

MEASURES OF DATA DISPERSION

Several rough measures of data dispersion will be covered in this section. They tell a controller how spread out the projected outcomes are from a central average point. By reviewing the several measurements, one can obtain a good feel for the extent to which projections cluster together. If they are tightly clustered, then the risk of not meeting the estimated outcome is low, whereas a large degree of dispersion reflects considerable dissension over the projected outcome; a greater degree of risk is associated with this situation.

The first task when determining data dispersion is to determine the center, or midpoint, of the data, so that we can see how far the group of estimates vary from this point. There are several ways to arrive at this point. They are:

- *Arithmetic mean.* This is the summary of all projections, divided by the total number of projections. It rarely results in a specific point that matches any of the underlying projections, because it is not based on any single projection—just the average of all points. It simply balances out the largest and smallest projections. It tends to be inaccurate if the underlying data includes one or two projections that are significantly different from the other projections, resulting in an average that is skewed in the direction of the significantly different projections.

- *Median.* This is the point at which half of the projections are below and half are above it. On the assumption that there are an even number of projections being used, the median is the average of the two middle values. By using this method, one can avoid the affect of any outlying projections that are radically different from the main group.

- *Mode.* This is the most commonly observed value in a set of underlying projections. As such, it is not impacted by any extreme projections. In a sense, this represents the most popular projection.

When selecting which of the preceding measures to use for the midpoint of the data, we must remember why we are using the midpoint. With the determination of the level of risk being the goal, we want to determine how far apart the projections are from a midpoint. Since we will be including the extreme values in our next set of measurements, we do not have to include them in the determination of the center of the projections. Accordingly, we will use the median, which ignores the size of outlying values, as the measurement of choice for our determination of the middle of the set of projected outcomes.

The next step is to determine how far apart the projections are from the median. Given the small number of projections, this is easy enough. Just pick the highest and lowest values from the list of outcomes. Then, we must determine the percentage by which the highest and lowest values vary from the median. To do so, we divide the difference between the lowest and median values by the median and calculate the same variance between the median and the highest value. This is a good way to determine the range of possible outcomes. For example, as shown in Exhibit 17.1, if the difference between the median and the highest possible estimate is only 25 percent, but the dif-

Exhibit 17.1   Calculating the Dispersion of a Set of Projections

1. The set of projections for estimated cash flow is: $250, $850, $400, $725, $875, and $675
2. When rearranged into increasing order, the estimates are: $250, $400, $675, $725, $850, and $875
3. The median is the average of the third and fourth values, which is: $700
4. The percentage difference between the median and highest projection is: ($875 − $700) / $700 = 25%
5. The percentage difference between the median and lowest projection is: ($700 − $250) / $700 = 64%

ference between the median and the lowest possible estimate is 64 percent, then we see that there is a modest chance that the actual result will be higher than the estimate, but that there is a significant risk that it may turn out to be lower than expected.

Though reviewing the variation between the highest and lowest values from the median is a good starting point for the determination of risk, it does not tell us the dispersion of the data within the total range of values. To use the previous example from Exhibit 17.1, the bulk of the projections appear to be clustered relatively closely about the median, with just one projection far below this group. A simple way to obtain an overall view of the distribution of the data is to create a graph of all data points, which is described in the next section.

Another way to determine dispersion is to calculate the standard deviation of the data. This method measures the average scatter of data about the mean. In other words, it arrives at a number which is the amount by which the average data point varies from the midpoint, either above or below it. This is not a calculation to undertake by hand. Instead, refer to the STDEV formula in Microsoft Excel that is referenced in Chapter 14 and shown in Exhibit 17.2.

Exhibit 17.2   Calculating the Standard Deviation and Coefficient of Variation

1. The standard deviation formula in Excel, using the data from Exhibit 17.1, is as follows:
   = STDEV(250,400,675,725,850,875)
   = 252
2. The calculation of the mean of all data is:
   = (Sum of all data items) / (Number of data items)
   = (250 + 400 + 675 + 725 + 850 + 875) / 6
   = 629
3. The calculation of the coefficient of variation is:
   = (Standard deviation) / (Mean)
   = 252/629
   = 40%

To build on the standard deviation formula, we can divide it by the mean of the data to arrive at a percentage that is called the coefficient of variation. This is an excellent way to convert the standard deviation, which is expressed in units, into a percentage. This is a much better way of expressing the range of deviation within a group of projections, because one cannot always tell if a standard deviation of $23 is good or bad, but when converted into a percentage of deviation of 3 percent, we can see that the same number indicates a very tight clustering of data about the center-point of all data. In Exhibit 17.2, the data already noted in Exhibit 17.1 are used to determine the standard deviation, the mean, and the coefficient of variation.

Thus, the calculations in Exhibits 17.1 and 17.2 reveal that the set of projections used as our underlying data vary significantly from the midpoint of the group, especially in a downward direction, which would give a controller cause to report on a high degree of risk that the expected outcome will not be achieved. These are not difficult calculations to make and are sufficient in many cases to arrive at a rough conclusion regarding the dispersion of estimates in a data sample, which is the primary form of risk that a controller must evaluate. Another format, that of graphical analysis, is of considerable use in persuading other members of management, who may not be so versed in statistics, regarding the relative risk of projections. The next section deals with this form of analysis.

GRAPHICAL REPRESENTATIONS OF DATA DISPERSION

Sometimes, the management team to whom risk information is reported will not be awed by a reported coefficient of variation of a whopping 80 percent, nor by a standard deviation of 800 units. They do not know what these measures mean, and they do not have time to find out. For them, a graphical representation of data dispersion may be a better approach. They can see the spread of estimates on a graph and then decide for themselves if there appears to be a problem with risk.

When constructing a graph that shows the dispersion of data, one can modify the baseline against which measurements are made, so that the data appears to be extremely closely packed, which would keep management from believing that there is a risk problem. For example, if a set of projected sales data covered the sales range of $17,000 to $34,000 (a difference between the two of 100 percent, and so certainly a widely diverse set of projections), the data points would appear very close together if the baseline on which the graph was created was for all sales from $0 to $1 million. On this scale, with a baseline of $1 million, the difference between the two appears to be only 1.7 percent (derived by dividing the difference between the estimates, which is $17,000, by the total baseline, which is $1 million). Consequently, the choice of baseline has an enormous impact on the perceived dispersion of data. A better approach is to lay out the data set in terms of the percentage difference between each item and the midpoint, which avoids the issue of what baseline

Exhibit 17.3   Data Dispersion, Measured in Percentages

Projection	Variance from the Median (%)
$250	−64
$400	−43
$675	−4
$700 (median)	**0**
$725	4
$850	21
$875	25

to use. As noted in Exhibit 17.3, we have taken the projection information used in Exhibit 17.1 and 17.2 and converted it into percentages from the median.

Note that in Exhibit 17.3 we have shown the smallest projections as having a negative percentage variance, while those greater than the median have a positive variance. When translated into a graph, this gives us a wide percentage distribution of data on either side of the "X" axis that gives a good indication of the true distribution of data about the mean. The data in Exhibit 17.3 have been translated into the graph at the top of Exhibit 17.4.

Note that there are two additional graphs in Exhibit 17.4. The one in the middle of the page assumes that we have a number of projections clustered under each of the variance points. In the example, we have arbitrarily expanded the number of projections to 26, with eight clustered at the median point, six each at the −4 percent and +4 percent variance points, and lesser amounts at the outlying variance points. This is close to a classic "bell curve" distribution, in which the bulk of estimates are clustered near the middle and a rapidly declining number are located at the periphery. This is an excellent way to present information, but for the types of projections that a controller works with, there will rarely be a sufficient number of projections to present this type of graph. If there are, a variation that may arise is the final graph at the bottom of Exhibit 17.4, which shows data that are skewed toward the right-hand side of the chart. This indicates a preponderance of estimates that lean, or "skew," toward the higher end of the range of estimates. A reverse graph that had "negative skew" would present a decided lean toward the left side of the graph. For more information on using Microsoft Excel to calculate the degree of skew, refer to Chapter 14.

Of the graphs presented in Exhibit 17.4, only the first one, the "Percent Distribution from Median," is likely to see consistent use, because there are so few data points available for a controller to work with in most situations. Nonetheless, any of these graphs should be used as much as possible when making presentations to management about the riskiness of projections, because they are so easy to understand.

Exhibit 17.4   Graphical Illustration of Data Dispersion

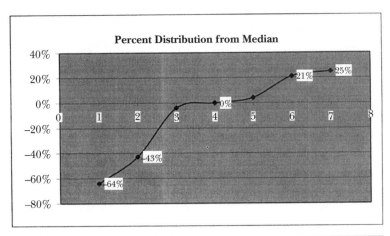

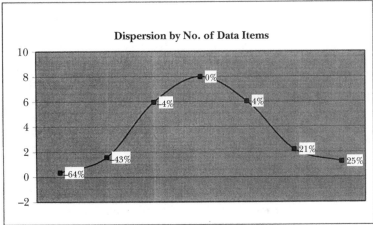

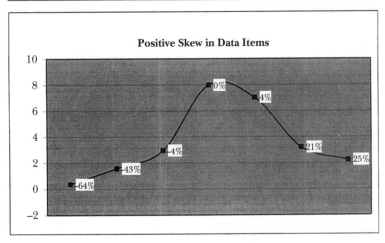

REGRESSION ANALYSIS

Sometimes, a controller is called on to issue a prediction, usually in the area of sales for a specific class of products or an entire company. Although this is a more common task for the sales manager, the controller may be in the role of verifying the prediction made by this person. If so, how to do it? The sales manager has forward-looking information already, with the best access to field reports from the sales staff regarding projected sales by individual customer, as well as the best estimates of how sample customer groups are responding to new products. With all of the information available to the sales manager, why should the controller be involved at all? Because the controller has the best access to historical information about the unit and dollar sales of all products and can verify the sales manager's predictions against past experience. This is a particularly common activity for the controller when the sales manager's predictions have a history of being somewhat exuberant in comparison to actual results, and a calmer head is needed to arrive at a lesser predicted sales level.

A good way to create a prediction in which there is a sufficient volume of historical information on hand is to use regression analysis. This method fits the best possible prediction line into a set of preexisting data points and extrapolates it forward to arrive at a predicted value. The simplest form of regression forecast is the establishment of a linear (i.e., straight line) relationship that extends a straight line forward from a mass of historical data into the future. The trouble with this method is that there may actually be a decided upward or downward trend in the data in the most recent few periods, which results in a curvilinear result—one that either curves upward (a positive curvilinear relationship) or downward (a negative curvilinear relationship). If there is a curvilinear relationship of any kind, then a curvilinear regression line will yield a much more accurate prediction than if a forecast were calculated under the assumption of a linear relationship, which does not factor in the results of the last few periods as strongly as does the curvilinear calculation.

The formula used to plot a linear regression is the least-squares method, which essentially creates a straight line through the available data that yields the intercept point on the "Y" axis and shows the angle of the line, which can then be extended to reveal the predicted value for future periods. Rather than delve into the details of this formula, we will use the Microsoft Excel spreadsheet to run the calculation for us. The historical sales data listed in Exhibit 17.5 will be used as the basis for the calculation. The purpose of the example is to determine the linear and curvilinear trend lines for the sales of "Boom Box" computer speakers for the next sales period. The underlying sales data for the last 12 months is shown in Exhibit 17.5.

To create a graph of this information, as well as linear and curvilinear trend lines that extend three months into the future, we now go to Microsoft Excel and enter into a spreadsheet all the information noted in Exhibit 17.5. We then highlight both the month and sales columns, click on the Chart Wiz-

Exhibit 17.5   Historical Sales Data for Regression Analysis

Month	Sales (000s)
January	$1,200
February	1,450
March	2,000
April	2,150
May	2,250
June	2,400
July	2,650
August	2,780
September	3,000
October	3,025
November	3,035
December	3,050

ard icon, and plot a graph using the XY (scatter) charting option (described in more detail in Chapter 14). Then, when the graph is complete, click on the graph, position the mouse in the area of the plotted data points, and press the right mouse button. Select the "Add Trendline" option. There are six options available. Pick the "Linear" option, which will fit a linear trend line through the data points. Then, position the cursor on the trend line and press the right mouse button. Select the "Format Trendline" option, followed by the "Options" button. Set the "Forecast Forward" field to 3 units, which will extend the trend line out by three months. Also, click on the "Display Equation on Chart" option, so that the mathematical formula for the trend line will be displayed on the chart. The resulting graph is shown at the top of Exhibit 17.6. To plot the same data using a curvilinear equation, create another chart using the same XY (scatter) option, but this time, in the "Add Trendline" screen, select the "Polynomial" option. Then, complete the graph, using the same options just noted for the linear trend line. The result is shown at the bottom of Exhibit 17.6. The differences in the two graphs are considerable. The linear trend line shows a much higher projected sales figure, despite the obvious drop in the rate of growth in the most recent four sales periods. The curvilinear trend line, on the other hand, takes into account the late drop in sales, and projects a drop in sales through the next three months. Best of all, both graphs include the exact formula that Excel has derived for each trend line, so one can use the formulas to determine the exact sales estimate for the period three months in the future. To find the numerical value for the projected sales figure three months in the future for the linear trend line, take the formula printed on the graph and enter the

Exhibit 17.6   Linear and Curvilinear Trend Lines

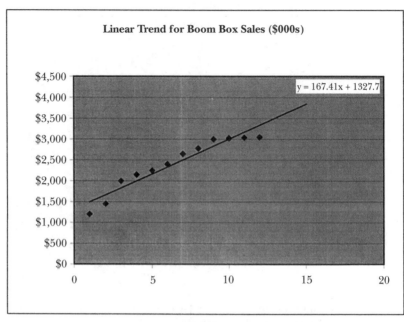

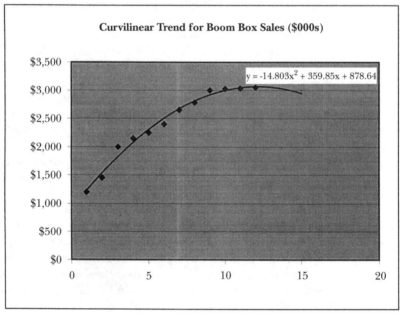

number "15" (for the fifteenth period in the data series for which we are solving). The calculation is as follows:

$$Y = 167.41(x) + 1327.7$$
$$Y = 167.41(15) + 1327.7$$
$$Y = \$3,839$$

Thus, according to the linear trend line, the sales level in the fifteenth period, which is three months in the future, is $3,839.

Then, when we use the formula shown on the curvilinear graph for the predicted value of sales three months in the future based on the curvilinear projection, we can use the following formula:

$$Y = -14.803(x)^2 + 359.85(x) + 878.64$$
$$Y = -14.803(15)^2 + 359.85(15) + 878.64$$
$$Y = -14.803(225) + 5397.75 + 878.64$$
$$Y = \$2,946$$

The difference between the two projections is $893, which is a difference of 30 percent between the lower and higher value. Given the large difference in projected amounts, it would be of great value for a controller to include not only the graphical representation of the differences in projections, but also the numerical and percentage differences, which are easy to calculate with the formulas provided by Excel. In this manner, one can clearly inform management of the degree of separation between different trend line projections, which tells management about the degree of forecasting risk with which it must deal.

REPORTING ON RISK

The risk analysis methods detailed in the previous sections can give a controller a good idea of the degree of risk associated with either a range of predictions or a forecast based on historical data. However, the results are mathematical in nature and not easy to convey to those members of the management team who are not versed in the study of risk analysis. Stating boldly that the coefficient of variation exceeds 60 percent, or that there is a 25 percent variance between the predictions of the linear and curvilinear regression models will probably *not* result in the entire management committee's shouting in appalled consternation—more likely, a dead silence, punctuated only by the gentle snoring of the marketing manager, is likely to result. Instead, a different method for conveying this information is necessary.

One alternate approach is to convert the data into graphics, such as those shown in Exhibit 17.6. This method clearly shows the difference in prediction methods. Also, the two types of regression can be combined in one chart to juxtapose the trend lines together more closely, resulting in an easier comparison of forecasts. However, even though this is a better method than describing risk with arcane statistical terms, it may not convey the true riski-ness of a cash flow projection or sales forecast if the chart is so small that the differences in cash flow projections or sales forecasts appear to be minor. Consequently, the graphical approach must be supplemented with additional information that is easy to understand.

A good way of adding this information is to convert statistical risk mea-sures into a high–medium–low interpretation. For example, if the coefficient of variation is less than 10 percent, we can describe the risk of not achieving a predicted cash flow level, based on a set of projections, as low, while a coeffi-cient of between 11 percent and 25 percent has a moderate degree of risk, and anything greater has a high degree of risk. The exact ranges assigned to each level of risk can be worked out by the accounting and finance staffs. The rating can even be color coded, with a red bar on the analysis for a high-risk projection (similar to the red color used by the Forest Service for a high fire danger situation!).

Another alternative is to translate the amount of risk into dollars. For example, if the difference between a forecasted sales level using the linear and curvilinear regressions is $700,000, then say so—this is a hard number that management understands. One can even go further and project gross margins or net profits using the lowest forecasted figure. Also, when dealing with a set of projections for a cash flow forecast, one should always calculate the net present value of the lowest possible cash flow projection and include it in the presentation to management. All of these methods quantify the low-est possible projection or forecast and translate it into a monetary impact, which is a language that the management team is trained to understand.

Finally, a controller may feel it necessary to report on the extent to which the projections of the company's review board (the one that issues cash flow projections) has been inaccurate in the past. This information is useful when the review board generates consistently incorrect predictions of cash flows for company projects. If so, the management team needs to know how much it can trust the newest projections of this group. Having the cumulative track record of that group in front of them yields this information. This report should also be provided if the review board has a strong record of mak-ing accurate predictions, because this bolsters the confidence of the manage-ment team in the latest projections. In either case, this information should be made available to the management team.

In summary, reporting on risk with raw statistical measures is not a good idea, because few managers can understand the information. Instead, an interlocking set of graphics, high–low risk interpretations, and translations into dollar amounts at risk are a much better way to report risk levels for pro-jected cash flows or sales forecasts to management.

SUMMARY

In this chapter, a number of statistical techniques have been distilled down into a few practical methods for determining the risk associated with cash flow projections for capital projects, as well as for sales forecasts. The analyses rely heavily on reviewing the comparative range of outcomes, with high-risk outcomes having a very broad band of outcomes and low-risk ones having the reverse. When calculating these results, it is very important to remember that a controller is usually working with a very small set of cash flow projections or historical data as the basis for sales projections; in both cases, the results will be incorrect if the underlying data is incorrect. Consequently, a fundamental part of any risk analysis is to carefully investigate and validate all underlying data before rendering an opinion regarding risk.

APPENDICES

A

Symptoms and Solutions

There are a relatively small number of symptoms that a controller will see in a company's performance, each of which indicates the presence of a multitude of potential illnesses. In this appendix, we note the most common financial symptoms, and then describe the forms of financial analysis one should undertake in order to precisely determine the nature of the illness, followed by brief descriptions of possible solutions.

The symptoms are ones that a typical controller, armed with an adequate financial reporting system, can spot with a cursory review of the financial statements. However, each level of analysis recommended in this appendix requires much more time to complete, so one should expect the most thorough analysis to require days or weeks of effort. When it looks as though the analysis work will be substantial, a controller should always consider two options. One is to immediately stop further analysis work as soon as preliminary analysis results indicate that the underlying problem has probably been found, so that corrective action can be taken as soon as possible. After all, a highly detailed proof of the problem, accompanied by a tastefully packaged analysis and presentation, does not do much good if a terse e-mail summarizing preliminary results could have warned the management team a week sooner. The second option is to construct new financial reporting systems that quickly and accurately collect and summarize much of the financial analysis work that was previously completed by hand, thereby saving large amounts of time. This second approach can be very expensive if a controller is determined to build reporting systems to spot every conceivable problem area. However, an intelligent review of the most likely problem areas can lead one to authorize the construction of management information systems that report on only the most commonly encountered problems, thereby leaving manual data collection and analysis for the least likely problem areas that are most rarely encountered. A combination of both approaches allows a controller to rapidly determine problem areas and disseminate information to management about not only the problem, but also suggested solutions.

The remainder of this appendix describes the most commonly encountered symptoms, first listing those found on the balance sheet, and then proceeding to the income statement and then the statement of cash flows. Beneath each described symptom are bullet points, each of which describes an area of analysis to complete that will point toward a likely problem area. Beneath each bullet point there is a check mark, followed by possible solutions for the indicated problems. By using this multistep approach, a controller can quickly hone in on a problem area, determine the precise cause of the problem, and recommend solutions.

1. **The investment in accounts receivable is increasing.**

   - *Check the turnover trend.* The first step is to see if the increase in accounts receivable is based on an increase in sales volume. For example, if a customer has purchased far more than the usual amount recently, the company will be funding the customer for the amount of this purchase until the contractually agreed-upon payment date has been reached. Consequently, to determine if the accounts receivable turnover rate has changed, run a trend line for this measure for at least the last quarter by dividing accounts receivable into the annualized sales for each month being measured.

      ✓ *Management recommendation.* Review sales to see if the increase in sales will continue. If so, arrange for more debt funding to cover the projected increase in accounts receivable.

   - *Check turnover trend by customer.* If the accounts receivable turnover trend is worsening, the next step is to determine which customers are not paying on time. This can be done either by calculating the turnover trend for each customer or by skimming through the accounts receivable aging to see which customers have large overdue balances.

      ✓ *Management recommendation.* If a specific customer is not paying on time, then possible remedies range from a visit to the customer to discuss payment terms, to cutting off additional credit, reducing the preset credit limit, or even filing a lawsuit to collect funds.

   - *Check the credit granting process.* If a customer is clearly unable to pay for goods received, an additional question is how did the customer ever receive credit terms sufficient to allow for significant bad debt to accumulate? This calls for a review of the credit granting process to ensure that credit checks are conducted and credit limits approved by authorized personnel.

      ✓ *Management recommendation.* Besides the corrective actions just noted, the management team should ensure that credit reviews for existing customers are done at regular intervals, to ensure that changes in the financial condition of customers are spotted in a timely manner and credit terms changed to match the new financial situation.

- *Review for fraud.* If there is some difficulty in contacting the customer, or if further review reveals that the customer no longer exists, there may be some chance of a fraudulent situation where the customer never had any intention of paying for the goods or services delivered.

  ✓ *Management recommendation.* Not only should there be a detailed review of the credit granting process to ensure that newly incorporated customers are especially carefully screened, but also that there is no linkage between employees granting credit and the customers who have fraudulently taken delivery of company goods or services.

2. The investment in inventory is increasing.

- *Check the turnover trend.* If sales are increasing, then the amount of inventory needed to support those sales may be justified. To verify if this is the case, calculate a trend line for inventory turnover for at least the last quarter of a year. To do so, divide the current inventory balance into the annualized cost of goods sold. If the turnover proportion has dropped, then there is proportionally more inventory on hand than is justified by the increase in sales.

  ✓ *Management recommendation.* Review the cause of any increase in sales to see if the increase is projected to continue. If so, the increased inventory level is unlikely to decline, and additional funding will be necessary to support the added inventory investment.

- *Review the last date on which inventory was used.* If inventory turns have worsened, then one possible problem is that some of the inventory is obsolete. One way to check this is to review the dates when inventory was last used. One approach is to see if there is such a date tracked by the computer system, or if there are dated inventory tags on the inventory items or dated shipping labels on the inventory. Then, compile the dollar value of all items that have not been used in some time to determine the level of obsolescence.

  ✓ *Management recommendation.* Institute a periodic inventory liquidation procedure, so that all old inventory items are regularly reviewed and sold off.

- *Verify where parts are used.* Another way to determine inventory obsolescence is to see where parts are being used. The best way is to use the "where used" feature that is common in most manufacturing computer systems, allowing one to enter a part number and have the system feed back information about the products in which those parts are used. If there are no products in which they are used, the parts are clearly obsolete.

✓ *Management recommendation.* There must be a reason why parts are in stock, even though there are no products in which they are used. The usual reason is that the engineering staff has changed to a new part without first using up the old stock of parts. Accordingly, one action for management is to review the unused parts to see if they can still be used in the newer, revised products, and secondly, to set up a procedure so that the engineering staff is forced to use up existing inventories before switching to a new part.

- *Review the sales trend for all finished goods kept in stock.* If it is evident that the bulk of the inventory is in finished goods, one should verify the sales trends for all products for which there is some inventory. If sales trends are declining and the amount of on-hand inventories are high, there may be a problem liquidating the inventory.

  ✓ *Management recommendation.* Set up a procedure with the production scheduling staff to ensure that additional production is not scheduled for any item that is experiencing a drop in sales. Also, have the sales staff run a promotion or temporary price decrease to clear out all excess finished goods inventories for products that are experiencing slow sales volume.

- *Review the turnover for work-in-process inventories.* If there are no problems with either raw materials or finished goods inventories, we are left with work-in-process (WIP) inventory. See if the inventory turnover level for WIP has changed significantly over the last few months by creating a trend line for WIP inventory turnover (calculated by dividing the current WIP inventory total by the annualized cost of goods sold).

  ✓ *Management recommendation.* See if there are any partial assemblies that have not been completed for lack of parts or machine capacity, and finish them. Also, verify that there is not an excessive quantity of WIP kept in a quality hold area for repair work. Also, verify that WIP is not piling up in front of a bottleneck operation; if there is, either cut back on the production coming from upstream work centers, or increase the capacity of the bottleneck operation. Finally, see if WIP is being held up at off-site locations or suppliers for finishing work; if so, expedite all such completion activity.

- *Verify the size of purchased quantities.* It is possible that the purchasing department is trying to obtain low per-unit costs by purchasing in excessively large quantities. If so, there will be very large on-hand quantities of selected parts.

  ✓ *Management recommendation.* Have the purchasing staff review the cost of buying in smaller multiples, and buy in this manner if there is a reasonable cost–benefit tradeoff. If not, then buy in large multiples, but issue releases from the suppliers' stock in weekly or smaller increments, so that the company is paying for only a portion of the total purchase at one time.

- *Look for costing errors.* If there is no evident change in the quantities of any inventories, it is possible that the per-unit cost has been accidentally changed in the inventory database. If so, compare the per-unit cost of each item for the current period and for the same items in a previous period. If there are significant differences, review the reasons for the costing changes.

  ✓ *Management recommendation.* Lock down the inventory costing database so that only authorized personnel are allowed to make changes. Also, audit the more expensive material costs to ensure that costs are accurate. Further, restrict access to the unit of measure field in the inventory database; for example, if the unit of measure for a roll of tape costing $1.00 per roll is changed to inches (with 1,760 inches on the roll), the cost of the roll will suddenly increase from $1 to $1,760.

3. The investment in fixed assets is increasing.

- *Compare assets purchased to the original budget.* There may be nothing wrong with a rapid increase in the asset base, as long as the additions were purchased in accordance with the original fixed asset budget. Simply compare all purchases to the original budget, and verify that all authorizations are in place for everything purchased.

  ✓ *Management recommendation.* Institute a tight capital budgeting procedure to ensure that no assets are purchased that have not gone through the entire budget approval process. Also, verify that capital approval levels are low enough to ensure that the correct managers are affixing their signatures to the purchase orders for the bulk of the dollar volume spent on fixed assets.

- *See if the depreciation method has changed.* If someone has inadvertently altered the depreciation method being used, this can result in a significant change in the net value of all fixed assets. Review the fixed asset register to ensure that the same depreciation method is being used for all items within each fixed asset category.

  ✓ *Management recommendation.* Create an internal audit procedure for checking the depreciation method used for a sample of all fixed assets in the assets register.

- *Verify that asset values are removed from the books when disposed of.* Some companies have such poor accounting systems that there is no record of asset removals once they have been sold or otherwise disposed of. If so, the asset value on the books will be excessively high. To verify this problem, conduct an audit of the fixed assets and compare all items found to those listed on the accounting books.

✓ *Management recommendation.* Institute a procedure for properly removing all assets from the books of record once they have been disposed of. Also, institute a policy of conducting a fixed asset audit at fixed intervals that is designed to spot any asset dispositions that have not been properly recorded.

- *Verify that only assets exceeding the capitalization limit are capitalized.* It is possible that asset values are increasing because the accounting staff is incorrectly capitalizing assets that are too low in cost, and which should actually be expensed. Sample the fixed-asset register and verify that all recorded assets exceed the capitalization limit.

  ✓ *Management recommendation.* Implement additional training of the accounting staff to ensure that they do not capitalize items that are below the capitalization limit.

4. The funding supplied by accounts payable is shrinking.

- *Verify that no additional discounts are being taken.* The amount of accounts payable may drop if the accounting staff becomes more aggressive in taking early payment discounts on all billings from suppliers that offer a discount rate exceeding the company's cost of capital. The best way to check this is to review the accounts payable to determine the dollar value of discounts taken.

  ✓ *Management recommendation.* Create a discounts tracking system that records the dollar amount of all discounts taken in a separate general ledger account, thereby making it easier to track changes in the dollar value of total discounts taken.

- *See if payments are being made too soon.* It is possible that the accounts payable staff is paying suppliers prior to the dates on which their invoices are due. To review this, audit a sample of recent payments and compare due dates on the supplier invoices to the dates on the check copies that are attached to the invoices.

  ✓ *Management recommendation.* Provide additional training for the accounting staff to ensure that they know when to pay suppliers. Also, include this training in a detailed accounts payable procedure.

- *Verify if supplier payment terms have changed.* If the previous two possibilities turn up no variations from previous periods, then it is possible that supplier terms have been changed by the suppliers. To test this, either audit a sample of billings and compare supplier terms to those from previous periods, or else use the keystroke tracking function in the accounting software (if it exists) to determine which supplier terms have been changed in the computer system.

✓ *Management recommendation.* Have the purchasing staff renegotiate payment terms with suppliers to lengthen the time required before payment. Also, set up a warning system whereby the accounts payable staff issues a notice to the purchasing staff whenever a supplier tries to shorten its payment terms.

- *Ascertain if suppliers with shorter payment terms have been added.* When new suppliers are added, possibly to replace old ones, their payment terms may be shorter than those of the suppliers they are replacing, which causes a net decline in the accounts payable balance. To see if this is the case, compare the payment terms on all newly added suppliers to those of the suppliers they are replacing.

  ✓ *Management recommendation.* Have the purchasing staff negotiate longer payment terms with new suppliers.

5. The return on equity is worsening.

- *Check the amount of equity.* The return on equity may be worsening simply because more equity was added since the last time this measurement was calculated and the amount of profit must now be spread over a larger equity base, resulting in a reduced rate of return. To test this, compare the dollar amount of equity at the time of the previous measurement to the amount currently on the books.

  ✓ *Management recommendation.* Maintain tight control over additions to equity. There should be CFO-level approval required before any additional stock is issued, as well as for any options that can be converted into stock.

- *Check the profit level.* If the level of equity has remained the same, then the primary option left is that profit levels have dropped in comparison to the amount of equity on hand. To see if this is true, divide total equity into total earnings for all time periods being compared to see if the trend line drops.

  ✓ *Management recommendation.* Review all of the management recommendations related to sales and expenses in this appendix in order to improve profitability. Also, consider using debt or cash generated from operations to buy back equity, which will improve the return on equity, though there is more risk in this approach, in the event that future cash flows cannot support payments on the added debt levels.

6. Sales are declining.

- *Review market share.* If sales are in decline, it is possible that the entire market is shrinking, and that the company is actually doing quite a good job of maintaining its proportion of a shrinking sales "pie." To see if this is the case, review industry statistics and projections of current total sales levels for those regions in which the company does business. Keep in mind that any such estimate will be extremely rough and will give only a general indication of actual sales levels.

✓ *Management recommendation.* If the overall market is shrinking, there are several options. One is to cut off all further cash investments in favor of milking all possible cash out of the business while letting it die out. Another option is to do the reverse and invest cash in hopes of taking over the smaller market as other competitors pull out. It may also be possible to invest cash in hopes of creating greater efficiencies, while the final options are to invest funds in either creating products targeted at new markets or to purchase companies or product lines that are already positioned in new markets.

- *Check sales by customer.* Individual customers may not be buying as much as was previously the case. To review this, conduct a Pareto analysis of all sales, reviewing the 20 percent of the customer list that accounts for 80 percent of total sales. Compare current or year-to-date sales of each customer in this subgroup to sales in an earlier period to determine which customers are not buying as much as was formerly the case.

  ✓ *Management recommendation.* One option is to intensify the sales and customer service effort with those customers who are no longer buying as much or at all from the company. This may involve questioning them about problems with customer service, offering special pricing deals, or changing the type of product or service delivered. Alternatively, if sales from these customers will not recur, turn the sales effort toward new customers, instead.

- *Check sales by product.* If there is a general downward sales trend for many customers, the reason may be that specific products sold to all of them are not doing well in the marketplace. To test this, go to the sales reports and create sales trend lines for all major products or product lines on either a unit or dollar basis.

  ✓ *Management recommendation.* There are several ways to deal with this problem. One approach is to reduce prices, though this approach will result in increased profits only if there will be a resulting disproportionate improvement in sales volume. Another option is to run short-term promotions to briefly capture more market share, which may result in some longer-term (though marginal) increases in sales. Yet another possibility is to have the engineering staff enhance the product and re-release it to the market, though this possibility is time consuming and may be expensive. Another option is to have the marketing staff repackage the product and sell it in a different market. Finally, it may be necessary for the engineering staff to completely replace the product with something else, which is usually the most expensive option of all.

- *Check seasonality.* If there is a reduction in sales volume for specific products or all of them, it may be that the market is highly seasonal, and that sales declines are normal at some times of the year, such as for Christmas ornaments right after the holidays. Management is probably well aware of seasonality factors already but may not be able to quantify it. To test this, calculate the percentage changes in sales by month for each of the last two years and compare the results for the two years to see if there is a strong correlation between them.

    ✓ *Management recommendation.* There is not much to be done about seasonality besides producing different products that are counter-cyclical. The best management approach is to adopt a budget plan that directs the company to alter inventory, production, and staffing levels to match the reality of seasonal sales levels.

- *Check the business cycle.* If there is no seasonality, it is still possible that a general downturn in business is causing a reduction in sales. This problem can be researched only through either an examination of industry publications or contacts with other companies in the same industry to see if there is a general decline in business activity. This can be very hard to spot and quantitatively prove.

    ✓ *Management recommendation.* If there is a general downturn, the best approach is always to institute draconian cost reduction measures, as well as to obtain extra funding sources, in case extra debt must be procured in order to ride out the lows in the business cycle. For those companies with excess cash or available debt, this may be an excellent time to purchase competing companies that are suffering more severely, and whose valuations have correspondingly declined.

- *Check customer complaints.* Sometimes the reason for a sales decline is more difficult to spot than by a short review of sales by market, customer, or product. Perhaps there are issues with product quality, inconsistent or inaccurate shipments, or poor customer service. The best way to find out is for the quality assurance or customer service departments to collect and summarize all customer complaints. The controller can then conduct a Pareto analysis of the complaints to determine where the main problems are arising.

    ✓ *Management recommendation.* Based on the just-noted Pareto analysis, target the most common causes of customer complaints, correct them, and continue to monitor complaints to ensure that they do not arise again.

7. The company is no longer making money at historical sales levels.

- *Construct a breakeven chart.* Sometimes a company is plodding along, garnering sales at the same old historical rate but is unaccountable, earning less (or losing more!) money than in previous periods when sales were the same. What happened? The cause can only be declines in the gross margin or increases in the underlying fixed costs. To determine which one is at fault, construct a breakeven chart, using the analysis described in Chapter 8.

✓ *Management recommendation.* Based on the results of the breakeven analysis, create a trend line of expenses, either in the gross margin or fixed cost areas, and focus attention on those items for which the trend of expenses has increased, with a strong emphasis on cost reduction.

8. Material costs are increasing.

- *Check the product mix.* When material costs increase, it may not be because material costs for individual products have gone up at all. Instead, the mix of products sold may have changed, so that a greater proportion of products with a greater amount of material costs in them is being sold. As a result, the material cost on the financial statements is increasing. To see if this is the case, construct a detailed cost of goods sold analysis that breaks out the cost of each product sold, using standard costs for the most recent reporting period, and compare it to the same analysis for a prior period.

  ✓ *Management recommendation.* If products with greater material costs are being sold, make sure that those products do not also have correspondingly lower margins. If so, it may be necessary to increase the prices on those products in order to restore overall margin levels. After all, if customers have discovered that a product is priced too low, they may order inordinate amounts of it, resulting in a permanent decline in gross margins.

- *Review the purchase price variance.* A material price increase may be caused by an increase in material costs on specific raw materials or subassemblies. To test this possibility, compare the standard cost of all purchased items received in the last reporting period to the amount actually paid for them, as noted on either the supplier invoice or the original purchase order.

  ✓ *Management recommendation.* Follow up on all purchase price variances, especially those resulting in large material cost increases, determine the underlying cause for the increase, and take action, either through negotiation with the supplier or sourcing with a new supplier, to bring material costs back down. If the cost increase appears to be permanent, then try to pass the increase through to customers with a price increase.

- *Compare new products to target costs.* It is exceedingly common for the engineering and purchasing teams that design new products to arrive at a solution that costs more than the originally targeted cost. This variance will not show up on the bill of materials, because the initial cost usually incorporates the actual costs at the time the product was first introduced. Accordingly, there does not appear to be a purchase price variance, just a new product with relatively poor margins. To test this problem, compare the original cost targets for each new product to the first bill of material created at the point of production, and note specific differences in costs between the two documents.

✓ *Management recommendation.* Actively review target and actual costs well before a product reaches the market and force the products back into redesign if costs are not in line with expectations. This may mean that some products should not reach the market at all if targeted material costs cannot be reached. The only alternative is to either raise prices on the new product or adopt an aggressive cost reduction plan for the next few years to gradually bring costs down to expected levels (though prices may also drop as competition increases through the time period).

- *Review scrap costs.* A common problem is that the manufacturing process is spinning off an excess amount of scrap, which is contributing to an excessive amount of materials cost. An increased level of scrap cost can be caused by an improperly engineered product that is difficult to manufacture, undertrained production employees, or shoddy supplier parts that are caused by poor supplier qualification or an attempt to shave the cost of purchased parts by buying substandard parts. No matter what the cause, there are several ways to detect scrap. One is to implement a scrap reporting system, which requires the production staff to report on scrap they produce; because this makes them look bad, underreporting of scrap is quite common. Another approach is to tightly control the materials flow from the production floor, so that all outgoing scrap must pass through a control point, where it is counted and its cost determined.

✓ *Management recommendation.* Research the underlying reasons for the occurrence of scrap (there may be several), determine which ones cause the largest amounts of scrap, and target those areas for immediate improvement.

- *Verify the accuracy of the cutoff.* Sometimes, there is no real material cost increase, but rather an increase in billings from suppliers that is not associated with a corresponding increase in inventory, which results in the false recording of extra expenses. This is a common condition that arises at the end of a reporting period, and which is known as "cutoff." To have a proper cutoff, go to the receiving log and verify that supplier invoices have been received for all items physically received prior to the last few days of the month. Also, verify that there has been a receipt for all invoices booked. By ensuring that both supplier invoices and receipts are posted to the correct period, one can avoid an improper cutoff that will result in the reporting of incorrect material costs.

✓ *Management recommendation.* Implement the tightest possible cut-off procedures, verifying that there is a properly recorded supplier invoice in the accounting system that matches a receipt of goods for the same period. This can be done manually, though most high-end enterprise resource planning (ERP) systems contain this feature and will not allow improper cutoffs to occur.

- *Investigate changes in pricing in contracts.* Another reason for a material cost increase is that a company has a contract with a supplier that allows the supplier to raise prices from time to time. If so, the proper investigative action is to compare all supplier price changes to the underlying contracts and verify that the price changes are within the proper percentage limits (if any), and at the designated times.

  ✓ *Management recommendation.* If appropriate, management should consider engaging in long-term contracts with relatively fixed prices, if, through experience, management believes that the prices obtained are reasonable and will not be higher than future market rates. Alternatively, if contractual rates are too variable, management can consider avoiding all contracts for some items and instead procure parts on the open market, on the assumption that current pricing is low enough, and that the company will not run short of supplies due to industry undercapacity.

- *Verify purchase volumes achieved.* Material prices may have increased because the company is no longer buying from its suppliers at volume levels that allow it to be charged discounts. This may be caused by less sales volume or the decision to switch to just-in-time purchasing, whereby individual shipments will be smaller, in order to keep inventory levels down. To see if this is the problem, one can call the supplier to see why they are charging more per unit, compare unit volumes per shipment to contract prices, or run a trend line of total unit volumes per month over a number of months to see if there is a volume decline.

  ✓ *Management recommendation.* Renegotiate prices with suppliers to see if it is still possible to obtain better pricing even though unit volumes have declined. Also, if individual order quantities have declined due to a switch to a just-in-time system, but total volumes are still the same, it may be possible to issue blanket orders to suppliers for a full year of production, thereby allowing for lower pricing while still arranging for a multitude of small order releases against the blanket purchase order.

9. Freight costs are increasing.

When freight costs increase, it can be extremely difficult to determine the exact reason why, because there are usually many invoices to sort through. Accordingly, there are a variety of approaches itemized here that one can use as a checklist that should eventually yield the answer to higher freight expenses.

- *Review the product mix.* Freight costs on a per-shipment basis may not have gone up at all, but the product mix during the reporting period may have shifted to different types of products with a greater cube size, which means that the shipper will charge more because the product takes up more room in the truck, railcar, or shipping container. To see if this is the case, determine the cube size for each product, ascertain the quantity of each product shipped, and multiply the two to determine the total cubic footage shipped during the reporting period. Then, track this information on a trend line to see if there are significant changes from month to month.

  ✓ *Management recommendation.* If the volume shipped is the reason for a freight expense increase, there is little to be done to improve the situation, unless the high-volume shipments can be consolidated into full-truckload deliveries, which are much less expensive than less-than-truckload (LTL) deliveries. The ability to do this is closely tied to the degree of dispersion of the product; if it is going to just a few distributors or retailers, it may be possible to consolidate shipments, but deliveries to many customers in many locations will almost certainly require LTL shipments.

- *Check rates in shipping contracts.* Contracts with individual shipping companies normally allow for a set percentage reduction from posted shipping rates, as long as a minimum volume of shipment is maintained. To see if discounts are being given by shippers, compare the billed rates to the contractual rates for a sample of shipping invoices. Because this can be a very high-volume review, many companies prefer to bring in an outside freight auditor to conduct this review.

  ✓ *Management recommendation.* Have the purchasing staff follow up with the shippers who are not billing in accordance with the terms of their contracts. If they continue to bill incorrectly, these suppliers should be terminated in favor of shippers who can invoice more accurately (assuming that shippers with good delivery service can be found).

- *Review shipment volumes by shipper.* If shippers are not giving discounts based on their shipping contracts, the reason may be that the company's shipment volumes with those shippers are not meeting the minimum levels required by the contracts. To see if this is the case, compare total volumes by shipper to the minimum contractual shipment volumes.

  ✓ *Management recommendation.* Consolidate shipments with the smallest possible number of shipping companies in order to obtain the highest volumes, and therefore the greatest freight cost reductions, with each one.

- *Check on rush deliveries caused by logistics or production.* It is possible that an increase in freight costs is caused by sudden changes in the production schedule that require a rapid reshuffling of purchase orders to suppliers. If any of these new purchase orders require short delivery times, there may be added freight charges for overnight or air freight deliveries. These types of deliveries are usually easily identified, since the carrier doing the billing is a specialist in rush deliveries (e.g., FedEx), and so sorting billing records by the name of the shipper will quickly result in the total amount of rush delivery costs.

  ✓ *Management recommendation.* Back track through the rush freight charges to determine the cause of each one. Specifically, this should include the reason why a change in the production schedule (or some similar causation factor) was deemed necessary. Also, create a rebilling system, so that customers are charged back for rush freight charges when they are requesting short delivery times.

- *Check the distance of shipments.* Local shipments cost less than long-distance ones. Accordingly, an increase in freight costs can be caused by a shift to suppliers or customers who are located further away. To see if this is the case, compare the zip codes or states in which current suppliers and customers are located to those of several reporting periods in the past to see if there has been a significant change. Alternatively, select the 20 percent of freight bills that account for 80 percent of the total freight cost, trace these items back to specific supplier and customer deliveries, and compare this distribution to the same data from prior reporting periods.

  ✓ *Management recommendation.* One way to reduce freight costs is to purchase parts from suppliers who are located closer to the company, though this cost reduction must be offset against any possible increases in unit costs to see if there is an overall cost reduction. Another possibility is to have customers pay the bill for freight on products shipped to them, rather than having the company foot the bill.

- *Review the cost of in-house freight versus outside freight.* Freight expenses may not just be for the charges of outside shippers; they may also include the cost of an in-house delivery fleet. If so, compare the cost of the in-house fleet to the cost from previous months to see if any components of the fleet costs have risen in comparison to those of previous periods. It is also possible that the fleet costs have not risen, but revenues have declined, so that freight costs have increased as a proportion of total sales.

  ✓ *Management recommendation.* If the cost of the internal fleet on a per-shipment basis exceeds the per-shipment cost of outside shippers, it is clearly time to trim back the internal fleet. Also, if the cost of the internal fleet has not risen, but sales have declined, then the internal fleet must be reduced in size to match the lower sales level.

10. Direct labor costs are increasing.

- *Review the product mix.* It may be no fault of the production managers if the direct labor cost increases, because the mix of products produced may have shifted to ones that require much more labor. To see if this is the case, create a report that lists the quantities of all products made during the reporting period, multiplied by the standard labor cost per unit produced. When tracked over time, this will clearly show any changes in the total cost of standard direct labor per month.

  ✓ *Management recommendation.* If the mix of products has changed to ones that require a large amount of direct labor, be sure to run a margin analysis on each of these products to ensure that the price is sufficient to cover the added direct labor cost. If not, see if the price can be increased to improve margins. If not, consider eliminating the product if the manufacturing facility can more profitably create other products with a lower labor cost. Also, have an industrial engineer review the production process to see if the labor content of those products with high labor costs can be reduced.

- *Verify differences between the actual and standard labor cost.* Labor costs may be increasing in terms of the cost per hour, even though the number of hours worked may be steady or even declining. This problem is most common in a tight labor market, where workers have better-paying alternatives, which forces employers to offer higher wages. Also, if it is necessary to hire a more senior and experienced workforce, perhaps due to the complexity of the production process, wages will also increase. To see if this is a problem, summarize all direct labor hours for the most recent reporting period and divide this into the total direct labor payroll for the same period, which yields the average wage per hour. Compare this information to the same calculation for previous periods to see if there is a trend of increasing wages.

  ✓ *Management recommendation.* One option is to move the production facility to another location where wage rates are lower, though this is a good option only when the labor cost component of a product is so high that major cost reductions can be achieved by making the move. Another alternative is to use industrial engineering reviews to make the production process simpler and in need of fewer workers, which has the byproduct benefit of requiring less trained and therefore less expensive workers. It may also be possible to invest in various kinds of automation to completely eliminate direct labor costs, though this option has the downside of requiring greater overhead costs, such as depreciation and machine maintenance.

- *Compare total hours worked to standard.* The per-hour cost of labor may be in line with expectations, but the number of hours may have increased. To see if this possibility is true, summarize the number of direct labor hours worked in the last reporting period and compare this to the number of hours at standard, which is collected by multiplying the standard hours listed on the bill of materials by the total number of products produced. If the number of actual hours exceeds the standard, then management should work on making the labor force more efficient.

  - ✓ *Management recommendation.* Besides the recommendations noted under the last item, management can also focus on the scheduling of direct labor personnel. If employees are coming in and waiting around with no work to do, then there is a disconnect caused either by the absence of materials with which to make products (which requires better control over the purchasing function or the scheduling of products that require purchases), or by the absence of scheduling for machine downtime that stops the production process. To solve either issue requires close and continual coordination between the production scheduling staff and the maintenance and purchasing departments.

- *Check on overtime costs.* An increase in labor costs may be brought about by additional employee overtime, which increases labor costs by a minimum of 50 percent for each overtime hour worked. To see if this is the problem, summarize all overtime dollars paid in the most recent reporting period, and compare this to the same calculation for previous periods to see if there is a change in the amount of dollars paid. Another measure is to divide the total dollars (or hours) of overtime by the grand total cost (or hours) for all labor in the period, which yields the overtime percentage for the period. This measure can also be compared to prior periods.

  - ✓ *Management recommendation.* Examine the reasons for overtime, and eliminate them. One may be that customers require shipments by a specified date, which cannot be met unless the staff works overtime. If so, can the extra cost be charged to the customer? Alternatively, could the production scheduling staff have done a better job of completing the work in an earlier period when more production capacity might have been available?

- *Investigate shift premiums.* Direct labor costs will go up if there are multiple shifts, with the second and third shifts being paid a premium. To determine the extent of this cost, summarize the shift premium expense for the second and third shifts in the reporting period. The analysis can be further refined by dividing this cost by the total direct labor cost to see if the proportion of shift premium cost is changing over time.

✓ *Management recommendation.* If there is a third shift, see if it is possible to cut back on or eliminate this shift, thereby eliminating the largest of the shift premiums. The same analysis can be applied to the second shift. These two shifts should only be used only when there are firm customer orders in hand, or very reliable sales forecasts that call for more product than the day shift can create on its own.

11. Departmental costs are increasing.

- *Compare the department head count against the budget.* In most departments, the primary cost is the salaries of the employees and all related payroll taxes and benefits. To see if this is causing the problem, compare either the budgeted head count or total payroll-related costs against the budget to see if there are discrepancies.

  ✓ *Management recommendation.* Investigate the need for extra personnel who have been hired, as well as how the hiring could have taken place despite the budgeted head count level. Also, see if the transaction volumes have changed significantly in the department, since a volume increase could account for extra staffing to handle the added workload.

- *Compare salaries to the budget.* If the head count matches the budget, the amount of salaries paid to those budgeted employees may not. To see if this is the case, obtain the year-to-date total payroll for the department and compare it to the year-to-date amount that was budgeted. If there is a difference, investigate by position to see where pay levels have changed. The difference may also be due to one-time bonuses.

  ✓ *Management recommendation.* Institute a procedure that requires higher-level management approval before pay changes of any kind are allowed. The approval process should include documentation of the budgeted pay level for the current period, so that any manager signing off on a pay raise knows what the budget should be for the position and is in a better position to protest if the pay rate being asked for is higher than the budget.

- *Compare overtime to the budget.* If pay rates per person are exceeding the budget, but the pay rate per person matches the budget, it is likely that the underlying problem is an increase in overtime. To see if this is the case, summarize all year-to-date overtime and compare the dollar amount to the budget. This can also be calculated as a percentage. However, be aware that some departments incur overtime only at certain times of the year, followed by slack periods. For example, the accounting staff will work longer hours in January to prepare for the annual audit (assuming that the fiscal year matches the calendar year), so the year-to-date overtime for the first quarter of the year will look horrendous, even though there will be little additional overtime for the remainder of the year.

✓ *Management recommendation.* Require advance management approval, in writing, for all overtime worked. Also, people who chronically work overtime may have an excessive need for cash, rather than an excessive workload; these people should be identified and their overtime hours reviewed with special care.

- *Look for full-time equivalents.* If a department manager needs more staff to handle the workload but is not budgeted for additional staff, a common solution is to hide additional employees by hiring temporary workers and listing the expense under other accounts. To see if this is the case, review the detail for other accounts, such as "miscellaneous" or "temporary help" to see if there is an excessive degree of part-time employee usage going on. Also, review the general and administrative expenses for excessive temporary help charges, since the cost of temporary workers is frequently charged to this area, even if they work for a different department.

  ✓ *Management recommendation.* Require all temporary help to be hired from a select number of temporary help agencies, so that all requests for help of this kind can be channeled through a single individual or department, which can compare work requests against the remaining departmental budgets for these costs. Alternatively, make sure that the accounting department is charging all temporary help costs against the correct department and account, so that managers can easily compare these costs against the budget. Yet another alternative is to require a purchase order for all temporary help, which needs management approval of the purchase orders prior to the workers' being brought in. This last approach ensures that temporary help costs will not exceed the budget.

- *Compare employee benefits to the budget.* To see if employee benefits are exceeding budgeted amounts, begin with the variance between the two costs for each department and break down the analysis into smaller components. For example, determine the cost per person of medical, dental, and life insurance, and other costs, and track this information on a trend line. Any sudden changes in these costs is caused by one of three possible conditions: Benefit costs have increased on a per-employee basis, employees have elected to take or stop taking a benefit, or the number of employees has changed.

  ✓ *Management recommendation.* If the per-employee cost of a benefit has changed, contact the supplier of the benefit to see if a different benefit package can be used that has a lower cost, or switch to a less expensive supplier. If a cost increase is due to the number of employees having risen, then compare the head count to the budget and take corrective action to reduce the head count.

- *Index other costs against head count and run a comparison.* The remaining departmental costs tend to be relatively small in comparison to payroll-related costs. They also tend to fluctuate in relation to the number of employees. For example, telephone costs, office supplies, and travel are directly related to the number of staff. To see if these remaining costs are varying excessively, construct a comparison of all nonpayroll costs to the number of employees in each department, which yields an expense amount per employee. For example, there is an average telephone cost per month of $75 per person, office supplies of $119, and travel of $542. As the number of employees changes over time, these costs per person should not vary significantly. If they do, investigate further to see if some expense accounts are being abused, such as flying first class, or taking home office supplies.

  ✓ *Management recommendation.* Unless all other company areas are well regulated and no longer in need of daily management attention (a rare situation), management generally does not have the time to investigate nonpayroll department costs in any degree of detail. Consequently, there are only two recommendations. First, make sure that department managers are allowed to spend only budgeted amounts for each expense line item, after which they are cut off until the start of the next fiscal year. Second, the travel budget is the only large-dollar item in the typical department budget, so use the internal audit staff to investigate large expenses in this area.

12. **Interest costs are excessive.**

- *Compare billed interest to debt agreements.* It is possible that the lender is charging an incorrect interest rate. To investigate this possibility, construct a schedule that shows all fixed interest rates and additional charges (if any), as per the loan or lease agreements. Then, add the exact interest rate agreements for variable rates, which tend to be a bit more complicated, and compare the cost of all interest billings to the amounts specified in the loan agreements to see if there is a disparity.

  ✓ *Management recommendation.* Meet with the lender at once if there is a clear billing discrepancy, in order to determine the reason for the problem, as well as how to obtain credits for earlier overpayments. If there are continuing problems with overbillings, management should be seriously concerned with the reliability and honesty of the lender and should investigate moving all debt to a different lender.

- *Verify that variable rate changes are justified.* If there have been interest rate changes based on alterations in underlying interest rates, such as a bank's prime rate or the London Interbank Offer Rate (LIBOR), one should conduct a comparison between the dates on which these underlying rates changed, and the amount of change, to the corresponding rate changes charged by the lender on debt owed by the company. Any differences should be brought to the attention of management.

✓ *Management recommendation.* If there are differences between the timing or amounts of interest charges and the underlying rates, these changes should be brought to the attention of the lender for corrective action. As was the case with the preceding recommendation, management should seriously consider switching to a new lender if the current one exhibits a continuing tendency to falsely alter the timing or amounts of interest charges in its favor.

- *Compare actual to budgeted debt levels.* The reason for an increase in the interest expense may simply be that the amount of debt has increased beyond budgeted expectations. To test this supposition, create a trend line that shows actual debt levels for the last few reporting periods in comparison to expected debt levels. This analysis is rarely sufficient, because management will want to know why the extra debt was incurred. Refer to the next item, "The company is running out of cash," for a complete review of investigative actions regarding this issue.

  ✓ *Management recommendation.* As just noted, refer to the next section for a complete set of management recommendations regarding cash flow issues.

13. The company is running out of cash.

- *Review working capital.* One of the main uses of cash in any company is working capital. To see if this is where the cash has gone, create a trend line that compares working capital levels for the past year. For each period measured on this trend line, add accounts receivable to inventory and subtract accounts payable. If there is an increase in working capital, then this is where the cash has gone.

  ✓ *Management recommendation.* Compare the working capital amount to sales to see of the ratio of the two has changed significantly. If the proportion of working capital has increased, then management should work on either reducing accounts receivable through better credit granting and collection efforts or reducing inventory through the methods noted earlier, under problem number two. Accounts payable can also be lengthened, using the recommendations noted earlier under problem number four. However, if the proportion of working capital to sales is the same and simply reflects an increase in sales, then the increase in working capital is probably permanent, and the company will have to find a funding source to cover the increase in working capital.

- *Review the level of profitability.* If there are losses net of noncash expenditures, then the cash balance will decline. To test this, take the profit or loss noted on the financial statements and add back the total amount of depreciation and amortization expense. If the resulting amount is negative and has been this way for some time, then profitability is the issue.

✓ *Management recommendation.* Conduct a sweeping review of all expenses for all departments. Verify that head count levels match what was originally budgeted, as well as targeted pay levels by position. Ensure that all cost of goods sold categories match budgeted percentages. Verify that sales levels and sales mix by product line are matching expectations. If any of these items are not consistent with original plans, take steps to bring them back into line. If sales levels are permanently lowered, then reduce costs proportionately.

- *Review the amount of assets purchased.* Asset purchases may exceed budgeted levels. To verify this, compare year-to-date asset purchases to the specific items identified in the original budget, and notify management of any assets purchased for which there was no budget. Also, verify that only items exceeding the capitalization limit are being purchased, that the depreciation method has not been altered, and that assets are being properly disposed of in the accounting books.

✓ *Management recommendation.* Institute all recommendations noted under problem number three, which include strict controls over fixed-asset purchases, as well as using training and procedures to ensure the consistency in usage of depreciation methods, disposal procedures, and use of capitalization limits.

- *See if debt agreements have terminated.* The reason for a cash outflow may be as simple as having to return a loan to a bank, which no one may have noticed if the loan was a relatively small one. To detect this issue, go back through the termination dates for all loans to see when they expire and if balloon payments are required.

✓ *Management recommendation.* Create a listing of all loan termination dates, including the amounts due at termination, and review it regularly. If there is any risk of a cash shortfall, be sure to begin negotiations to roll over any terminating debt instruments into new loans many months in advance of the termination date, so that there is no risk of a cash shortfall.

B

Commonly Used Ratios

Ratios and the explanations of their usage are liberally sprinkled throughout this book. This appendix has been created for those readers who need quick access to a ratio for some financial analysis and do not want to spend the time searching through the main body of the text to ascertain this information. For those readers, this appendix contains a variety of the most common ratios, grouped by type of analysis for which they would be used. The main groupings are:

- Analysis of profitability

- Analysis of the balance sheet

- Analysis of corporate growth

- Analysis of cash flow

- Analysis of specific departments:

  ✓ Accounting

  ✓ Customer service

  ✓ Distribution

  ✓ Engineering

  ✓ Human resources

  ✓ Materials management

  ✓ Production

  ✓ Sales and marketing

The layout shown here for several ratios is a heavily modified version of similar ratios taken from Chapter 7 of the sixth edition of *Controllership* (James D. Willson, Jan Roehl-Anderson, and Steven Bragg; New York: John Wiley & Sons, 1999) with the permission of the authors.

Analysis of Profitability

Ratio	Explanation	Derivation
Breakeven point	Pinpoints the revenue level at which a company begins to turn a profit. Useful for determining if this point is so high that a company cannot earn a good profit without major cost reductions.	$\dfrac{\text{Revenue}}{\text{Average gross margin}}$
Number of times interest earned	Indicates the level of risk of taking on more debt. A low ratio indicates that paying the interest on more debt is very risky.	$\dfrac{\text{Average interest expense}}{\text{Cash flow}}$
Operating margin	Indicates the adequacy of margins to cover additional sales and general and administrative costs, as well as interest costs. Also very useful for tracking by profit center or division.	$\dfrac{\text{Revenues}}{\text{Cost of goods sold}}$
Overhead rate	Shows the cost of nondirect expenses that are charged to products when determining product costs and prices. A high overhead rate can indicate excessive overhead costs, but also that there may be a better allocation base than direct labor, resulting in a reduced overhead cost per unit of allocation.	$\dfrac{\text{Overhead expenses}}{\text{Direct labor}}$
Percent return on net sales	Shows the net operating results of a company, but is subject to manipulation because of special accruals or charge-offs. It also does not account for cash flow issues.	$\dfrac{\text{Net sales}}{\text{Net profit}}$
Ratio of sales returns to gross sales	Indicates the quality of goods sold, because high returns usually equate to a poor product. A high return rate can also mean that there is too much product in the distribution pipeline.	$\dfrac{\text{Sales returns}}{\text{Gross sales}}$
Sales per person	Indicates high internal efficiency levels if the existing staff can churn out sales that exceed the industry average.	$\dfrac{\text{Sales}}{\text{Total full-time equivalents}}$
Profit per person	Indicates high internal efficiency levels if the existing staff can create profits that exceed the industry average.	$\dfrac{\text{Profits}}{\text{Total full-time equivalents}}$

Analysis of the Balance Sheet

Ratio	Explanation	Derivation
Debt/equity ratio	Reveals the leverage that management has imposed on the balance sheet by acquiring debt.	$\dfrac{\text{Long-term debt} + \text{short-term debt}}{\text{Total equity}}$
Return on assets	Reveals the proportion of assets needed to generate a certain amount of sales volume. This shows the efficiency of asset usage.	$\dfrac{\text{Total sales}}{\text{Total assets}}$
Return on shareholder equity	Shows the return generated for each dollar of equity invested, but does not show the associated risk, because the measure can be skewed if debt is used to reduce equity.	$\dfrac{\text{Net income}}{\text{Total equity}}$
Current ratio	Compares current assets to liabilities to see if assets are sufficient to pay off current liabilities.	$\dfrac{\text{Current assets}}{\text{Current liabilities}}$
Quick ratio	Similar to the current ratio, but does not include inventory, which is not as easily liquidated to pay off liabilities.	$\dfrac{\text{Cash} + \text{accounts receivable} + \text{investments}}{\text{Current liabilities}}$
Ratio of sales to accounts receivable	Shows the proportion of accounts receivable needed for a given sales volume, which indicates if the receivables are being collected in a timely manner.	$\dfrac{\text{Net sales}}{\text{Total accounts receivable}}$
Accounts payable turnover	Reveals if payments are being made in a timely manner. A low turnover ratio means that either payment terms are very long or payables are not being paid on time.	$\dfrac{\text{Total purchases}}{\text{Ending accounts payable balance}}$
Ratio of repairs and maintenance expense to fixed assets	Useful for determining the condition of corporate assets, since many repairs indicate old or overused equipment.	$\dfrac{\text{Total repairs and maintenance expense}}{\text{Total fixed assets before depreciation}}$
Ratio of depreciation to fixed assets	Determines the general age of company equipment. A ratio close to 1:1 indicates that assets are almost fully depreciated.	$\dfrac{\text{Accumulated depreciation}}{\text{Total fixed assets}}$
Fixed asset turnover	Shows the asset base needed by management to generate a certain level of sales.	$\dfrac{\text{Net sales}}{\text{Fixed assets}}$
Ratio of retained earnings to capital	Used by a lender to determine how much earnings are retained in a business. If low, then management is trying to fund activities through debt instead of equity.	$\dfrac{\text{Retained earnings}}{\text{Total stockholder's equity}}$

Ratio	Explanation	Derivation
Economic value added	Shows the incremental rate of return in excess of the cost of capital on the net investment. If negative, a company is not generating a return in excess of its capital costs.	(Net investment) × (Actual return on assets − required minimum rate of return)
Market value added	Shows the net difference between a company's market value and the cost of its invested capital. A negative amount indicates that management has done a poor job of creating value with the equity base.	(Number of shares outstanding × share price) + (Market value of preferred stock and debt) − (Invested capital)
Working capital productivity	Shows the amount of working capital needed to generate sales. A low ratio reveals that management is using too much working capital to support sales.	$\dfrac{\text{Annual net sales}}{\text{Working capital}}$

Analysis of Corporate Growth

Ratio	Explanation	Derivation
Percentage change in cash flow	This is an excellent first indicator of cash flow–related problems. Although it does not provide the answer for why cash flows change, it is the primary indicator, upon which more detailed analyses may then be conducted.	$\dfrac{\text{Incremental change in cash flow}}{\text{Cash flow from previous period}}$
Percentage change in earnings per share (EPS)	Indicates problems with either an increasing base of equity that is not being matched by increased earnings, or else a reduction in earnings in comparison to a steady equity base.	$\dfrac{\text{Incremental change in EPS}}{\text{EPS from previous period}}$
Percentage change in market share	Is one of the best absolute indicators of company performance, since an improvement in this area means that it has taken sales away from competitors. However, there is not necessarily a correlation between market share and earnings.	$\dfrac{\text{Incremental change in market share}}{\text{Market share from previous period}}$
Percentage change in sales	A necessary trend line for all companies, not only in total, but also for individual product lines or products. A decline should result in either renewed sales activity or new product configurations to boost sales.	$\dfrac{\text{Incremental change in sales}}{\text{Sales from previous period}}$

Analysis of Cash Flow

Ratio	Explanation	Derivation
Cash flow adequacy	Reveals if the cash flow from continuing operations is sufficient to meet all major payment commitments.	$\dfrac{\text{Cash flow from operations}}{\text{All scheduled payments for long-term debt, asset purchases, and dividends}}$
Cash flow return on assets	If there is a large proportion of noncash expenses, such as depreciation or amortization, this ratio will look much better than the profit-based return on assets measurement.	$\dfrac{\text{Cash flow}}{\text{Total assets}}$
Cash flow to sales	Reveals the total amount of cash flow attributable to each sales dollar.	$\dfrac{\text{Cash flow from operations}}{\text{Total revenue}}$
Dividend payout ratio	Shows the proportion of cash flow that goes toward the payment of dividends. A worsening ratio shows an investor that a company is more likely to cut the dividend.	$\dfrac{\text{Total dividend payments}}{\text{Cash flow from operations}}$
Long-term debt repayment	Reveals if current cash flows are sufficient for paying off regularly scheduled debt payments.	$\dfrac{\text{Total long-term debt payments for the period}}{\text{Cash flow from operations for the period}}$
Operating cash flow	Shows the basic underlying elements of cash flow, excluding one-time contributors to cash, such as the sale of assets.	Profits + noncash expenses ± changes in working capital

Analysis of Specific Departments

Accounting

Ratio	Explanation	Derivation
Average collection period	Shows the number of days over which an average invoice goes unpaid. A long collection period is evidence of several possible problems, such as customers with poor credit, incorrect invoices, or shipping problems.	$\dfrac{\text{Average annualized accounts receivable}}{\text{Average daily credit sales}}$
Overdue accounts receivable	Shows the proportion of overdue accounts receivable as compared to total receivables. An increase in this ratio is a sign of worsening collection problems.	$\dfrac{\text{Total of overdue accounts receivable}}{\text{Total accounts receivable}}$

Ratio	Explanation	Derivation
Ratio of purchase discounts to total purchases	Reveals if the accounting staff is alertly taking all available purchase discounts. However, a failure to do so may be driven more by a lack of available cash to make the early payments.	$\dfrac{\text{Total purchase discounts taken}}{\text{Total purchases}}$
Time to produce financial statements	Reveals the speed with which statements are issued. However, this will necessarily take longer in a more complex environment, such as when there are multiple divisions to consolidate.	(Financial statement issue date) − (First day of month)
Transaction error rate	A prime indicator of not only the management ability of a controller, but also the level of training and overall skill of the accounting staff.	$\dfrac{\text{Number of errors}}{\text{Total number of transactions}}$
Transactions processed per person	This is the best measure of the efficiency of the accounting staff, though it does not indicate if some transactions should be completed at all, since automation may be an option that is being ignored.	$\dfrac{\text{Number of transactions completed}}{\text{Number of full-time equivalents required to complete transactions}}$

Customer service

Ratio	Explanation	Derivation
Customer turnover	Shows the proportion of customers who are no longer being serviced by the company. A high turnover figure may have many possible causes, such as rude customer service, poor products, or inconsistent delivery.	$\dfrac{\text{(Total customer list) − (Invoiced customers)}}{\text{Total customer list}}$
Number of customer complaints	This is the prime source of information for the use of management in determining the amount and type of complaints, so that management can determine a course of action to resolve them.	Summarize complaints from complaints database for specified date range
Response time to customer complaints	Shows the time needed to fix customer problems. When used on a trend line, this is an excellent way to see if customer problems are being fixed more rapidly over time.	(Final resolution date) − (Initial contact date)

Distribution

Ratio	Explanation	Derivation
Average delivery time	This is a high level measure that reveals overall delivery time problems, but requires additional analysis to find the underlying problems.	(Delivery date) – (Date order was sent to shipping area)
Percentage of on-time deliveries	Similar to the prior measure, but can be enhanced by including notations on the causes of delivery problems.	(Required date) – (Actual delivery date)
Percentage of products damaged in transit	Reveals either packaging problems in the facility or trouble at any third-party carriers that are delivering products.	$\dfrac{\text{Damage-related complaints in complaints database}}{\text{Total complaints in complaints database}}$

Engineering

Ratio	Explanation	Derivation
Bill of material accuracy	Reveals if there are problems with the list of components used to purchase parts for products. Problems in this area lead to errors in purchasing and picking, which can greatly reduce the efficiency of the production operation.	$\dfrac{\text{Number of accurate parts in bill of material (BOM)}}{\text{Total list of parts on BOM}}$
Number of patent applications filed	Shows the creativity not only of the engineering staff, but also of the legal staff in converting ideas into protected competitive concepts.	Number of patent applications logged in as having been filed during the period
Percentage of new products introduced in the period	Shows the ability of the engineering staff to convert product ideas into new products on a regular basis.	$\dfrac{\text{Number of new products introduced in the period}}{\text{Number of products available at the beginning of the period}}$
Percentage of sales from new products	Shows if new products are original enough and sufficiently closely targeted at specific markets to result in significant sales increases.	$\dfrac{\text{Revenues from new products}}{\text{Total revenues}}$
Percentage of new parts used on products	Shows if the engineering staff is trying to reduce the amount of parts on hand by reusing existing parts in new product designs.	$\dfrac{\text{Number of new parts in BOM}}{\text{Total number of parts in BOM}}$

Ratio	Explanation	Derivation
Percentage of products reaching market before competition	Shows the efficiency not only of the engineering department, but also the purchasing and production staffs in converting product designs into saleable products.	$\dfrac{\text{Number of products released before competition}}{\text{Total number of products released}}$
Percentage of released designs matching target costs	This crucial measure reveals the management ability of the engineering staff in ensuring that completed product designs match the originally targeted costs.	$\dfrac{\text{Summary of actual product costs}}{\text{Summary of target costs}}$
Time from design inception to production	When compared to budgeted time periods, this measure shows if the engineering, purchasing, and production staffs are capable of converting designs into products in a timely manner.	(Completed design sign-off date) – (Design start date)

Human resources

Ratio	Explanation	Derivation
Average time to fill requested positions	The time needed to fill positions is of great importance when a company is in rapid growth mode, and must fill positions in order to maintain its growth rate.	(Date offer letter is accepted by recruit) – (Date of receipt of position request)
Average yearly wage per employee	Reveals the average company pay level as compared to the industry average. This can be of more use on a position-by-position basis, since industry pay compilations are generally made on this basis.	$\dfrac{\begin{array}{c}\text{(Summary of all hourly wages} \times \text{number of annual working hours} + \text{(Summary of all salaries)}\end{array}}{\begin{array}{c}\text{Number of employees}\end{array}}$
Employee turnover rate	A high turnover rate usually results in high recruiting costs, as well as more transaction errors by new personnel, since they have less experience in company systems.	$\dfrac{\text{Number of employee departures}}{\text{Number of employees at beginning of period}}$
Indirect to direct personnel ratio	Reveals an excessive degree of overhead personnel as compared to the direct labor personnel who are actually creating products or providing services, especially when plotted on a trend line.	$\dfrac{\text{Number of personnel in overhead positions}}{\text{Number of personnel in direct labor positions}}$
Minorities percentage	Reveals the percentages of currently employed minorities on the staff, which may be of use when trying to meet federal minority hiring requirements.	Summarize by minority code in payroll or human resources systems

Human resources

Ratio	Explanation	Derivation
Percentage of employees with certifications	This is an indicator not only of the education level of employees, but also of the commitment of the corporation to further the training of its staff.	$$\dfrac{\text{Number of employees with certifications}}{\text{Total number of employees}}$$
Ratio of fringe benefits to direct labor	The amount of fringe benefit costs can be compared to that offered by other organizations, or to industry rates in general to see if a company is leading or lagging in this important compensation area.	$$\dfrac{\text{Total fringe benefit expense}}{\text{Total direct labor expense}}$$
Trend of head count	An excessively rapid increase in head count that does not correlate to a similar increase in sales or profits may be cause for a head count review by management to keep costs in line with revenues.	(Total full-time employees) + (Total full-time equivalents for part-time employees)

Materials management

Ratio	Explanation	Derivation
Inventory accuracy	One of the most important logistics measures, for an inaccurate inventory leads to incorrect purchasing decisions and expensive production downtime, not to mention rush freight charges, all because expected inventories are not actually on hand.	$$\dfrac{\text{Number of accurate test items}}{\text{Number of items sampled}}$$
Number of suppliers used by commodity code	An excessive number of suppliers within each commodity code points toward too much work by the purchasing staff in managing an excessive number of suppliers, and should lead to a reduction in the number of suppliers.	Sort accounts payable list of suppliers by commodity code
Obsolete inventory percentage	A high proportion of obsolete inventory is a cause for alarm, not only because the inventory must be written off, but also because there may be incorrect purchasing or production decisions that led to the accumulation of inventory in the first place.	$$\dfrac{\text{Cost of inventory items with no recent usage}}{\text{Total inventory cost}}$$

Ratio	Explanation	Derivation
Percentage of on-time part delivery	Reveals those suppliers who are incapable of delivering parts when asked, which interferes with the production process. This measure should be tracked by supplier, not in aggregate, since more problems are revealed.	(Actual arrival date) − (Requested arrival date)
Percentage of suppliers using electronic data interchange (EDI)	The purchasing staff can experience a higher degree of automation if a large proportion of suppliers use EDI, which allows the staff to conduct other, more value-added activities.	$\dfrac{\text{Number of suppliers with EDI linkages}}{\text{Total number of suppliers}}$
Total number of components	An excessive number of components requires an extensive storage and tracking system, not to mention a significant number of suppliers and purchasing staff.	Summary of all inventory line items

Production

Ratio	Explanation	Derivation
Average equipment setup time	A short equipment setup time allows a company to spread the cost of the setup over a shorter number of parts, so that short production runs become more economical.	(Start time for new production run) − (Stop time for last production run)
Percentage of acceptable products completed	Reveals the proportion of production lots resulting in products that pass acceptance criteria, which then requires additional analysis to improve the acceptance rate.	$\dfrac{\text{Number of rejected products}}{\text{Number of products in production run}}$
Percentage of scrap	Reveals the proportion of scrapped products, though much more investigation is needed to determine underlying causes.	$\dfrac{\text{(Actual cost of goods sold)}-\text{(Standard cost of goods sold)}}{\text{Standard cost of goods sold}}$
Unit output per employee hour	A good measure for those organizations emphasizing maximum throughput, though not useful for those using just-in-time manufacturing principles, which focus on only producing when there is specific customer demand, which may result in less unit output per employee hour.	$\dfrac{\text{Aggregate output per production area}}{\text{Total hours worked in production area}}$

Production

Ratio	Explanation	Derivation
Work-in-process turnover	A production process that is organized for the streamlined flow of materials will have a very high work-in-process turnover, while disorganized ones will experience the reverse.	$\dfrac{\text{Total work-in-process}}{\text{Annual cost of goods sold}}$

Sales and marketing

Ratio	Explanation	Derivation
Market share	This is a better measure of a company's sales performance than a simple change in sales, since sales may increase in an expanding market while the overall market share is declining in comparison to that of competitors.	$\dfrac{\text{Dollar volume of company shipments}}{\text{Dollar volume of industry shipments}}$
Number of major accounts for which the company is the preferred supplier	A major goal of any sales staff is to become the sole supplier for all key customers, which may allow a company to charge premium pricing for selected products and services.	$\dfrac{\text{Number of major sole-source suppliers}}{\text{Number of major customers}}$
Ratio of backlog to sales	A large backlog is generally indicative of a high customer demand for a company's products, but it may also indicate an inability to ship products on time.	$\dfrac{\text{Dollar volume of all orders not yet in production}}{\text{Average of sales for last three months}}$
Sales trend by product line	The sales and engineering staffs need to know when sales for specific products or product lines are beginning to slow down, so that reduced pricing, promotions, or new products can be planned to keep sales growth surging.	$\dfrac{(\text{Summary of current period sales}) - (\text{Summary of previous period sales})}{\text{Summary of previous period sales}}$

Suggested Readings

Aggarwal, R. (editor), *Capital Budgeting Under Uncertainty*. Englewood Cliffs, NJ: Prentice Hall, 1991.

Bandler, James P., *How to Use Financial Statements*. Burr Ridge, IL: Irwin, 1994.

Bogan, Christopher, and Michael English, *Benchmarking for Best Practices*. New York: McGraw-Hill, 1994.

Bragg, Steven, *Outsourcing*. New York: John Wiley & Sons, 1998.

Burgess, Deanna Oxender, "Buy or Lease: The Eternal Question," *Journal of Accountancy*, April 1999, pp. 25–33.

Burton, E. James, and W. Blan McBride, *The Total Business Manual*. New York: John Wiley & Sons, 1991.

Copeland, Tom, Tim Koller, and Jack Murrin, *Measuring and Managing the Value of Companies*. New York: John Wiley & Sons, 1991.

Damodaran, Aswath, *Damodaran on Valuation*. New York: John Wiley & Sons, 1994.

Drucker, Peter F., "The Information Executives Truly Need," *Harvard Business Review*, January/February 1995.

Hackel, Kenneth S., and Joshua Livnat, *Cash Flow and Security Analysis*. Burr Ridge, IL: Business-One Irwin, 1992.

Helfert, Erich A., *Techniques of Financial Analysis*. New York: McGraw-Hill, 1997.

Higgins, Robert, *Analysis for Financial Management*. Burr Ridge, IL: Irwin, 1997.

Kaplan, Robert S., and David P. Norton, *The Balanced Scorecard*. Boston: Harvard Business School Press, 1996.

Porter, Michael E., *Competitive Strategy*. New York: Free Press, 1998.

Rappaport, Alfred, *Creating Superior Shareholder Value*. New York: Free Press, 1986.

Reed, Stanley Foster, and Alexandra Reed Lajoux, *The Art of M&A*. New York: McGraw-Hill, 1998.

Roehl-Anderson, Jan, and Steven Bragg, *Controllership*, 6th ed., New York: John Wiley & Sons, 1999.

Stewart, G. Bennett III, *The Quest for Value*. New York: Harper Business, 1991.

Weber, Joseph, and Jeffrey Laderman, "The Market: Too High? Too Low? Why So Many Valuation Models Are Wrong," *Business Week*, April 5, 1999, pp. 92–93.

Index